Thank you for picking up *Haikyu!!* volume 8. It seems like rumors often become facts as they are spread around. Even if the actual facts are different, whatever is believed to be true by the most people is considered the truth. I can't help but think that, nowadays, things that seem to be true are more important than things that are actually true.

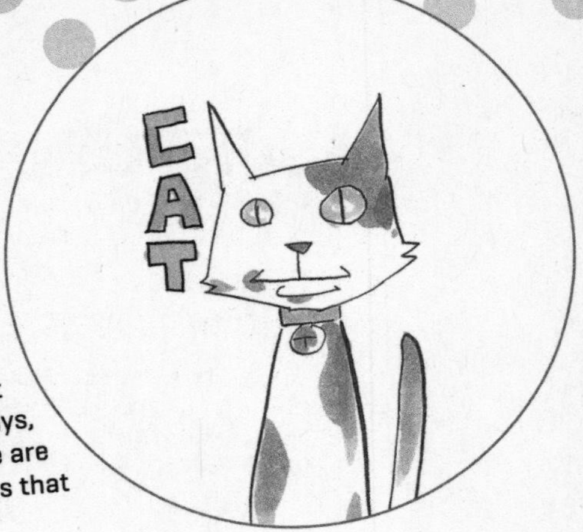
CAT

HARUICHI FURUDATE began his manga career when he was 25 years old with the one-shot *Ousama Kid* [King Kid], which won an honorable mention for the 14th Jump Treasure Newcomer Manga Prize. His first series, *Kiben Gakuha, Yotsuya Sensei no Kaidan* [Philosophy School, Yotsuya Sensei's Ghost Stories], was serialized in *Weekly Shonen Jump* in 2010. In 2012, he began serializing *Haikyu!!* in *Weekly Shonen Jump*, where it became his most popular work to date.

HAIKYU!!
VOLUME 8
SHONEN JUMP Manga Edition

Story and Art by
HARUICHI FURUDATE

Translation 1 ADRIENNE BECK
Touch-Up Art & Lettering 2 ERIKA TERRIQUEZ
Design 3 FAWN LAU
Editor 4 MARLENE FIRST

HAIKYU!! © 2012 by Haruichi Furudate
All rights reserved.
First published in Japan in 2012 by SHUEISHA Inc., Tokyo.
English translation rights arranged by SHUEISHA Inc.

The stories, characters and incidents mentioned
in this publication are entirely fictional.

Printed in the U.S.A.

Published by VIZ Media, LLC
P.O. Box 77010
San Francisco, CA 94107

10 9 8 7 6 5 4 3 2 1
First printing, February 2017

SHONEN JUMP MANGA

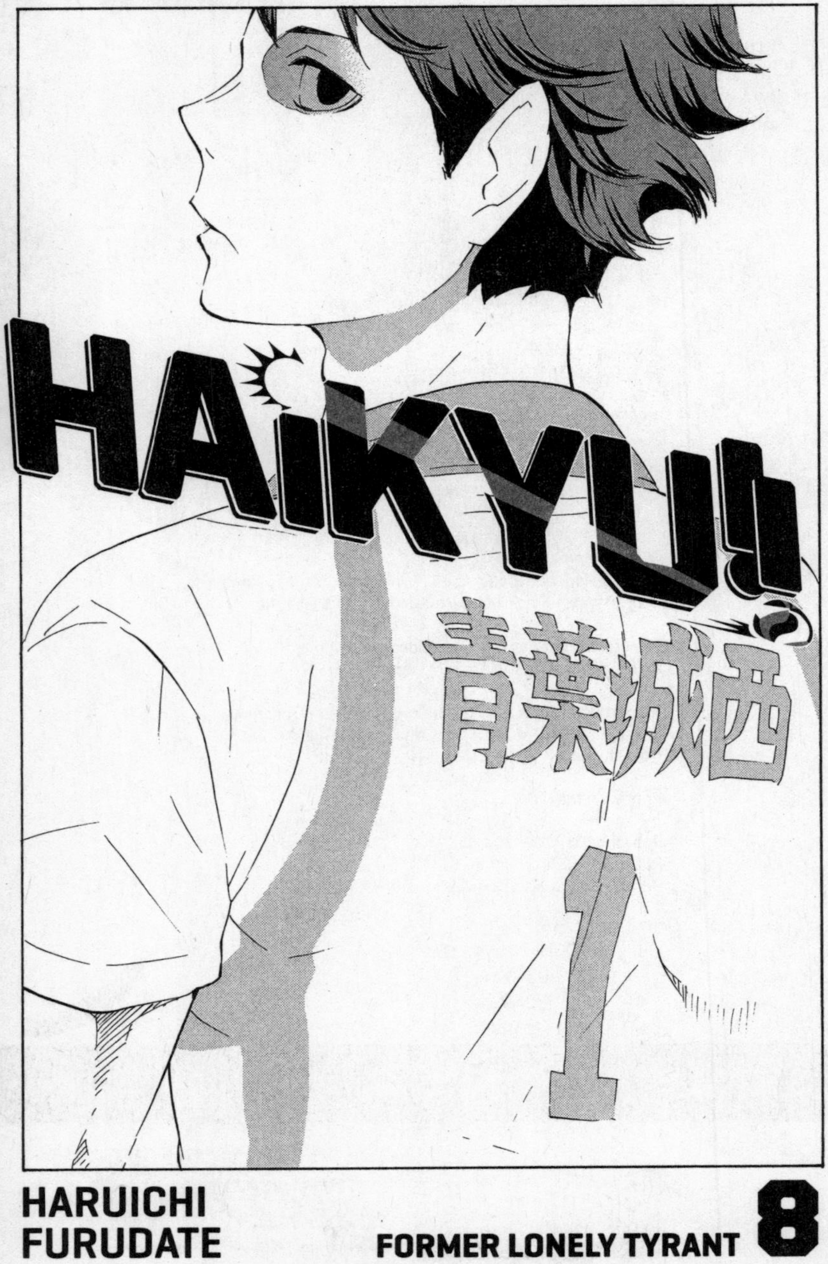
HAIKYU!!
青葉城西
1

HARUICHI
FURUDATE

8

FORMER LONELY TYRANT

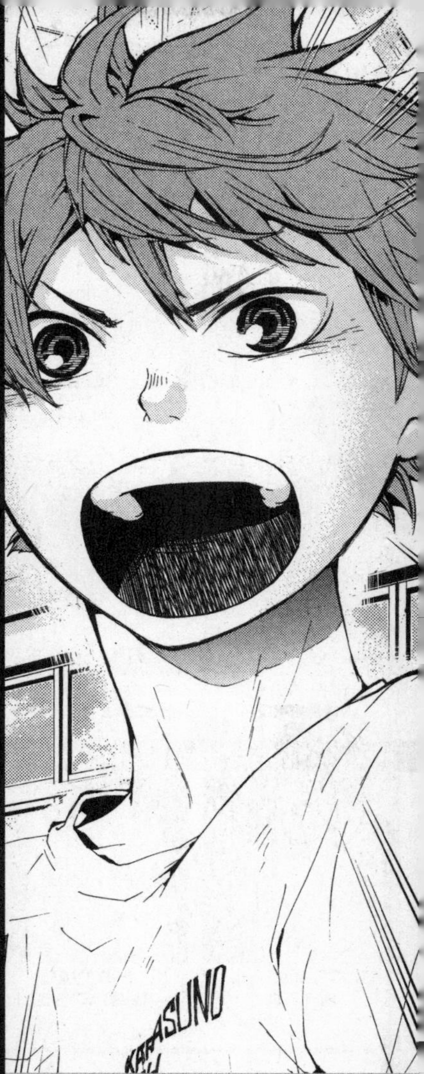

SHOYO HINATA

1ST YEAR / MIDDLE BLOCKER

Even though he doesn't have the best body type for volleyball, he is super athletic. Gets nervous easily.

TOBIO KAGEYAMA

1ST YEAR / SETTER

His instincts and athletic talent are so good that he's like a "king" who rules the court. Demanding and egocentric.

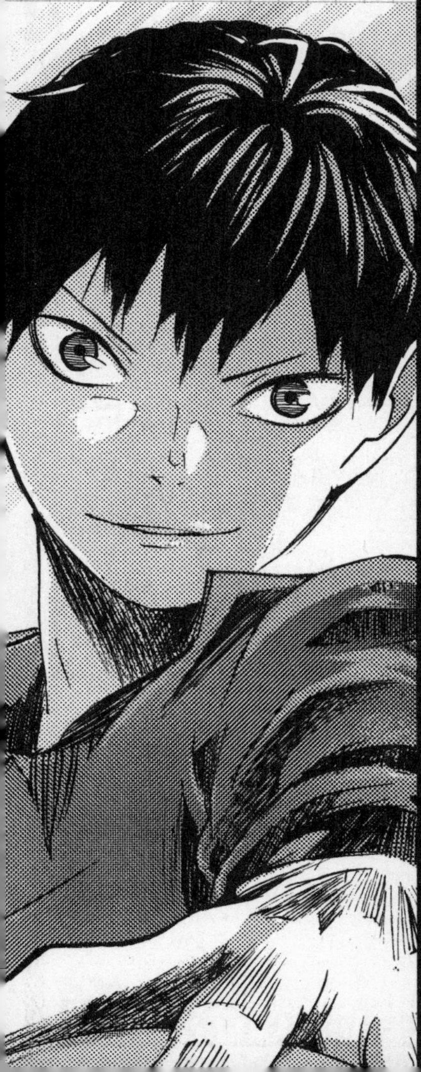

CHARACTERS

Karasuno High School Volleyball Club

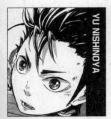

YU NISHINOYA

2ND YEAR
LIBERO

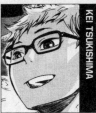

KEI TSUKISHIMA

1ST YEAR
MIDDLE BLOCKER

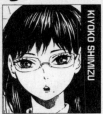

KIYOKO SHIMIZU

3RD YEAR
MANAGER

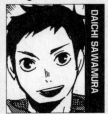

DAICHI SAWAMURA

3RD YEAR (CAPTAIN)
WING SPIKER

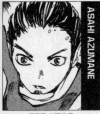

ASAHI AZUMANE

3RD YEAR
WING SPIKER

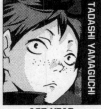

TADASHI YAMAGUCHI

1ST YEAR
MIDDLE BLOCKER

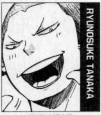

RYUNOSUKE TANAKA

2ND YEAR
WING SPIKER

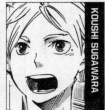

KOUSHI SUGAWARA

3RD YEAR (VICE CAPTAIN)
SETTER

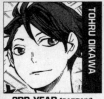

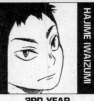

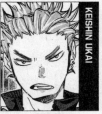

KEISHIN UKAI

COACH

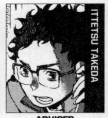

ITTETSU TAKEDA

ADVISER

Aoba Johsai High School Volleyball Club

TOHRU OIKAWA

3RD YEAR (CAPTAIN)
SETTER

HAJIME IWAIZUMI

3RD YEAR
WING SPIKER

Ever since he saw the legendary player known as "the Little Giant" compete at the national volleyball finals, Shoyo Hinata has been aiming to be the best volleyball player ever! He decides to join the volleyball club at his middle school and gets to play in an official tournament during his third year. His team is crushed by a team led by volleyball prodigy Tobio Kageyama, also known as "the King of the Court." Swearing revenge on Kageyama, Hinata graduates middle school and enters Karasuno High School, the school where the Little Giant played. However, upon joining the club, he finds out that Kageyama is there too! In Karasuno's practice game against Nekoma, Kageyama and Hinata figure out new ways to improve their skills but ultimately lose to their opponent's consistent teamwork. Promising to get payback on the national stage, Karasuno gets ready for the summer Inter-High Tournament! Round 3 is a rematch against Aoba Johsai! Kageyama loses his cool mid-game and is benched, and the one who replaces him is none other than Sugawara! With his guidance, Karasuno manages to take the second set! With Kageyama back on the court and Hinata shining as a decoy, can Karasuno manage to pull ahead of their 15-15 score?

HAIKYU!!

8 FORMER LONELY TYRANT

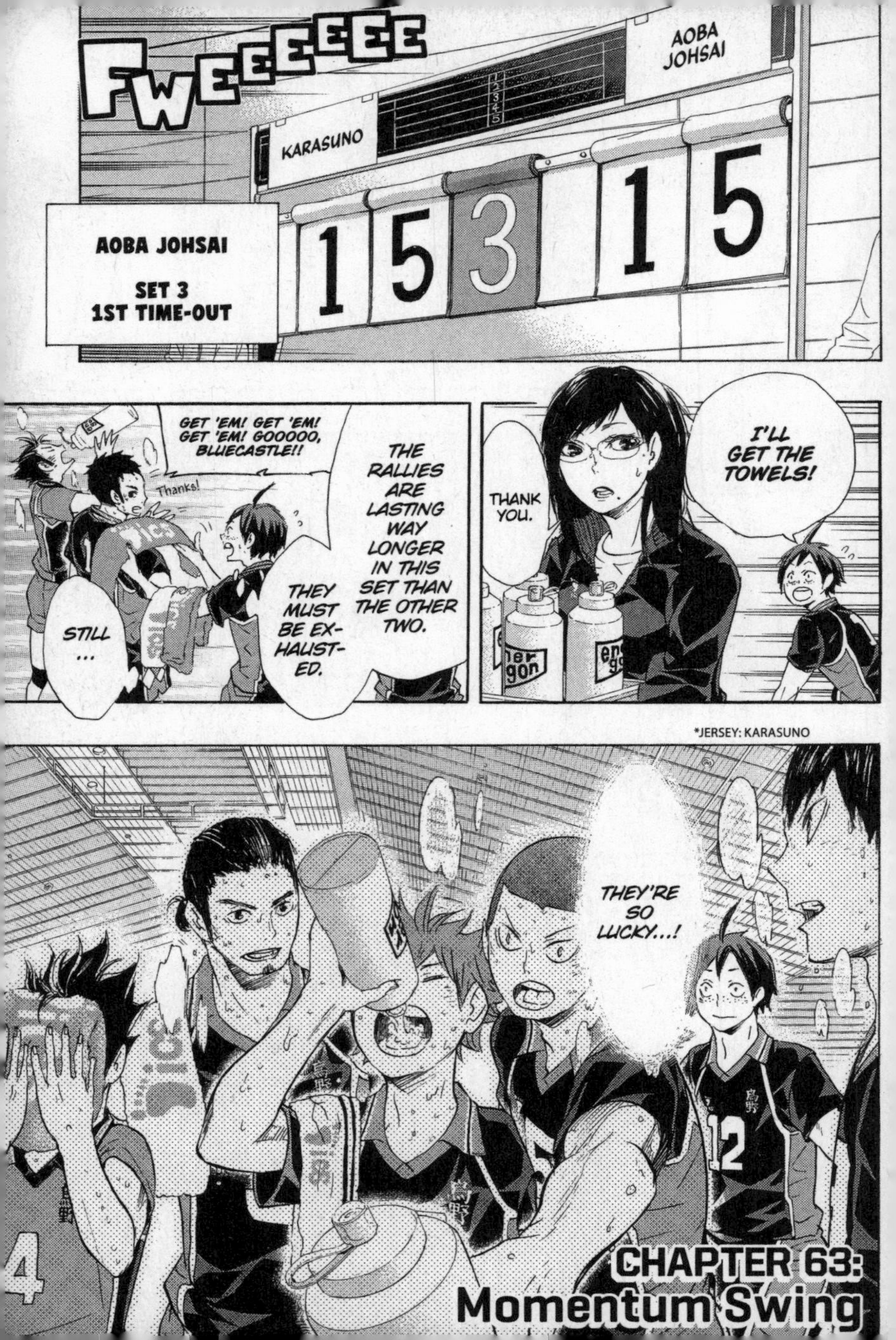
FWEEEEEE
AOBA JOHSAI
KARASUNO
1
2
3
4
5
15 3 15
AOBA JOHSAI
SET 3
1ST TIME-OUT
I'LL GET THE TOWELS!
THANK YOU.
GET 'EM! GET 'EM! GOOOOO, BLUECASTLE!!
THE RALLIES ARE LASTING WAY LONGER IN THIS SET THAN THE OTHER TWO.
THEY MUST BE EX-HAUST-ED.
Thanks!
STILL ...
*JERSEY: KARASUNO
THEY'RE SO LUCKY...!
CHAPTER 63:
Momentum Swing

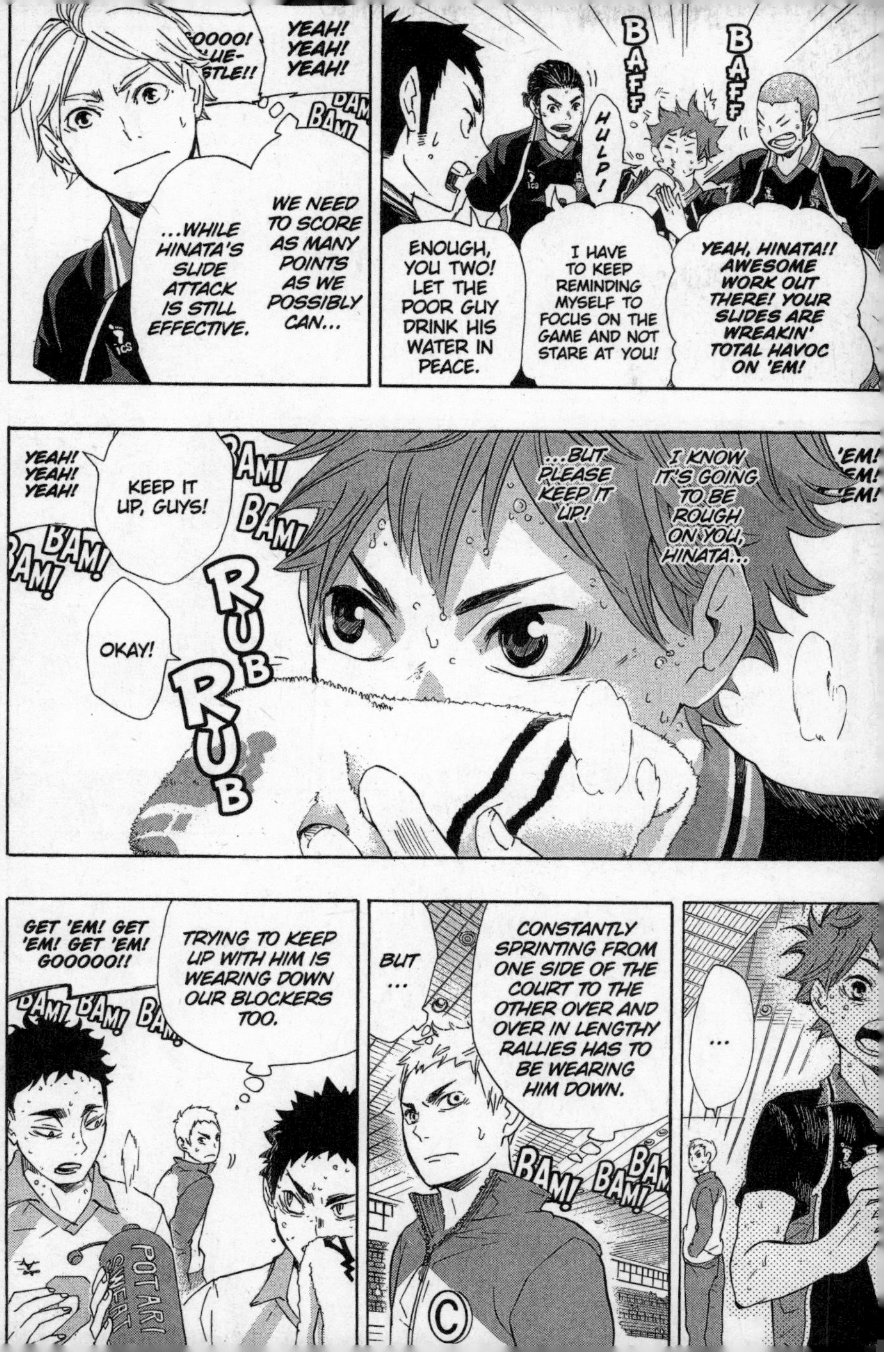
BAFF
BAFF
YEAH, HINATA!! AWESOME WORK OUT THERE! YOUR SLIDES ARE WREAKIN' TOTAL HAVOC ON 'EM!
I HAVE TO KEEP REMINDING MYSELF TO FOCUS ON THE GAME AND NOT STARE AT YOU!
HULP!
ENOUGH, YOU TWO! LET THE POOR GUY DRINK HIS WATER IN PEACE.
OOOO! LUE- STLE!!
YEAH! YEAH! YEAH!
BAM!
WE NEED TO SCORE AS MANY POINTS AS WE POSSIBLY CAN...
...WHILE HINATA'S SLIDE ATTACK IS STILL EFFECTIVE.
I KNOW IT'S GOING TO BE ROUGH ON YOU, HINATA...
...BUT PLEASE KEEP IT UP!
BAM! BAM!
KEEP IT UP, GUYS!
YEAH! YEAH! YEAH!
BAM! BAM!
OKAY!
RUB RUB
...
CONSTANTLY SPRINTING FROM ONE SIDE OF THE COURT TO THE OTHER OVER AND OVER IN LENGTHY RALLIES HAS TO BE WEARING HIM DOWN.
BUT ...
BAM! BAM! BAM!
GET 'EM! GET 'EM! GET 'EM! GOOOOO!!
TRYING TO KEEP UP WITH HIM IS WEARING DOWN OUR BLOCKERS TOO.
BAM! BAM!
POTARI
SWEAT

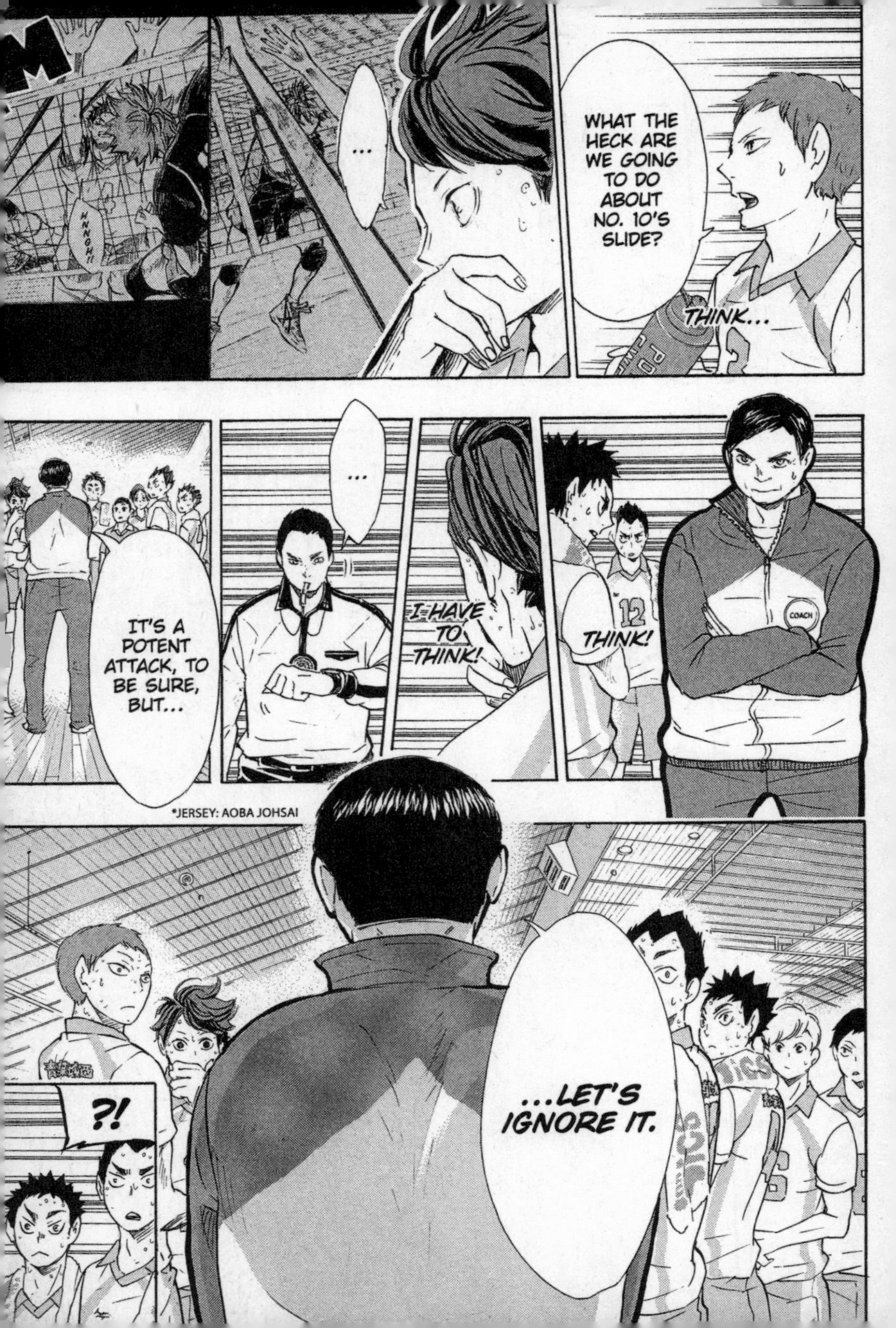
WHAT THE HECK ARE WE GOING TO DO ABOUT NO. 10'S SLIDE?
THINK...
...
HNNGH!!
THINK!
I HAVE TO THINK!
...
IT'S A POTENT ATTACK, TO BE SURE, BUT...
*JERSEY: AOBA JOHSAI
...LET'S IGNORE IT.
?!

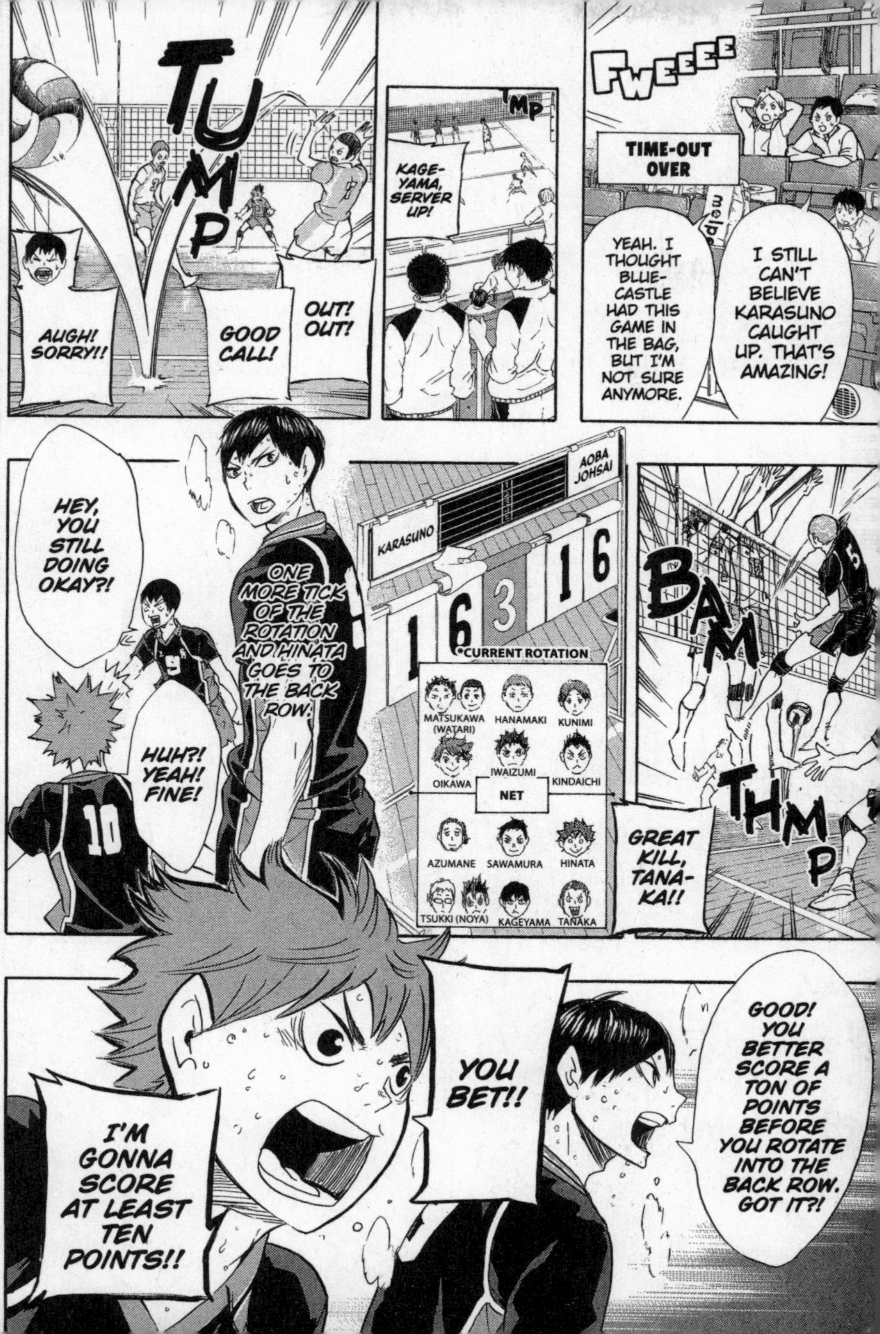
FWEEEE
TIME-OUT OVER
I STILL CAN'T BELIEVE KARASUNO CAUGHT UP. THAT'S AMAZING!
YEAH. I THOUGHT BLUE-CASTLE HAD THIS GAME IN THE BAG, BUT I'M NOT SURE ANYMORE.
TMP
KAGE-YAMA, SERVER UP!
TUMP
OUT! OUT!
GOOD CALL!
AUGH! SORRY!!
BAM
THMP
GREAT KILL, TANA-KA!!
AOBA JOHSAI
KARASUNO
16 3 16
*CURRENT ROTATION
MATSUKAWA (WATARI)
HANAMAKI
KUNIMI
OIKAWA
IWAIZUMI
KINDAICHI
NET
AZUMANE
SAWAMURA
HINATA
TSUKKI (NOYA)
KAGEYAMA
TANAKA
ONE MORE TICK OF THE ROTATION AND HINATA GOES TO THE BACK ROW.
HEY, YOU STILL DOING OKAY?!
HUH?! YEAH! FINE!
GOOD! YOU BETTER SCORE A TON OF POINTS BEFORE YOU ROTATE INTO THE BACK ROW. GOT IT?!
YOU BET!!
I'M GONNA SCORE AT LEAST TEN POINTS!!

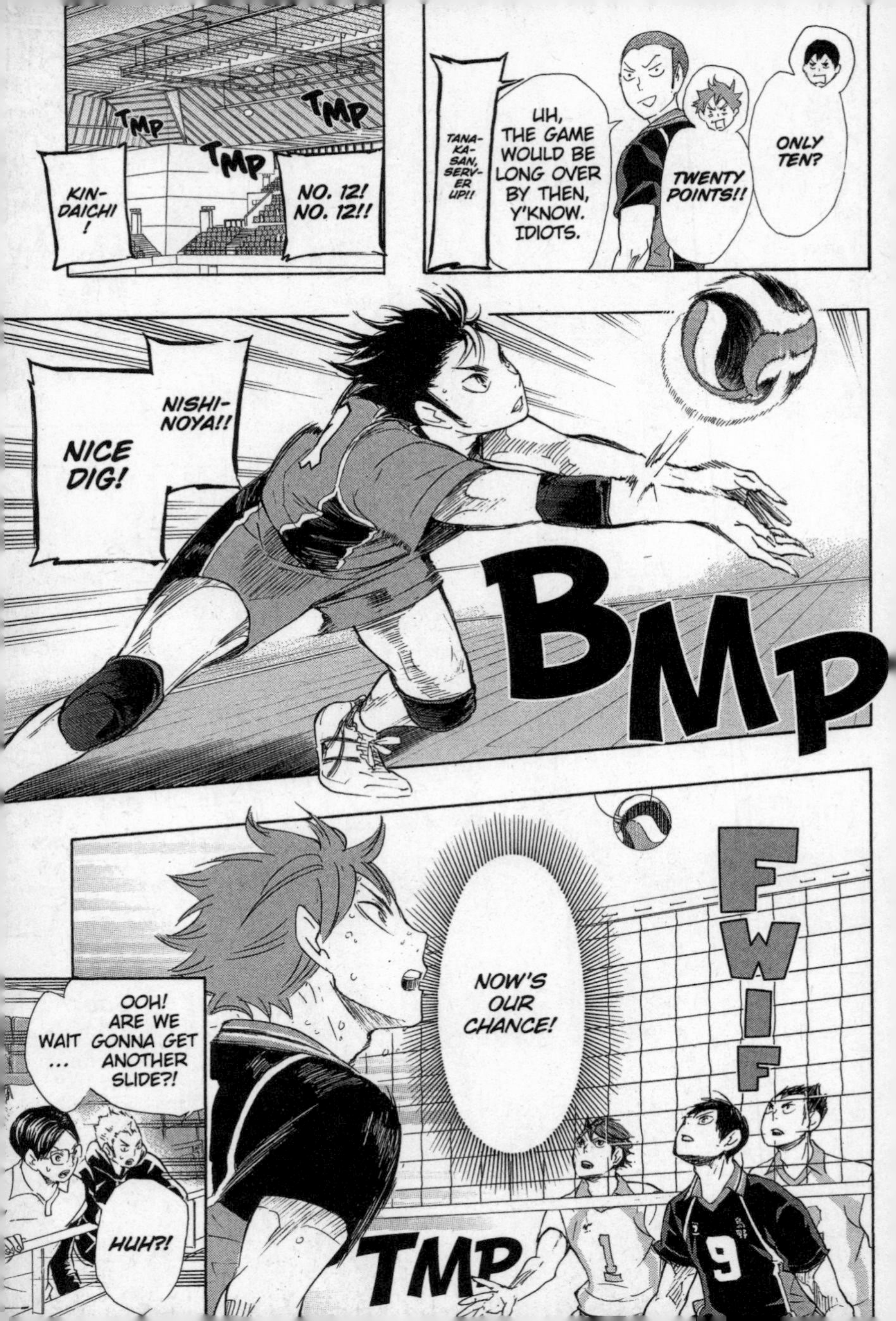
ONLY TEN?
TWENTY POINTS!!
UH, THE GAME WOULD BE LONG OVER BY THEN, Y'KNOW. IDIOTS.
TANAKA-SAN, SERVER UP!!
TMP
TMP
TMP
NO. 12! NO. 12!!
KIN-DAICHI!
NISHI-NOYA!!
NICE DIG!
BMP
FWIF
NOW'S OUR CHANCE!
OOH! ARE WE GONNA GET ANOTHER SLIDE?!
WAIT...
HUH?!
TMP

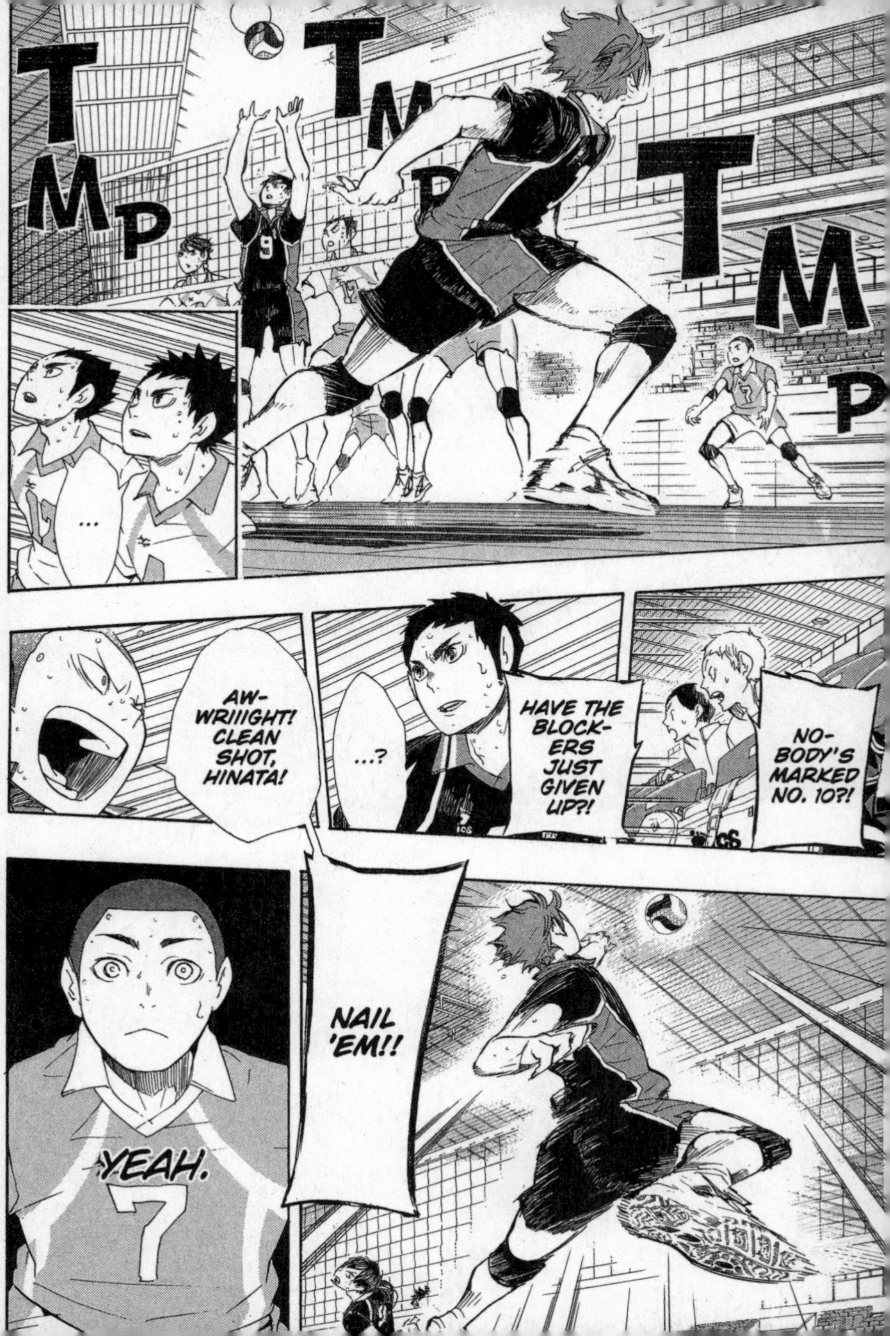
TMP
TMP
TMP
TMP
...
NOBODY'S MARKED NO. 10?!
HAVE THE BLOCKERS JUST GIVEN UP?!
...?
AWWRIIIGHT! CLEAN SHOT, HINATA!
NAIL 'EM!!
YEAH.

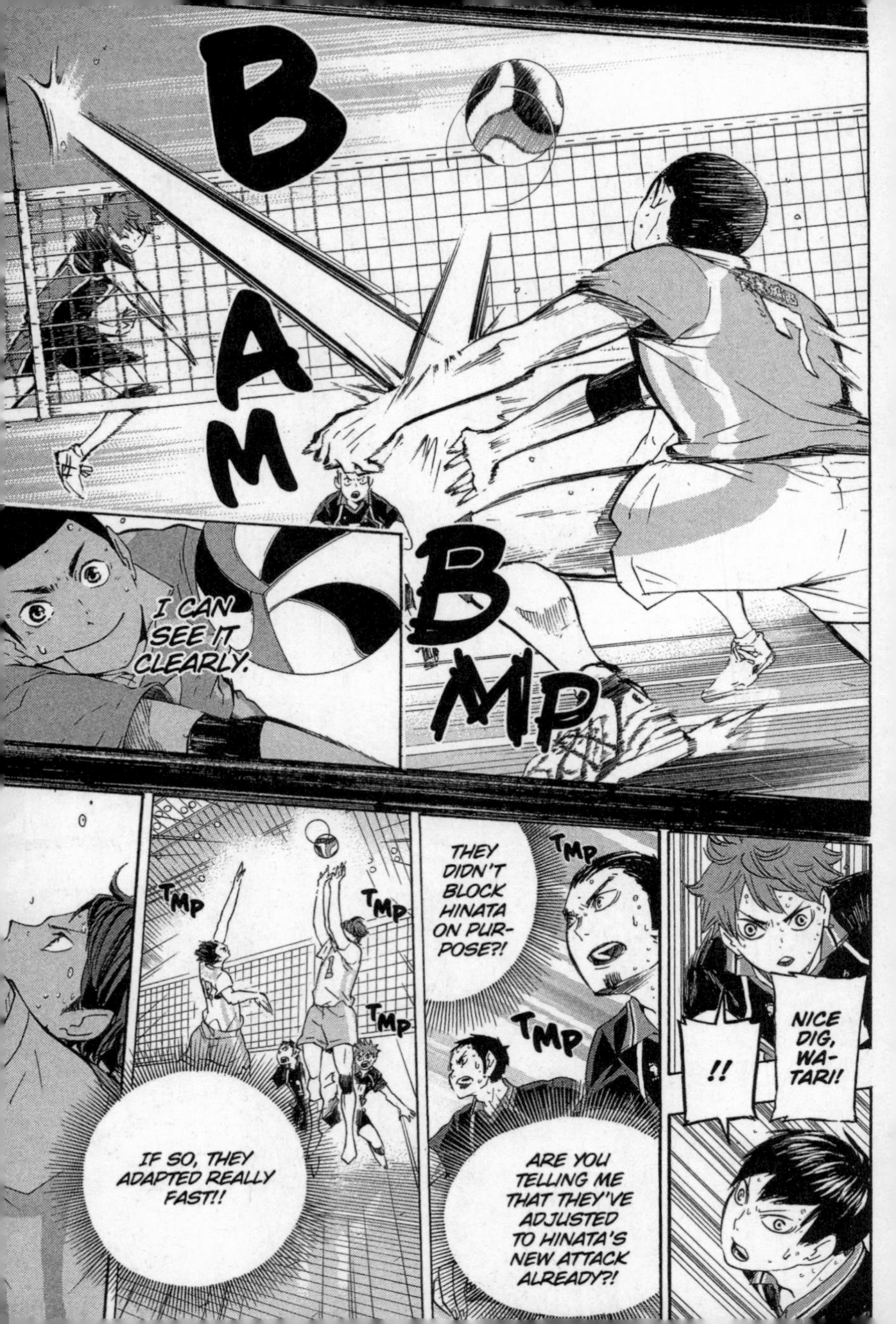
BAM
BMP
I CAN SEE IT CLEARLY.
NICE DIG, WATARI!
!!
THEY DIDN'T BLOCK HINATA ON PURPOSE?!
TMP
TMP
ARE YOU TELLING ME THAT THEY'VE ADJUSTED TO HINATA'S NEW ATTACK ALREADY?!
TMP
TMP
TMP
IF SO, THEY ADAPTED REALLY FAST!!

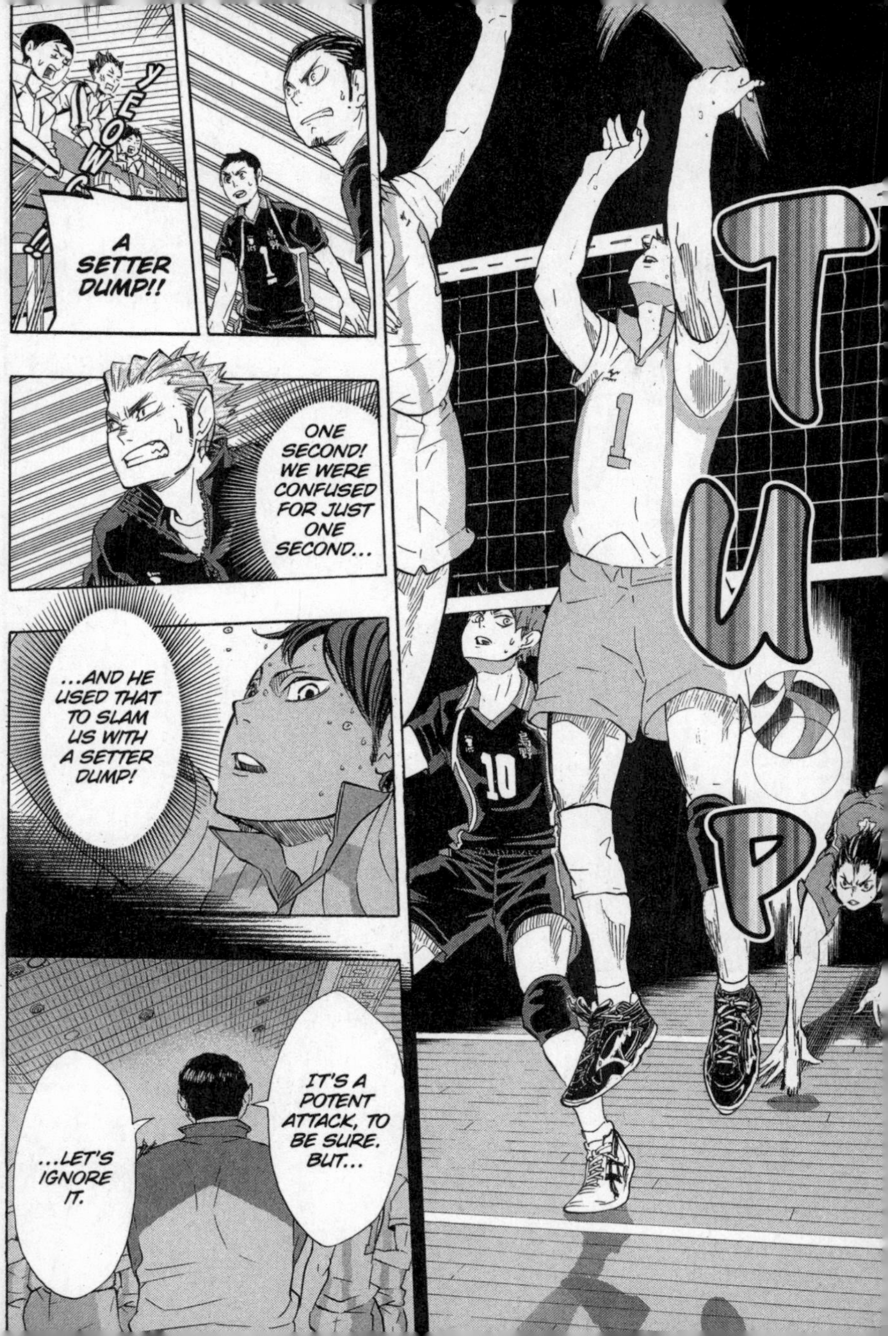
TUP
YEOWC
A SETTER DUMP!!
ONE SECOND! WE WERE CONFUSED FOR JUST ONE SECOND...
...AND HE USED THAT TO SLAM US WITH A SETTER DUMP!
IT'S A POTENT ATTACK, TO BE SURE. BUT...
...LET'S IGNORE IT.

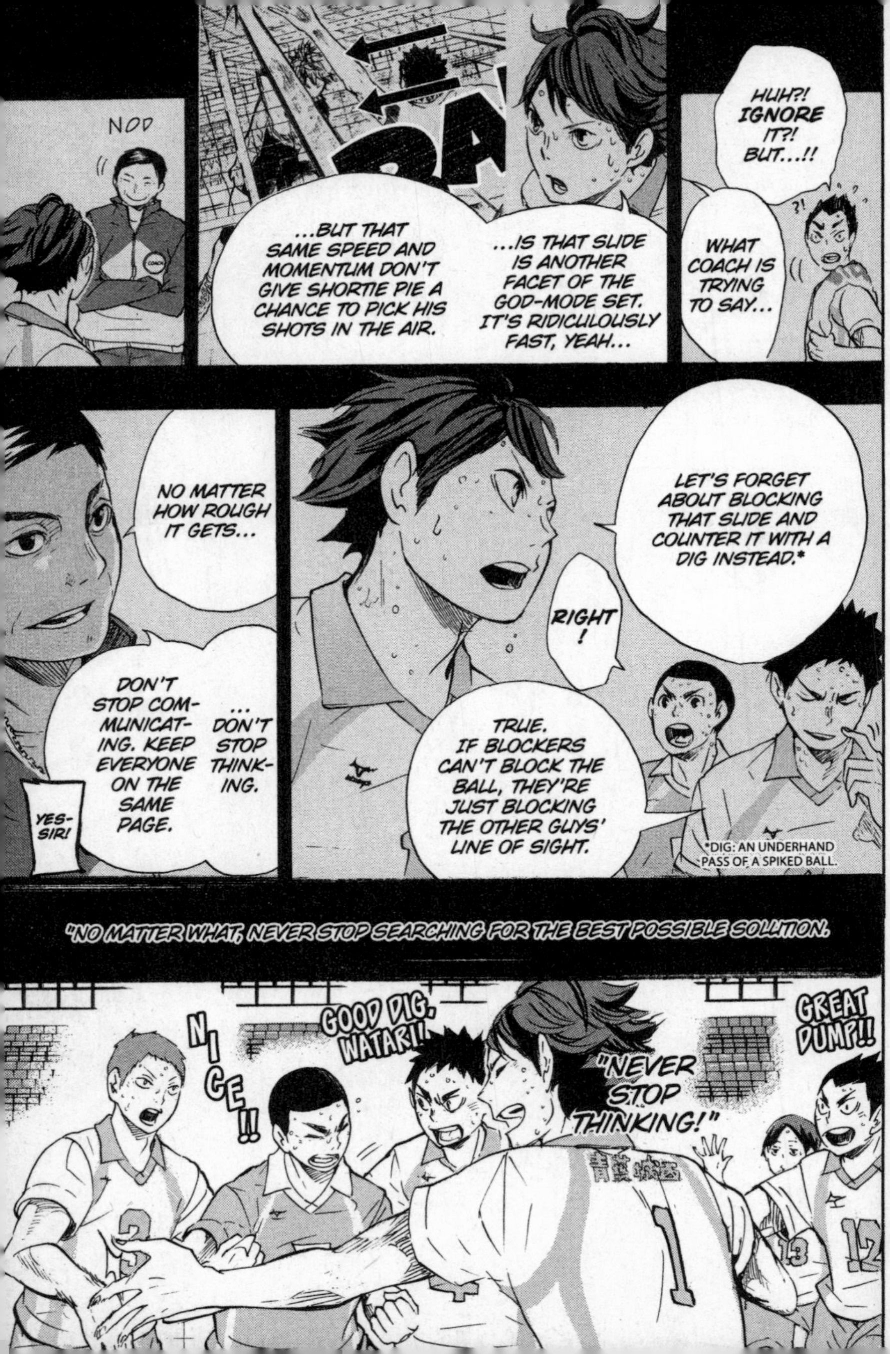
HUH?! IGNORE IT?! BUT...!!
?!
WHAT COACH IS TRYING TO SAY...
...IS THAT SLIDE IS ANOTHER FACET OF THE GOD-MODE SET. IT'S RIDICULOUSLY FAST, YEAH...
...BUT THAT SAME SPEED AND MOMENTUM DON'T GIVE SHORTIE PIE A CHANCE TO PICK HIS SHOTS IN THE AIR.
BA
NOD
LET'S FORGET ABOUT BLOCKING THAT SLIDE AND COUNTER IT WITH A DIG INSTEAD.*
RIGHT!
TRUE. IF BLOCKERS CAN'T BLOCK THE BALL, THEY'RE JUST BLOCKING THE OTHER GUYS' LINE OF SIGHT.
*DIG: AN UNDERHAND PASS OF A SPIKED BALL.
NO MATTER HOW ROUGH IT GETS...
...DON'T STOP THINKING.
DON'T STOP COMMUNICATING. KEEP EVERYONE ON THE SAME PAGE.
YES-SIR!
"NO MATTER WHAT, NEVER STOP SEARCHING FOR THE BEST POSSIBLE SOLUTION.
GREAT DUMP!!
"NEVER STOP THINKING!"
GOOD DIG, WATARI!!
NICE!!

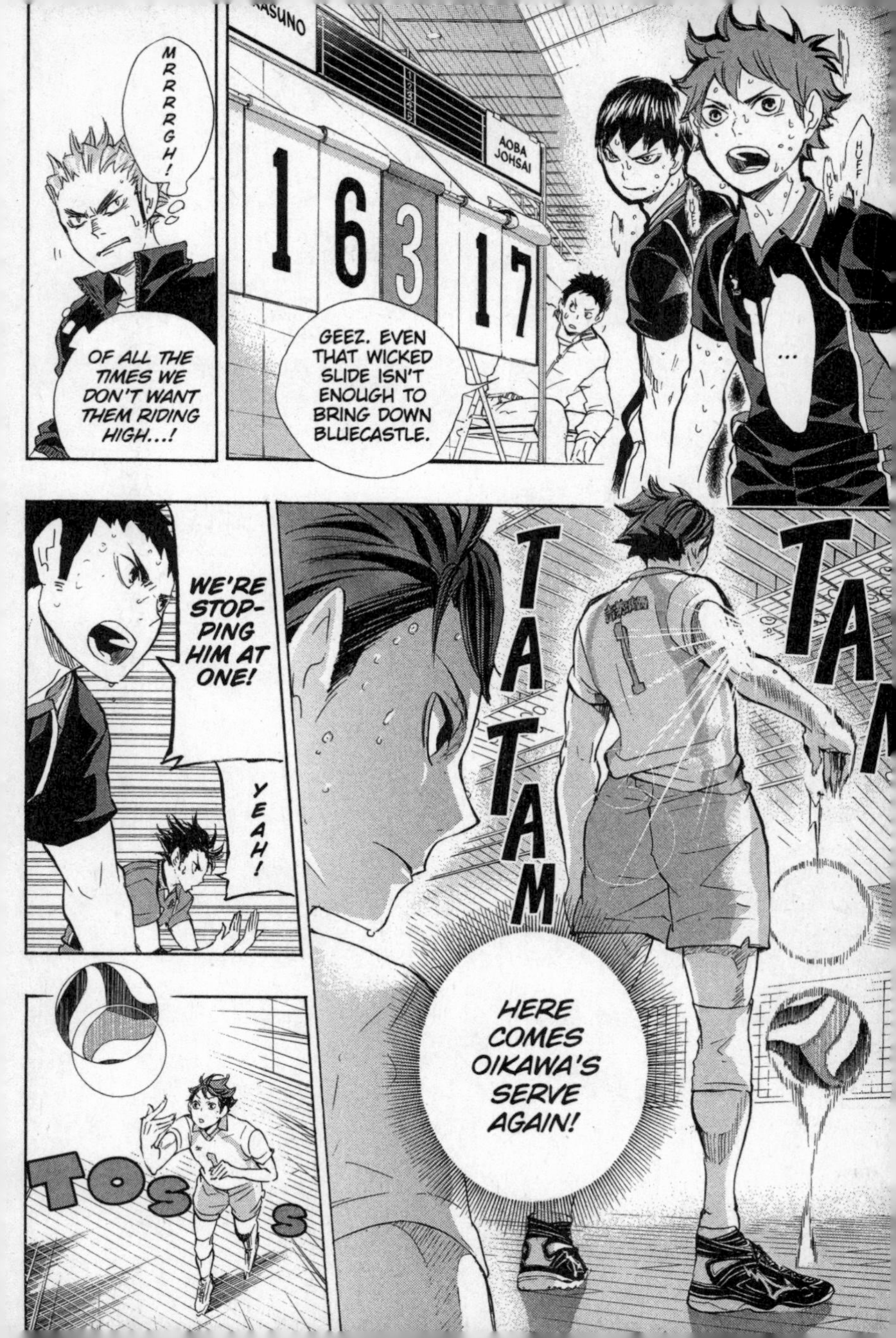
HUFF
HUFF
HUFF
...
AOBA JOHSAI
16 3 17
GEEZ. EVEN THAT WICKED SLIDE ISN'T ENOUGH TO BRING DOWN BLUECASTLE.
MRRRRGH!
OF ALL THE TIMES WE DON'T WANT THEM RIDING HIGH...!
TAM
TA TAM
HERE COMES OIKAWA'S SERVE AGAIN!
WE'RE STOP-PING HIM AT ONE!
YEAH!
TOSS

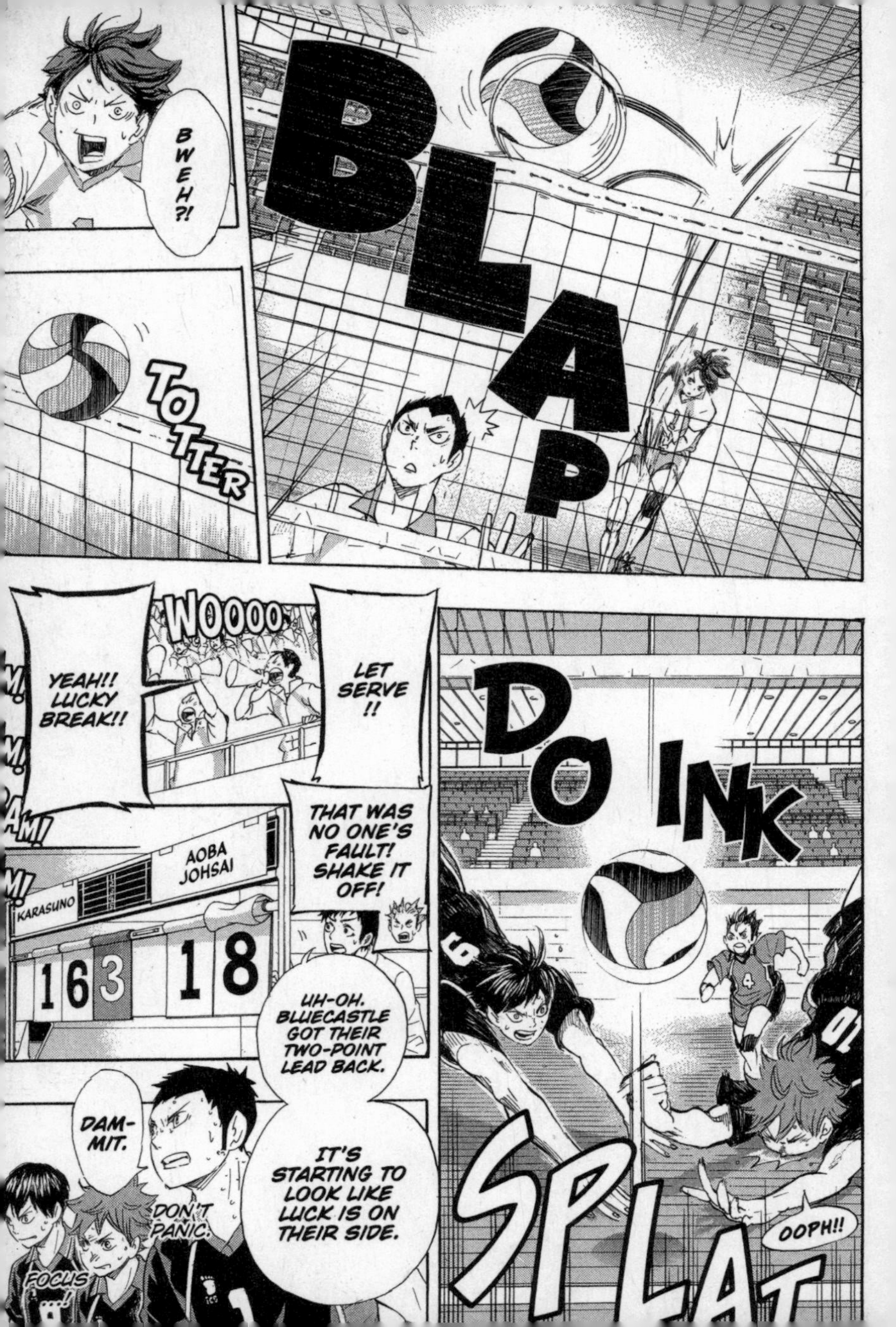
BLAP
BWEH?!
TOTTER
DOINK
SPLAT
OOPH!!
LET SERVE!!
WOOOO
YEAH!! LUCKY BREAK!!
THAT WAS NO ONE'S FAULT! SHAKE IT OFF!
AOBA JOHSAI
KARASUNO
16 3
18
UH-OH. BLUECASTLE GOT THEIR TWO-POINT LEAD BACK.
IT'S STARTING TO LOOK LIKE LUCK IS ON THEIR SIDE.
DAM-MIT.
DON'T PANIC.
FOCUS...!

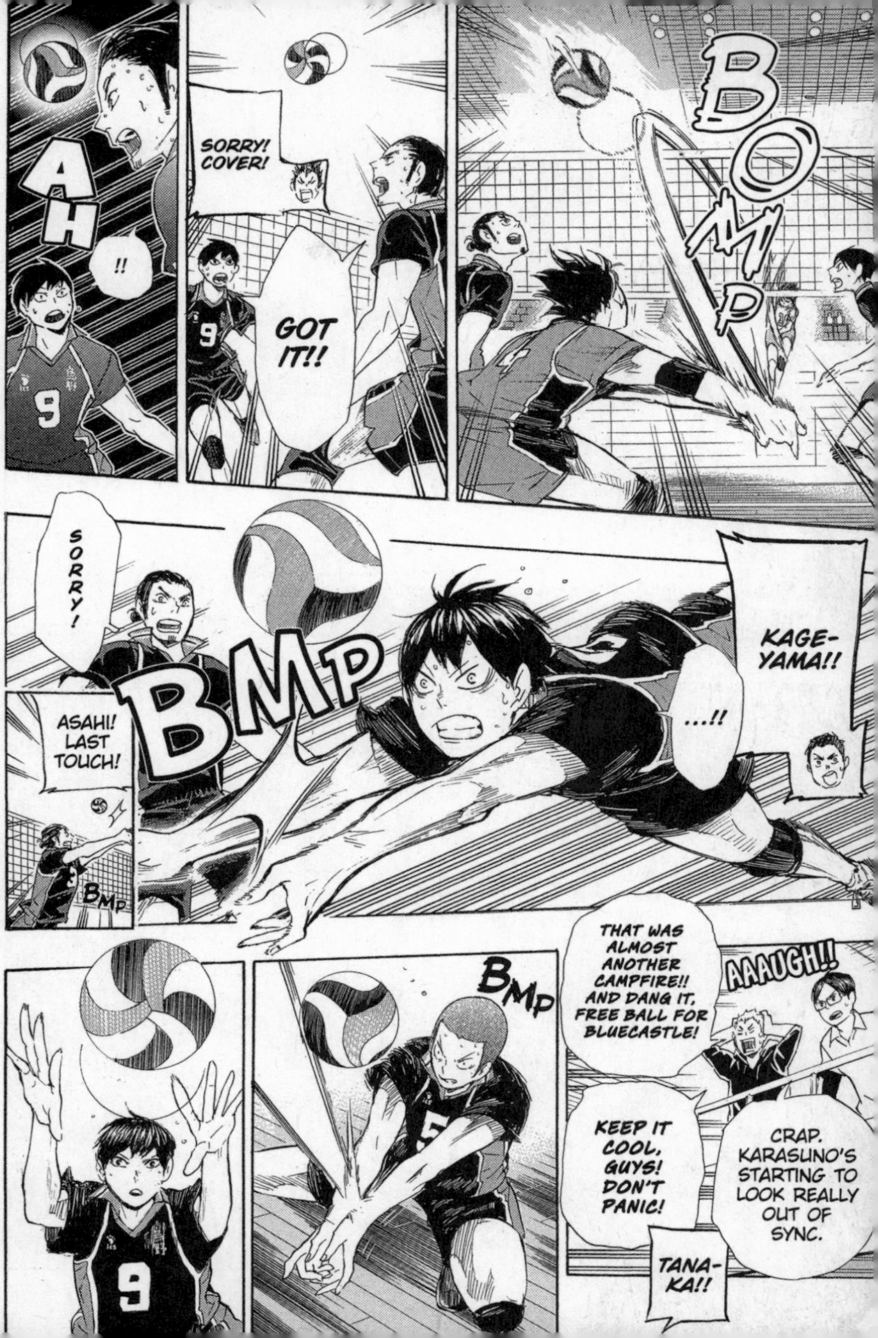
BOMMP
SORRY! COVER!
GOT IT!!
AH
!!
KAGE-YAMA!!
...!!
SORRY!
BMP
ASAHI! LAST TOUCH!
BMP
AAAUGH!!
THAT WAS ALMOST ANOTHER CAMPFIRE!! AND DANG IT, FREE BALL FOR BLUECASTLE!
CRAP. KARASUNO'S STARTING TO LOOK REALLY OUT OF SYNC.
KEEP IT COOL, GUYS! DON'T PANIC!
TANA-KA!!
BMP

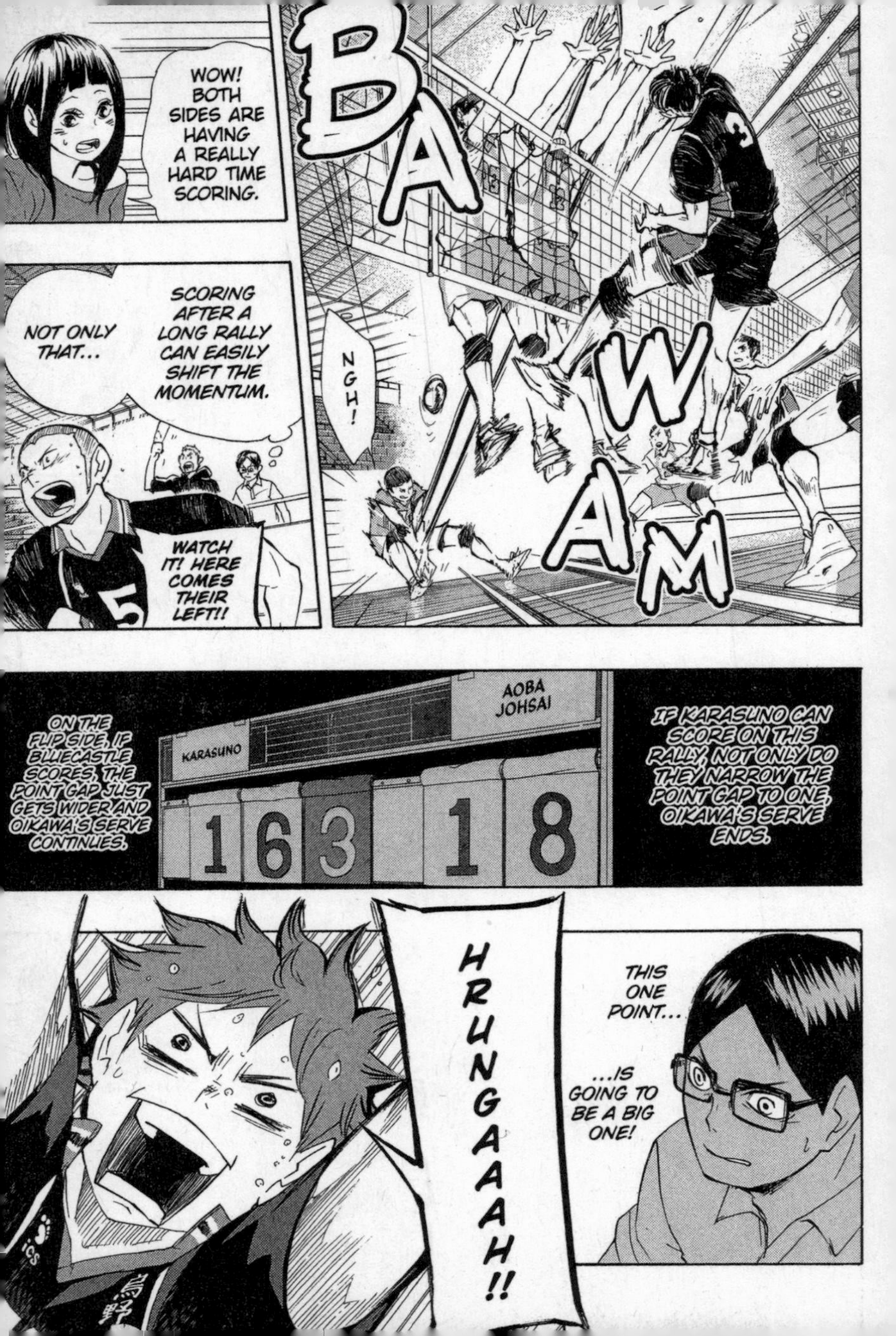
BAWAM
NGH!
WOW! BOTH SIDES ARE HAVING A REALLY HARD TIME SCORING.
SCORING AFTER A LONG RALLY CAN EASILY SHIFT THE MOMENTUM.
NOT ONLY THAT...
WATCH IT! HERE COMES THEIR LEFT!!
AOBA JOHSAI
KARASUNO
1 6 3 1 8
IF KARASUNO CAN SCORE ON THIS RALLY, NOT ONLY DO THEY NARROW THE POINT GAP TO ONE, OIKAWA'S SERVE ENDS.
ON THE FLIP SIDE, IF BLUECASTLE SCORES, THE POINT GAP JUST GETS WIDER AND OIKAWA'S SERVE CONTINUES.
THIS ONE POINT...
...IS GOING TO BE A BIG ONE!
HRUNGAAAH!!

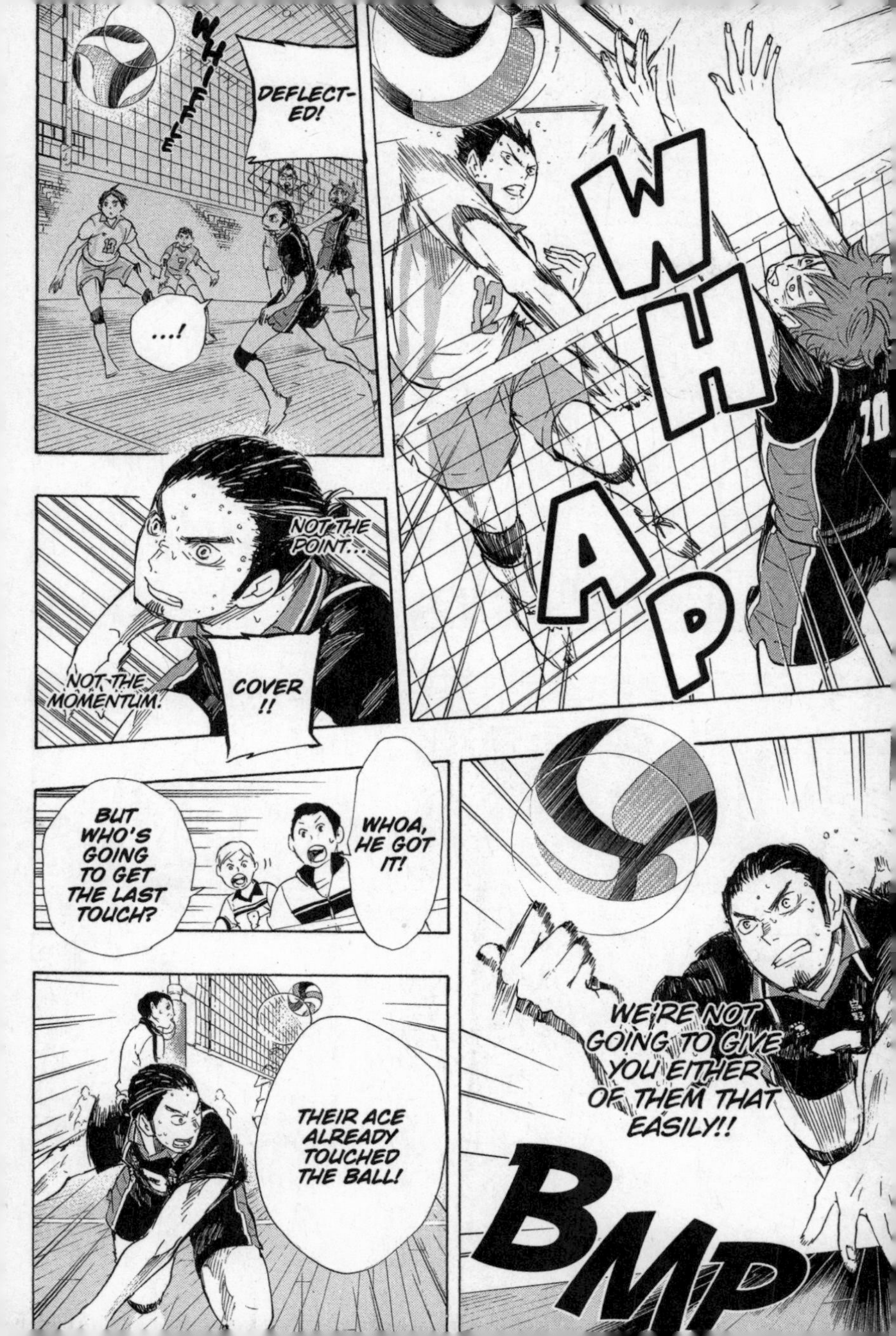
WHAP
DEFLECT-ED!
WHIFFLE
...!
NOT THE POINT...
COVER !!
NOT THE MOMENTUM.
WE'RE NOT GOING TO GIVE YOU EITHER OF THEM THAT EASILY!!
BMP
WHOA, HE GOT IT!
BUT WHO'S GOING TO GET THE LAST TOUCH?
THEIR ACE ALREADY TOUCHED THE BALL!

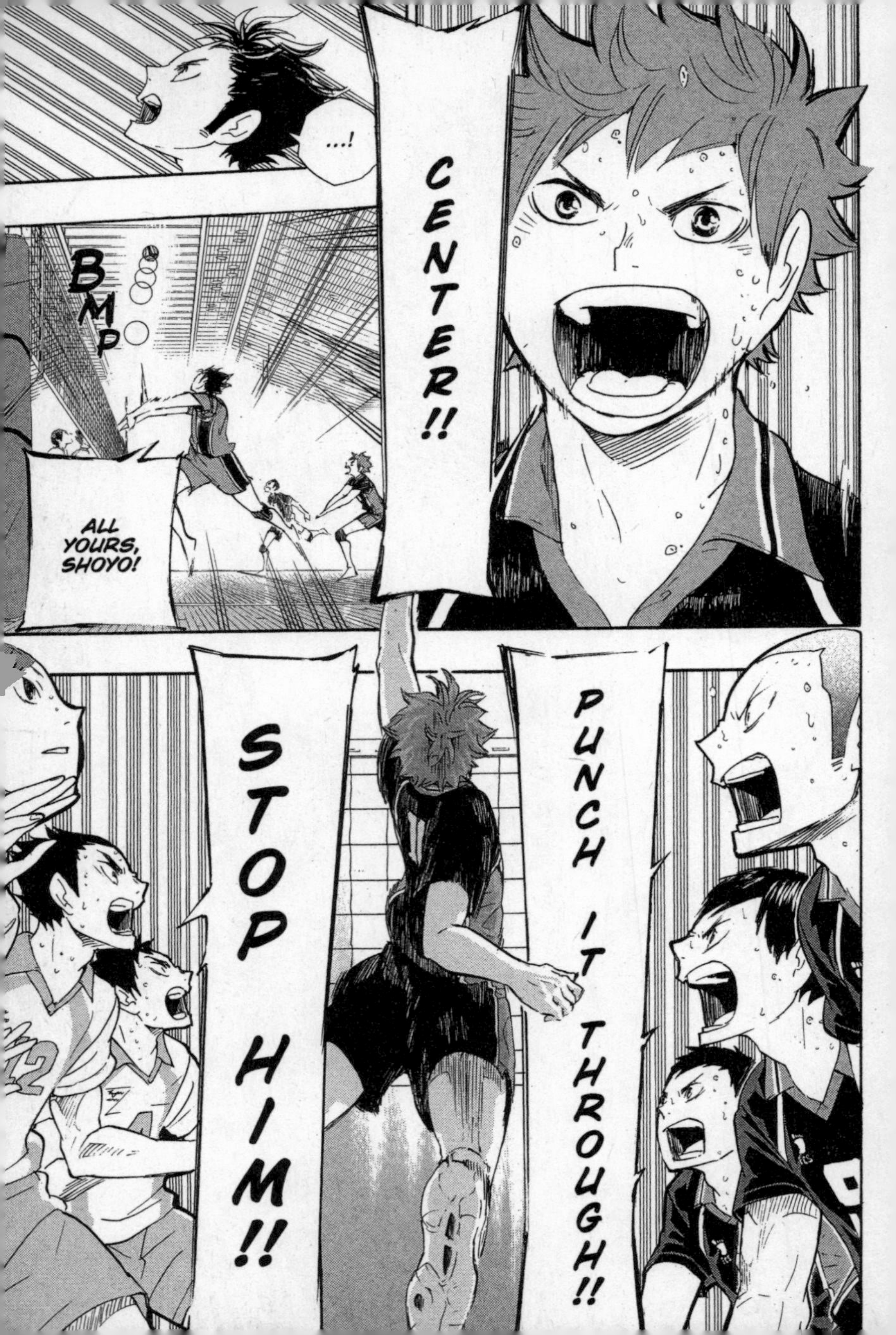
CENTER!!
...!
BMP
ALL YOURS, SHOYO!
PUNCH IT THROUGH!!
STOP HIM!!

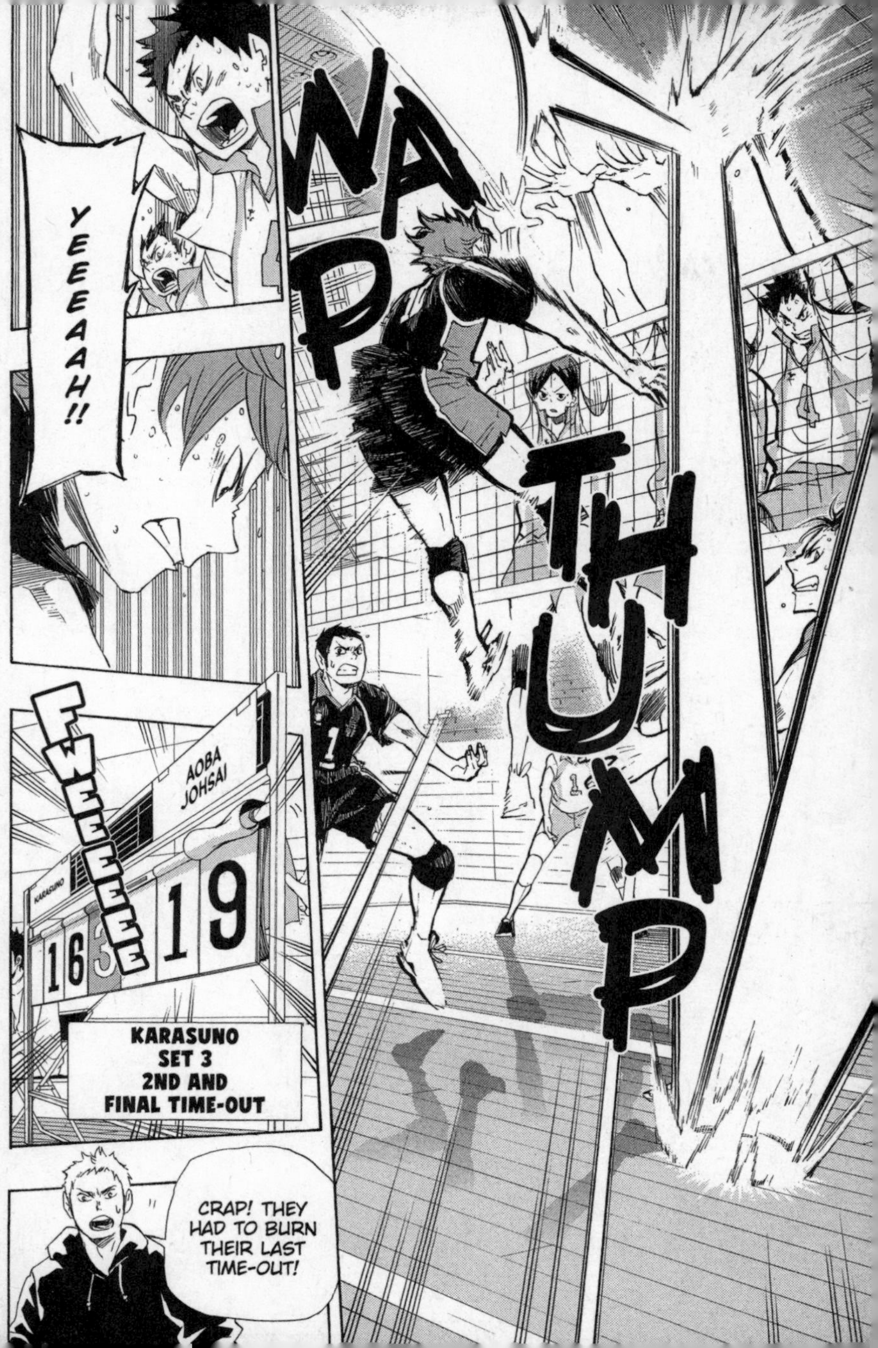
WAP
THUMP
YEEEAAH!!
FWEEEEEE
AOBA JOHSAI
KARASUNO
16
19
KARASUNO SET 3 2ND AND FINAL TIME-OUT
CRAP! THEY HAD TO BURN THEIR LAST TIME-OUT!

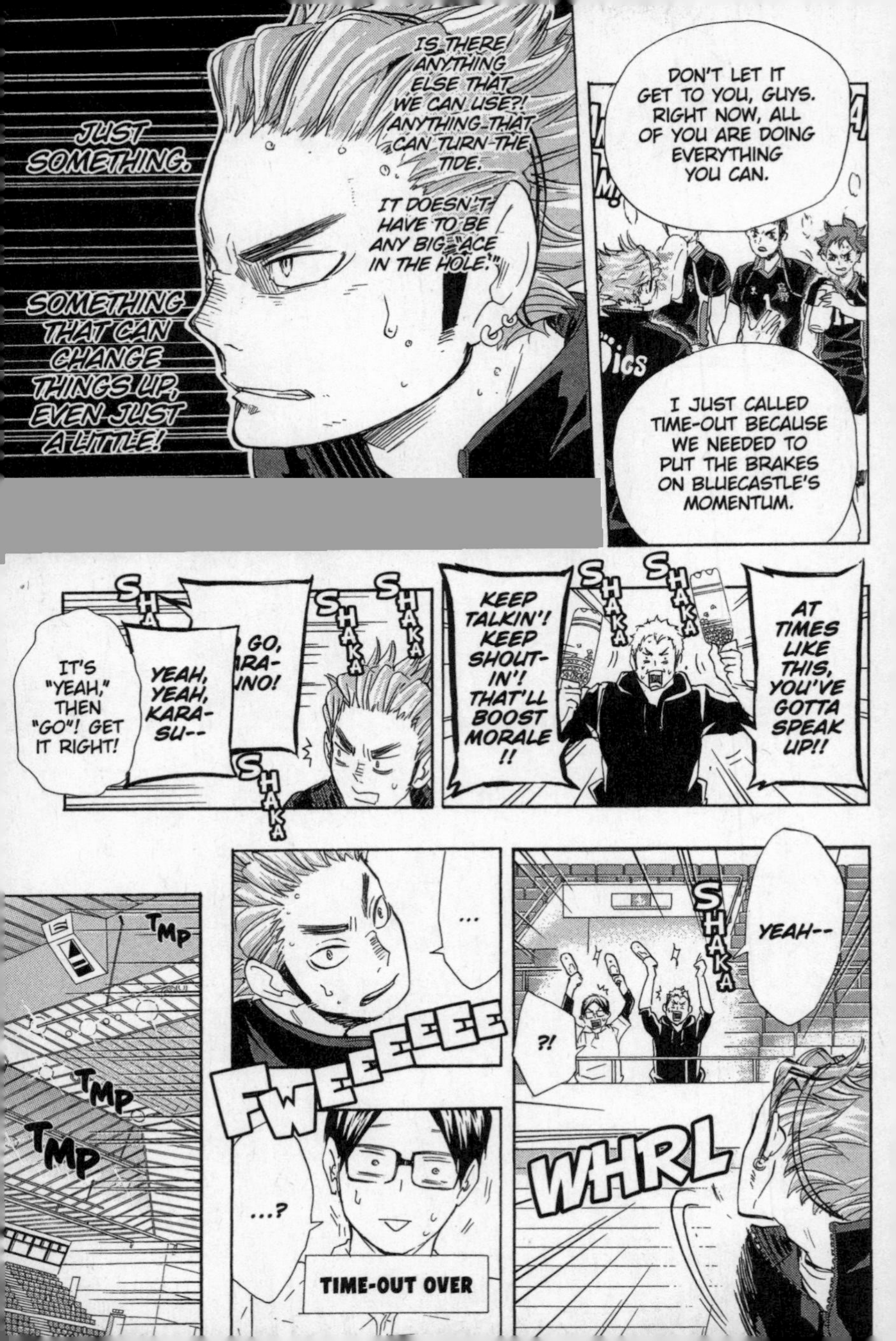
DON'T LET IT GET TO YOU, GUYS. RIGHT NOW, ALL OF YOU ARE DOING EVERYTHING YOU CAN.
I JUST CALLED TIME-OUT BECAUSE WE NEEDED TO PUT THE BRAKES ON BLUECASTLE'S MOMENTUM.
IS THERE ANYTHING ELSE THAT WE CAN USE?! ANYTHING THAT CAN TURN THE TIDE.
IT DOESN'T HAVE TO BE ANY BIG "ACE IN THE HOLE."
JUST SOMETHING.
SOMETHING THAT CAN CHANGE THINGS UP, EVEN JUST A LITTLE!
AT TIMES LIKE THIS, YOU'VE GOTTA SPEAK UP!!
SHAKA
SHAKA
KEEP TALKIN'! KEEP SHOUT-IN'! THAT'LL BOOST MORALE!!
SHAKA
SHAKA
GO, RA- UNO!
SHAKA
YEAH, YEAH, KARASU--
SHAKA
IT'S "YEAH," THEN "GO"! GET IT RIGHT!
SHAKA
YEAH--
SHAKA
?!
WHRL
...
FWEEEEEEE
...?
TIME-OUT OVER
TMP
TMP
TMP

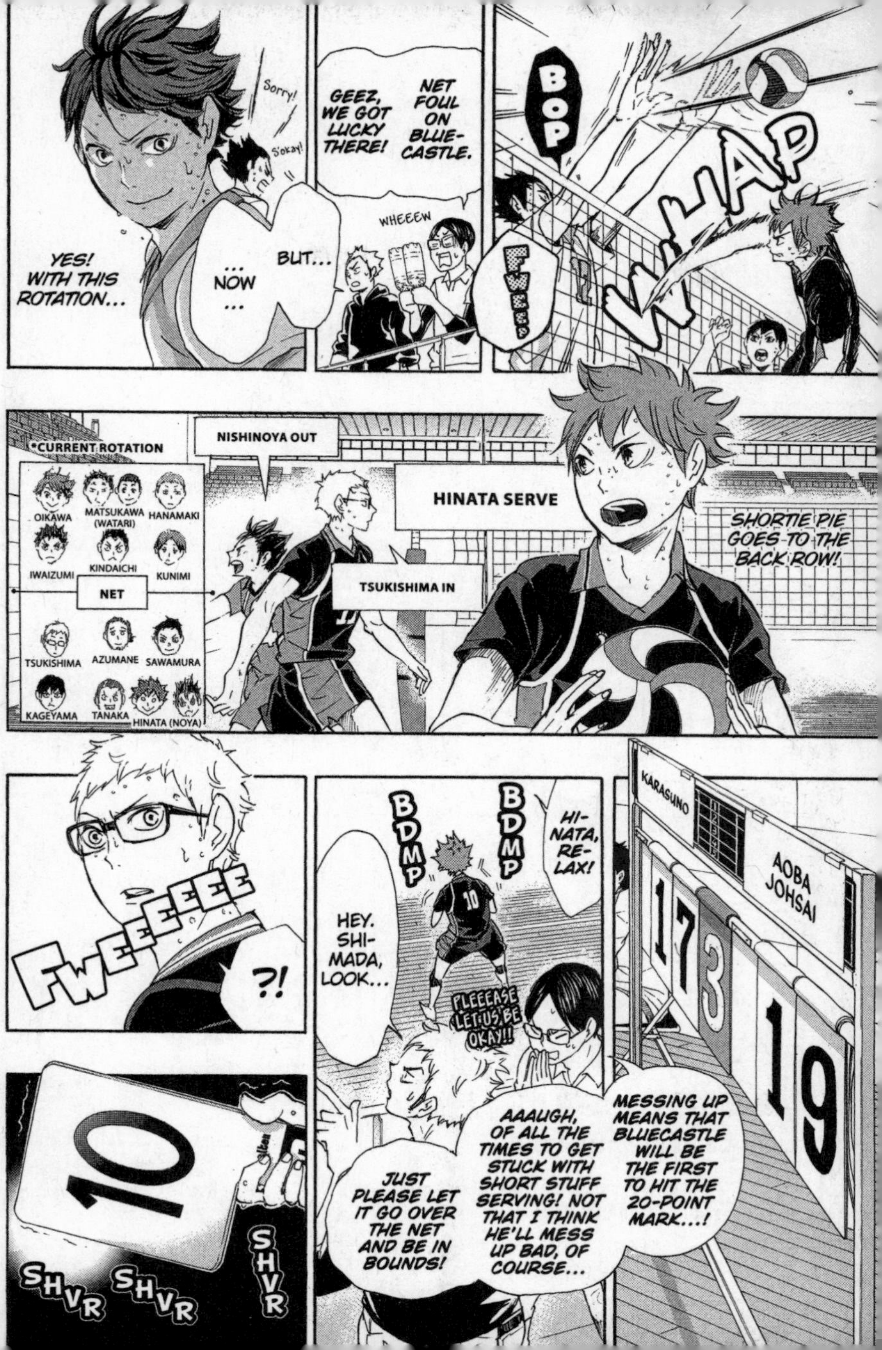
BOP
WHAP
FWEEP
NET FOUL ON BLUE-CASTLE.
GEEZ, WE GOT LUCKY THERE!
WHEEEW
Sorry!
S'okay!
BUT...
... NOW ...
YES! WITH THIS ROTATION...
HINATA SERVE
SHORTIE PIE GOES TO THE BACK ROW!
TSUKISHIMA IN
NISHINOYA OUT
*CURRENT ROTATION
OIKAWA
MATSUKAWA (WATARI)
HANAMAKI
IWAIZUMI
KINDAICHI
KUNIMI
NET
TSUKISHIMA
AZUMANE
SAWAMURA
KAGEYAMA
TANAKA
HINATA (NOYA)
KARASUNO
AOBA JOHSAI
17
3
19
HI-NATA, RE-LAX!
BDMP
BDMP
HEY. SHI-MADA, LOOK...
PLEEEASE LET US BE OKAY!!
MESSING UP MEANS THAT BLUECASTLE WILL BE THE FIRST TO HIT THE 20-POINT MARK...!
AAAUGH, OF ALL THE TIMES TO GET STUCK WITH SHORT STUFF SERVING! NOT THAT I THINK HE'LL MESS UP BAD, OF COURSE...
JUST PLEASE LET IT GO OVER THE NET AND BE IN BOUNDS!
FWEEEEEE
?!
10
SHVR
SHVR
SHVR

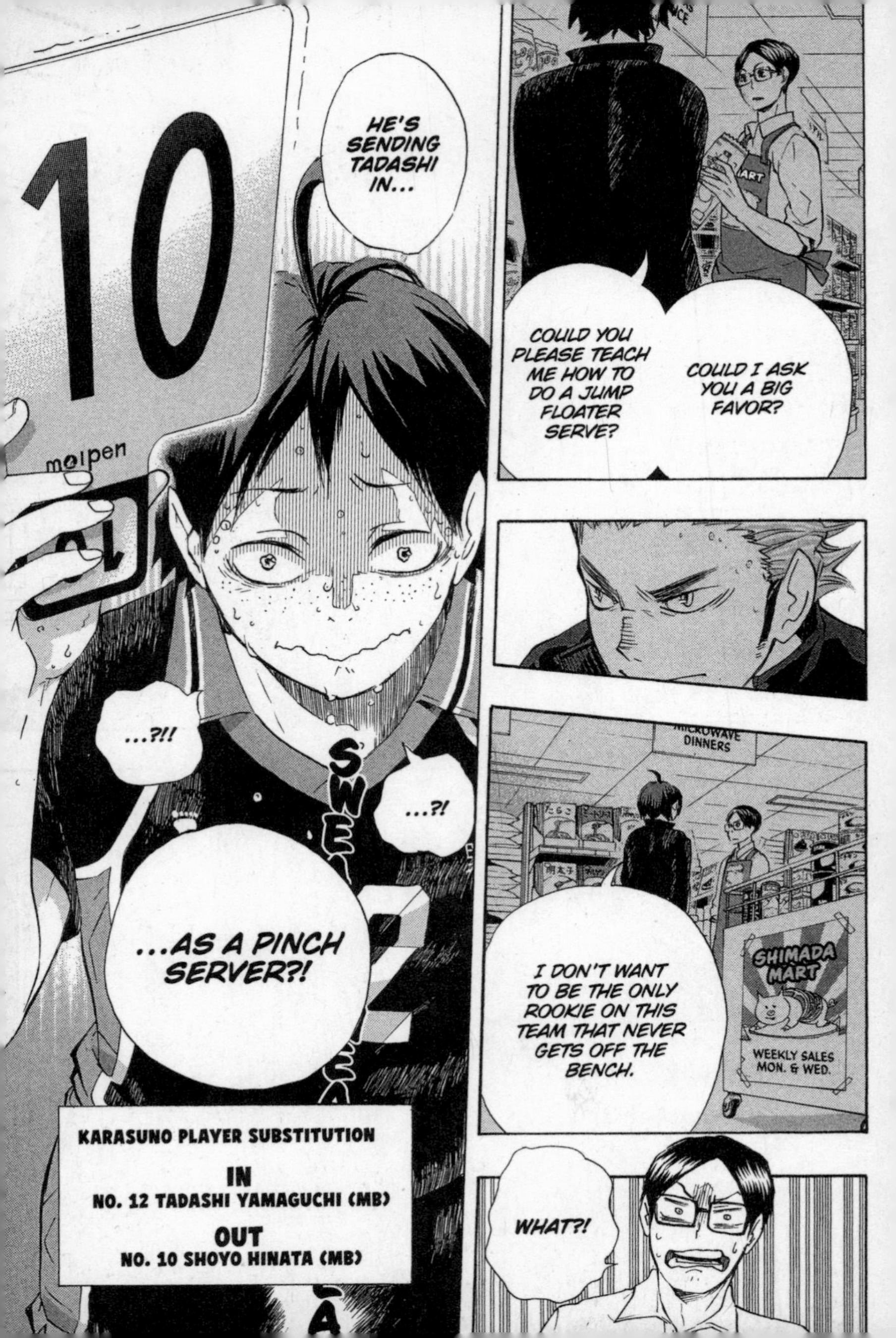
COULD I ASK YOU A BIG FAVOR?
COULD YOU PLEASE TEACH ME HOW TO DO A JUMP FLOATER SERVE?
DINNERS
I DON'T WANT TO BE THE ONLY ROOKIE ON THIS TEAM THAT NEVER GETS OFF THE BENCH.
SHIMADA MART
WEEKLY SALES MON. & WED.
WHAT?!
HE'S SENDING TADASHI IN...
...?!!
...?!
...AS A PINCH SERVER?!
KARASUNO PLAYER SUBSTITUTION
IN
NO. 12 TADASHI YAMAGUCHI (MB)
OUT
NO. 10 SHOYO HINATA (MB)

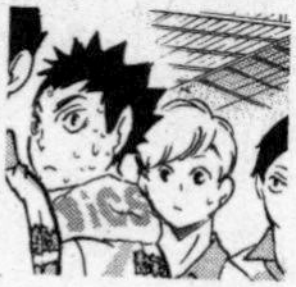

THIS GUY. HE'S THE ONE WHO PLAYED SETTER WHILE OIKAWA WAS OUT DURING THEIR FIRST PRACTICE GAME.

SHIGERU YAHABA

AOBA JOHSAI HIGH SCHOOL
CLASS 2-5

POSITION:
SETTER

HEIGHT: 5'11"

WEIGHT: 152 LBS.
(AS OF APRIL, 2ND YEAR OF HIGH SCHOOL)

BIRTHDAY: MARCH 1

FAVORITE FOOD:
SALMON ROE RICE BOWL

CURRENT WORRY:
BEING OIKAWA'S SUCCESSOR ISN'T EASY.

ABILITY PARAMETERS
(5-POINT SCALE)

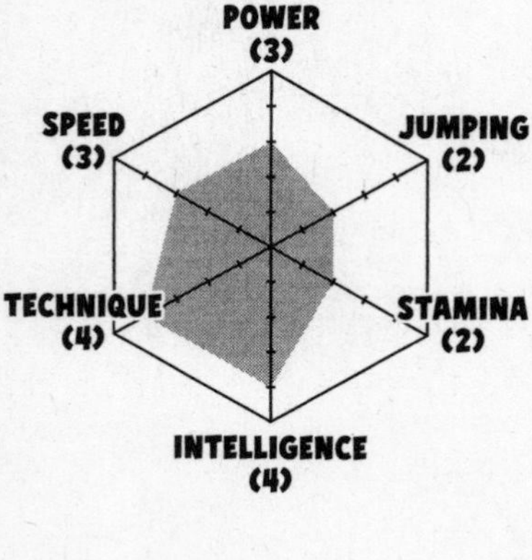
POWER
(3)
JUMPING
(2)
STAMINA
(2)
INTELLIGENCE
(4)
TECHNIQUE
(4)
SPEED
(3)

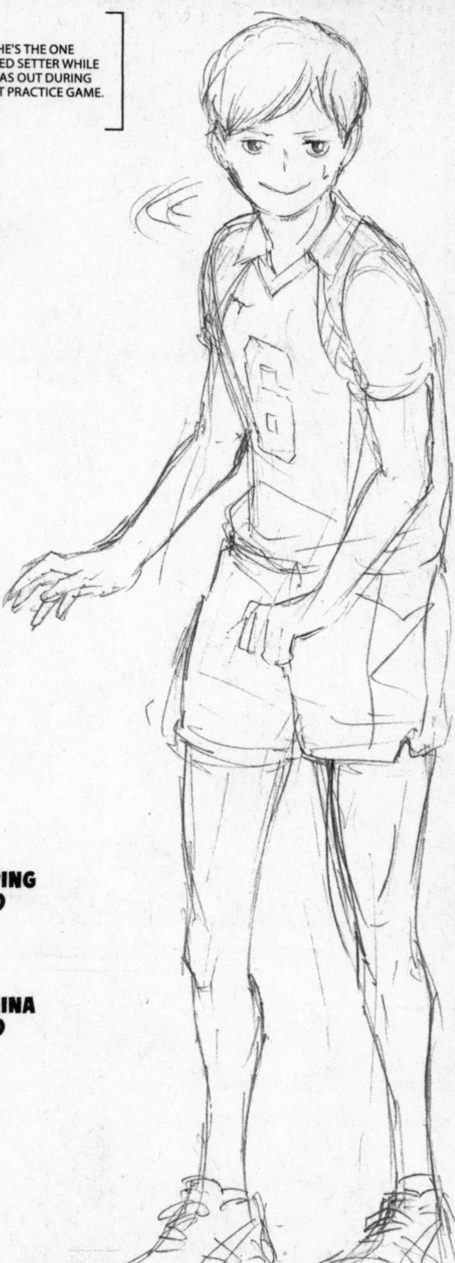

CHAPTER 64

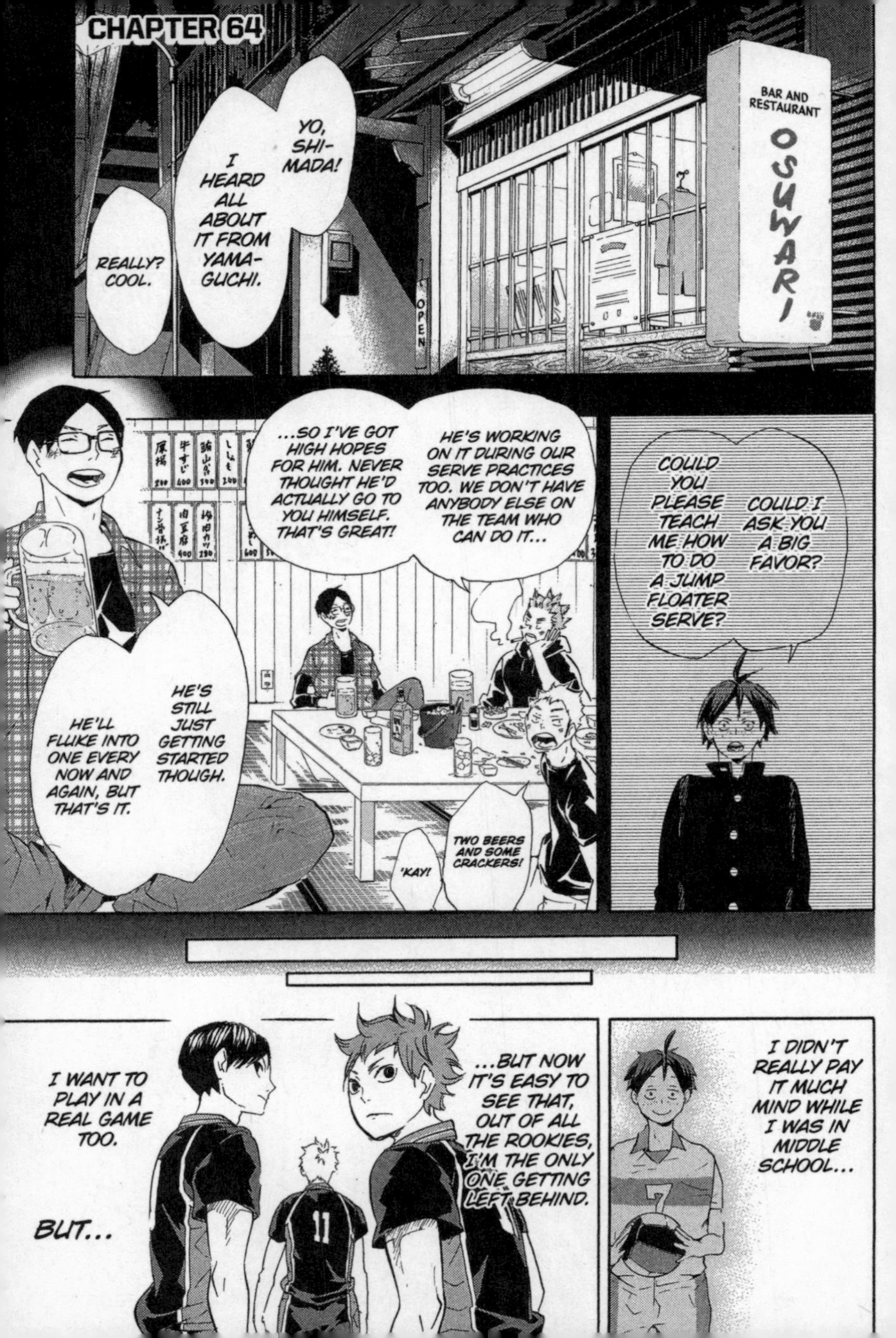
BAR AND RESTAURANT
OSUWARI
OPEN
YO, SHIMADA! I HEARD ALL ABOUT IT FROM YAMAGUCHI.
REALLY? COOL.
COULD I ASK YOU A BIG FAVOR?
COULD YOU PLEASE TEACH ME HOW TO DO A JUMP FLOATER SERVE?
HE'S WORKING ON IT DURING OUR SERVE PRACTICES TOO. WE DON'T HAVE ANYBODY ELSE ON THE TEAM WHO CAN DO IT...
...SO I'VE GOT HIGH HOPES FOR HIM. NEVER THOUGHT HE'D ACTUALLY GO TO YOU HIMSELF. THAT'S GREAT!
HE'S STILL JUST GETTING STARTED THOUGH.
HE'LL FLUKE INTO ONE EVERY NOW AND AGAIN, BUT THAT'S IT.
TWO BEERS AND SOME CRACKERS!
'KAY!
I DIDN'T REALLY PAY IT MUCH MIND WHILE I WAS IN MIDDLE SCHOOL...
...BUT NOW IT'S EASY TO SEE THAT, OUT OF ALL THE ROOKIES, I'M THE ONLY ONE GETTING LEFT BEHIND.
I WANT TO PLAY IN A REAL GAME TOO.
BUT...

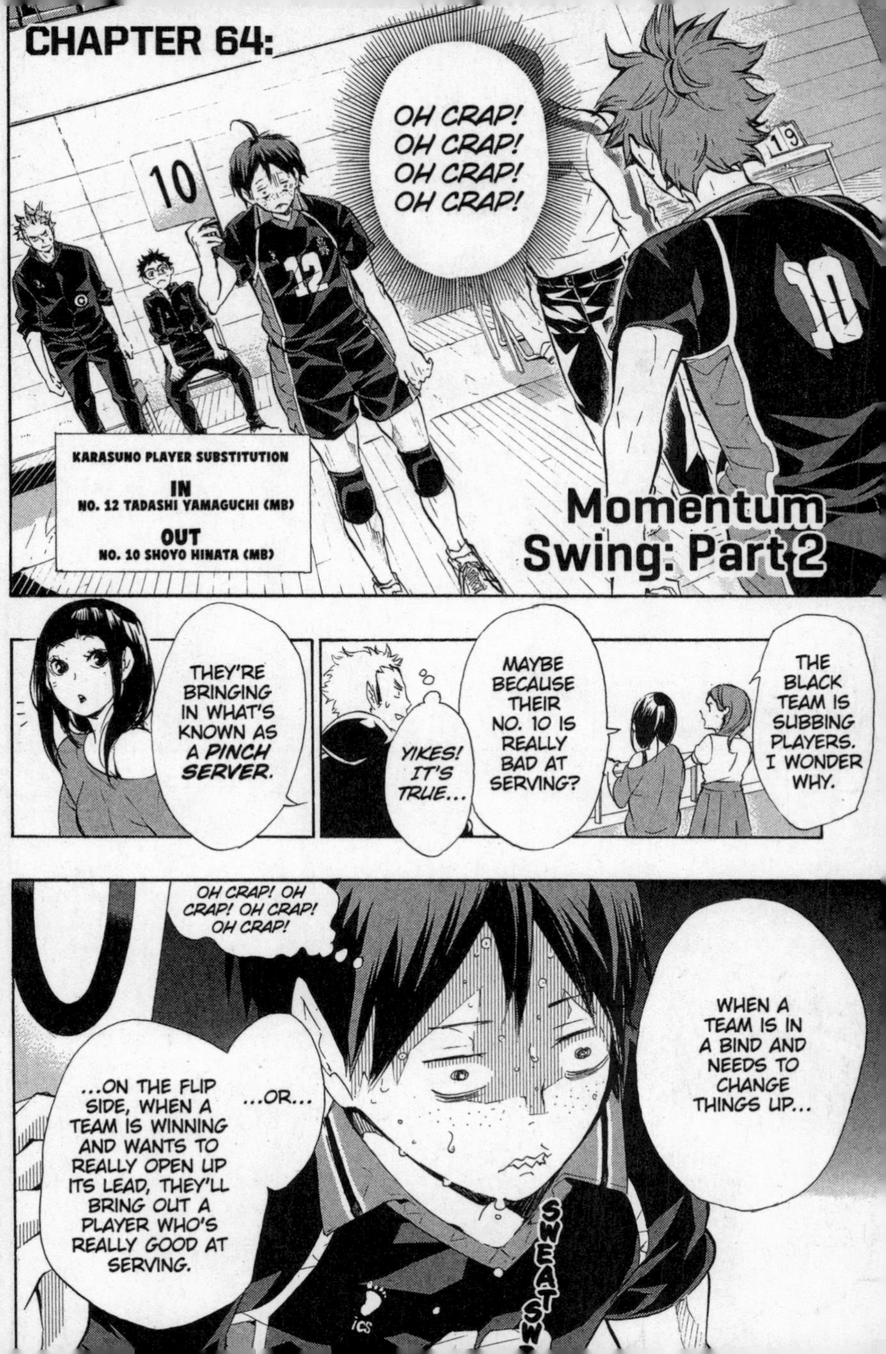
CHAPTER 64:
Momentum Swing: Part 2
OH CRAP! OH CRAP! OH CRAP! OH CRAP!
KARASUNO PLAYER SUBSTITUTION
IN
NO. 12 TADASHI YAMAGUCHI (MB)
OUT
NO. 10 SHOYO HINATA (MB)
THE BLACK TEAM IS SUBBING PLAYERS. I WONDER WHY.
MAYBE BECAUSE THEIR NO. 10 IS REALLY BAD AT SERVING?
YIKES! IT'S TRUE...
THEY'RE BRINGING IN WHAT'S KNOWN AS A PINCH SERVER.
WHEN A TEAM IS IN A BIND AND NEEDS TO CHANGE THINGS UP...
OH CRAP! OH CRAP! OH CRAP! OH CRAP!
...OR...
...ON THE FLIP SIDE, WHEN A TEAM IS WINNING AND WANTS TO REALLY OPEN UP ITS LEAD, THEY'LL BRING OUT A PLAYER WHO'S REALLY GOOD AT SERVING.
SWEAT

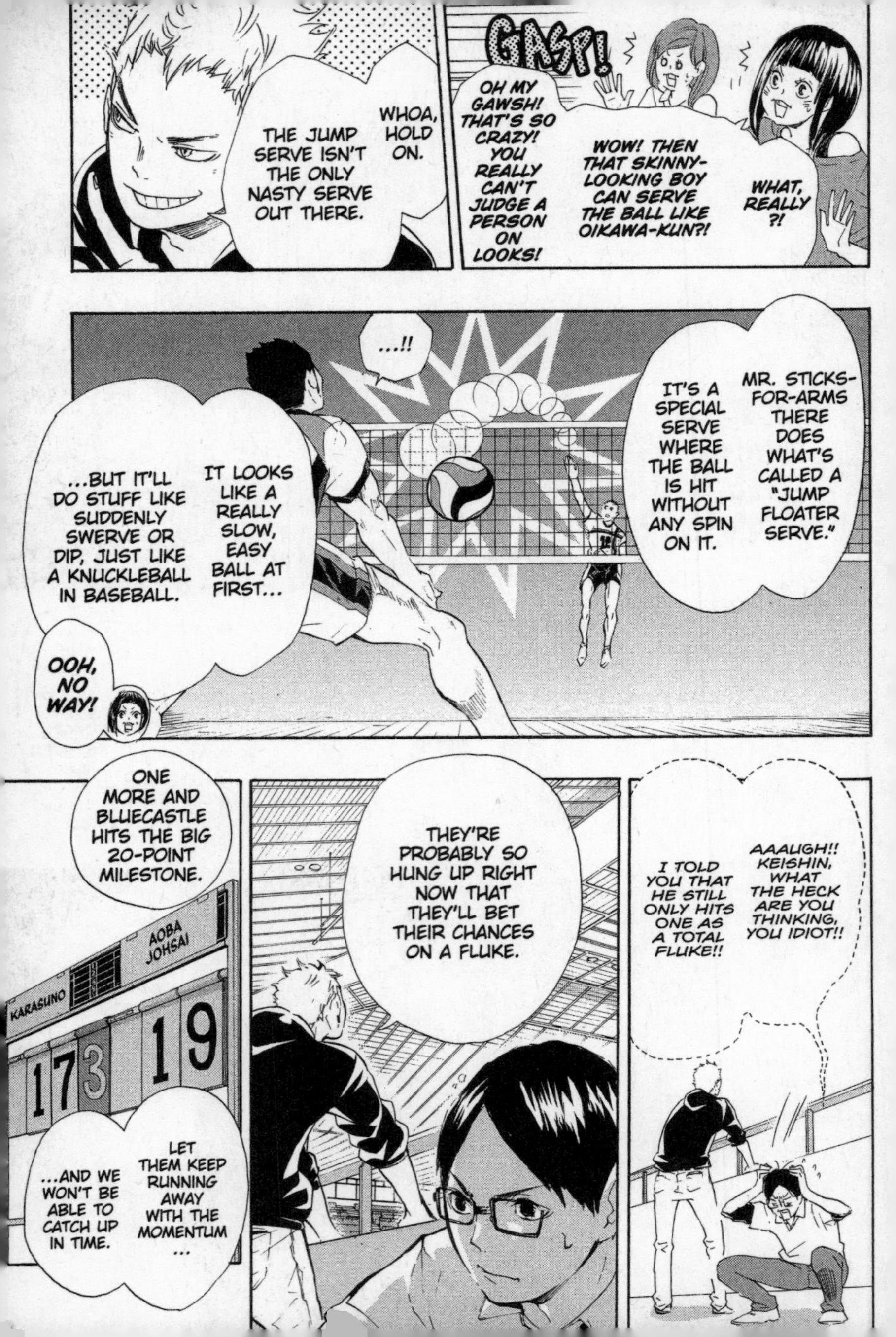
GASP!
WHAT, REALLY?!
WOW! THEN THAT SKINNY-LOOKING BOY CAN SERVE THE BALL LIKE OIKAWA-KUN?!
OH MY GAWSH! THAT'S SO CRAZY! YOU REALLY CAN'T JUDGE A PERSON ON LOOKS!
WHOA, HOLD ON.
THE JUMP SERVE ISN'T THE ONLY NASTY SERVE OUT THERE.
MR. STICKS-FOR-ARMS THERE DOES WHAT'S CALLED A "JUMP FLOATER SERVE."
IT'S A SPECIAL SERVE WHERE THE BALL IS HIT WITHOUT ANY SPIN ON IT.
...!!
IT LOOKS LIKE A REALLY SLOW, EASY BALL AT FIRST...
...BUT IT'LL DO STUFF LIKE SUDDENLY SWERVE OR DIP, JUST LIKE A KNUCKLEBALL IN BASEBALL.
OOH, NO WAY!
AAAUGH!! KEISHIN, WHAT THE HECK ARE YOU THINKING, YOU IDIOT!!
I TOLD YOU THAT HE STILL ONLY HITS ONE AS A TOTAL FLUKE!!
THEY'RE PROBABLY SO HUNG UP RIGHT NOW THAT THEY'LL BET THEIR CHANCES ON A FLUKE.
ONE MORE AND BLUECASTLE HITS THE BIG 20-POINT MILESTONE.
AOBA JOHSAI
KARASUNO
17
19
LET THEM KEEP RUNNING AWAY WITH THE MOMENTUM...
...AND WE WON'T BE ABLE TO CATCH UP IN TIME.

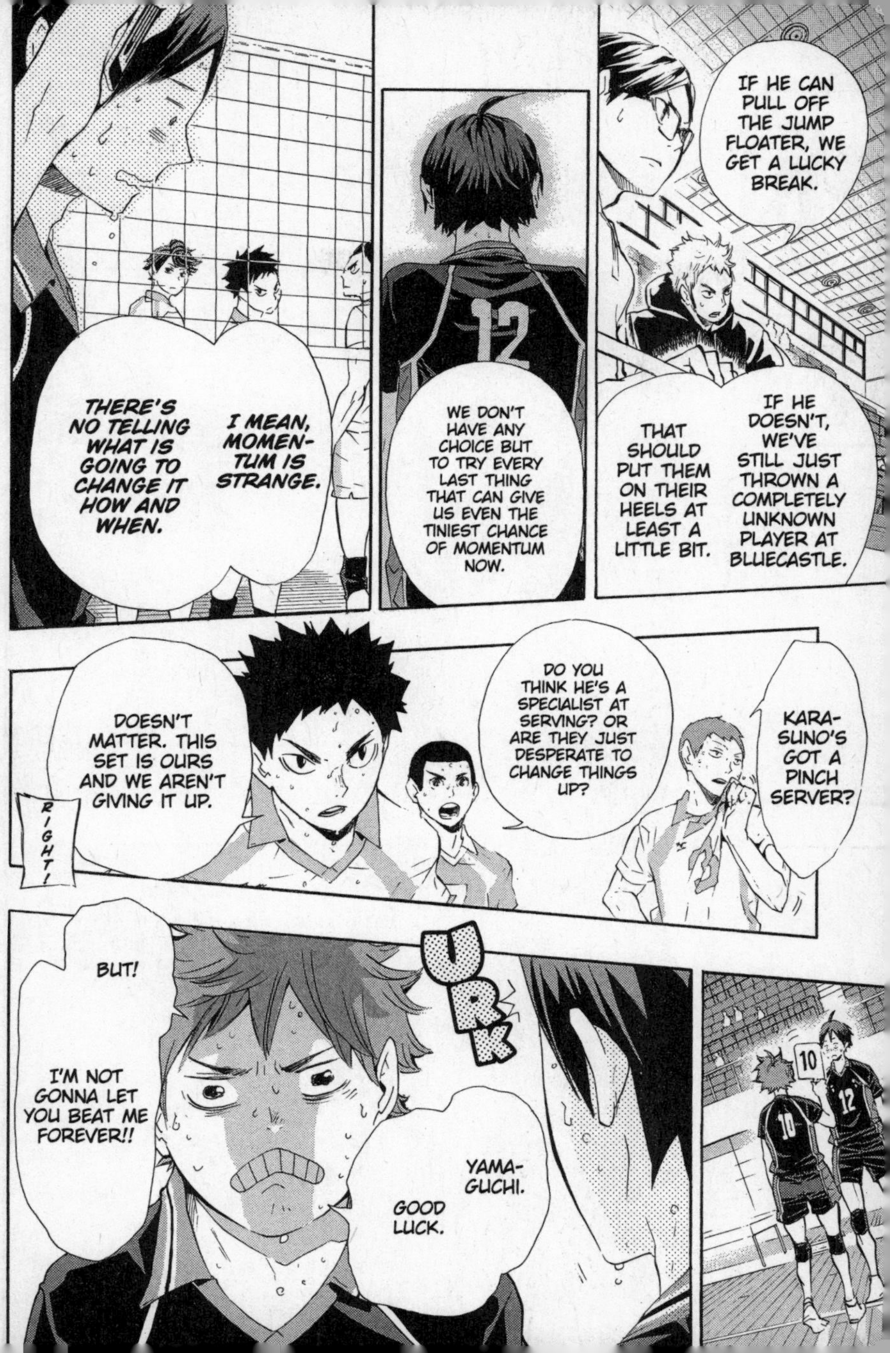
IF HE CAN PULL OFF THE JUMP FLOATER, WE GET A LUCKY BREAK.
IF HE DOESN'T, WE'VE STILL JUST THROWN A COMPLETELY UNKNOWN PLAYER AT BLUECASTLE.
THAT SHOULD PUT THEM ON THEIR HEELS AT LEAST A LITTLE BIT.
WE DON'T HAVE ANY CHOICE BUT TO TRY EVERY LAST THING THAT CAN GIVE US EVEN THE TINIEST CHANCE OF MOMENTUM NOW.
I MEAN, MOMENTUM IS STRANGE.
THERE'S NO TELLING WHAT IS GOING TO CHANGE IT HOW AND WHEN.
KARASUNO'S GOT A PINCH SERVER?
DO YOU THINK HE'S A SPECIALIST AT SERVING? OR ARE THEY JUST DESPERATE TO CHANGE THINGS UP?
DOESN'T MATTER. THIS SET IS OURS AND WE AREN'T GIVING IT UP.
RIGHT!
10
12
YAMAGUCHI.
GOOD LUCK.
URK
BUT!
I'M NOT GONNA LET YOU BEAT ME FOREVER!!

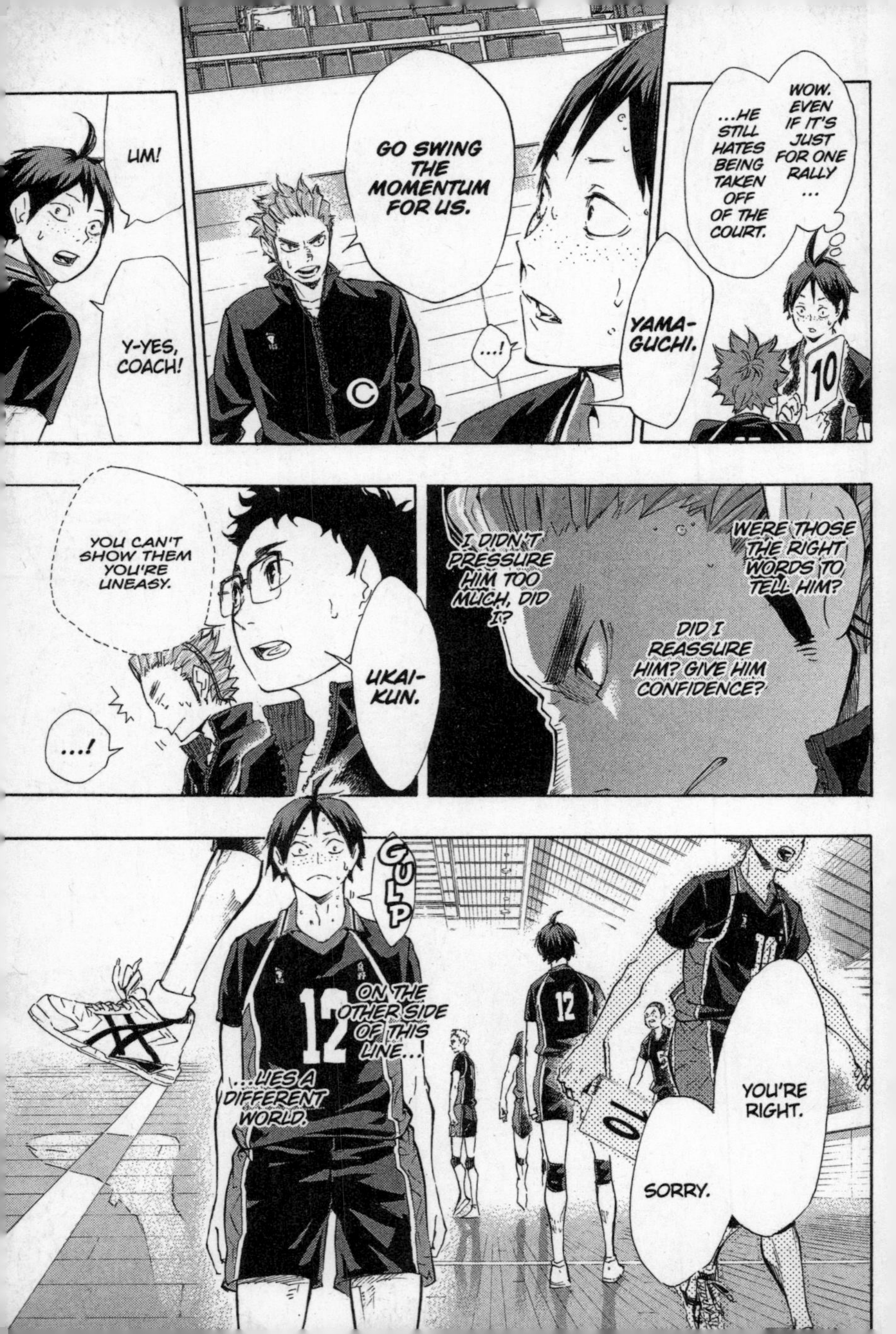
WOW. EVEN IF IT'S JUST FOR ONE RALLY ...
...HE STILL HATES BEING TAKEN OFF OF THE COURT.
YAMA-GUCHI.
GO SWING THE MOMENTUM FOR US.
...!
UM!
Y-YES, COACH!
WERE THOSE THE RIGHT WORDS TO TELL HIM?
I DIDN'T PRESSURE HIM TOO MUCH, DID I?
DID I REASSURE HIM? GIVE HIM CONFIDENCE?
UKAI-KUN.
YOU CAN'T SHOW THEM YOU'RE UNEASY.
...!
YOU'RE RIGHT.
SORRY.
GULP
ON THE OTHER SIDE OF THIS LINE...
...LIES A DIFFERENT WORLD.
10
12
12
10

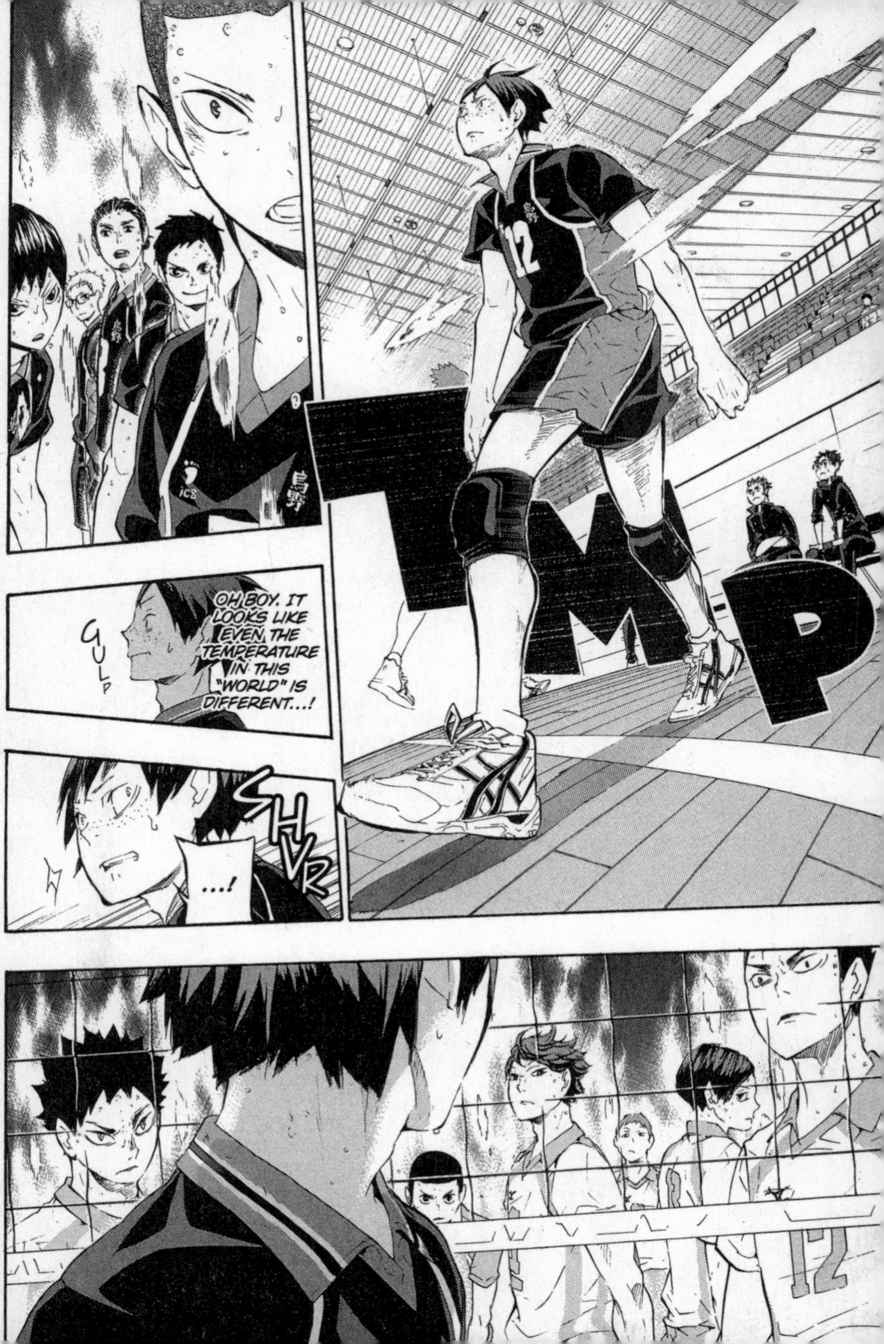
TMP
GULP
OH BOY. IT LOOKS LIKE EVEN THE TEMPERATURE IN THIS "WORLD" IS DIFFERENT...!
SHVR
...!

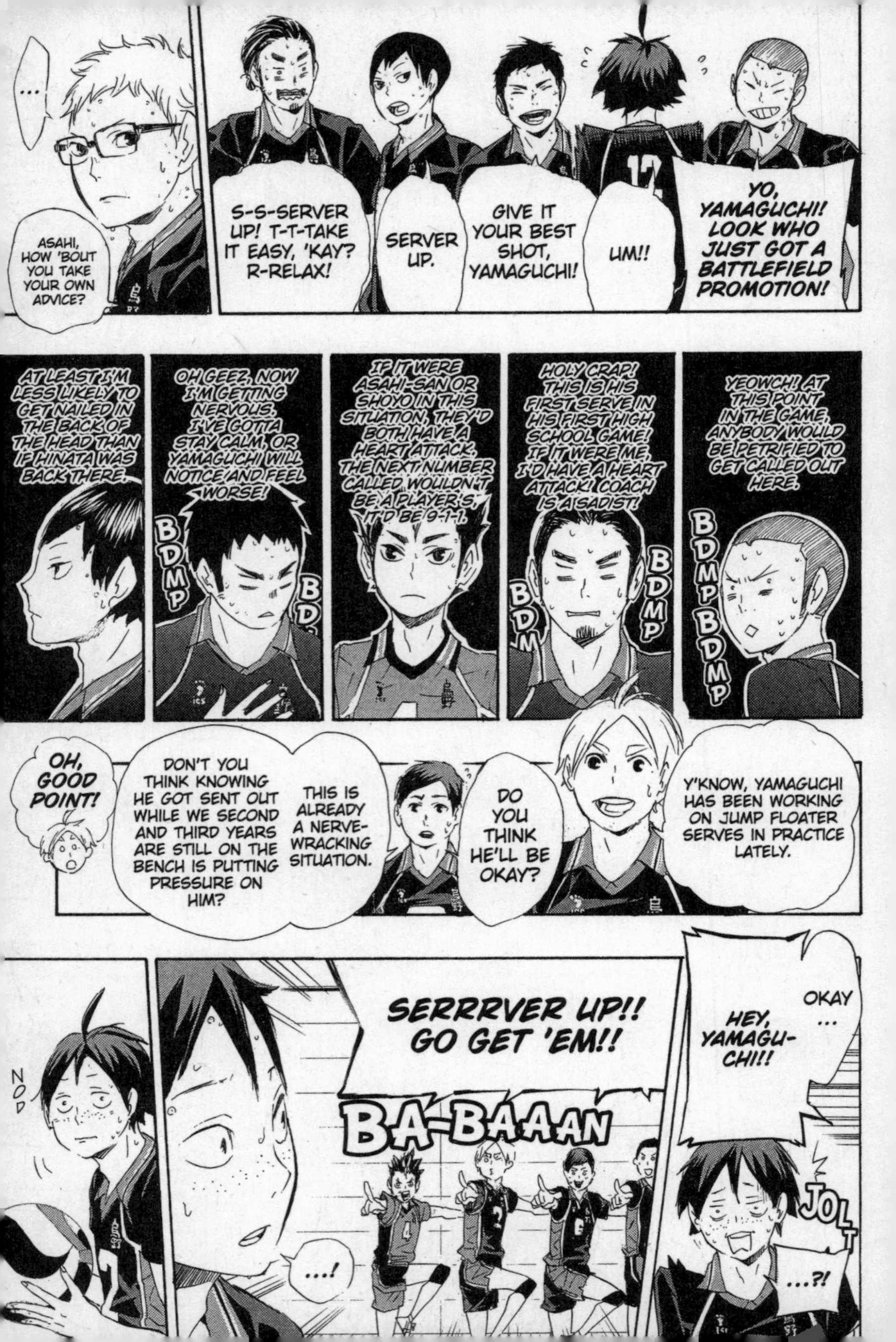
YO, YAMAGUCHI! LOOK WHO JUST GOT A BATTLEFIELD PROMOTION!
UM!!
GIVE IT YOUR BEST SHOT, YAMAGUCHI!
SERVER UP.
S-S-SERVER UP! T-T-TAKE IT EASY, 'KAY? R-RELAX!
...
ASAHI, HOW 'BOUT YOU TAKE YOUR OWN ADVICE?
YEOWCH! AT THIS POINT IN THE GAME, ANYBODY WOULD BE PETRIFIED TO GET CALLED OUT HERE.
BDMP BDMP BDMP
HOLY CRAP! THIS IS HIS FIRST SERVE IN HIS FIRST HIGH SCHOOL GAME! IF IT WERE ME, I'D HAVE A HEART ATTACK! COACH IS A SADIST!
BDMP
BDM
IF IT WERE ASAHI-SAN OR SHOYO IN THIS SITUATION, THEY'D BOTH HAVE A HEART ATTACK. THE NEXT NUMBER CALLED WOULDN'T BE A PLAYER'S, IT'D BE 9-1-1.
OH GEEZ, NOW I'M GETTING NERVOUS. I'VE GOTTA STAY CALM, OR YAMAGUCHI WILL NOTICE AND FEEL WORSE!
BDMP
AT LEAST I'M LESS LIKELY TO GET NAILED IN THE BACK OF THE HEAD THAN IF HINATA WAS BACK THERE.
Y'KNOW, YAMAGUCHI HAS BEEN WORKING ON JUMP FLOATER SERVES IN PRACTICE LATELY.
DO YOU THINK HE'LL BE OKAY?
THIS IS ALREADY A NERVE-WRACKING SITUATION.
DON'T YOU THINK KNOWING HE GOT SENT OUT WHILE WE SECOND AND THIRD YEARS ARE STILL ON THE BENCH IS PUTTING PRESSURE ON HIM?
OH, GOOD POINT!
OKAY ...
HEY, YAMAGUCHI!!
JOLT
...?!
SERRRVER UP!! GO GET 'EM!!
BA-BAAAN
...!
NOD

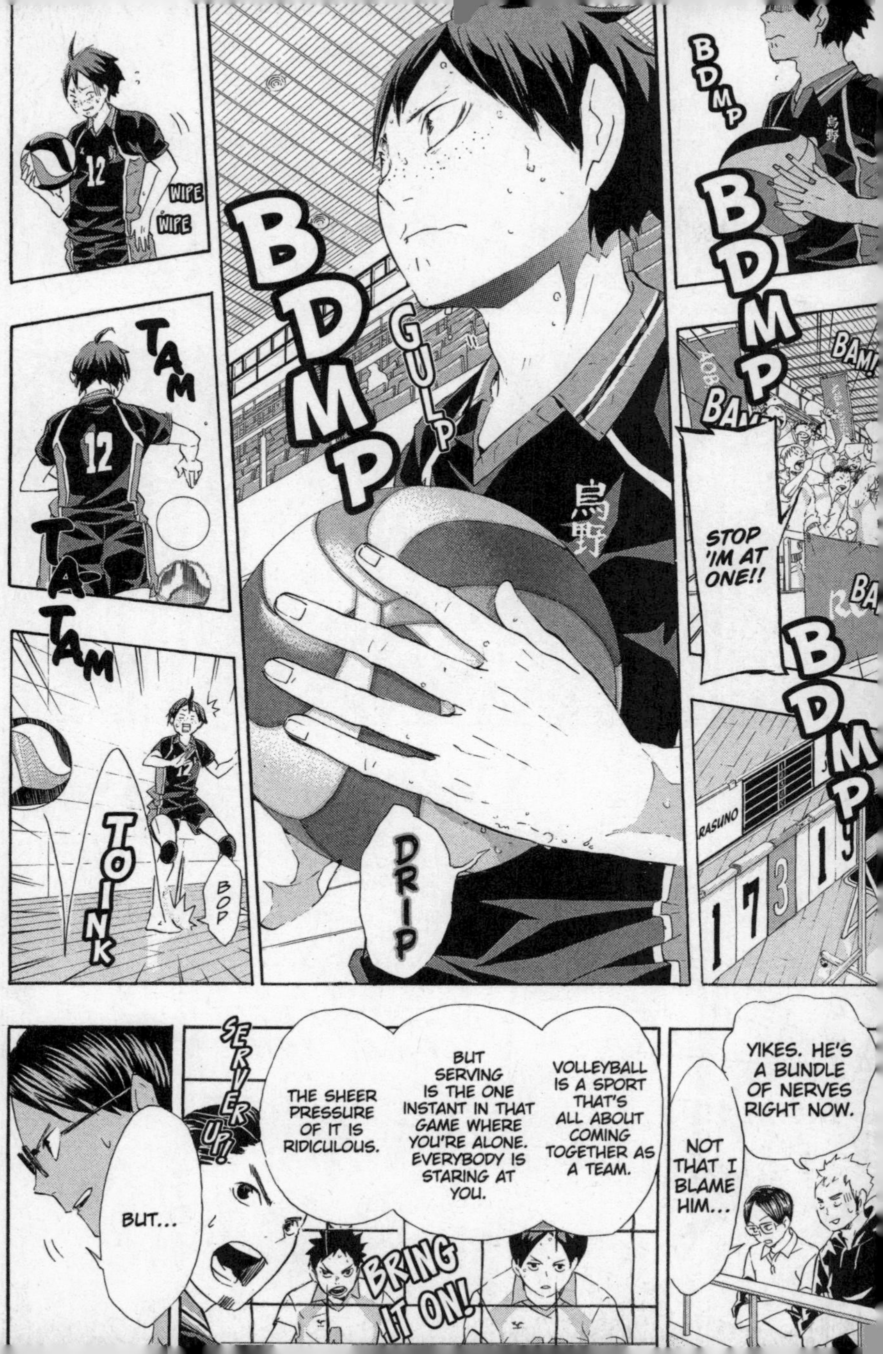
BDMP
BDMP
BAM!
BAM
STOP 'I'M AT ONE!!
BA
BDMP
RASUNO
17 3 1 9
BDMP
GULP
DRIP
WIPE
WIPE
TAM
TA-TAM
TOINK
BOP
YIKES. HE'S A BUNDLE OF NERVES RIGHT NOW.
NOT THAT I BLAME HIM...
VOLLEYBALL IS A SPORT THAT'S ALL ABOUT COMING TOGETHER AS A TEAM.
BUT SERVING IS THE ONE INSTANT IN THAT GAME WHERE YOU'RE ALONE. EVERYBODY IS STARING AT YOU.
THE SHEER PRESSURE OF IT IS RIDICULOUS.
SERVER UP!
BRING IT ON!
BUT...

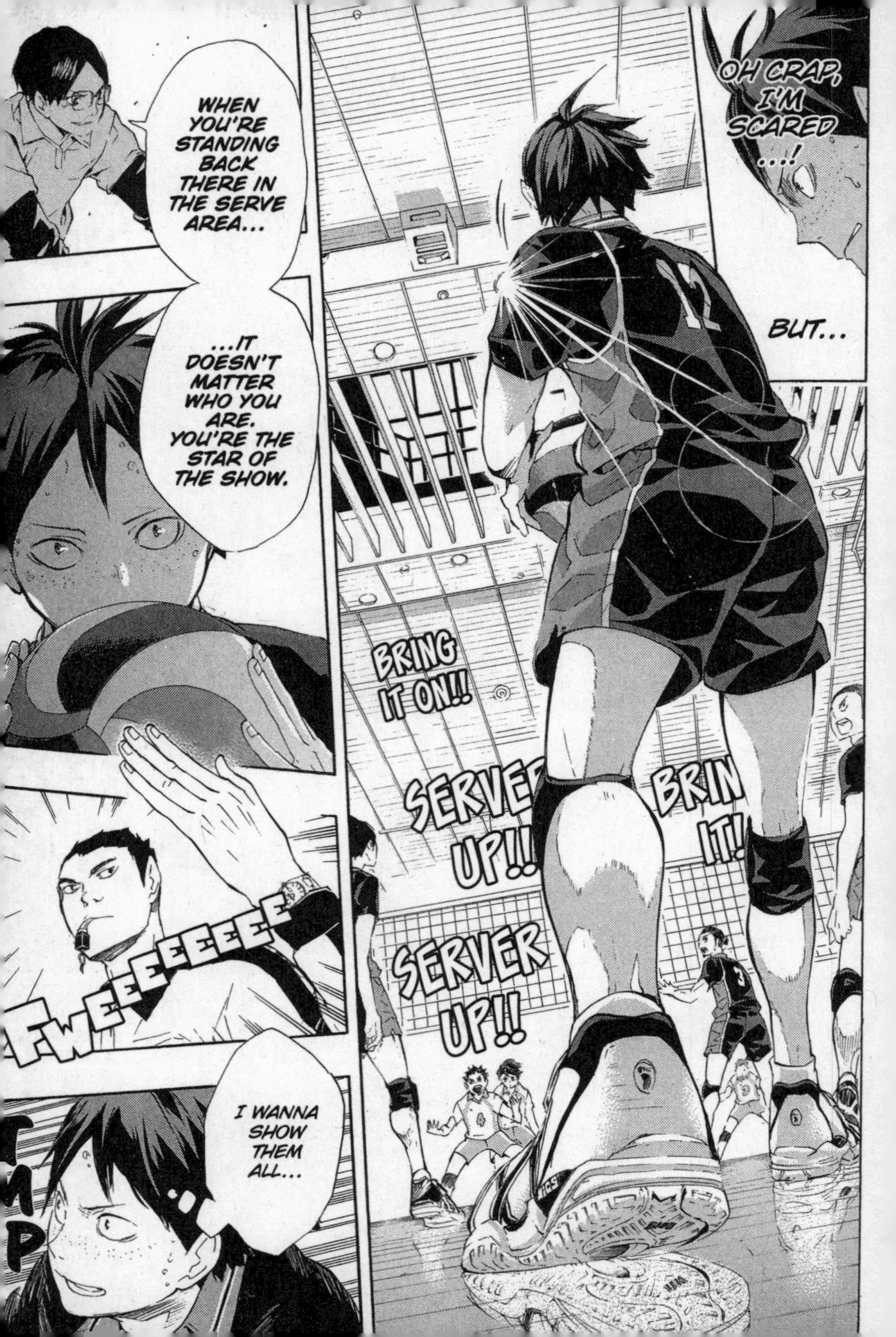
OH CRAP, I'M SCARED ...!
BUT...
BRIN IT!
BRING IT ON!!
SERVER UP!!
SERVER UP!!
WHEN YOU'RE STANDING BACK THERE IN THE SERVE AREA...
...IT DOESN'T MATTER WHO YOU ARE. YOU'RE THE STAR OF THE SHOW.
FWEEEEEEEE
I WANNA SHOW THEM ALL...
TMP

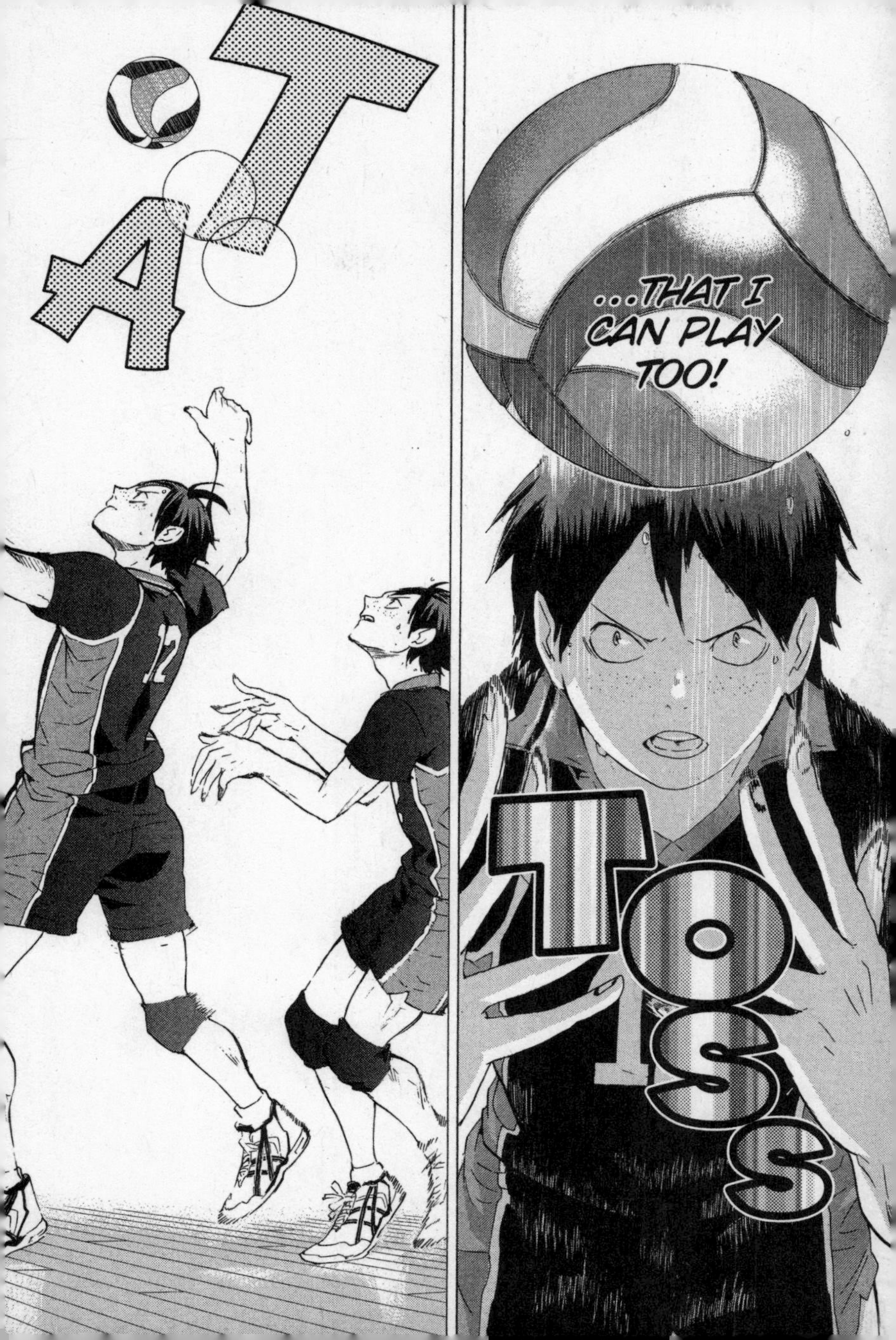
...THAT I CAN PLAY TOO!
TOSS
TA

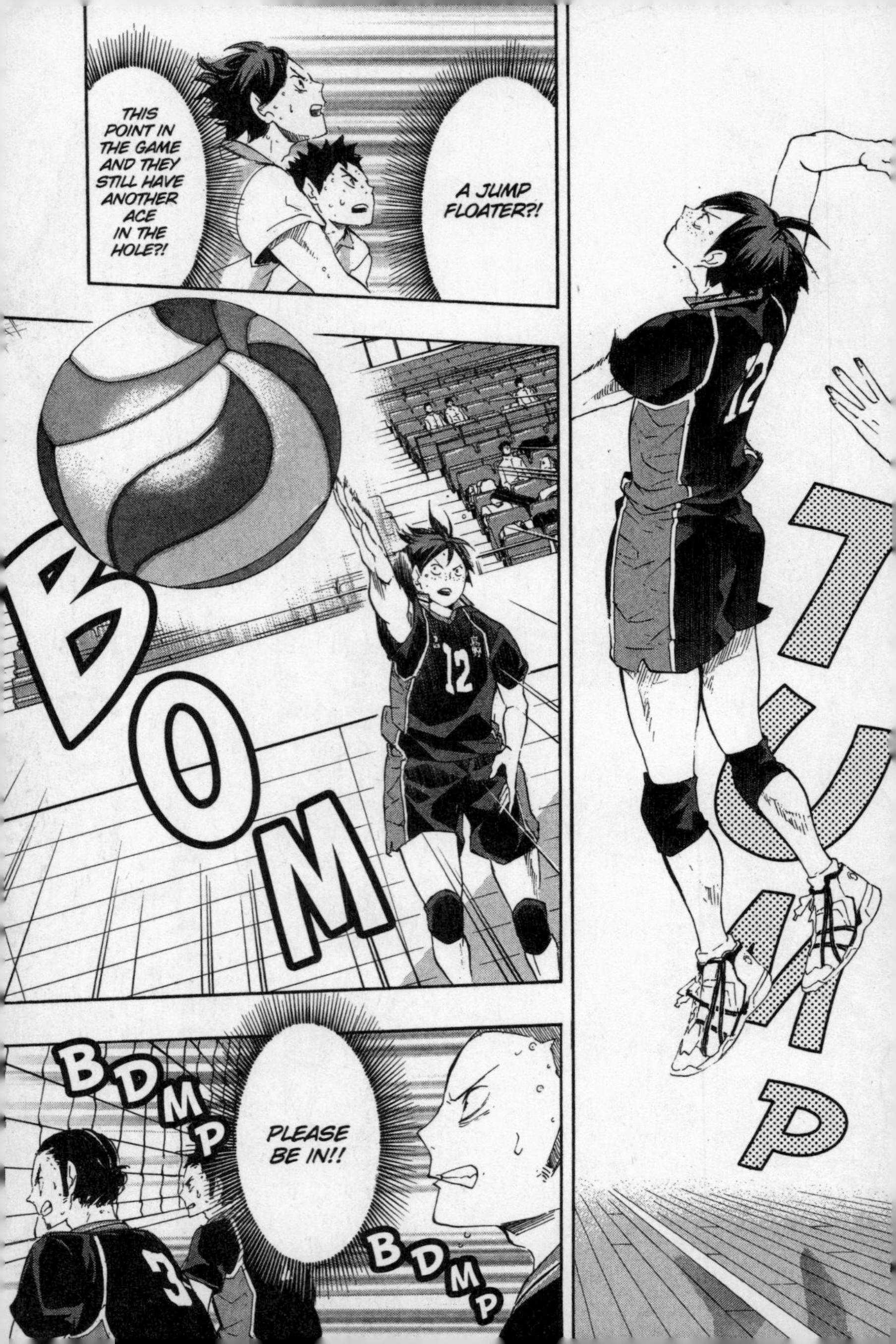
THUMP
A JUMP FLOATER?!
THIS POINT IN THE GAME AND THEY STILL HAVE ANOTHER ACE IN THE HOLE?!
BOOM
BDMP
PLEASE BE IN!!
BDMP

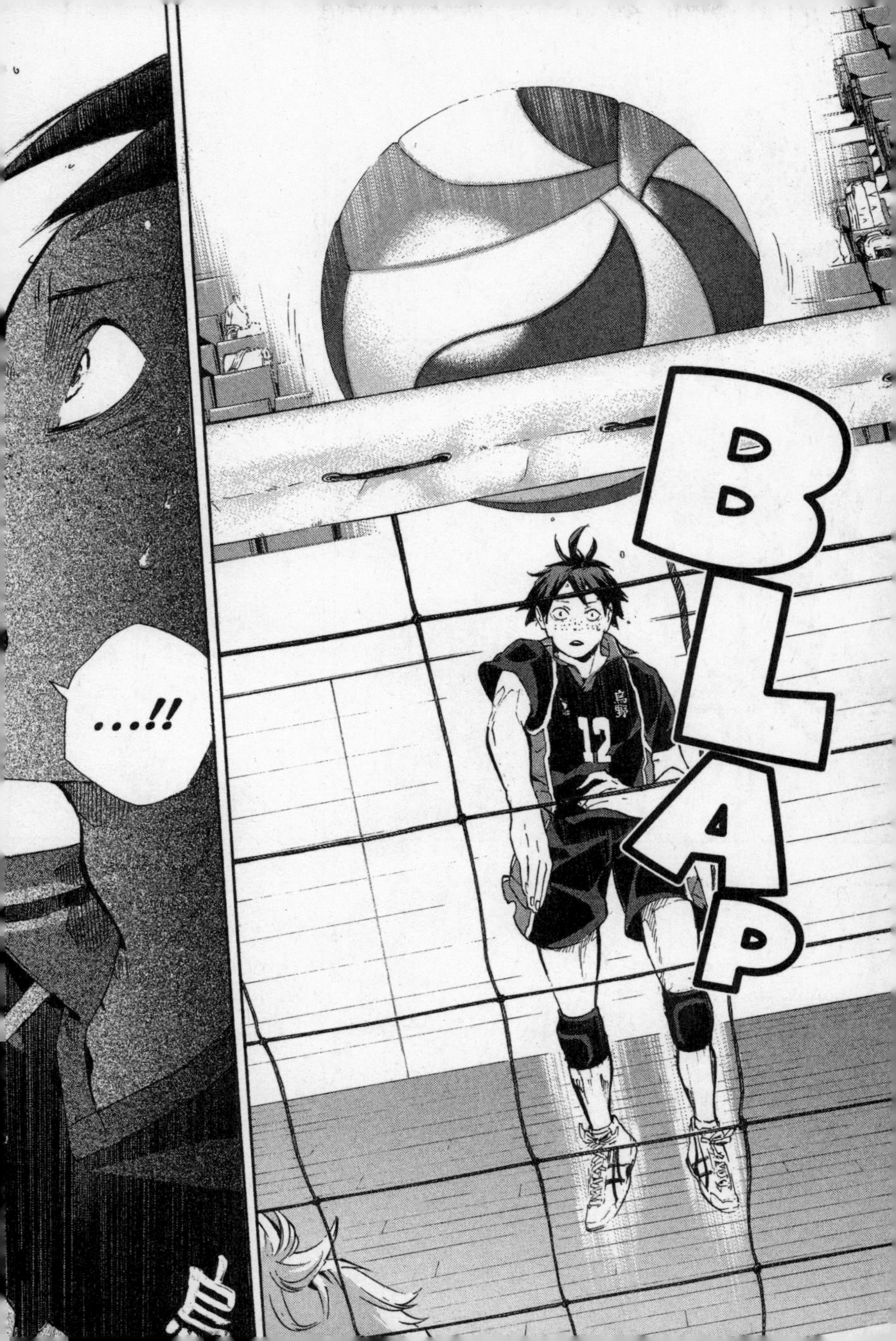
BLAP
...!!

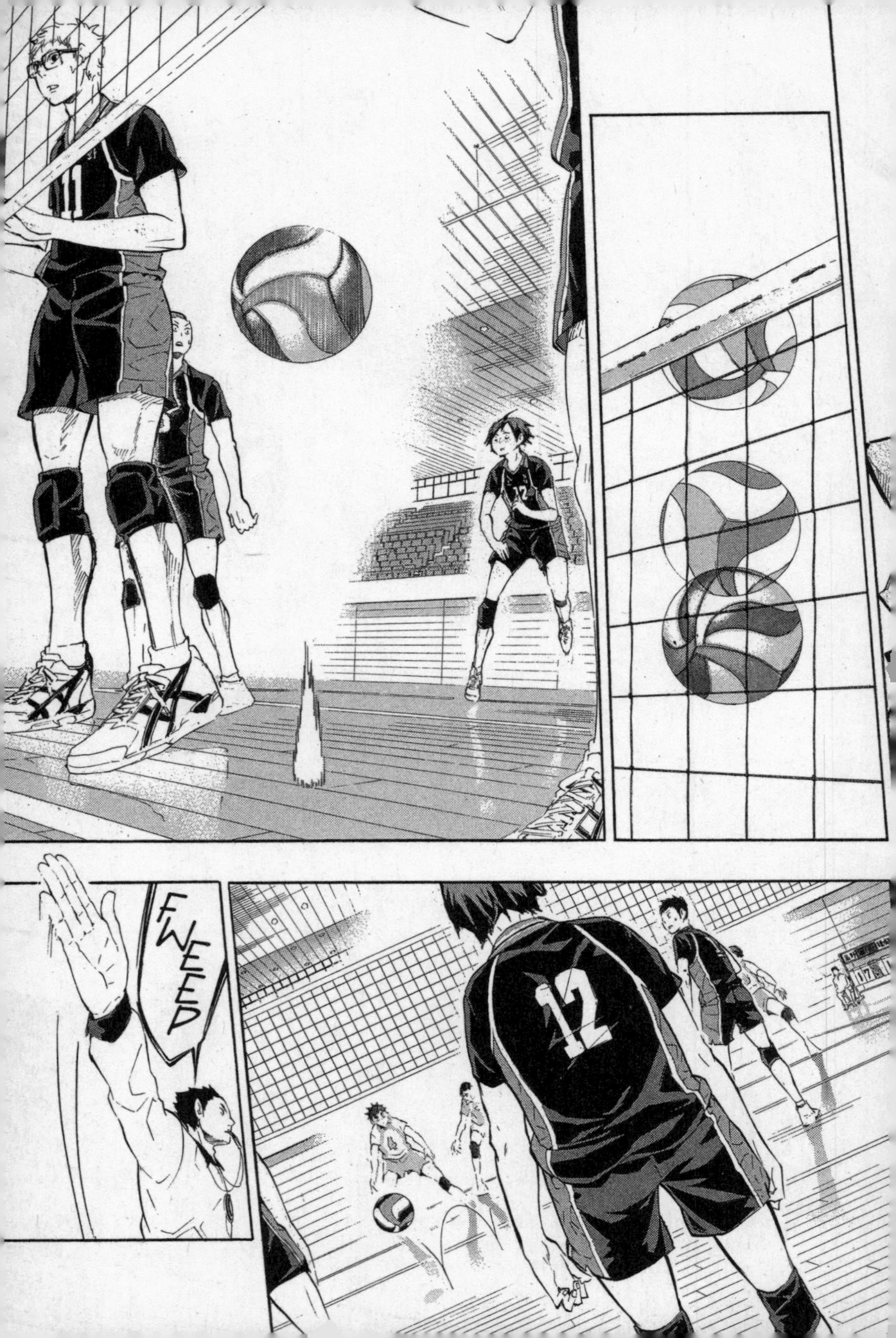
FWEED

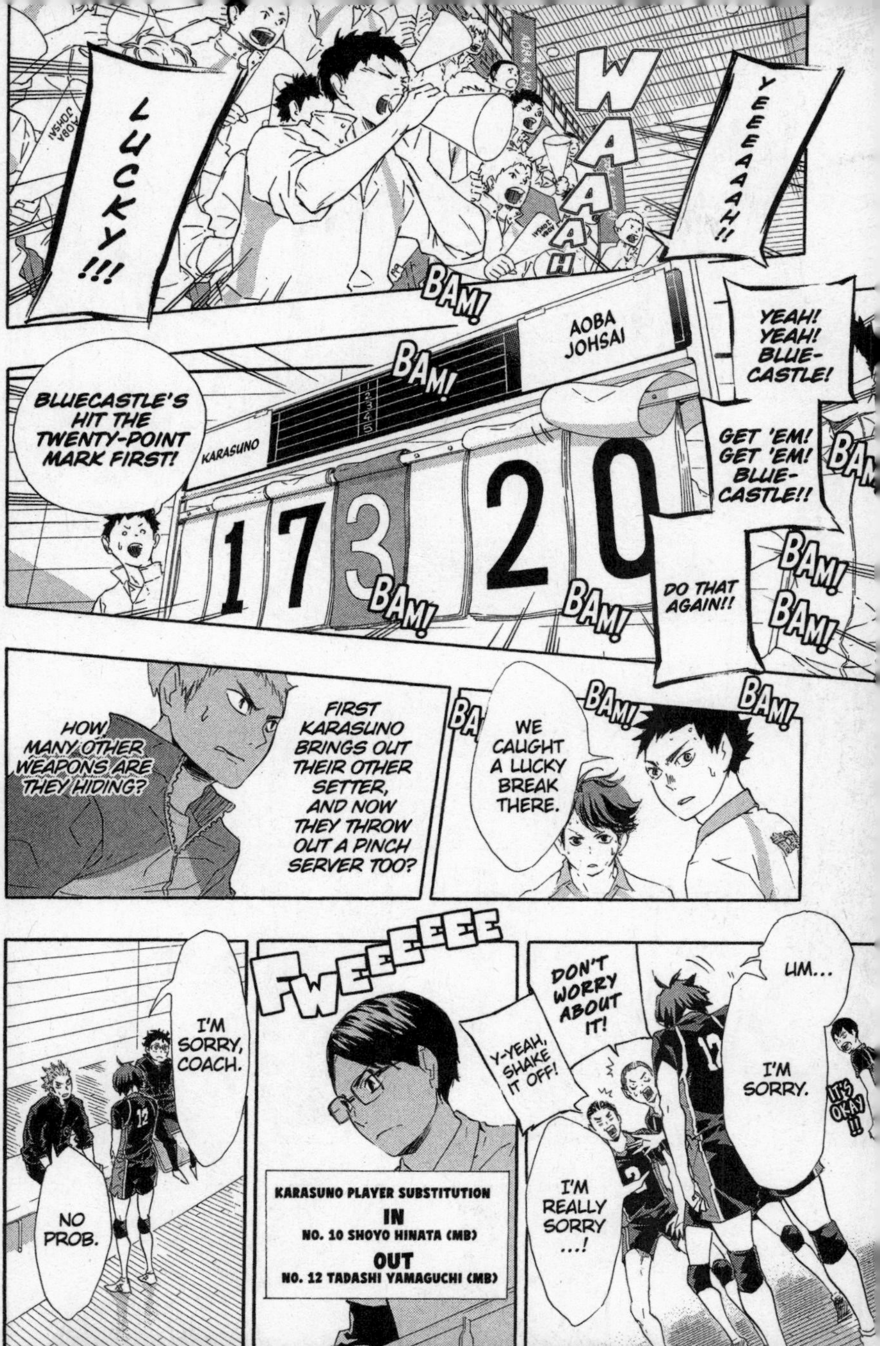
YEEEAAAH!!
WAAAAH
LUCKY!!!
AOBA JOHSAI
BAM!
YEAH! YEAH! BLUE-CASTLE!
GET 'EM! GET 'EM! BLUE-CASTLE!!
BAM!
BAM!
DO THAT AGAIN!!
BAM!
BAM!
AOBA JOHSAI
KARASUNO
17 3 20
BAM!
BAM!
BLUECASTLE'S HIT THE TWENTY-POINT MARK FIRST!
BAM!
BAM!
WE CAUGHT A LUCKY BREAK THERE.
FIRST KARASUNO BRINGS OUT THEIR OTHER SETTER, AND NOW THEY THROW OUT A PINCH SERVER TOO?
HOW MANY OTHER WEAPONS ARE THEY HIDING?
UM...
I'M SORRY.
IT'S OKAY!!
DON'T WORRY ABOUT IT!
Y-YEAH, SHAKE IT OFF!
I'M REALLY SORRY ...!
FWEEEEEE
KARASUNO PLAYER SUBSTITUTION
IN
NO. 10 SHOYO HINATA (MB)
OUT
NO. 12 TADASHI YAMAGUCHI (MB)
I'M SORRY, COACH.
NO PROB.

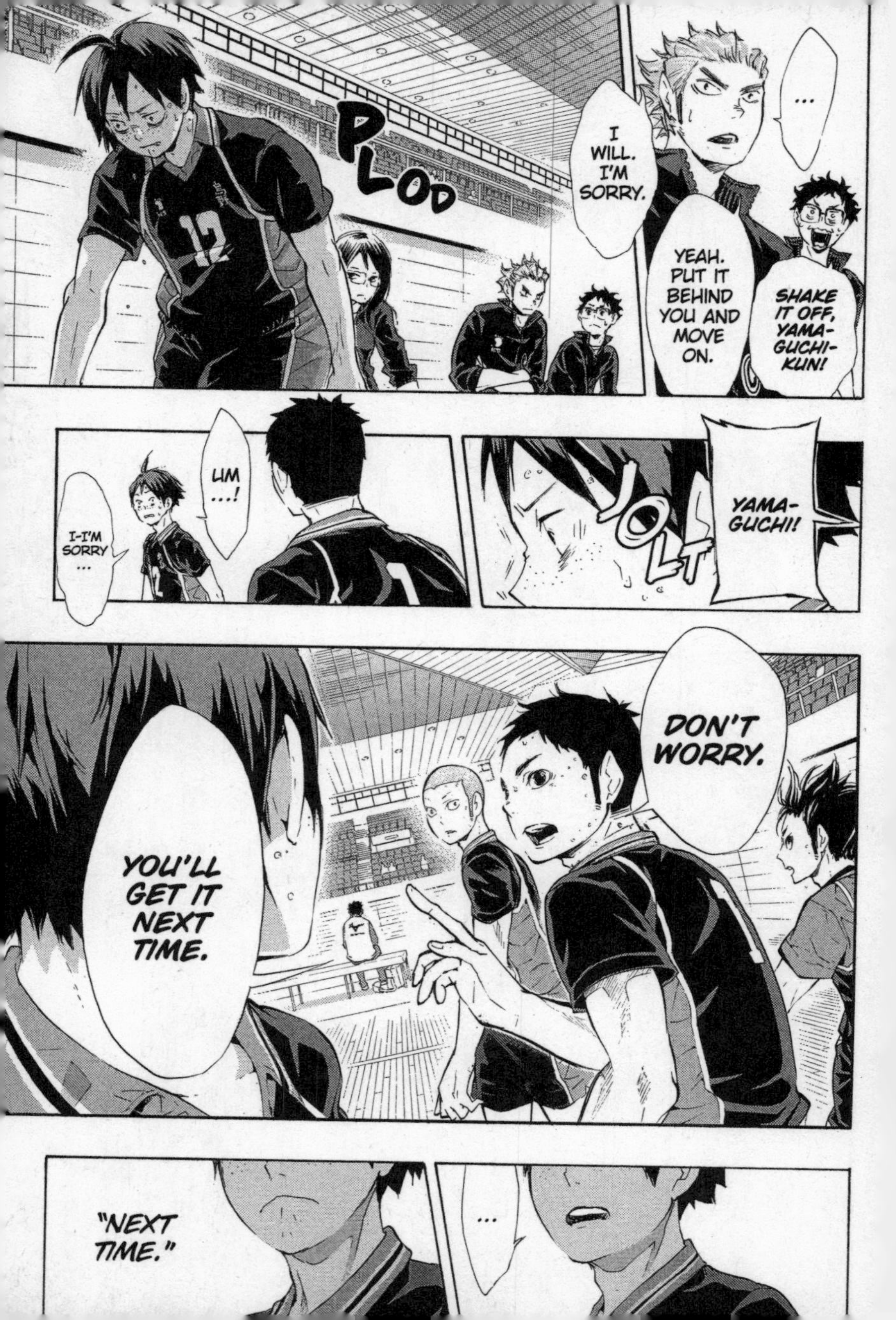
...
I WILL. I'M SORRY.
SHAKE IT OFF, YAMAGUCHI-KUN!
YEAH. PUT IT BEHIND YOU AND MOVE ON.
PLOD
YAMAGUCHI!
JOLT
UM ...!
I-I'M SORRY ...
DON'T WORRY.
YOU'LL GET IT NEXT TIME.
...
"NEXT TIME."

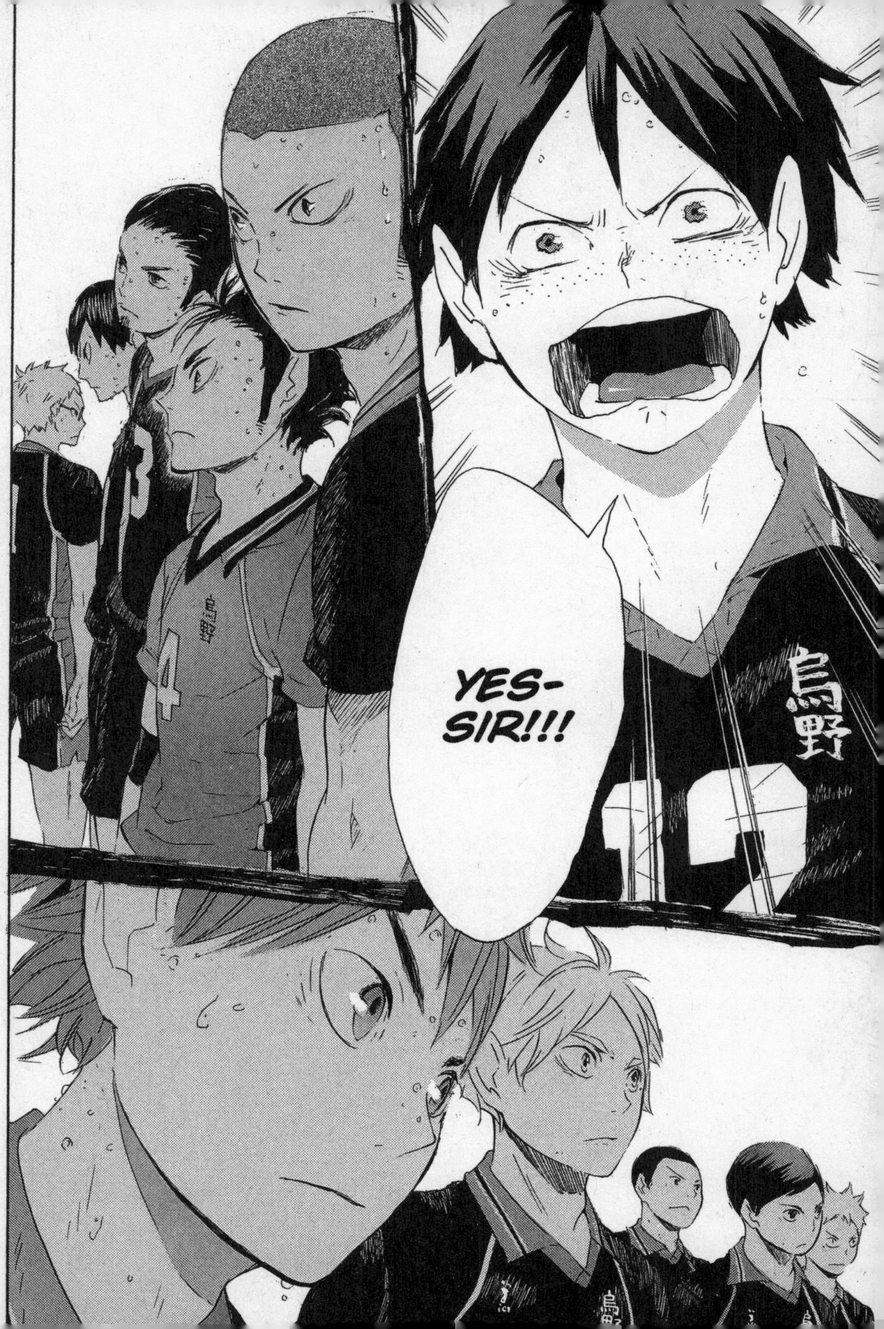
YES-SIR!!!

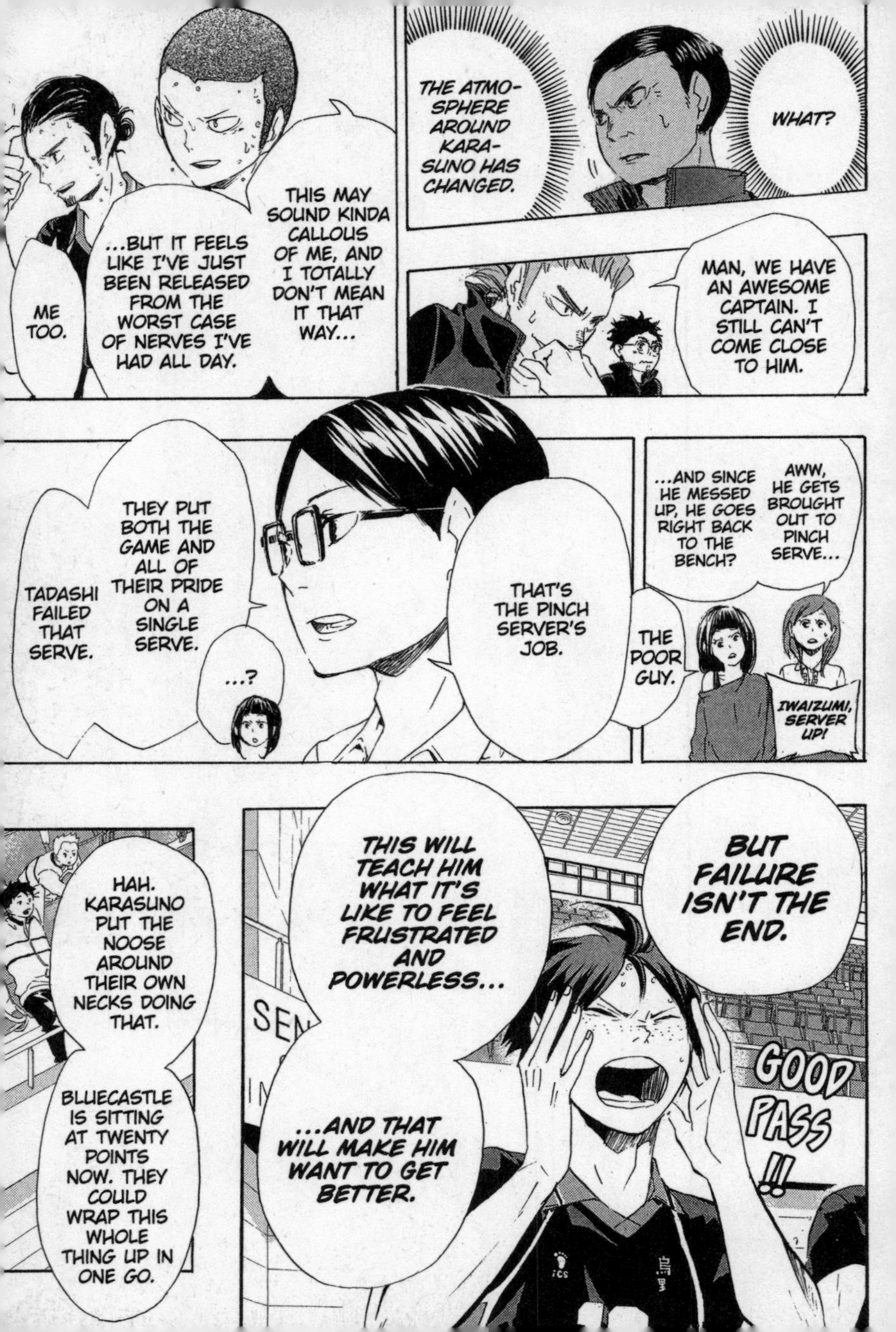
WHAT?
THE ATMOSPHERE AROUND KARASUNO HAS CHANGED.
MAN, WE HAVE AN AWESOME CAPTAIN. I STILL CAN'T COME CLOSE TO HIM.
THIS MAY SOUND KINDA CALLOUS OF ME, AND I TOTALLY DON'T MEAN IT THAT WAY...
...BUT IT FEELS LIKE I'VE JUST BEEN RELEASED FROM THE WORST CASE OF NERVES I'VE HAD ALL DAY.
ME TOO.
AWW, HE GETS BROUGHT OUT TO PINCH SERVE...
...AND SINCE HE MESSED UP, HE GOES RIGHT BACK TO THE BENCH?
THE POOR GUY.
IWAIZUMI, SERVER UP!
THAT'S THE PINCH SERVER'S JOB.
THEY PUT BOTH THE GAME AND ALL OF THEIR PRIDE ON A SINGLE SERVE.
TADASHI FAILED THAT SERVE.
...?
BUT FAILURE ISN'T THE END.
THIS WILL TEACH HIM WHAT IT'S LIKE TO FEEL FRUSTRATED AND POWERLESS...
GOOD PASS!!
...AND THAT WILL MAKE HIM WANT TO GET BETTER.
HAH. KARASUNO PUT THE NOOSE AROUND THEIR OWN NECKS DOING THAT.
BLUECASTLE IS SITTING AT TWENTY POINTS NOW. THEY COULD WRAP THIS WHOLE THING UP IN ONE GO.

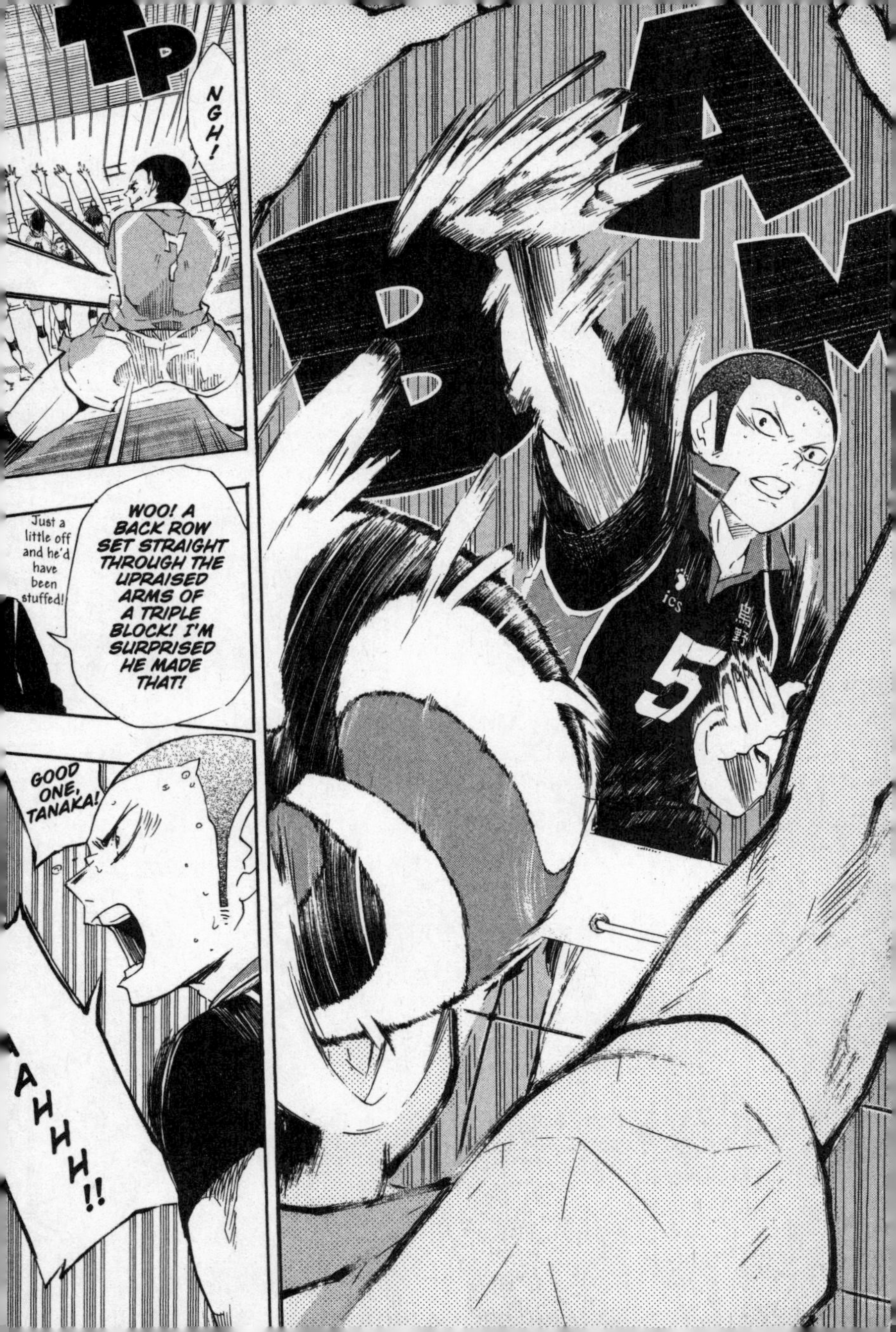
BAM
TP
NGH!
WOO! A BACK ROW SET STRAIGHT THROUGH THE UPRAISED ARMS OF A TRIPLE BLOCK! I'M SURPRISED HE MADE THAT!
Just a little off and he'd have been stuffed!
GOOD ONE, TANAKA!
AHHH!!

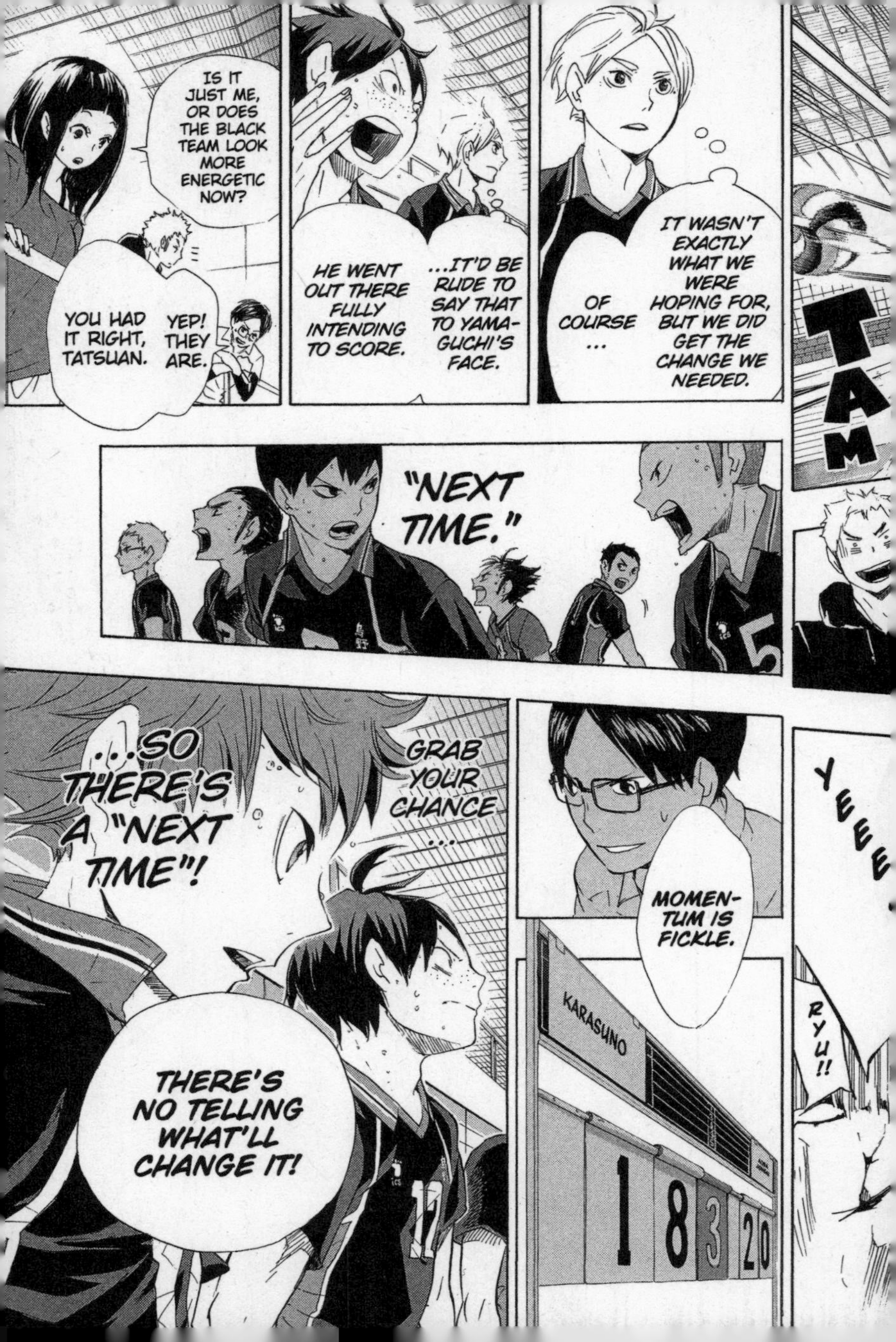
TAM
IT WASN'T EXACTLY WHAT WE WERE HOPING FOR, BUT WE DID GET THE CHANGE WE NEEDED.
OF COURSE ...
...IT'D BE RUDE TO SAY THAT TO YAMAGUCHI'S FACE.
HE WENT OUT THERE FULLY INTENDING TO SCORE.
IS IT JUST ME, OR DOES THE BLACK TEAM LOOK MORE ENERGETIC NOW?
YEP! THEY ARE.
YOU HAD IT RIGHT, TATSUAN.
"NEXT TIME."
YEEEE...
RYU!!
MOMENTUM IS FICKLE.
KARASUNO
18 3 20
GRAB YOUR CHANCE ...
...SO THERE'S A "NEXT TIME"!
THERE'S NO TELLING WHAT'LL CHANGE IT!

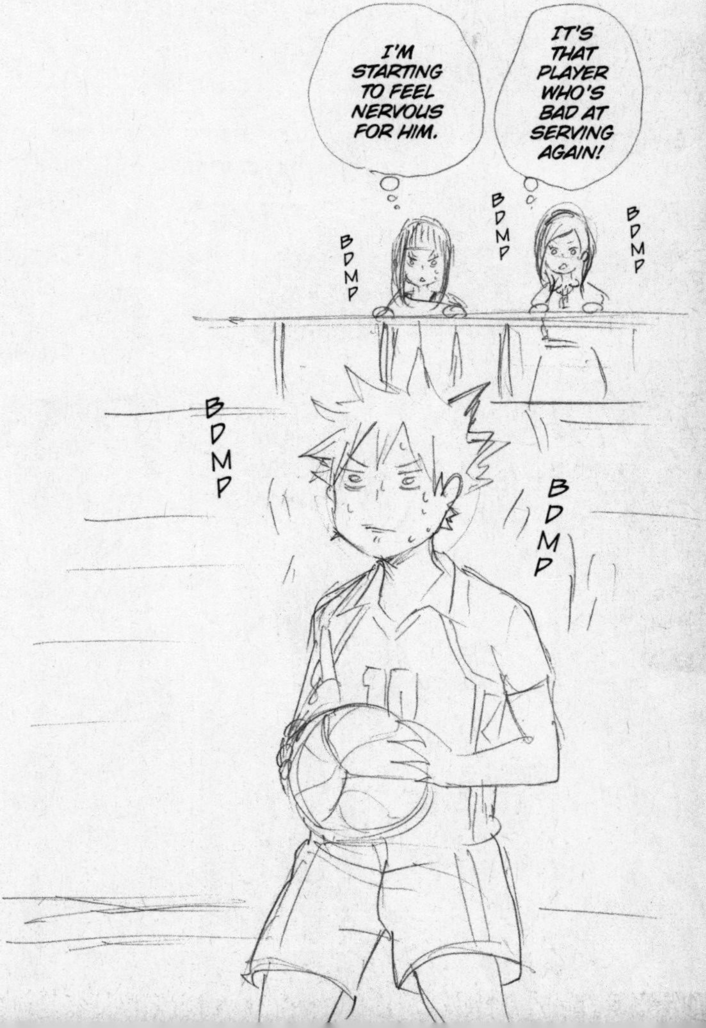
IT'S THAT PLAYER WHO'S BAD AT SERVING AGAIN!
I'M STARTING TO FEEL NERVOUS FOR HIM.
BDMP
BDMP
BDMP
BDMP
BDMP
BDMP

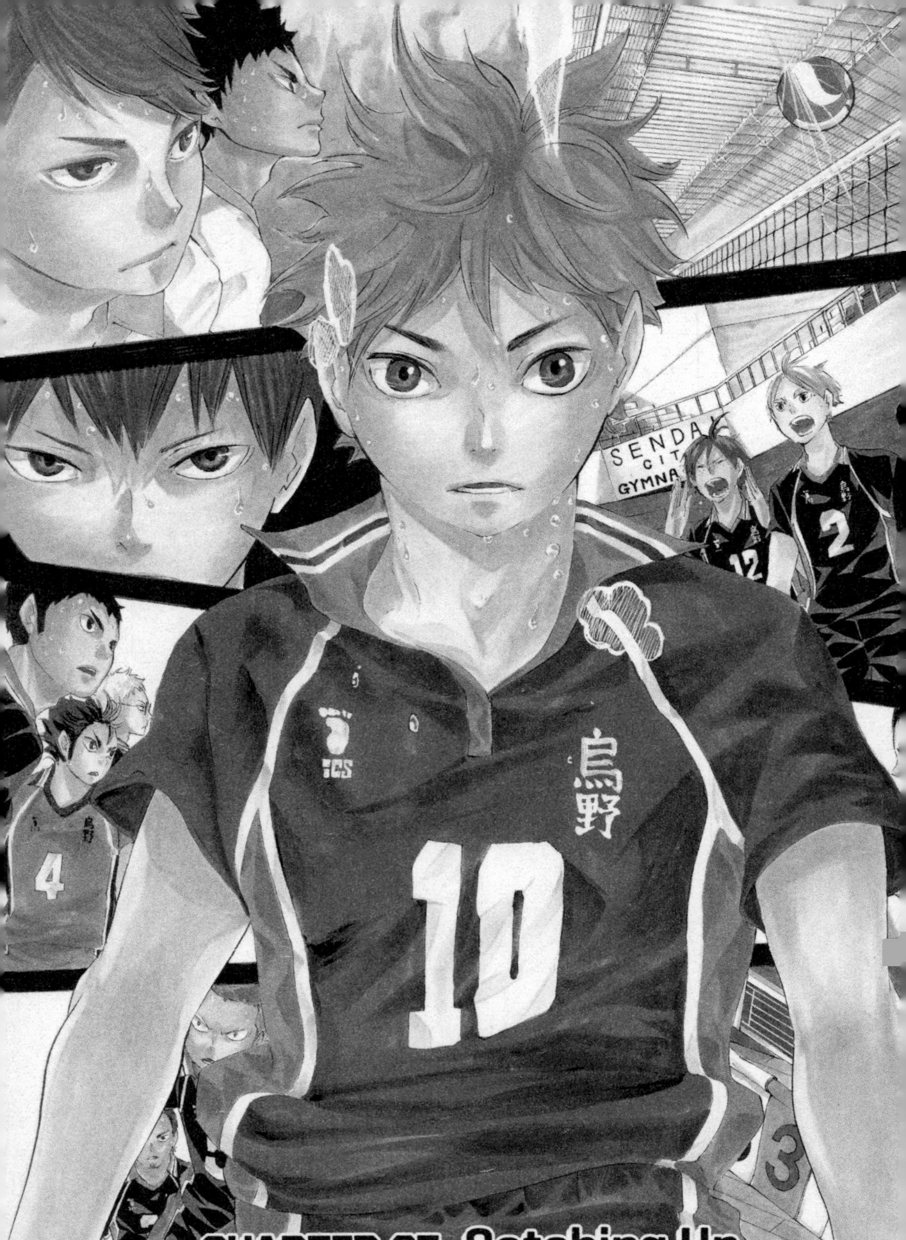
SENDA
CIT
GYMNA

CHAPTER 65: Catching Up

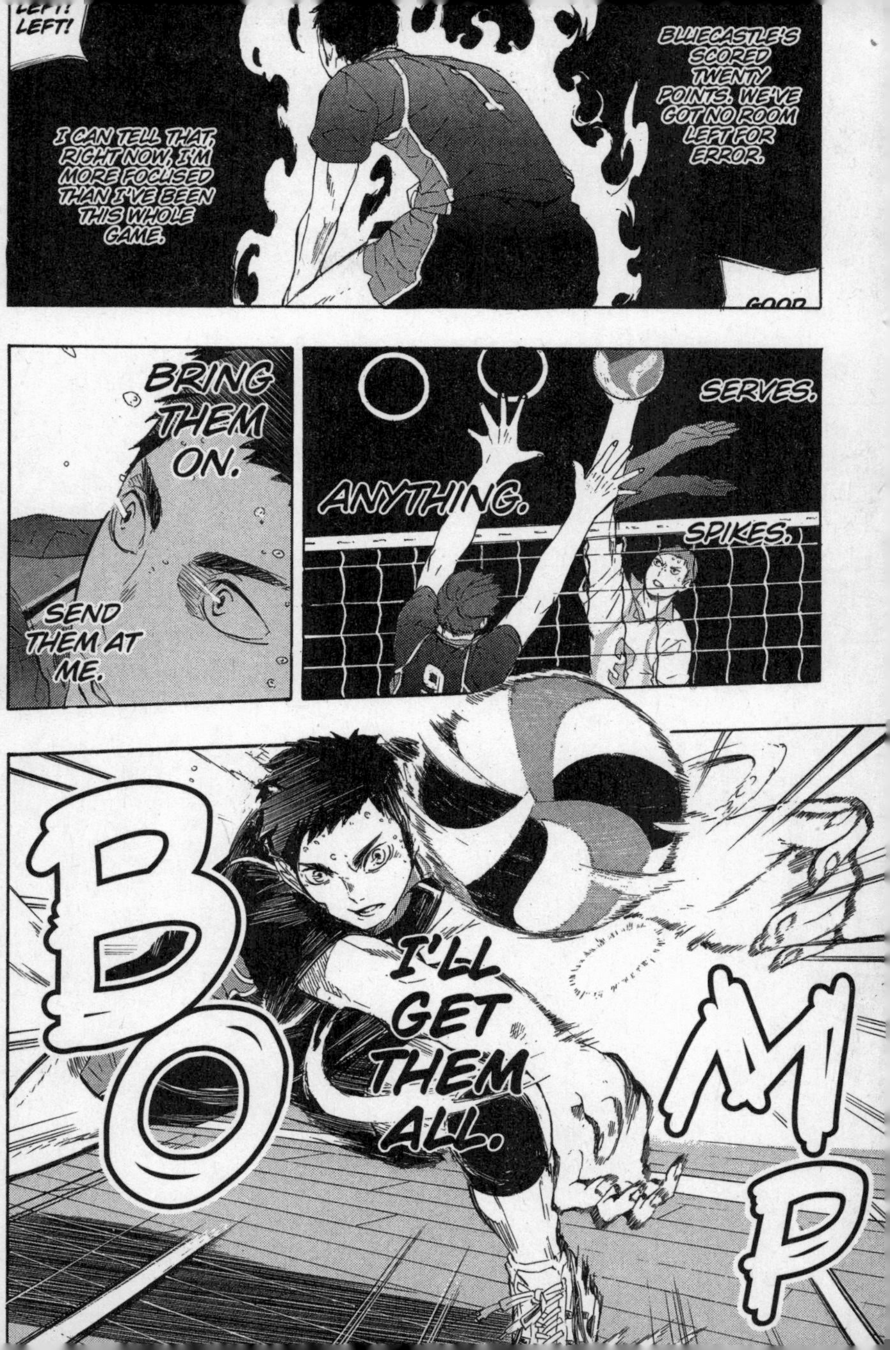
LEFT! LEFT!
BLUECASTLE'S SCORED TWENTY POINTS. WE'VE GOT NO ROOM LEFT FOR ERROR.
I CAN TELL THAT, RIGHT NOW, I'M MORE FOCUSED THAN I'VE BEEN THIS WHOLE GAME.
GOOD
SERVES.
SPIKES.
ANYTHING.
BRING THEM ON.
SEND THEM AT ME.
BOMP
I'LL GET THEM ALL.

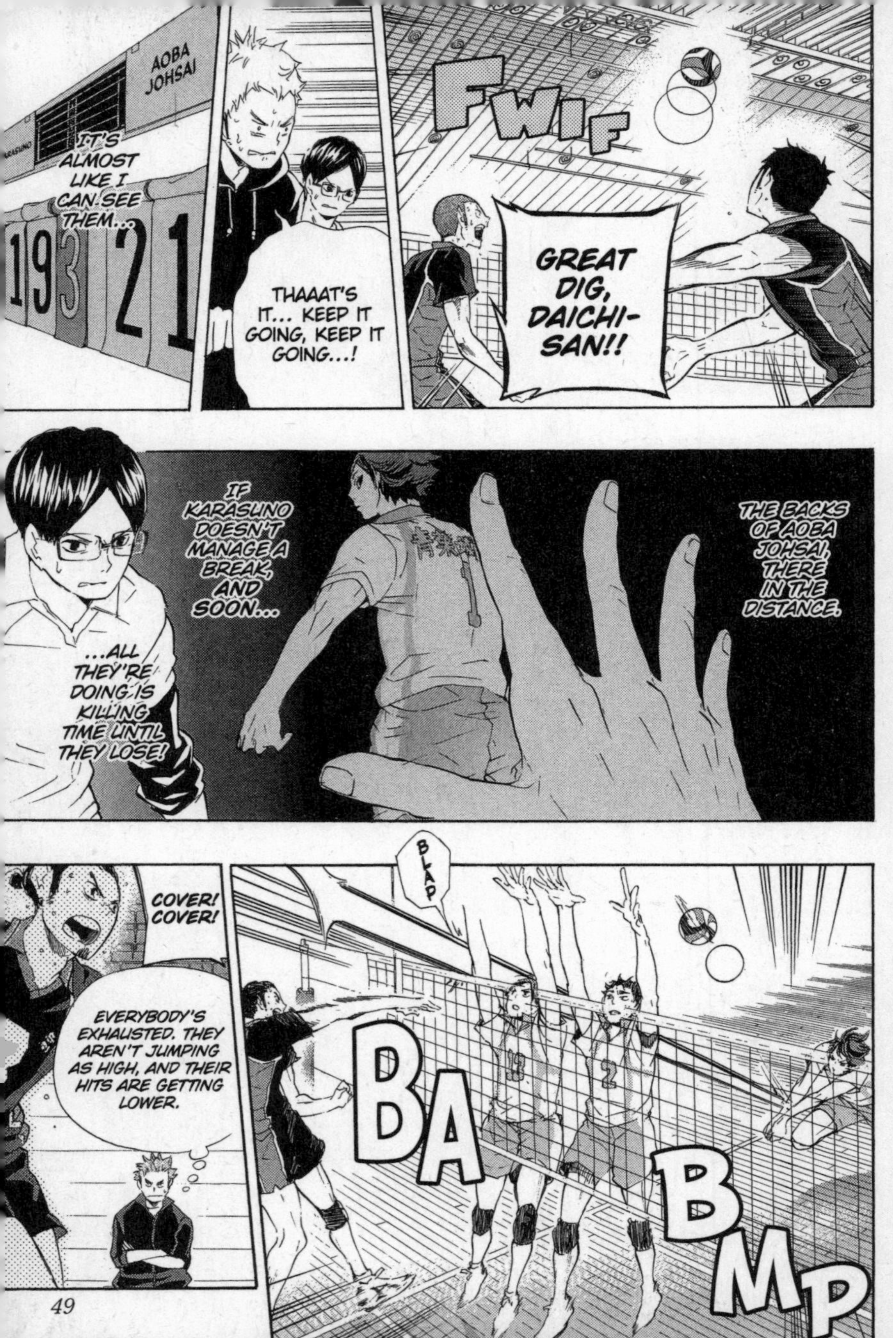

FWIF
GREAT DIG, DAICHI-SAN!!
THAAAT'S IT... KEEP IT GOING, KEEP IT GOING...!
AOBA JOHSAI
KARASUNO
IT'S ALMOST LIKE I CAN SEE THEM...
THE BACKS OF AOBA JOHSAI, THERE IN THE DISTANCE.
IF KARASUNO DOESN'T MANAGE A BREAK, AND SOON...
...ALL THEY'RE DOING IS KILLING TIME UNTIL THEY LOSE!
BLAP
BABMP
COVER! COVER!
EVERYBODY'S EXHAUSTED. THEY AREN'T JUMPING AS HIGH, AND THEIR HITS ARE GETTING LOWER.

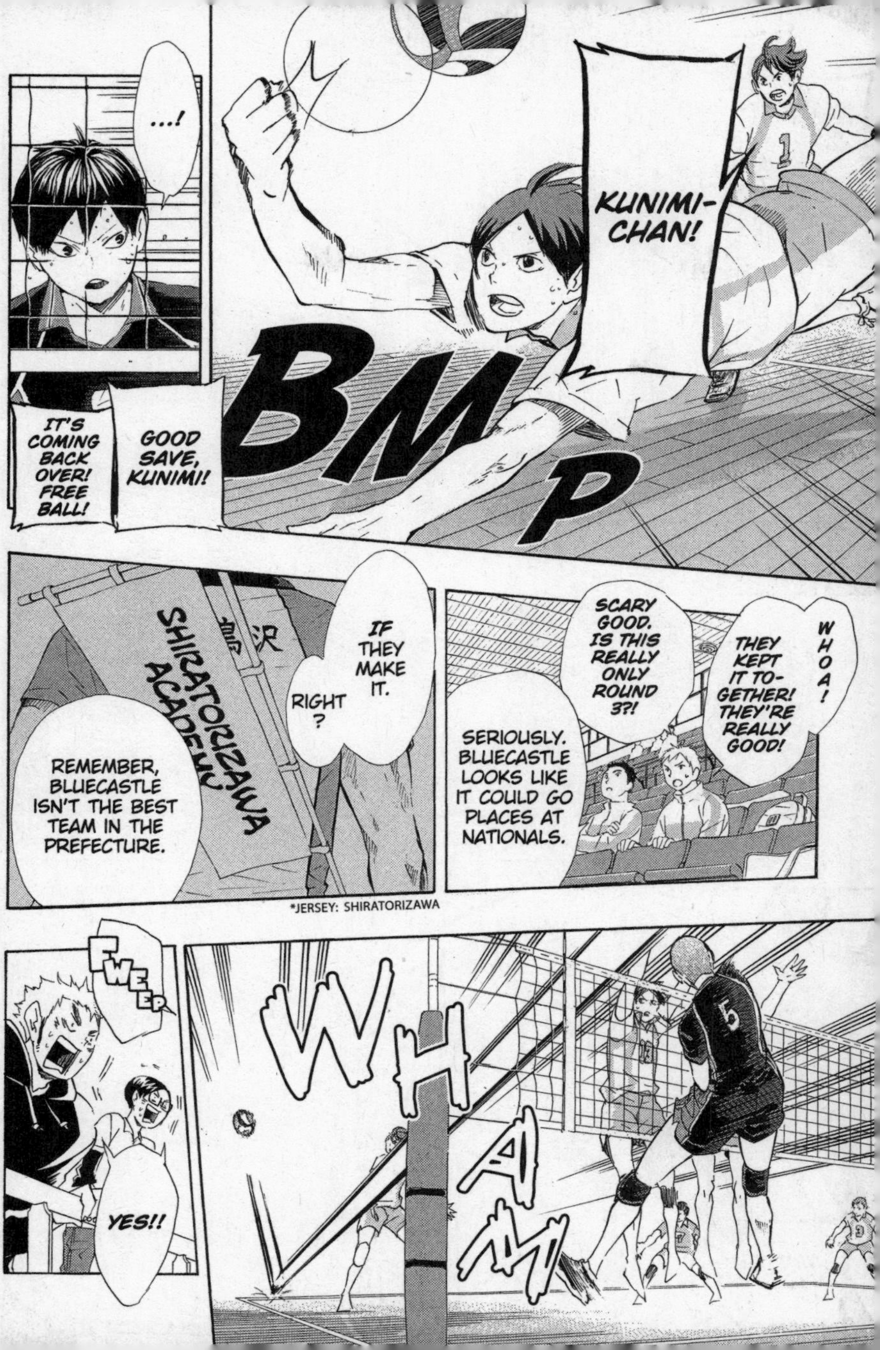
KUNIMI-CHAN!
BMP
...!
GOOD SAVE, KUNIMI!
IT'S COMING BACK OVER! FREE BALL!
WHOA!
THEY KEPT IT TO-GETHER! THEY'RE REALLY GOOD!
SCARY GOOD. IS THIS REALLY ONLY ROUND 3?!
SERIOUSLY. BLUECASTLE LOOKS LIKE IT COULD GO PLACES AT NATIONALS.
IF THEY MAKE IT.
RIGHT?
SHIRATORIZAWA ACADEMY
REMEMBER, BLUECASTLE ISN'T THE BEST TEAM IN THE PREFECTURE.
WHAM
FWEEP
YES!!
*JERSEY: SHIRATORIZAWA

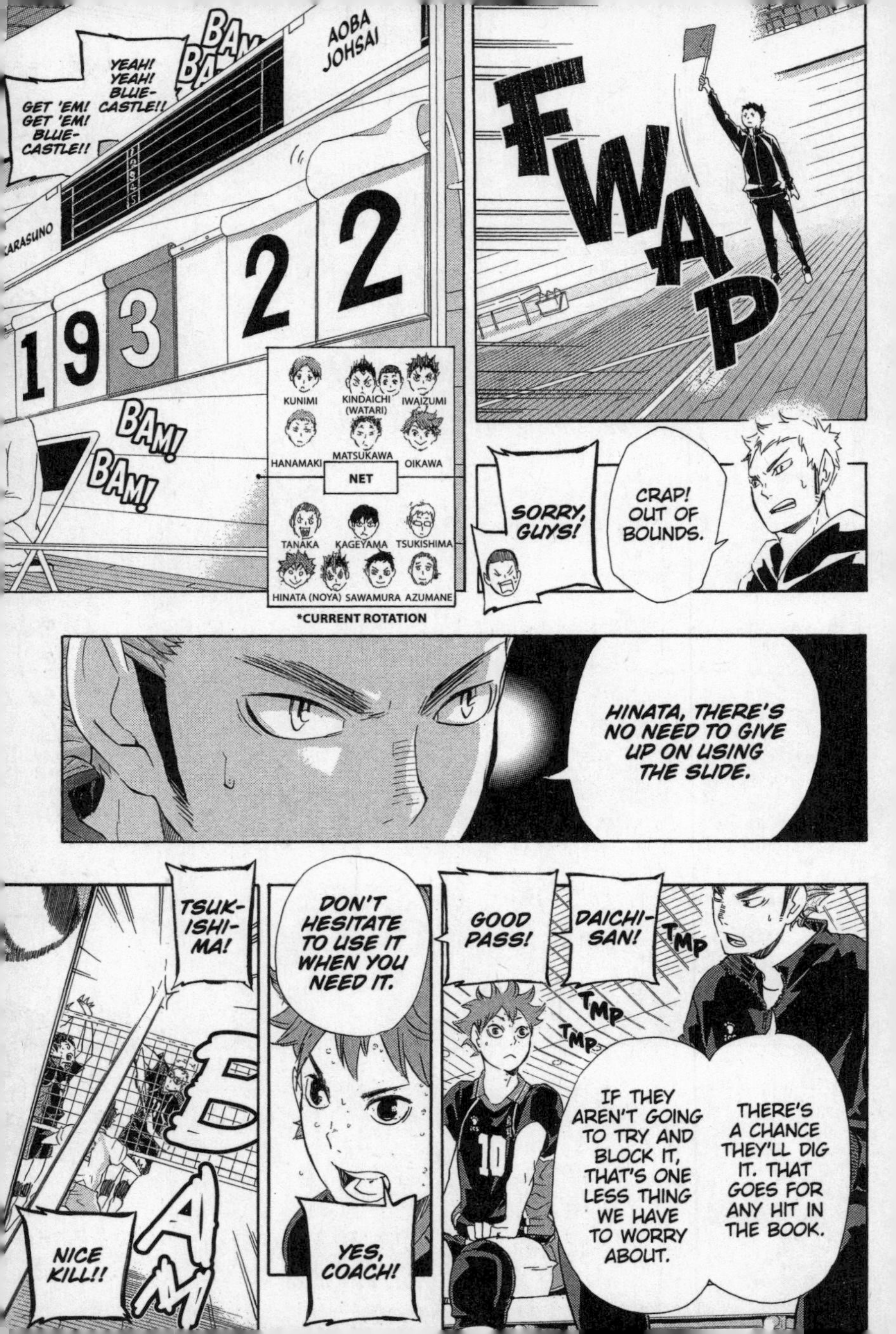
FWAP
AOBA JOHSAI
BAM
BAM
YEAH! YEAH! BLUE-CASTLE!!
GET 'EM! GET 'EM! BLUE-CASTLE!!
KARASUNO
19
3
22
BAM!
BAM!
KUNIMI
KINDAICHI (WATARI)
IWAIZUMI
HANAMAKI
MATSUKAWA
OIKAWA
NET
TANAKA
KAGEYAMA
TSUKISHIMA
HINATA (NOYA)
SAWAMURA
AZUMANE
*CURRENT ROTATION
CRAP! OUT OF BOUNDS.
SORRY, GUYS!
HINATA, THERE'S NO NEED TO GIVE UP ON USING THE SLIDE.
DAICHI-SAN!
TMP
GOOD PASS!
TMP
TMP
THERE'S A CHANCE THEY'LL DIG IT. THAT GOES FOR ANY HIT IN THE BOOK.
IF THEY AREN'T GOING TO TRY AND BLOCK IT, THAT'S ONE LESS THING WE HAVE TO WORRY ABOUT.
DON'T HESITATE TO USE IT WHEN YOU NEED IT.
YES, COACH!
TSUKI-SHIMA!
BAM
NICE KILL!!

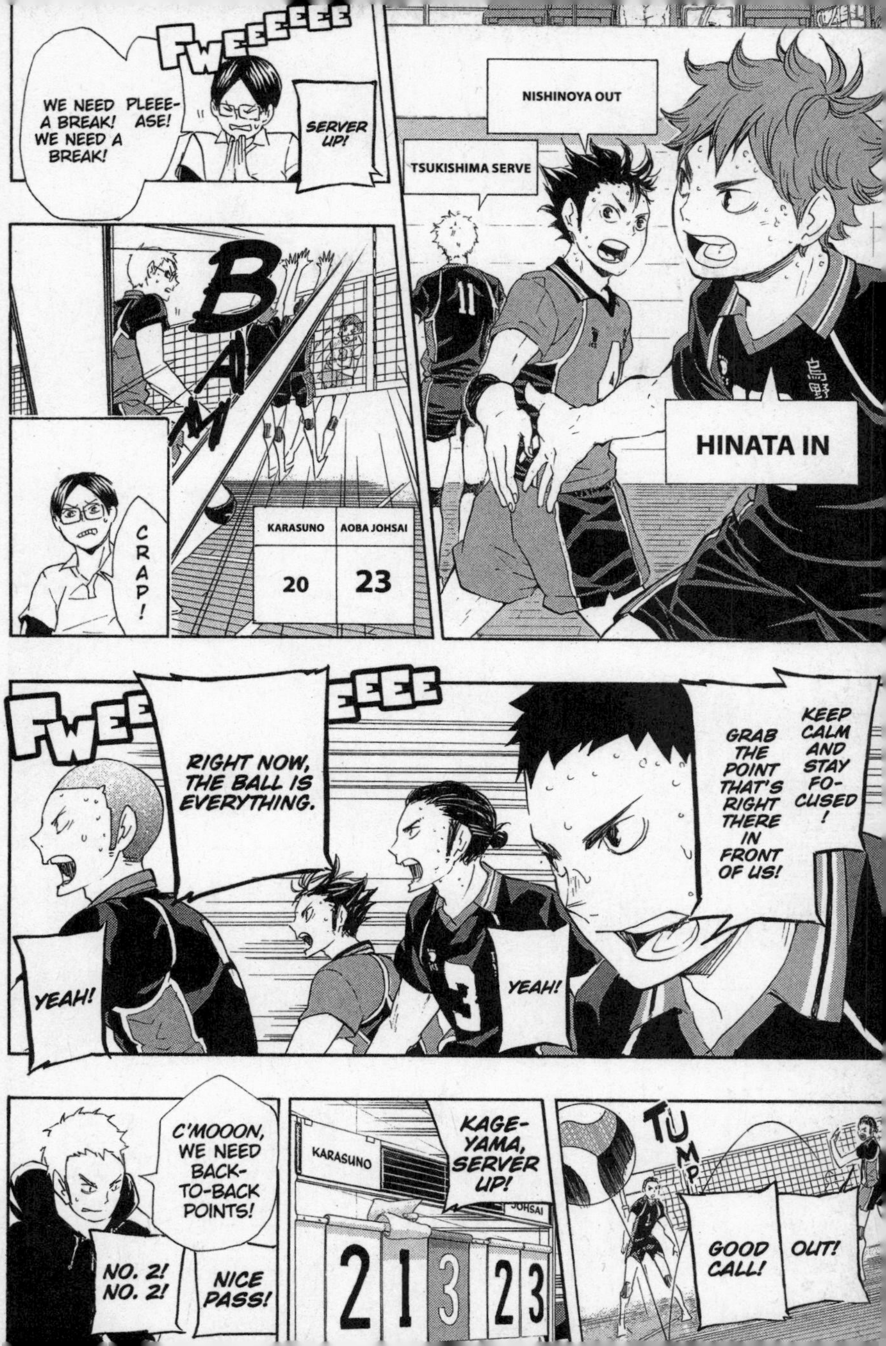
NISHINOYA OUT
TSUKISHIMA SERVE
HINATA IN
FWEEEEEE
SERVER UP!
PLEEE-ASE!
WE NEED A BREAK! WE NEED A BREAK!
BAM
CRAP!
KARASUNO
20
AOBA JOHSAI
23
FWEEEEEEE
KEEP CALM AND STAY FO-CUSED!
GRAB THE POINT THAT'S RIGHT THERE IN FRONT OF US!
RIGHT NOW, THE BALL IS EVERYTHING.
YEAH!
YEAH!
TUMP
OUT!
GOOD CALL!
KAGE-YAMA, SERVER UP!
KARASUNO
JOHSAI
21
23
C'MOOON, WE NEED BACK-TO-BACK POINTS!
NICE PASS!
NO. 2! NO. 2!

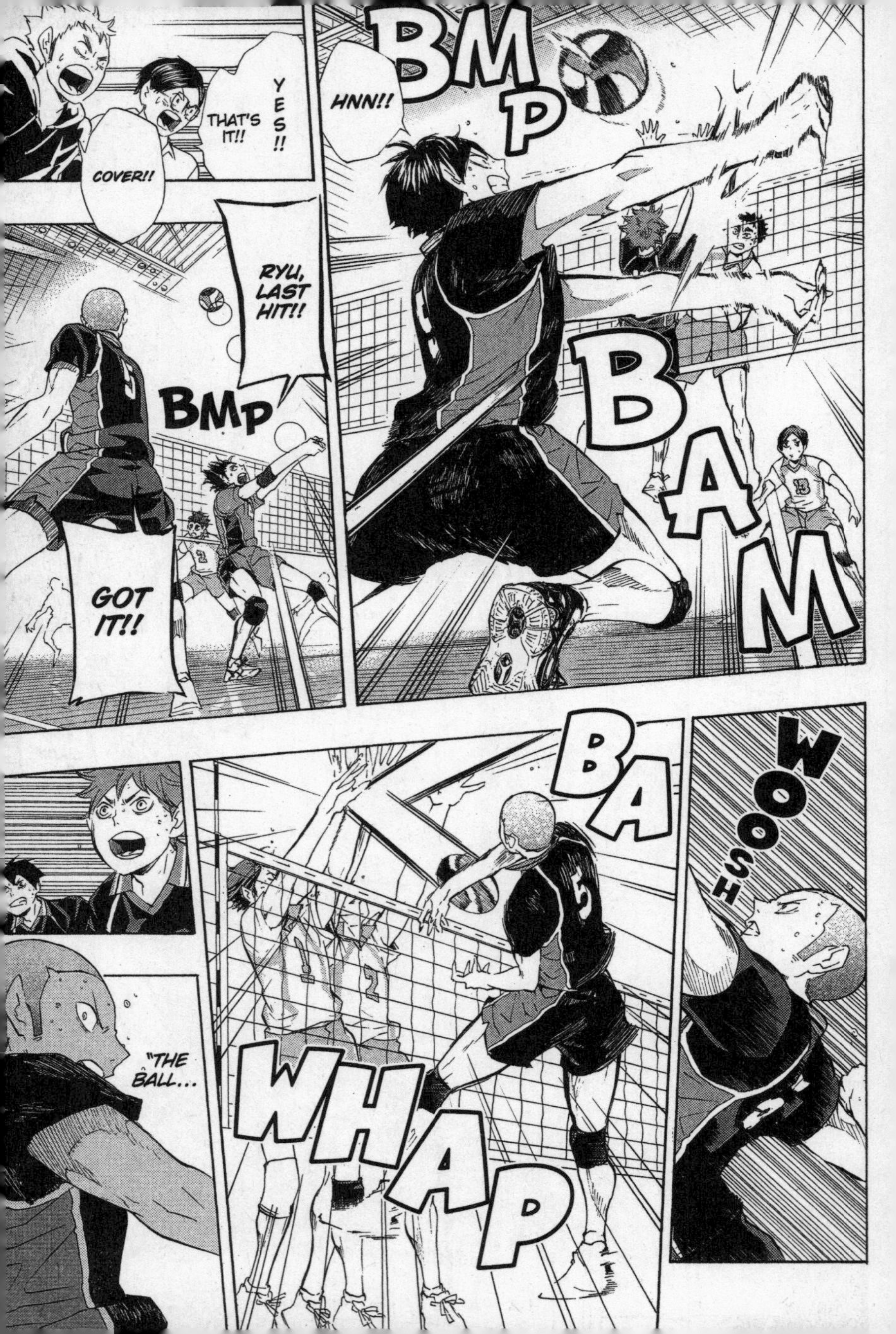
BMP
HNN!!
BAM
YES!!
THAT'S IT!!
COVER!!
RYU, LAST HIT!!
BMP
GOT IT!!
WOOSH
BA
WHAP
"THE BALL...

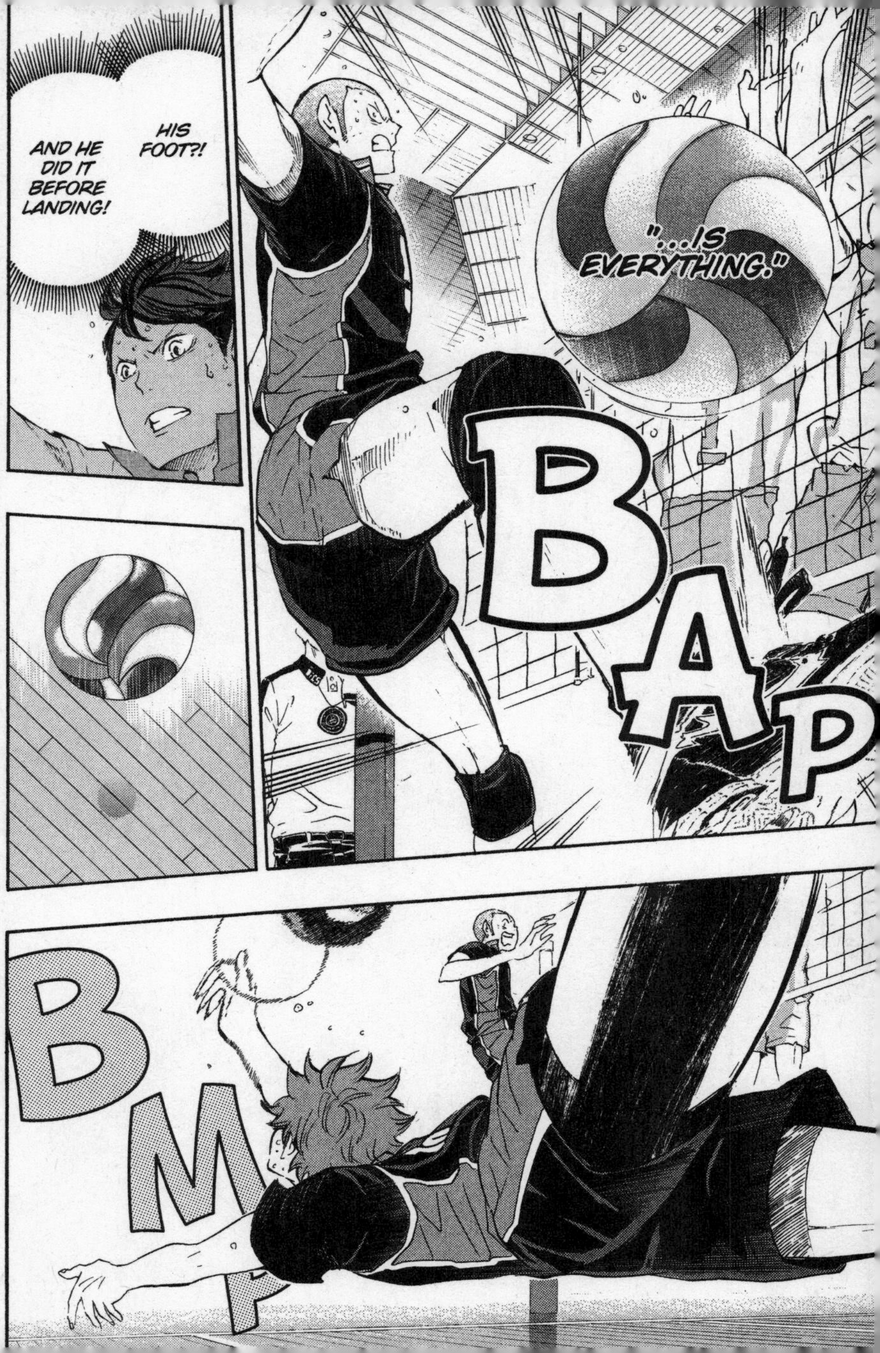
"...IS EVERYTHING."
BAP
HIS FOOT?!
AND HE DID IT BEFORE LANDING!
BMP

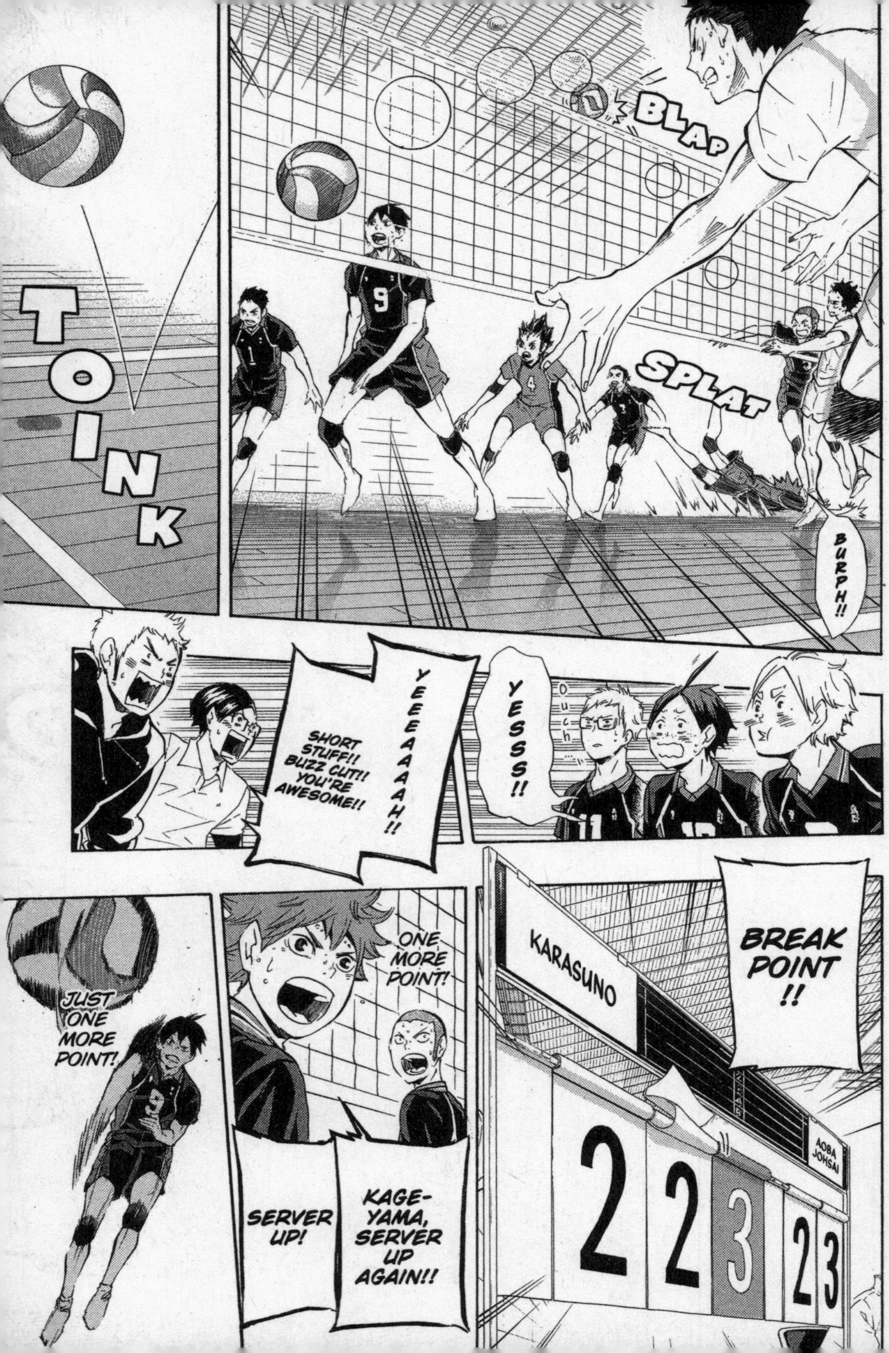
BLAP
SPLAT
BURPH!!
TOINK
YESS!!
Ouch...
YEEEAAAAAH!!
SHORT STUFF!! BUZZ CUT!! YOU'RE AWESOME!!
BREAK POINT!!
KARASUNO
AOBA JOHSAI
22
23
ONE MORE POINT!
KAGE-YAMA, SERVER UP AGAIN!!
SERVER UP!
JUST ONE MORE POINT!

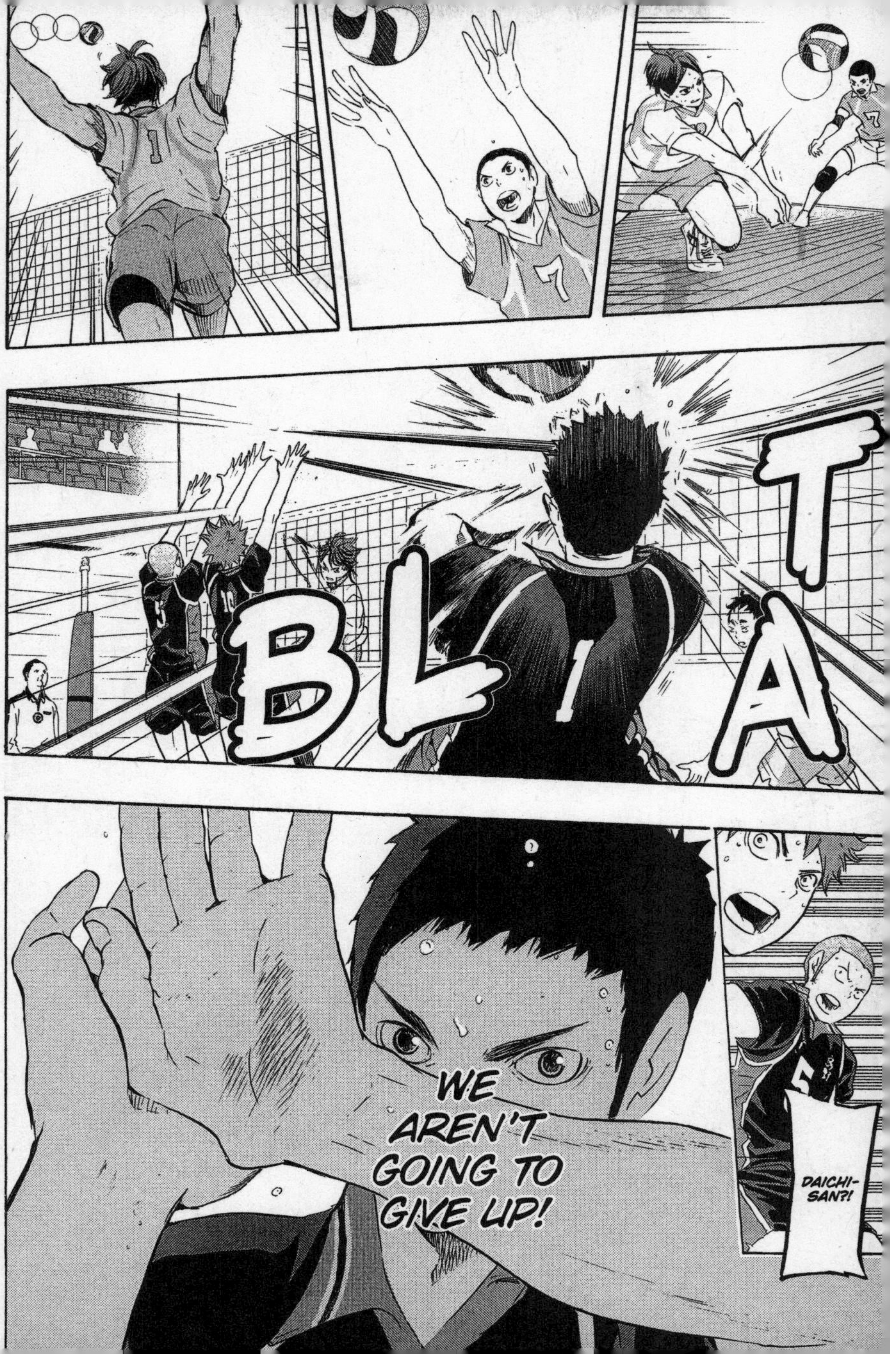
BLAT
DAICHI-SAN?!
WE AREN'T GOING TO GIVE UP!

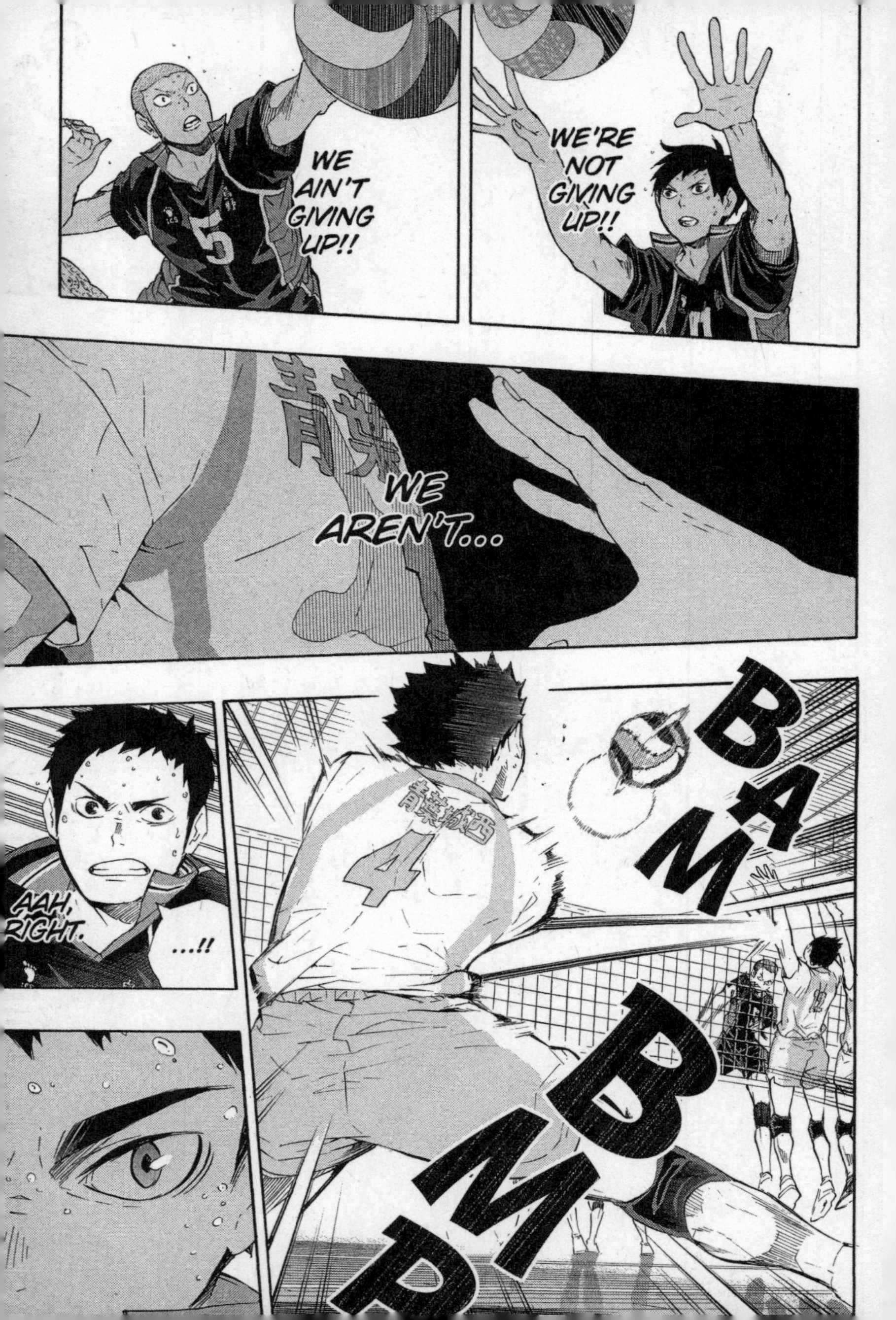
WE'RE NOT GIVING UP!!
WE AIN'T GIVING UP!!
WE AREN'T...
BAM
BMP
AAH, RIGHT.
...!!

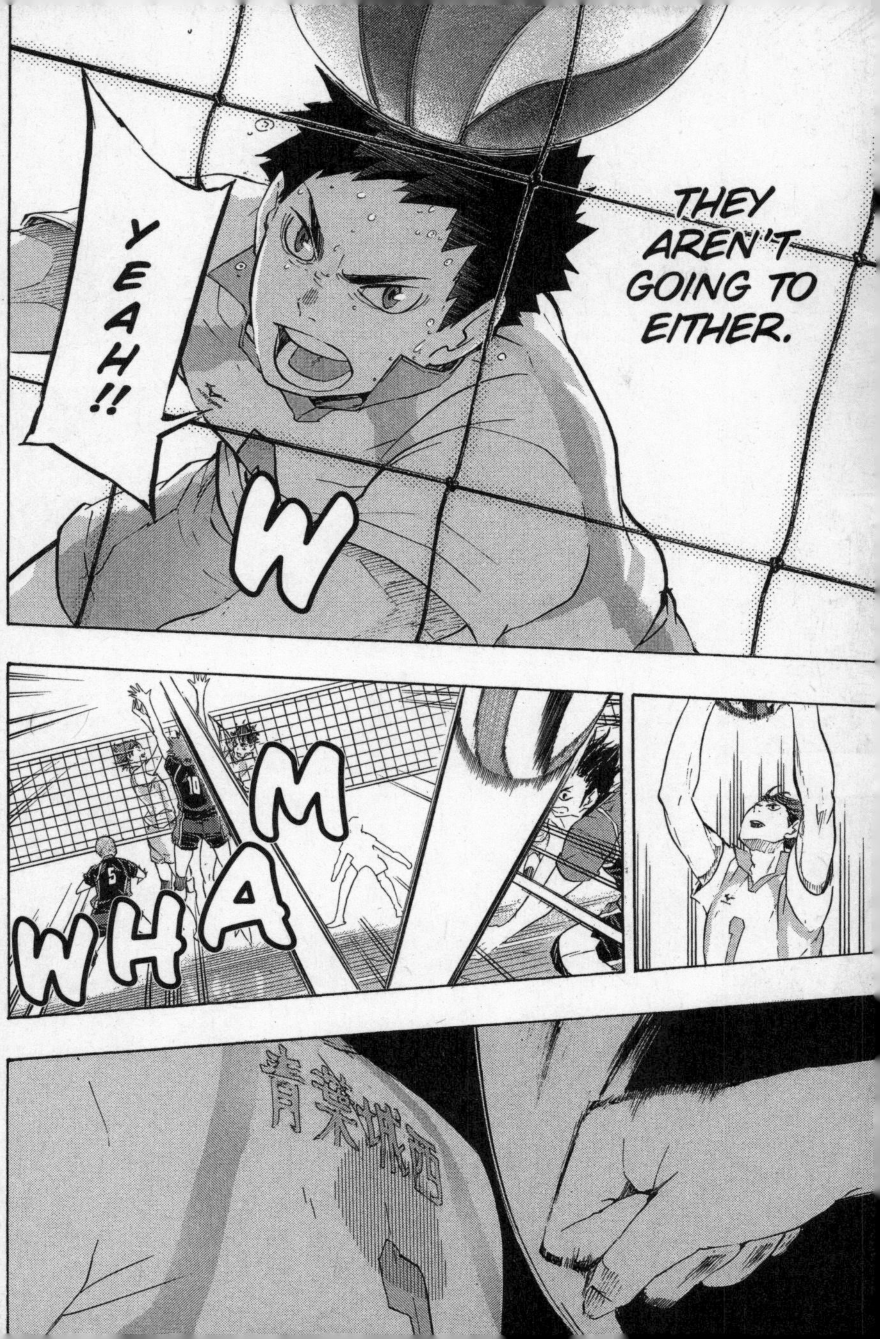
THEY AREN'T GOING TO EITHER.
YEAH!!
W
WHAM
青葉城西

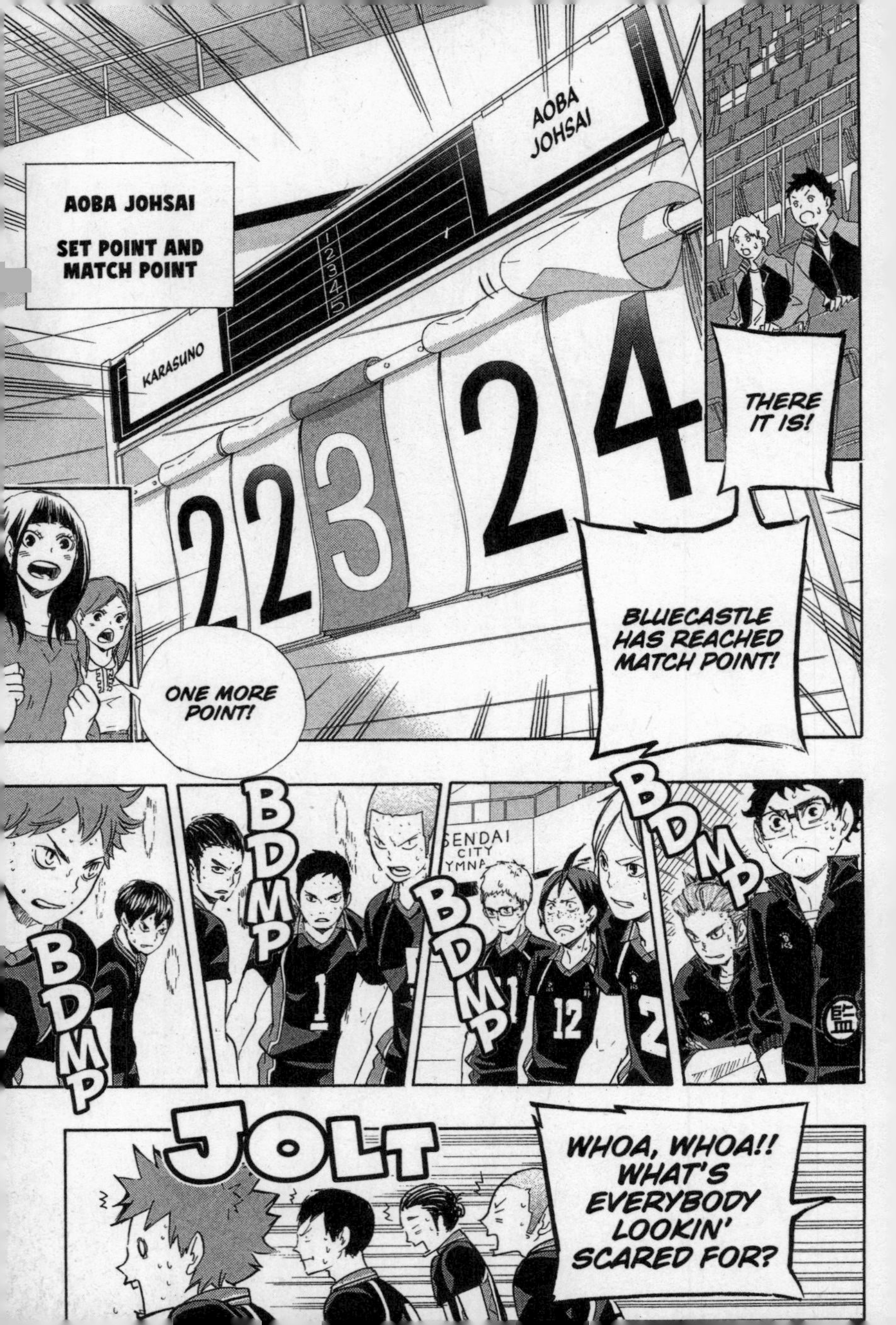
THERE IT IS!
AOBA JOHSAI
AOBA JOHSAI
SET POINT AND MATCH POINT
KARASUNO
BLUECASTLE HAS REACHED MATCH POINT!
ONE MORE POINT!
BDMP
BDMP
BDMP
BDMP
BDMP
WHOA, WHOA!! WHAT'S EVERYBODY LOOKIN' SCARED FOR?
JOLT

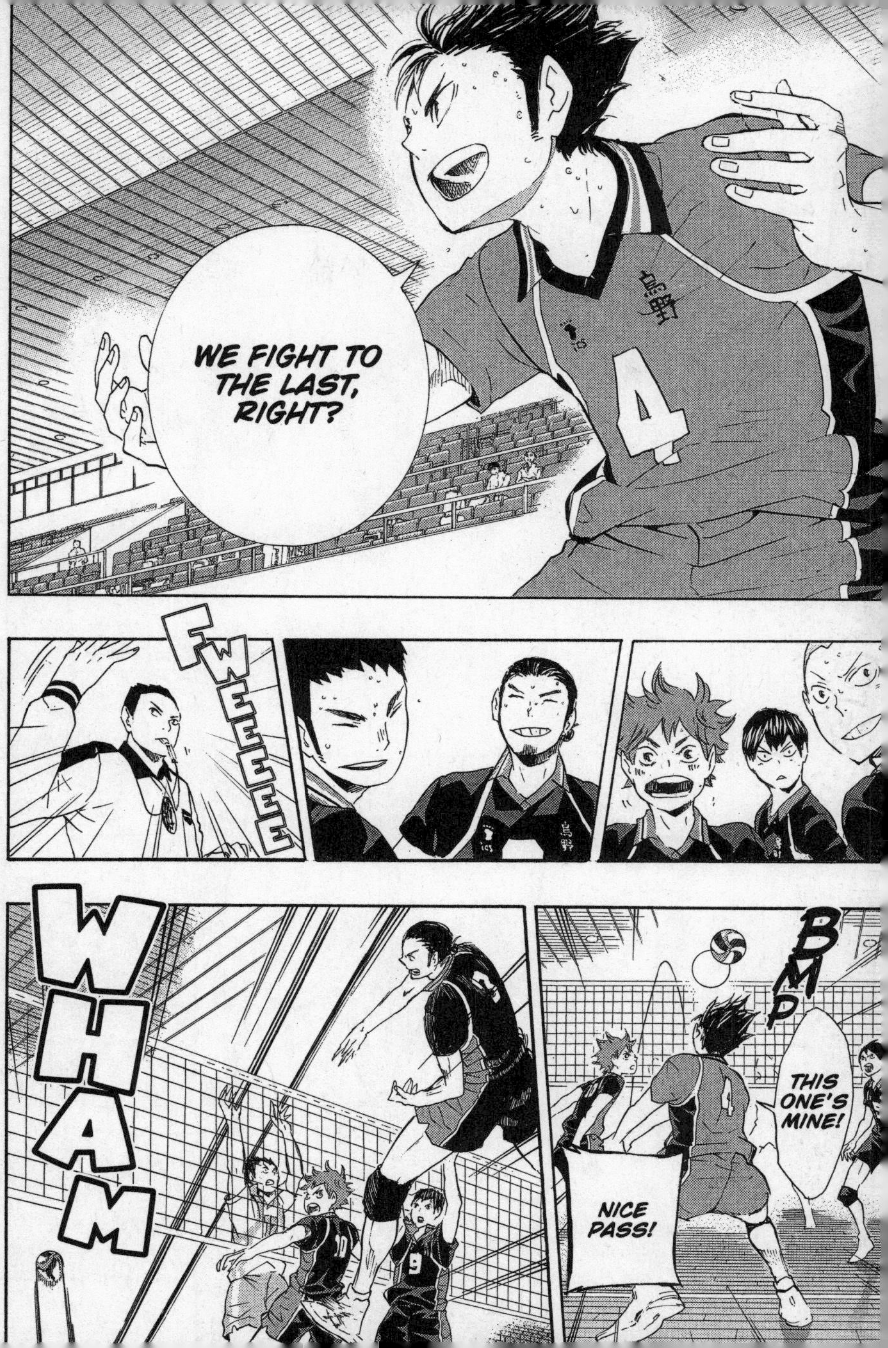
WE FIGHT TO THE LAST, RIGHT?
FWEEEEE
BMP
THIS ONE'S MINE!
NICE PASS!
WHAM

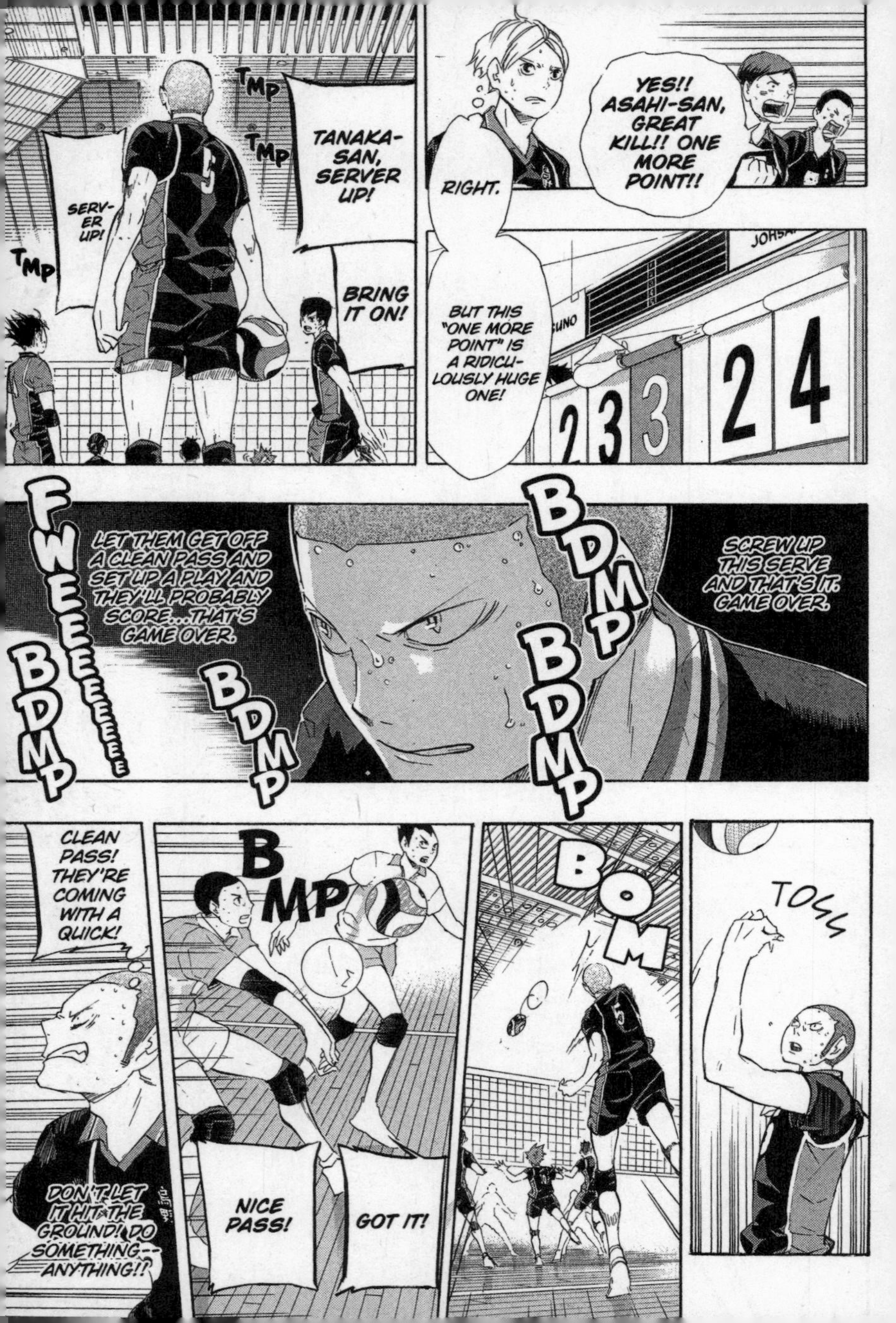
YES!! ASAHI-SAN, GREAT KILL!! ONE MORE POINT!!
RIGHT.
BUT THIS "ONE MORE POINT" IS A RIDICULOUSLY HUGE ONE!
TANAKA-SAN, SERVER UP!
TMP
TMP
SERVER UP!
TMP
BRING IT ON!
BDMP
SCREW UP THIS SERVE AND THAT'S IT. GAME OVER.
BDMP
BDMP
LET THEM GET OFF A CLEAN PASS AND SET UP A PLAY AND THEY'LL PROBABLY SCORE...THAT'S GAME OVER.
FWEEEEEEEE
BDMP
TOSS
BOOM
BMP
NICE PASS!
GOT IT!
CLEAN PASS! THEY'RE COMING WITH A QUICK!
DON'T LET IT HIT THE GROUND! DO SOMETHING--ANYTHING!!

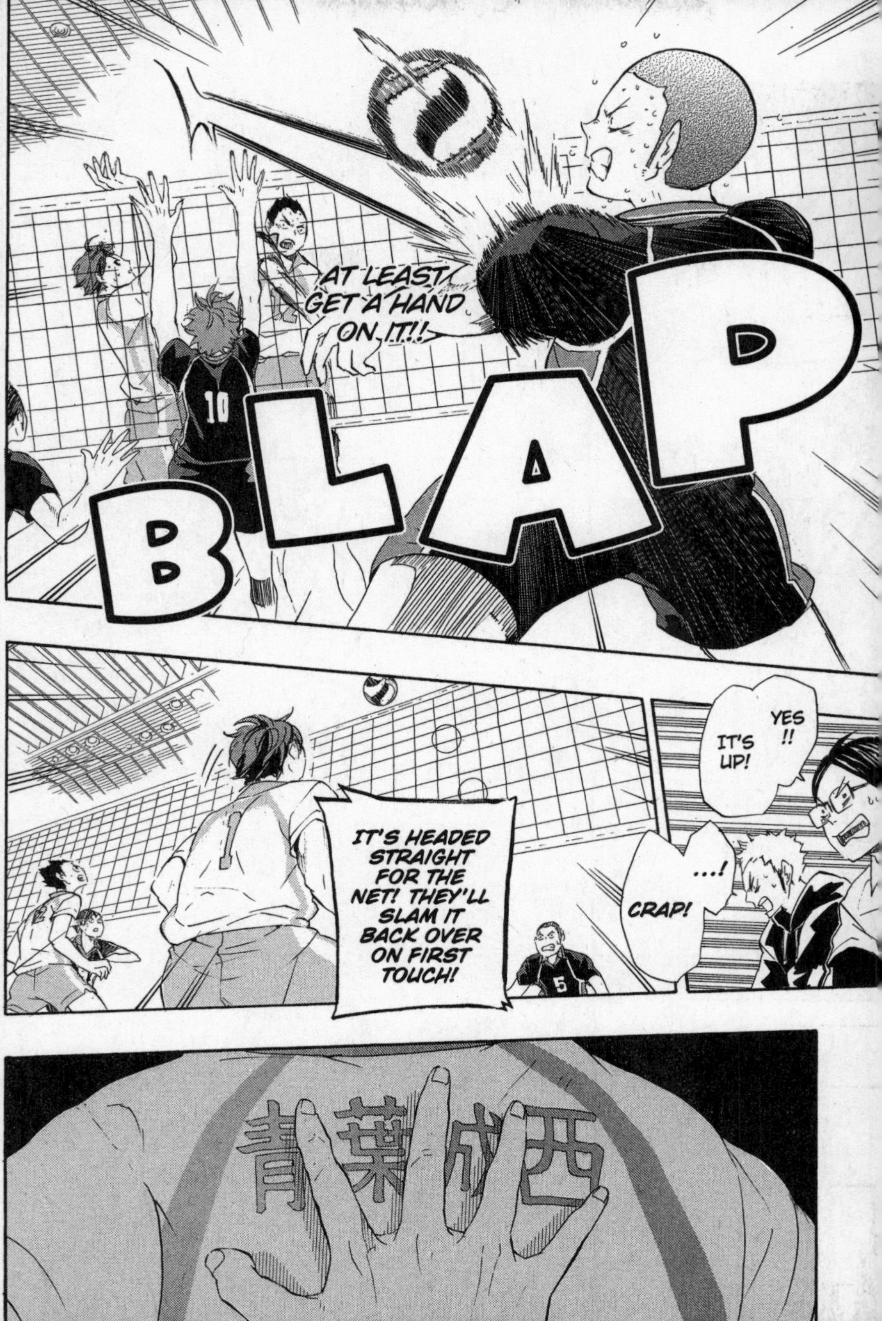
AT LEAST GET A HAND ON IT!!
BLAP
YES !!
IT'S UP!
...!
CRAP!
IT'S HEADED STRAIGHT FOR THE NET! THEY'LL SLAM IT BACK OVER ON FIRST TOUCH!

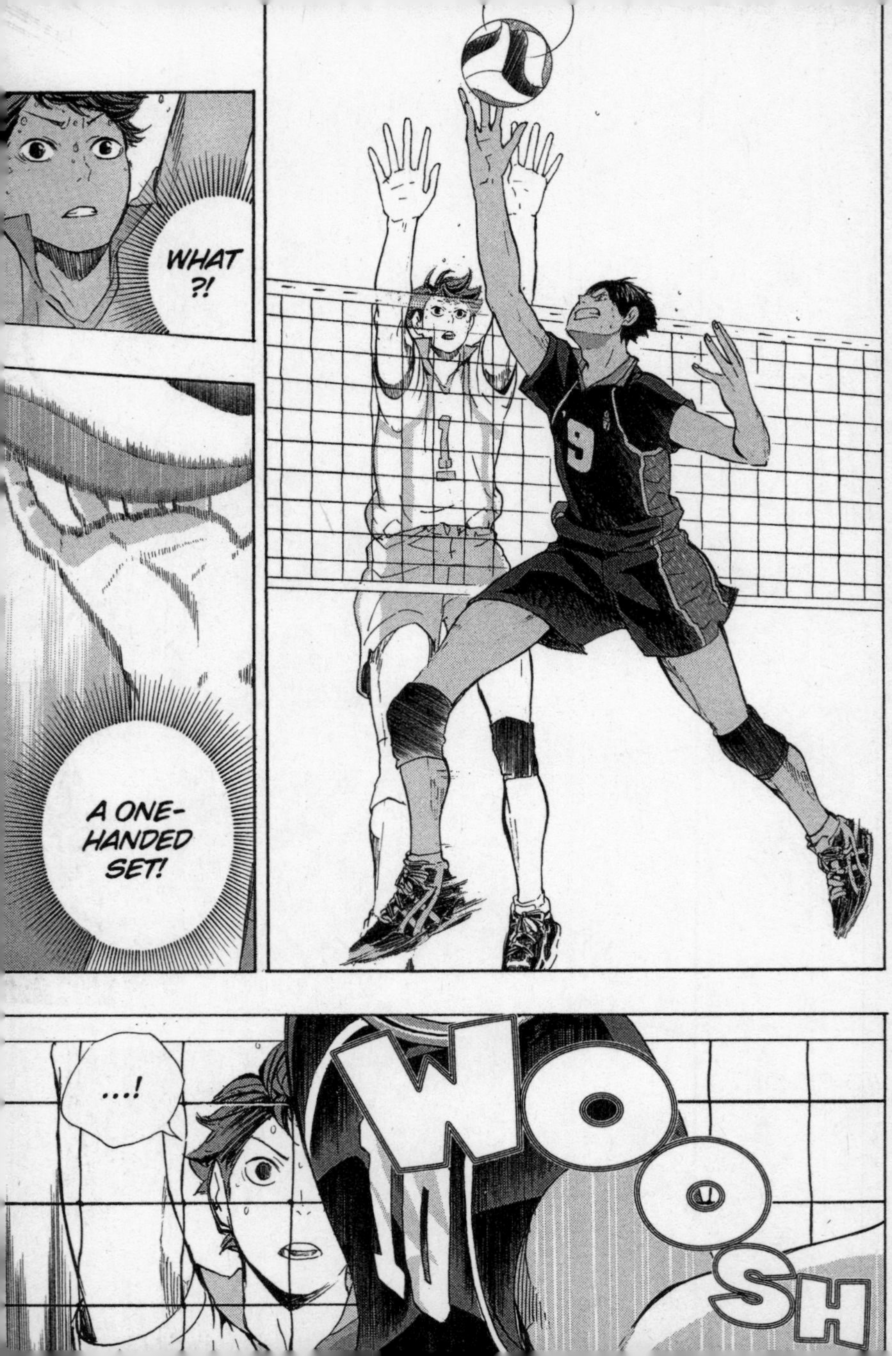
WHAT?!
A ONE-HANDED SET!
WOOSH
...!

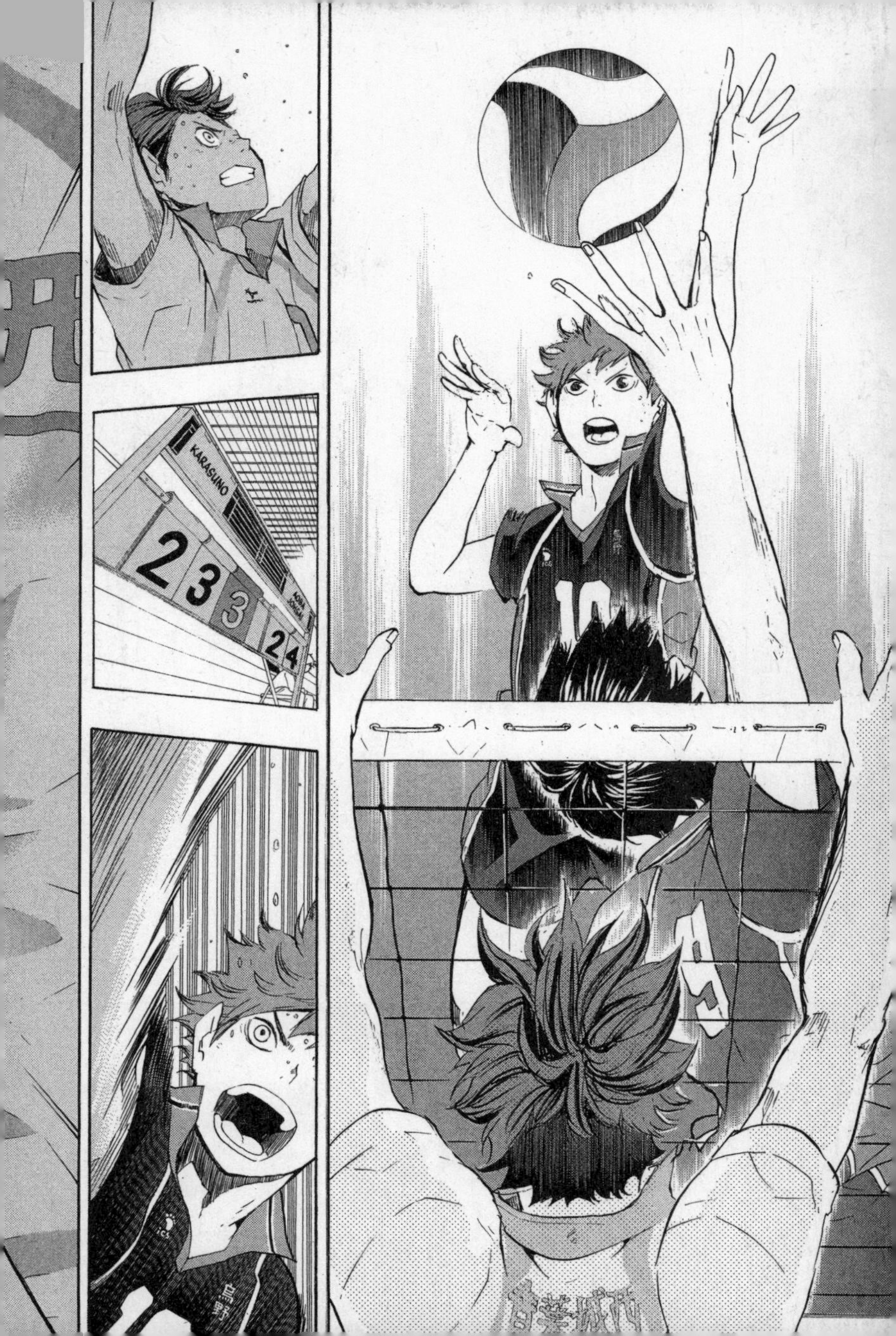
KARASUNO
23
3
24
AOBA JOHSAI

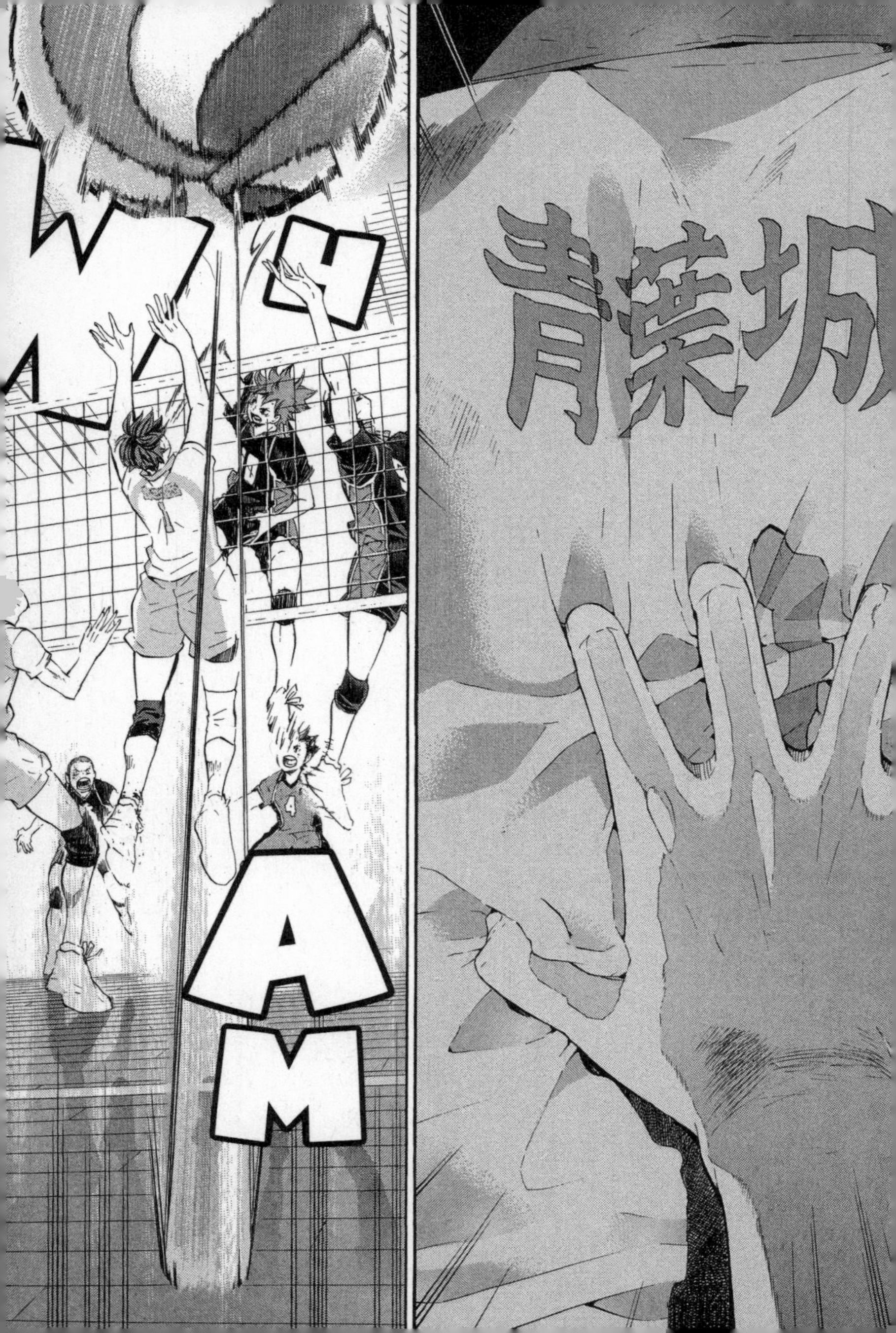
青葉
WHAM

CHAPTER 66: Again

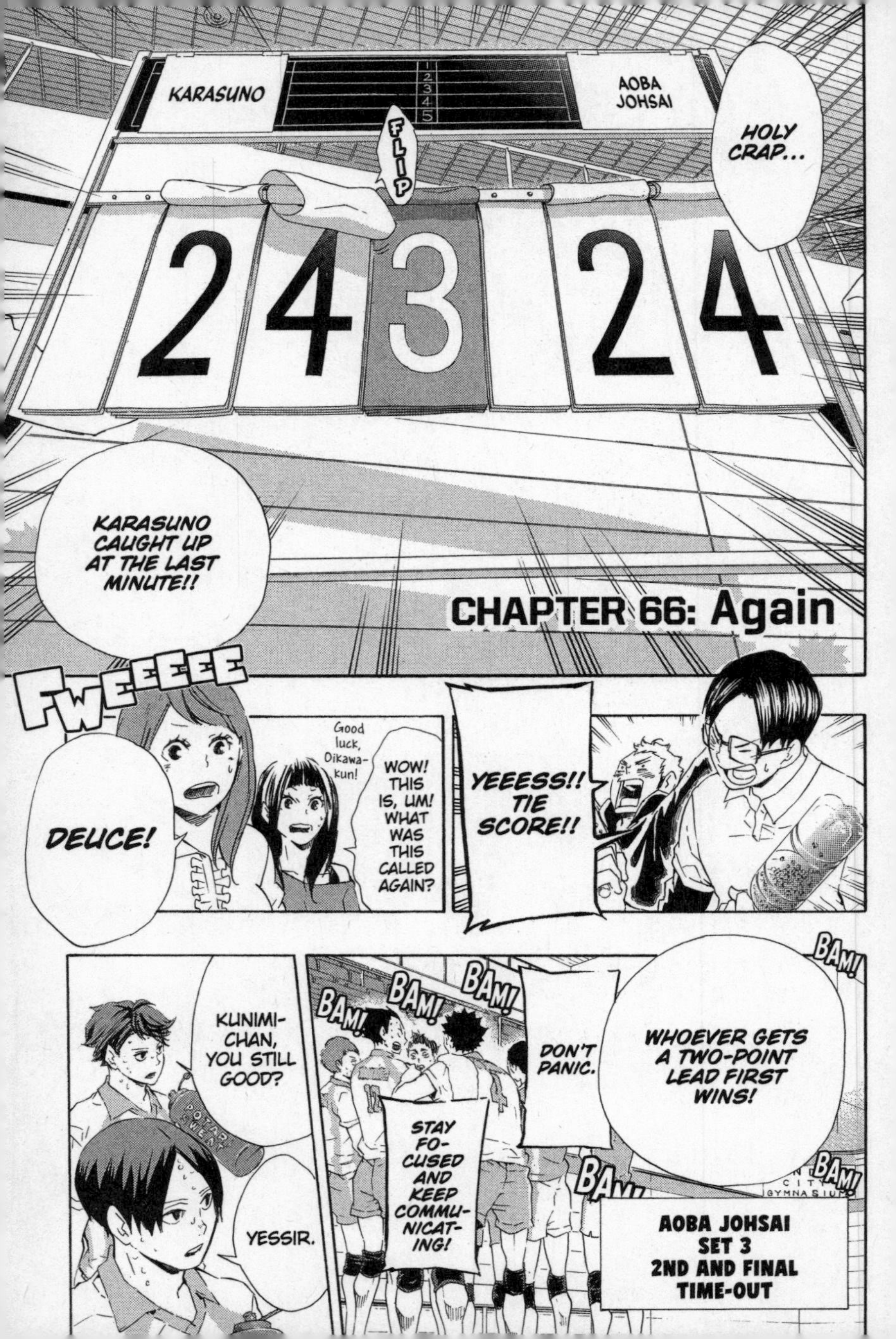
HOLY CRAP...
KARASUNO
AOBA JOHSAI
1 2 3 4 5
FLIP
24 3 24
KARASUNO CAUGHT UP AT THE LAST MINUTE!!
YEEESS!! TIE SCORE!!
WOW! THIS IS, UM! WHAT WAS THIS CALLED AGAIN?
Good luck, Oikawa-kun!
FWEEEEE
DEUCE!
BAM!
WHOEVER GETS A TWO-POINT LEAD FIRST WINS!
DON'T PANIC.
BAM!
BAM!
BAM!
STAY FO-CUSED AND KEEP COMMU-NICAT-ING!
BAM!
BAM!
AOBA JOHSAI SET 3 2ND AND FINAL TIME-OUT
KUNIMI-CHAN, YOU STILL GOOD?
YESSIR.

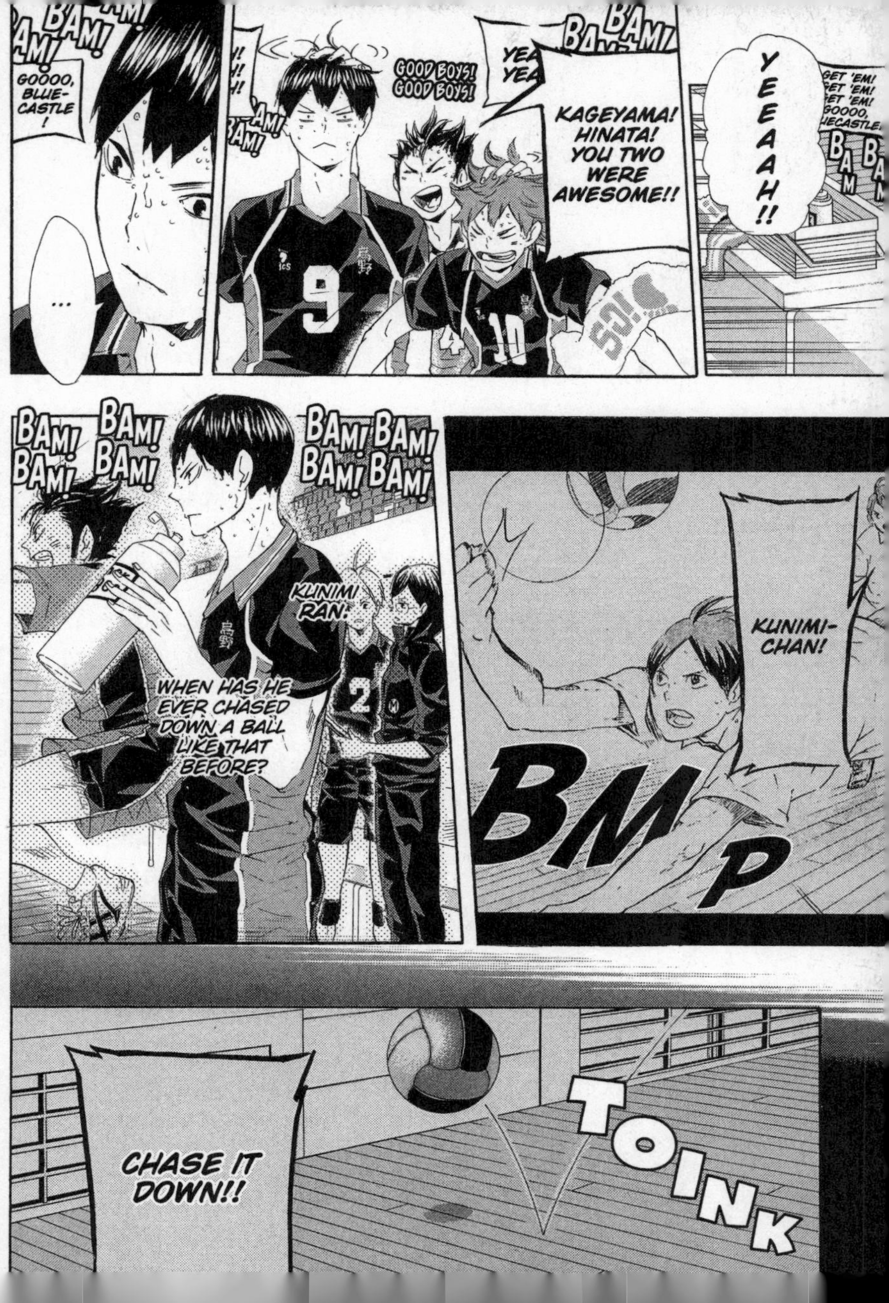
YEEAAH!!
GET 'EM! GET 'EM! GET 'EM! GOOOO,
BAM BAM
BAM! BAM!
KAGEYAMA! HINATA! YOU TWO WERE AWESOME!!
GOOD BOYS! GOOD BOYS!
BAM! BAM!
GOOOO, BLUE-CASTLE!
...
KUNIMI-CHAN!
BMP
BAM! BAM! BAM! BAM!
BAM! BAM!
BAM! BAM!
KUNIMI RAN!
WHEN HAS HE EVER CHASED DOWN A BALL LIKE THAT BEFORE?
TOINK
CHASE IT DOWN!!

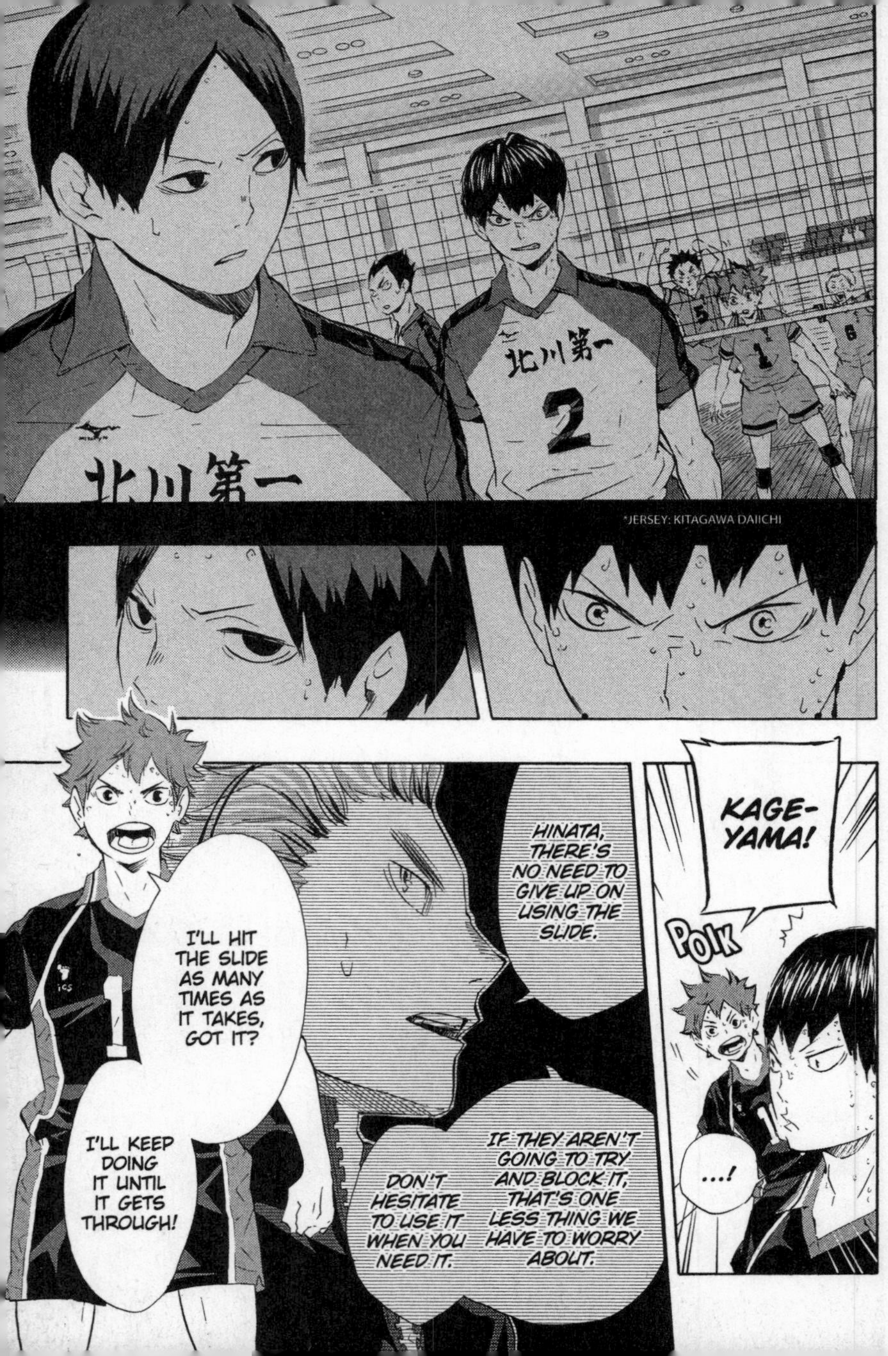
*JERSEY: KITAGAWA DAIICHI
KAGE-YAMA!
POIK
...!
HINATA, THERE'S NO NEED TO GIVE UP ON USING THE SLIDE.
IF THEY AREN'T GOING TO TRY AND BLOCK IT, THAT'S ONE LESS THING WE HAVE TO WORRY ABOUT.
DON'T HESITATE TO USE IT WHEN YOU NEED IT.
I'LL HIT THE SLIDE AS MANY TIMES AS IT TAKES, GOT IT?
I'LL KEEP DOING IT UNTIL IT GETS THROUGH!

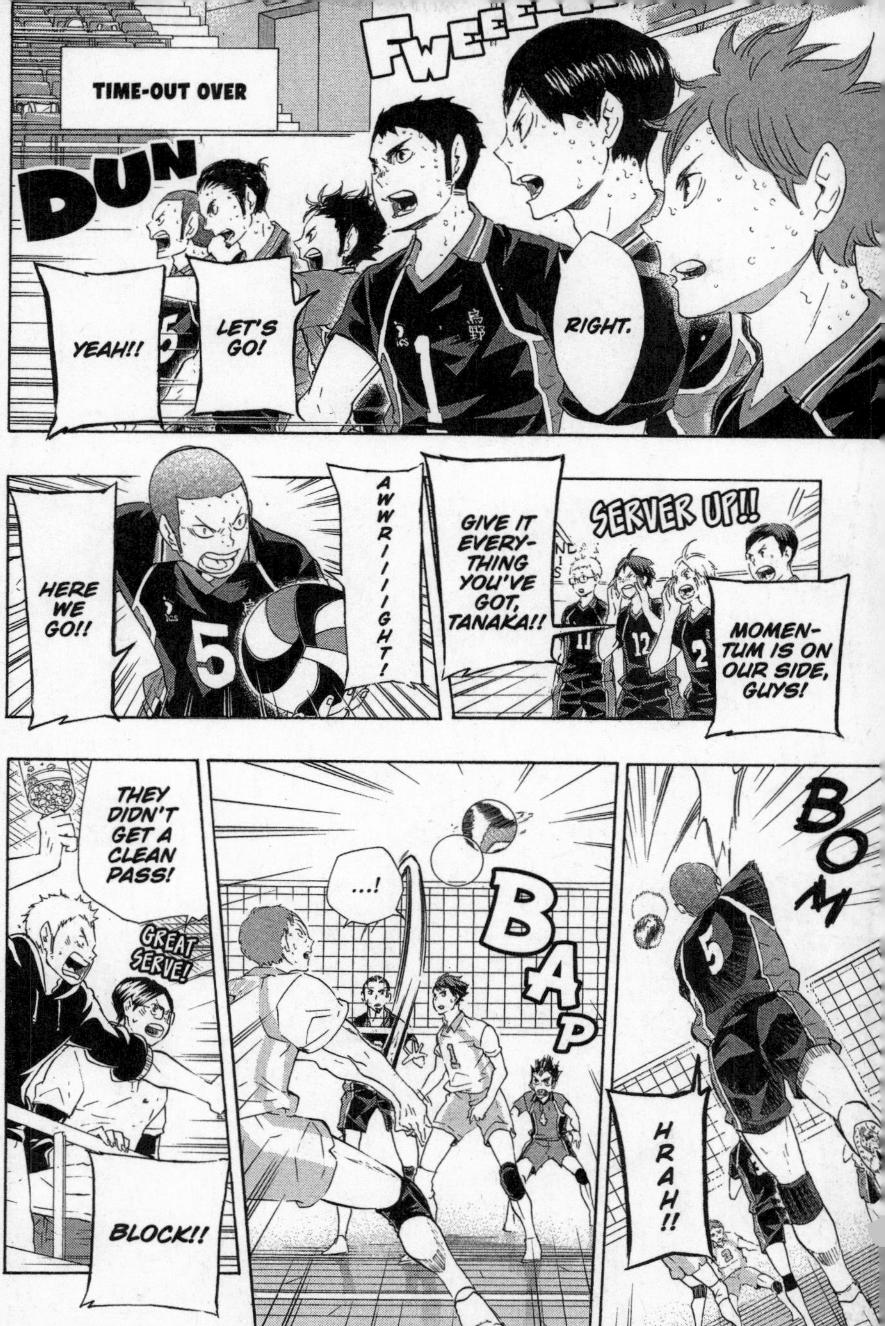
FWEEE-E
TIME-OUT OVER
RIGHT.
DUN
LET'S GO!
YEAH!!
SERVER UP!!
GIVE IT EVERYTHING YOU'VE GOT, TANAKA!!
MOMENTUM IS ON OUR SIDE, GUYS!
AWWRIIIIIGHT!
HERE WE GO!!
BOM
HRAH!!
BAP
...!
THEY DIDN'T GET A CLEAN PASS!
GREAT SERVE!
BLOCK!!

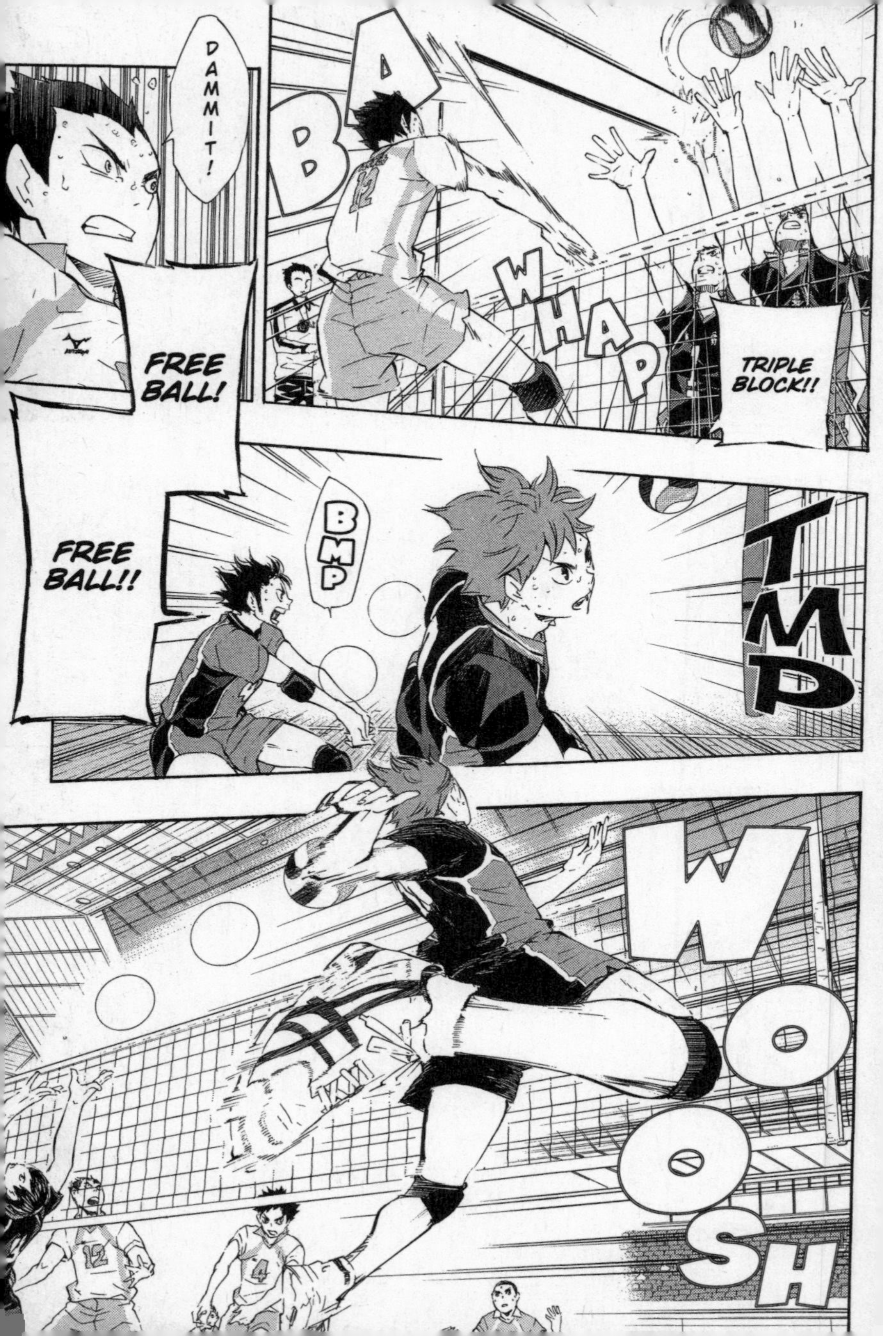

BA
WHAP
TRIPLE BLOCK!!
DAMMIT!
FREE BALL!
TMP
BMP
FREE BALL!!
WHOOSH

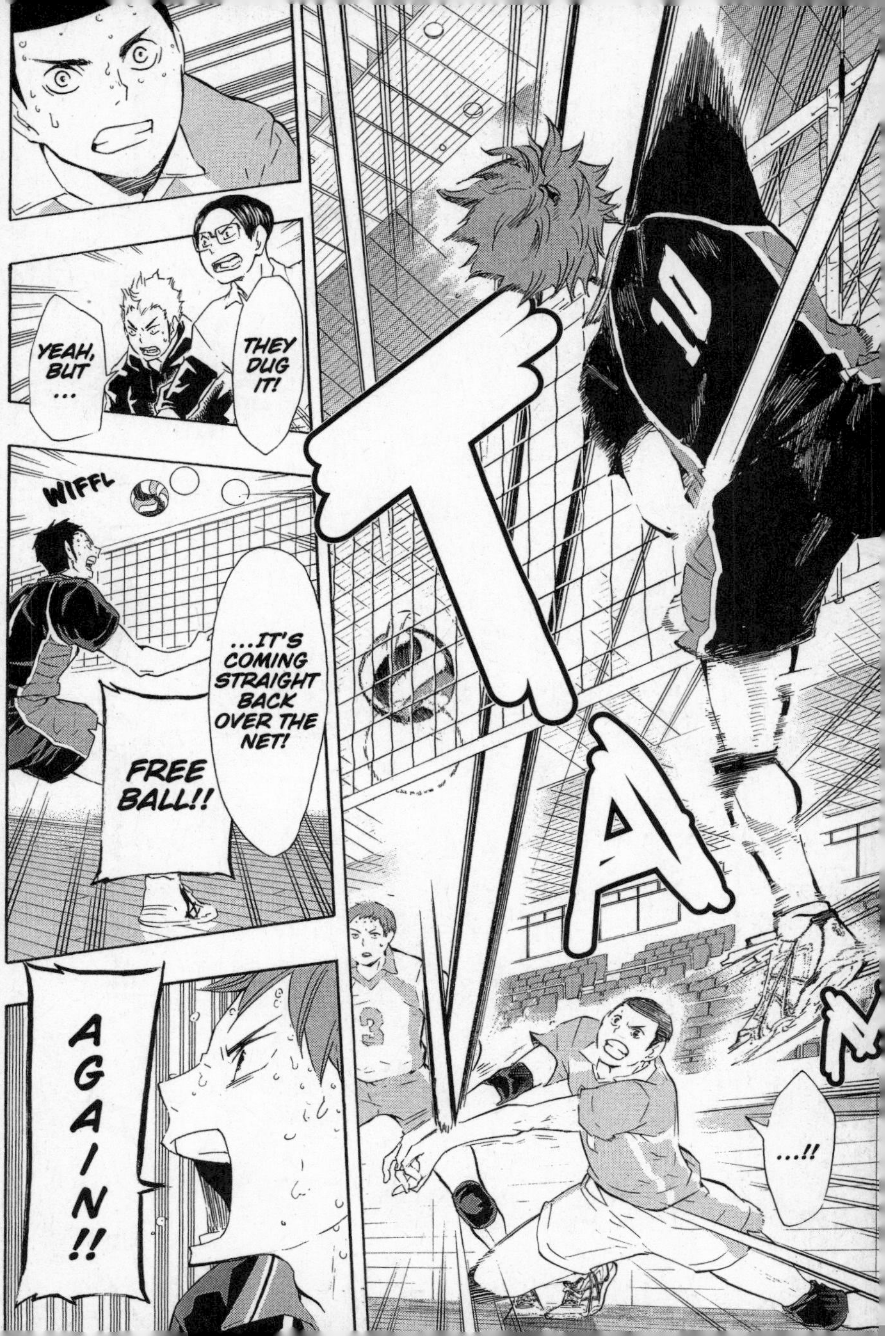
TAM
...!!
THEY DUG IT!
YEAH, BUT ...
WIFFL
...IT'S COMING STRAIGHT BACK OVER THE NET!
FREE BALL!!
AGAIN!!

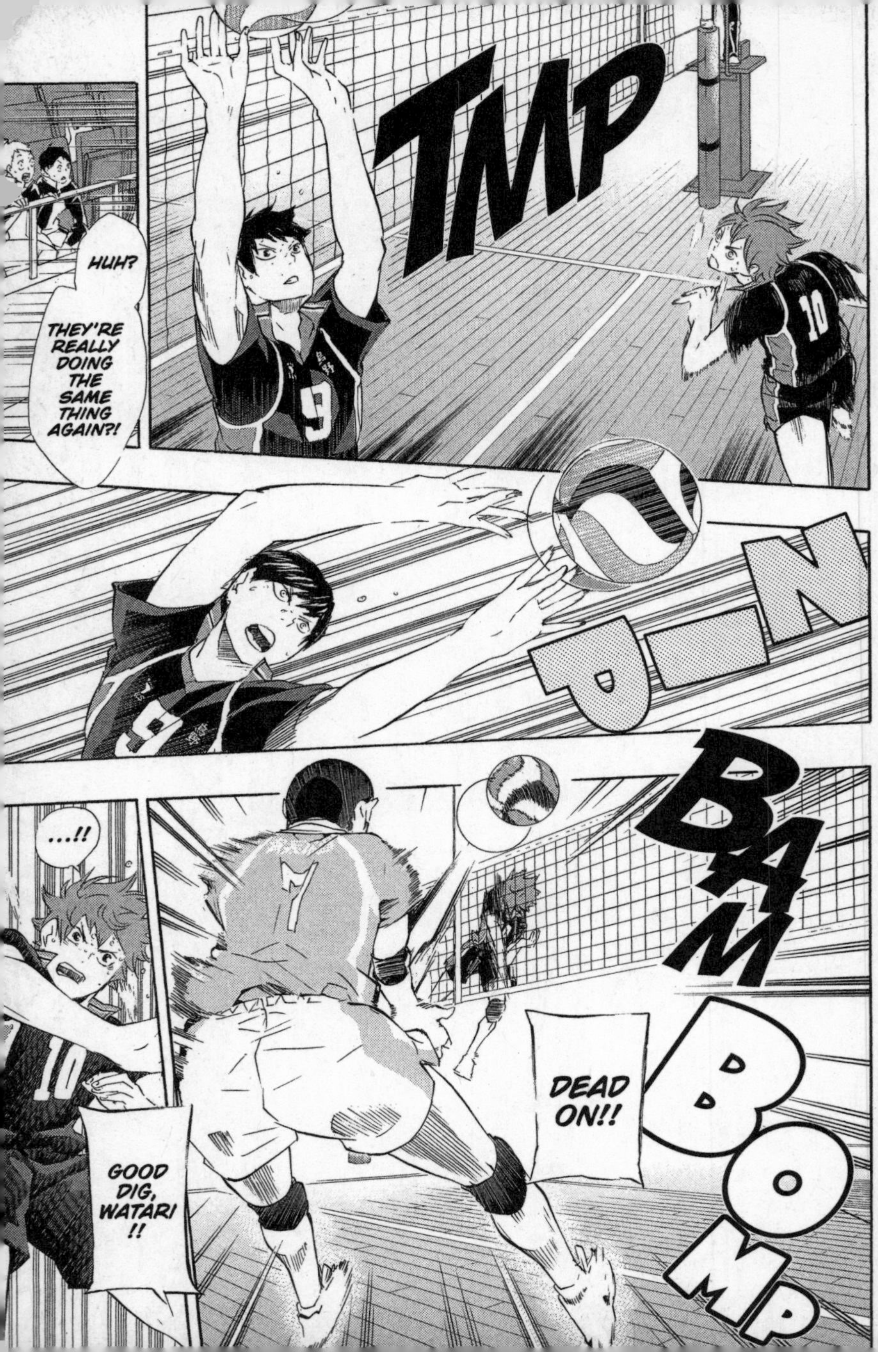
TMP
HUH?
THEY'RE REALLY DOING THE SAME THING AGAIN?!
P—N
BAM
BOMP
DEAD ON!!
...!!
GOOD DIG, WATARI!!

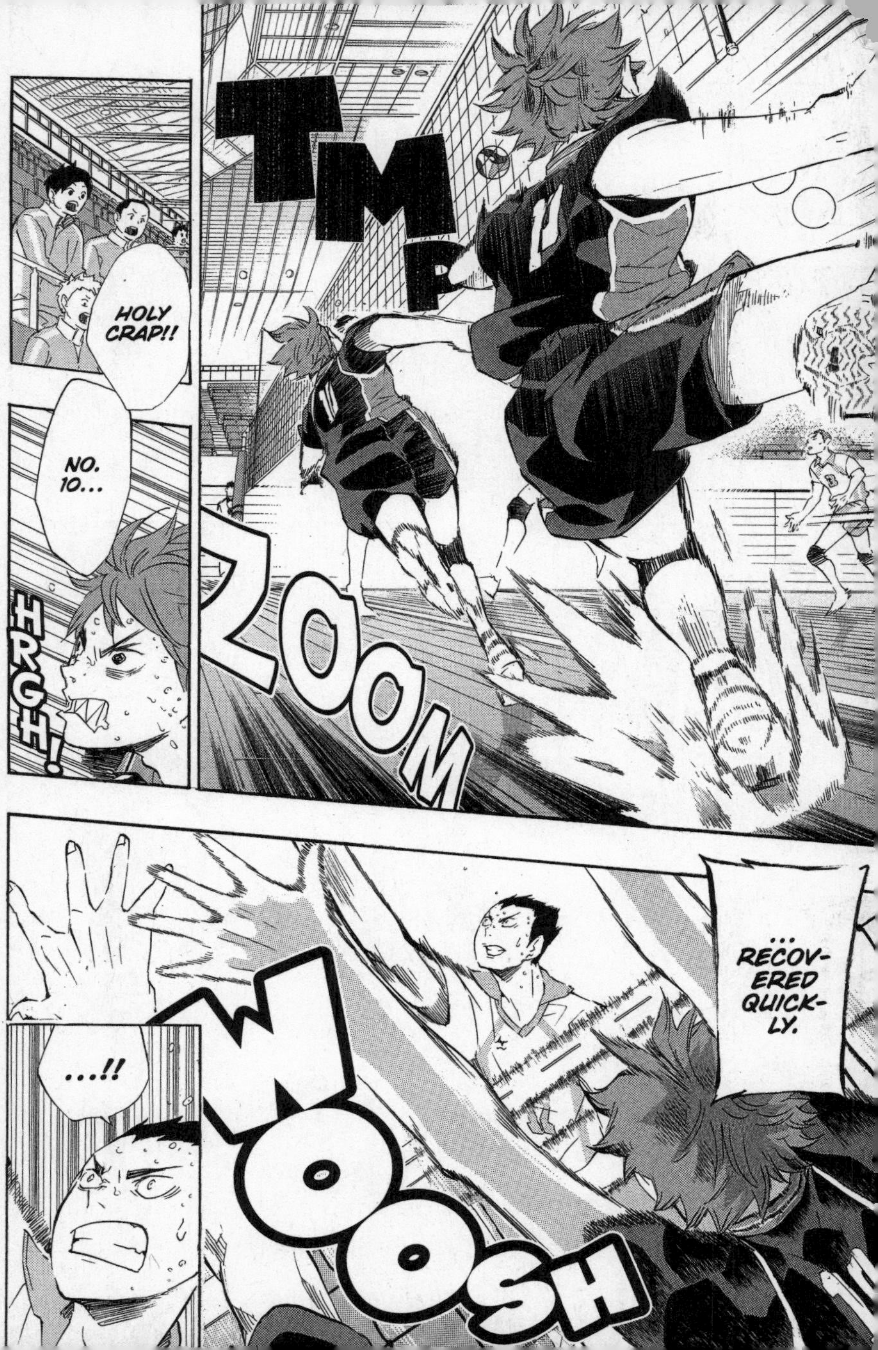
TMP
ZOOM
HOLY CRAP!!
NO. 10...
HRGH!
...RECOV-ERED QUICK-LY.
WHOOSH
...!!

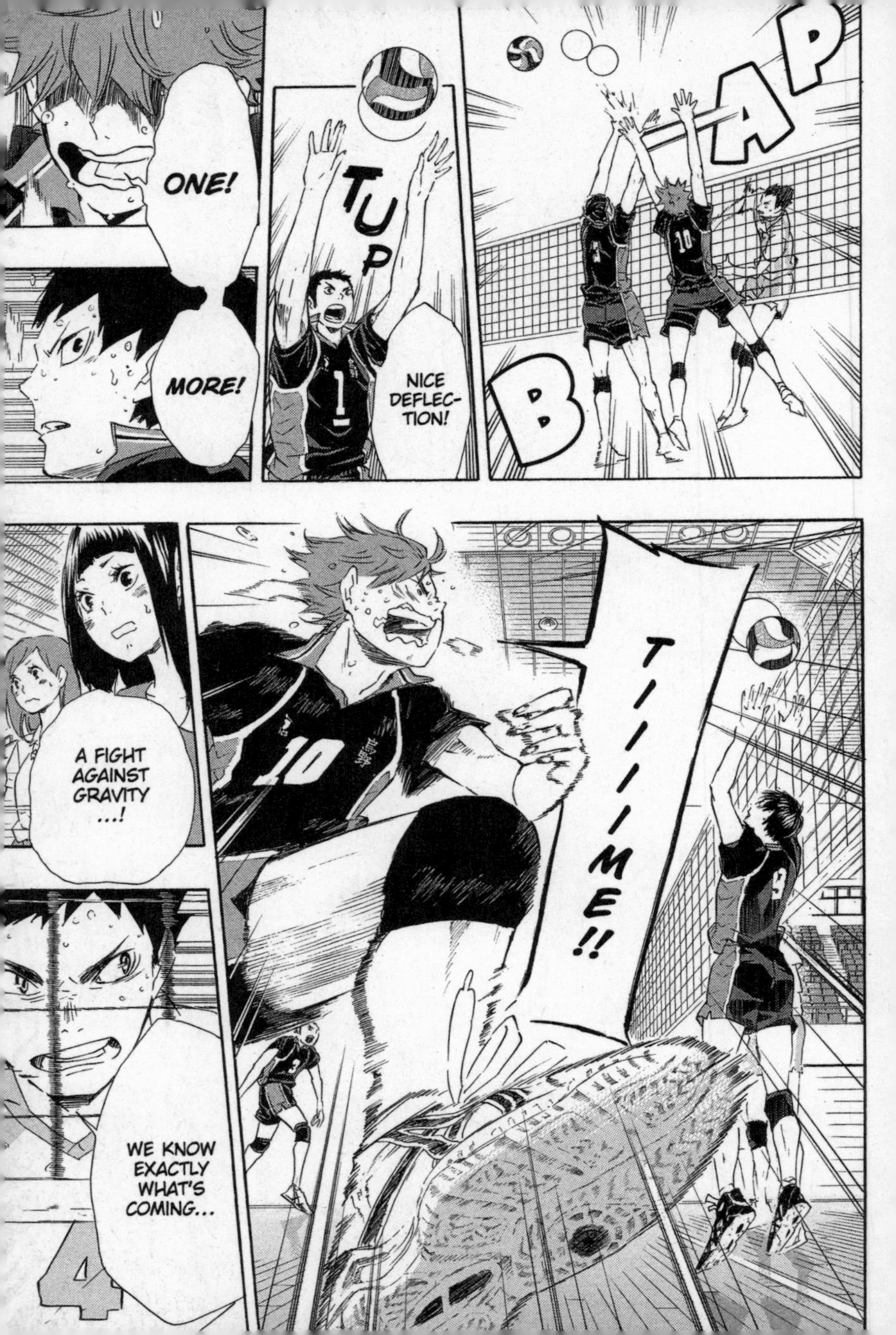
BAP
TUP
NICE DEFLECTION!
ONE!
MORE!
TIIIIME!!
A FIGHT AGAINST GRAVITY ...!
WE KNOW EXACTLY WHAT'S COMING...

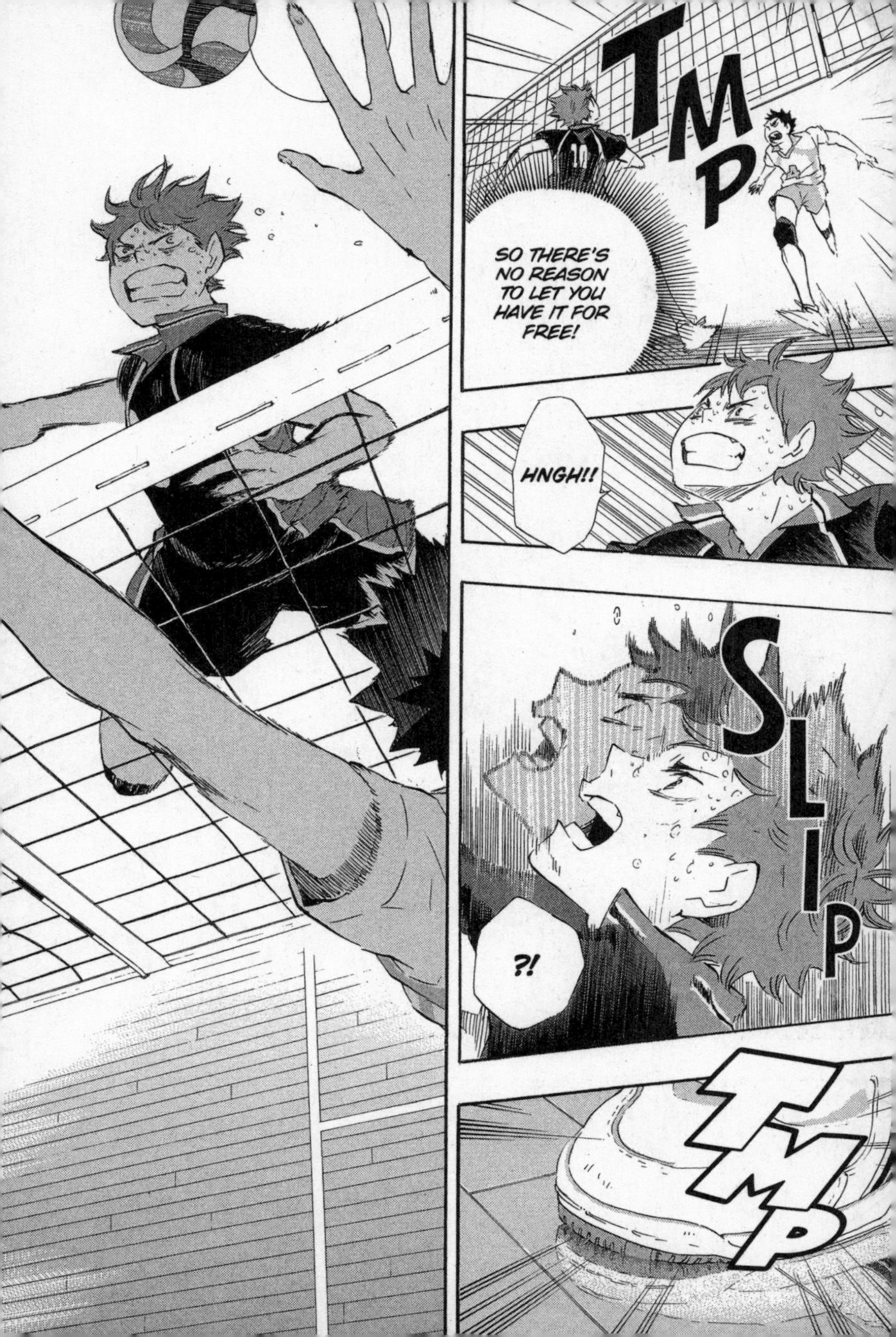
TMP
SO THERE'S NO REASON TO LET YOU HAVE IT FOR FREE!
HNGH!!
SLIP
?!
TMP

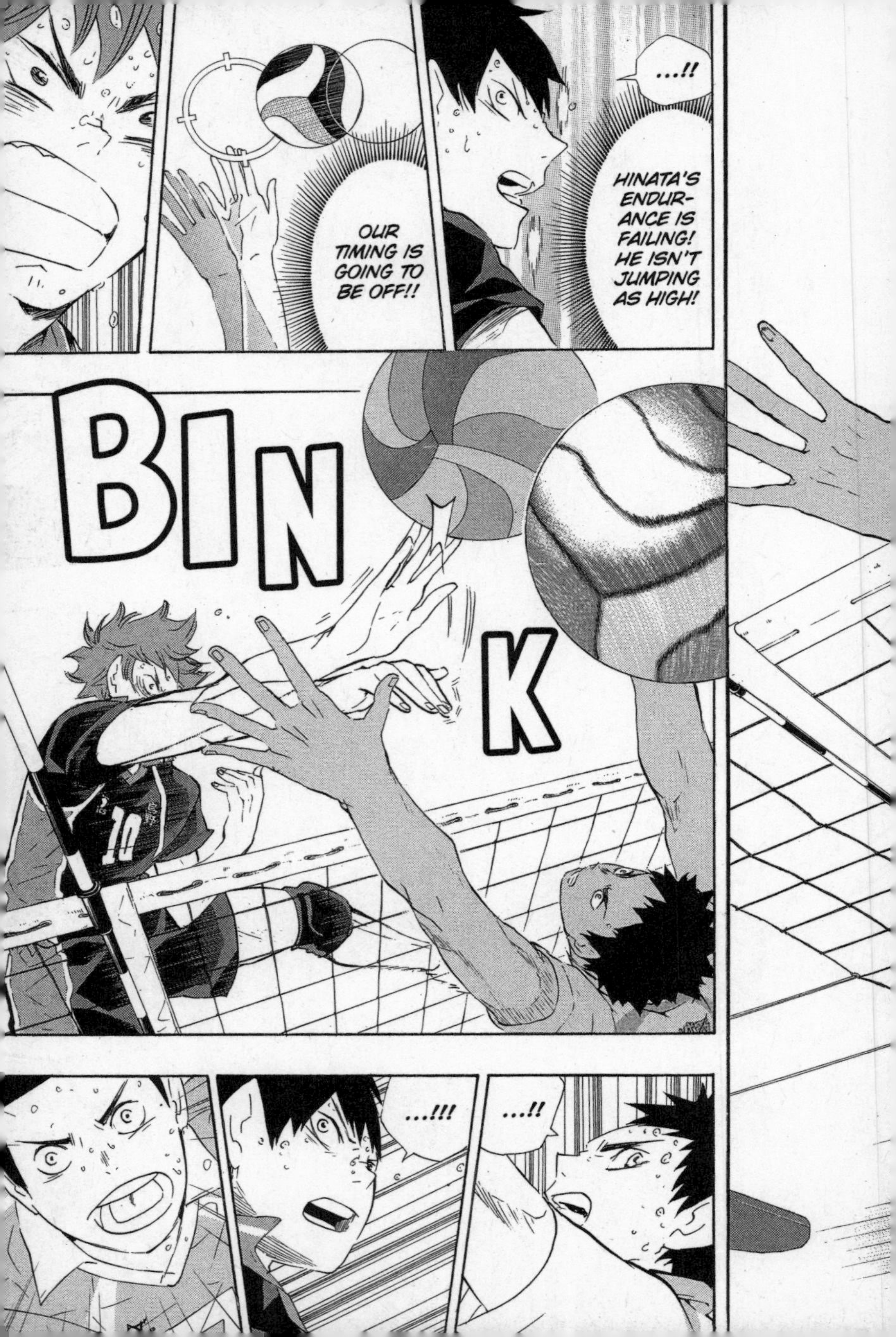
...!!
HINATA'S ENDURANCE IS FAILING! HE ISN'T JUMPING AS HIGH!
OUR TIMING IS GOING TO BE OFF!!
BINK
...!!
...!!!

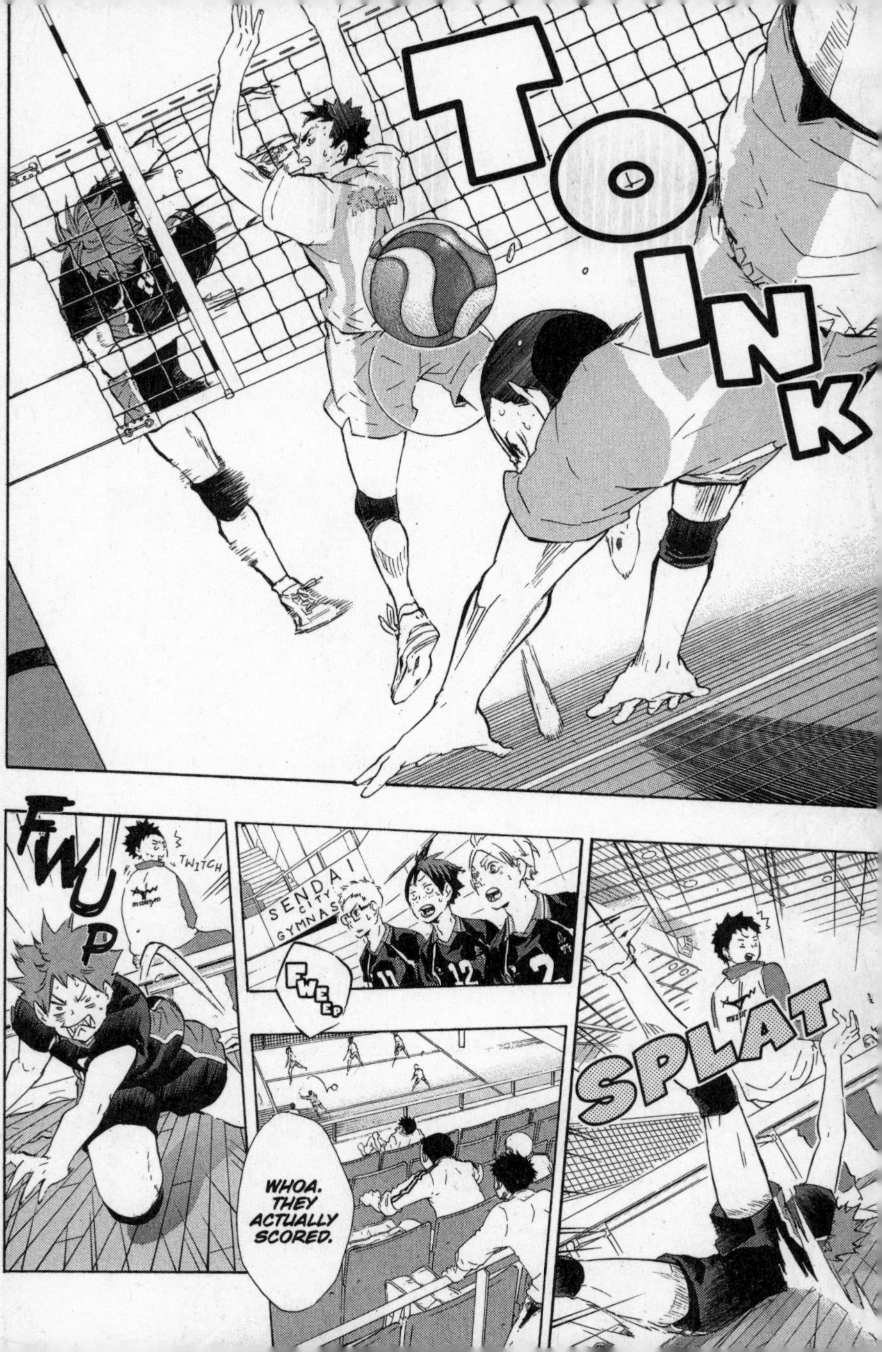
TOINK
SPLAT
SENDAI CITY GYMNAS
FWEEP
WHOA. THEY ACTUALLY SCORED.
FWUP
TWITCH

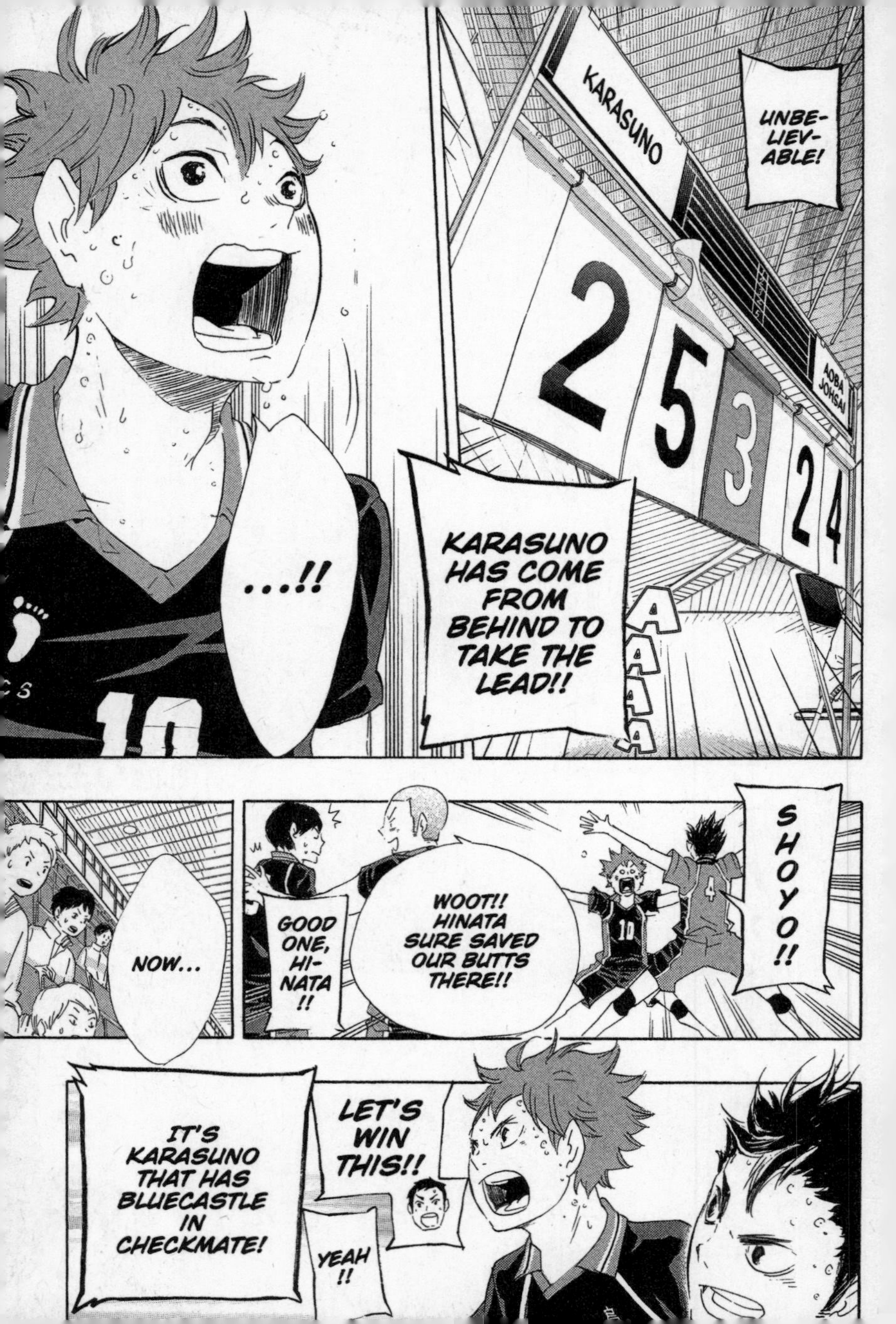
UNBE-LIEV-ABLE!
KARASUNO
AOBA JOHSAI
25
3
24
KARASUNO HAS COME FROM BEHIND TO TAKE THE LEAD!!
AAAAA
...!!
SHOYO!!
WOOT!! HINATA SURE SAVED OUR BUTTS THERE!!
GOOD ONE, HI-NATA!!
NOW...
LET'S WIN THIS!!
IT'S KARASUNO THAT HAS BLUECASTLE IN CHECKMATE!
YEAH!!

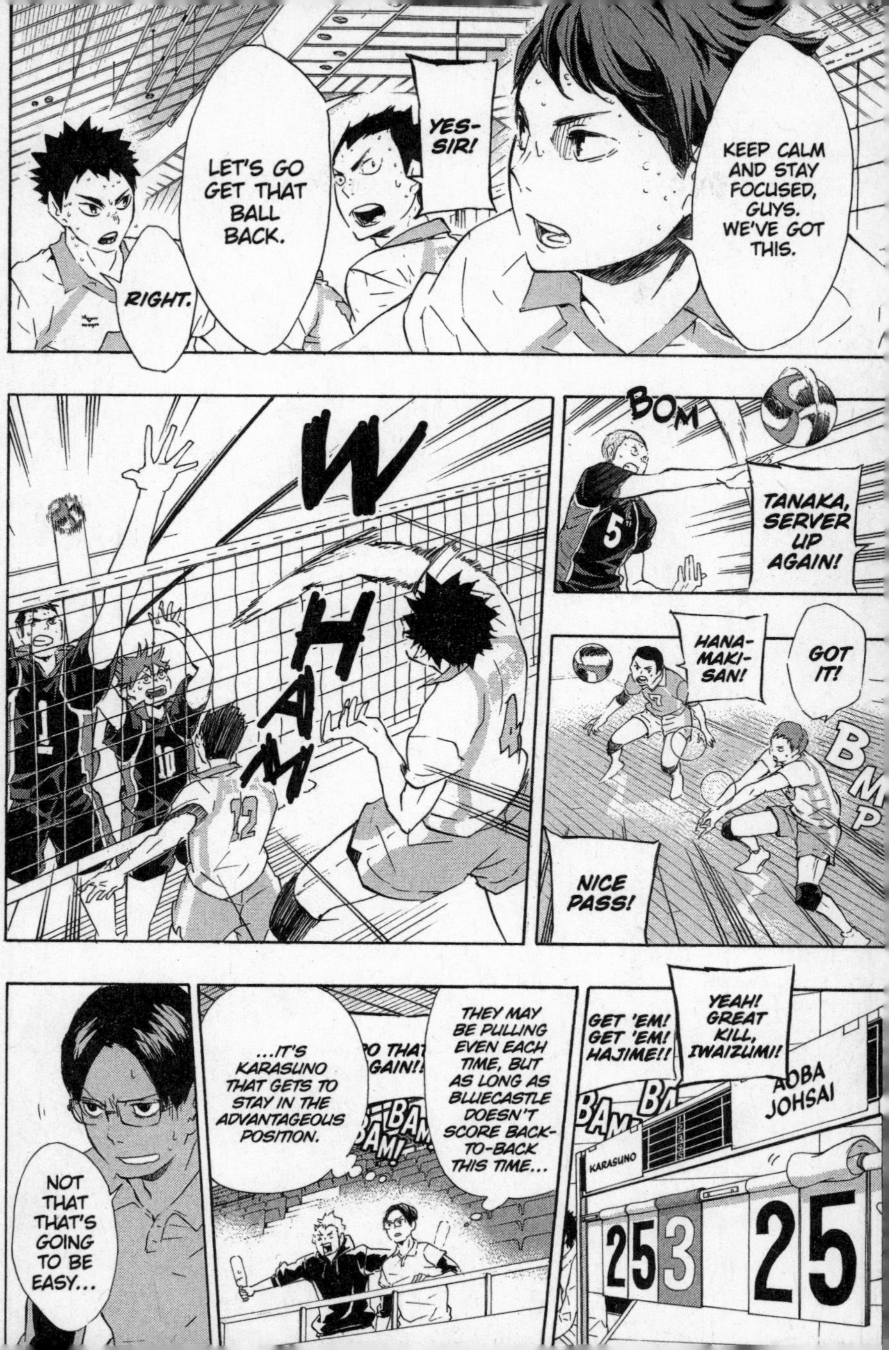
KEEP CALM AND STAY FOCUSED, GUYS. WE'VE GOT THIS.
YES-SIR!
LET'S GO GET THAT BALL BACK.
RIGHT.
BOM
TANAKA, SERVER UP AGAIN!
GOT IT!
HANA-MAKI-SAN!
BMP
NICE PASS!
WHAM
YEAH! GREAT KILL, IWAIZUMI!
AOBA JOHSAI
GET 'EM! GET 'EM! HAJIME!!
BAM BAM
KARASUNO
25
3
25
THEY MAY BE PULLING EVEN EACH TIME, BUT AS LONG AS BLUECASTLE DOESN'T SCORE BACK-TO-BACK THIS TIME...
...IT'S KARASUNO THAT GETS TO STAY IN THE ADVANTAGEOUS POSITION.
BAM BAM!
NOT THAT THAT'S GOING TO BE EASY...

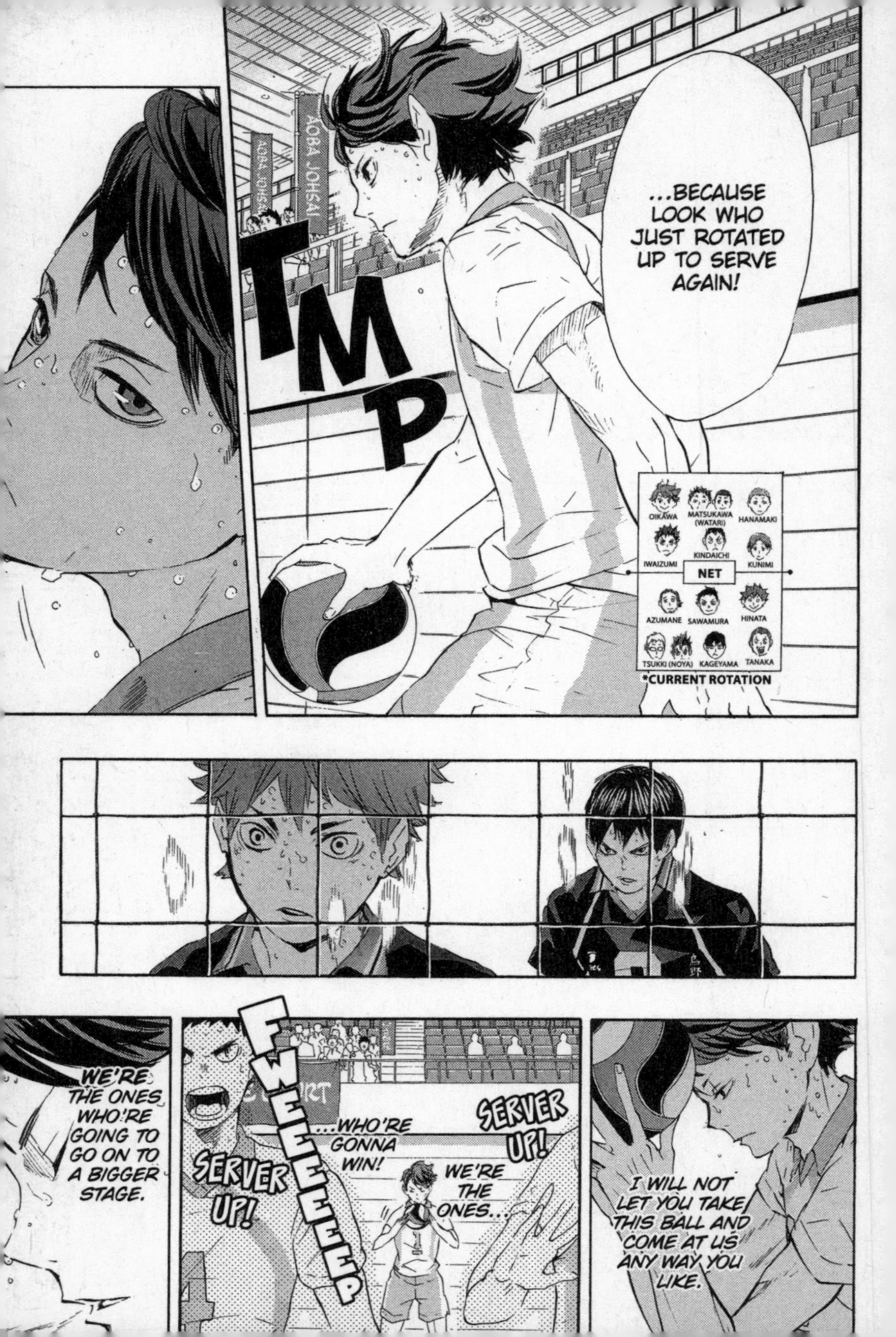
AOBA JOHSAI
AOBA JOHSAI
...BECAUSE LOOK WHO JUST ROTATED UP TO SERVE AGAIN!
TMP
OIKAWA
MATSUKAWA (WATARI)
HANAMAKI
IWAIZUMI
KINDAICHI
KUNIMI
NET
AZUMANE
SAWAMURA
HINATA
TSUKKI (NOYA)
KAGEYAMA
TANAKA
*CURRENT ROTATION
I WILL NOT LET YOU TAKE THIS BALL AND COME AT US ANY WAY YOU LIKE.
SERVER UP!
WE'RE THE ONES...
...WHO'RE GONNA WIN!
FWEEEEEEEP
SERVER UP!
WE'RE THE ONES WHO'RE GOING TO GO ON TO A BIGGER STAGE.

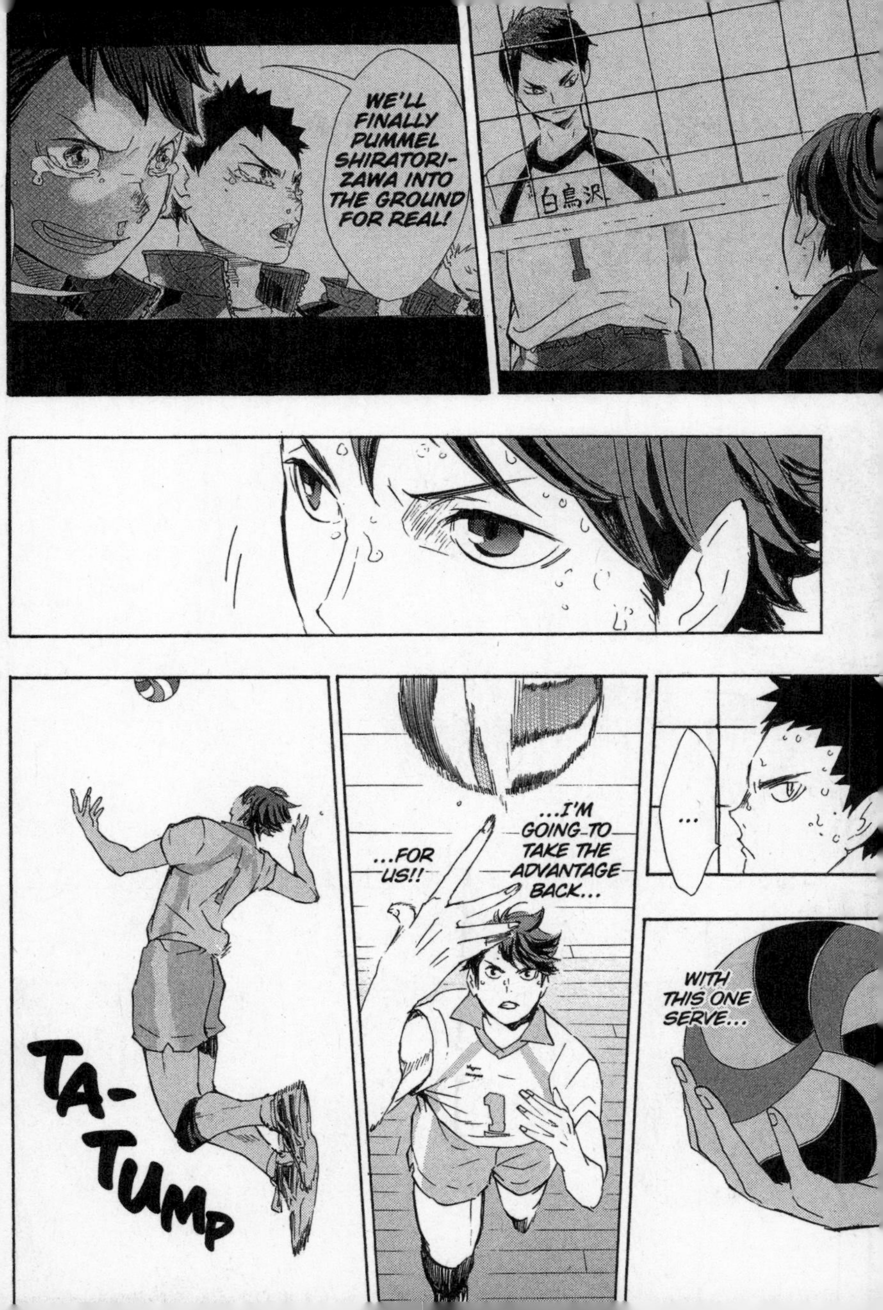
白鳥沢
WE'LL FINALLY PUMMEL SHIRATORI-ZAWA INTO THE GROUND FOR REAL!
...
WITH THIS ONE SERVE...
...I'M GOING TO TAKE THE ADVANTAGE BACK...
...FOR US!!
TA-TUMP

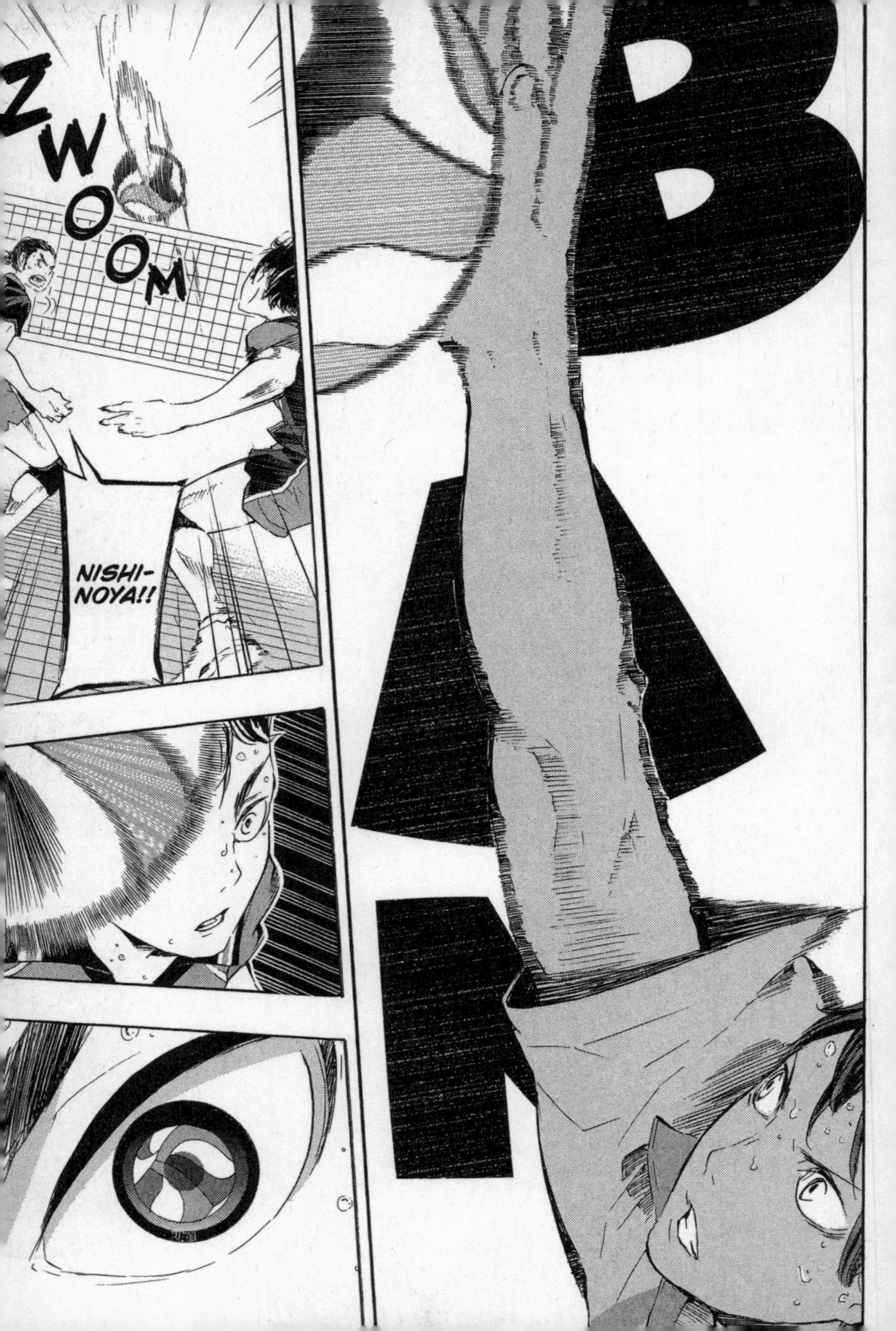
BAM
ZWOOOM
NISHI-
NOYA!!

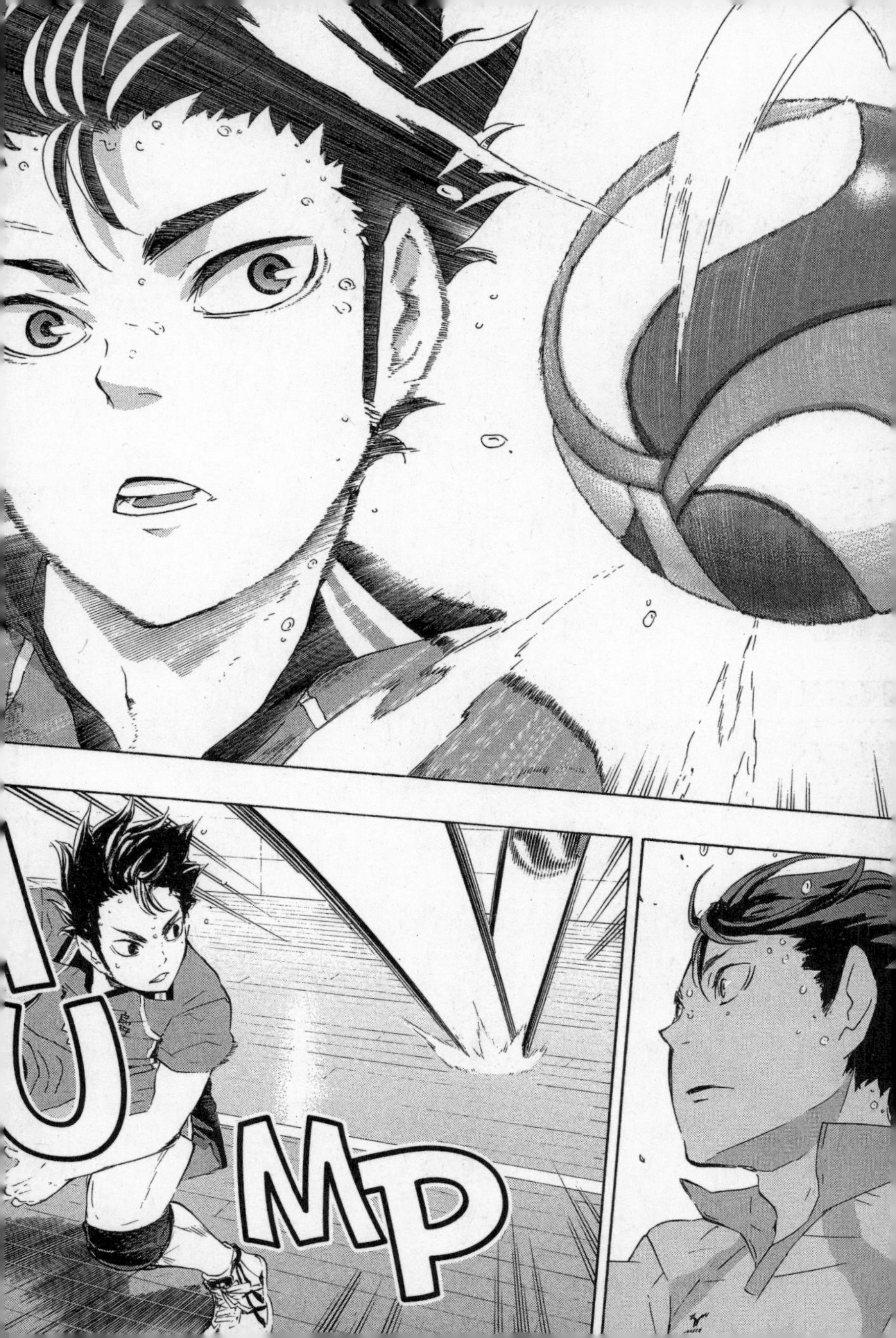
UMP

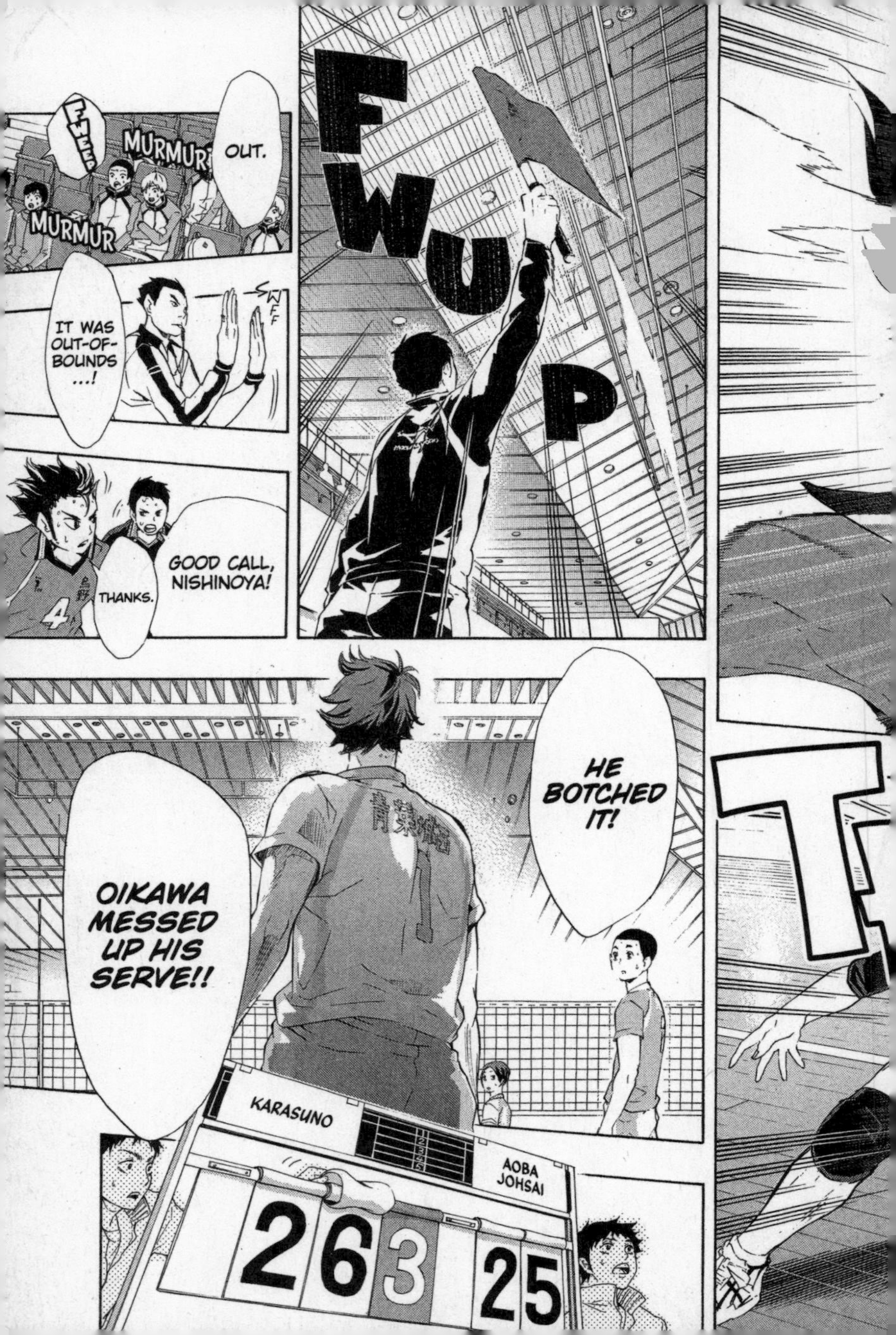
FWUP
OUT.
MURMUR
FWEEP
MURMUR
SWFF
IT WAS OUT-OF-BOUNDS ...!
GOOD CALL, NISHINOYA!
THANKS.
HE BOTCHED IT!
OIKAWA MESSED UP HIS SERVE!!
KARASUNO
AOBA JOHSAI
26 3 25

WHEN I WAS PULLING AN ALL-NIGHTER WORKING ON CHAPTER 66, I PUT THE HORROR FLICK *ONE MISSED CALL* ON IN THE BACKGROUND TO HELP KEEP ME AWAKE. NOW, WHENEVER I LOOK BACK OVER CHAPTER 66, I CAN'T HELP BUT REMEMBER SCENES FROM THAT MOVIE.

THE CREEPY RINGTONE...

DING CHING CHING

YEEP!

CHAPTER 67: Smiles

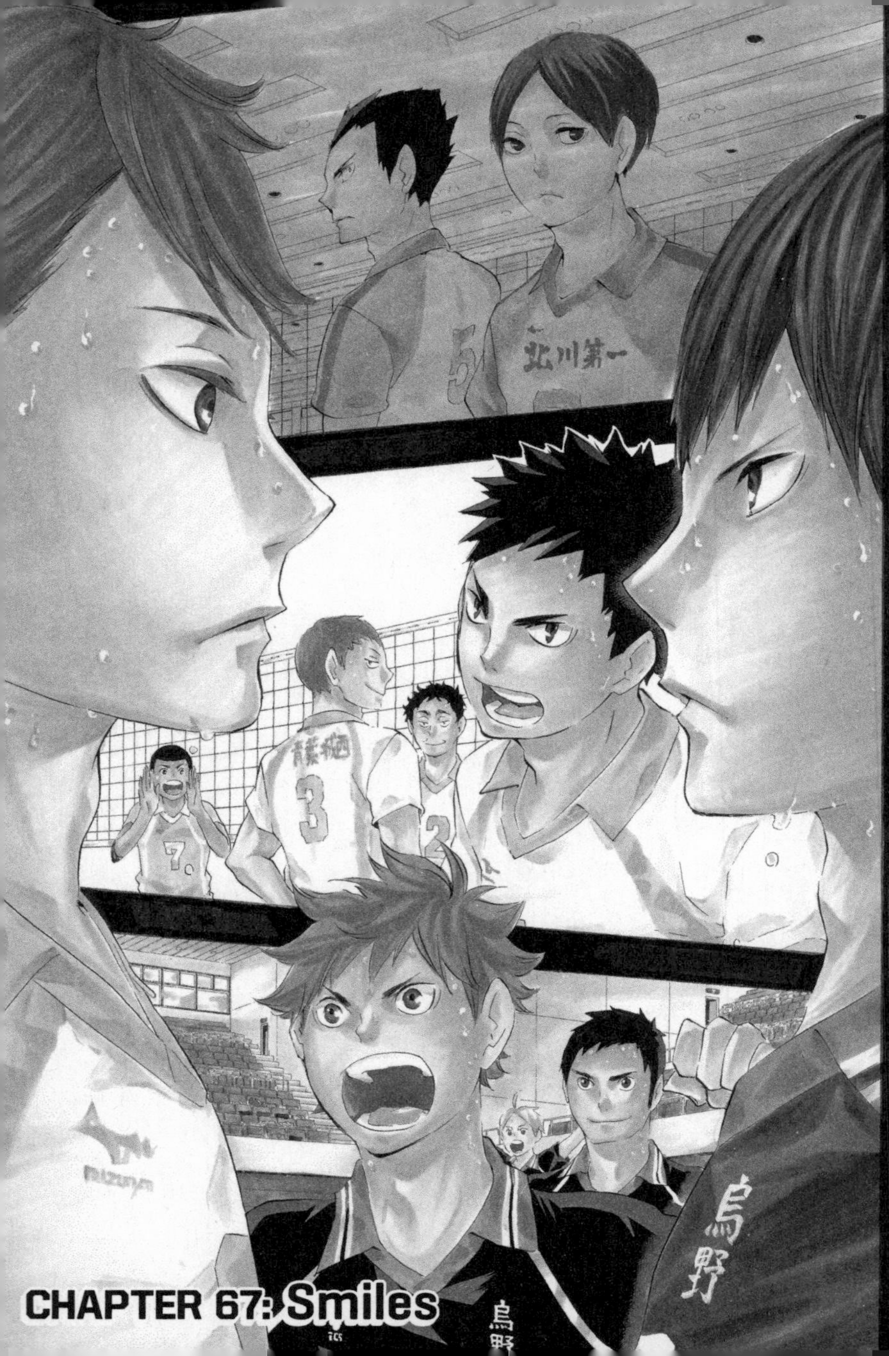
烏野

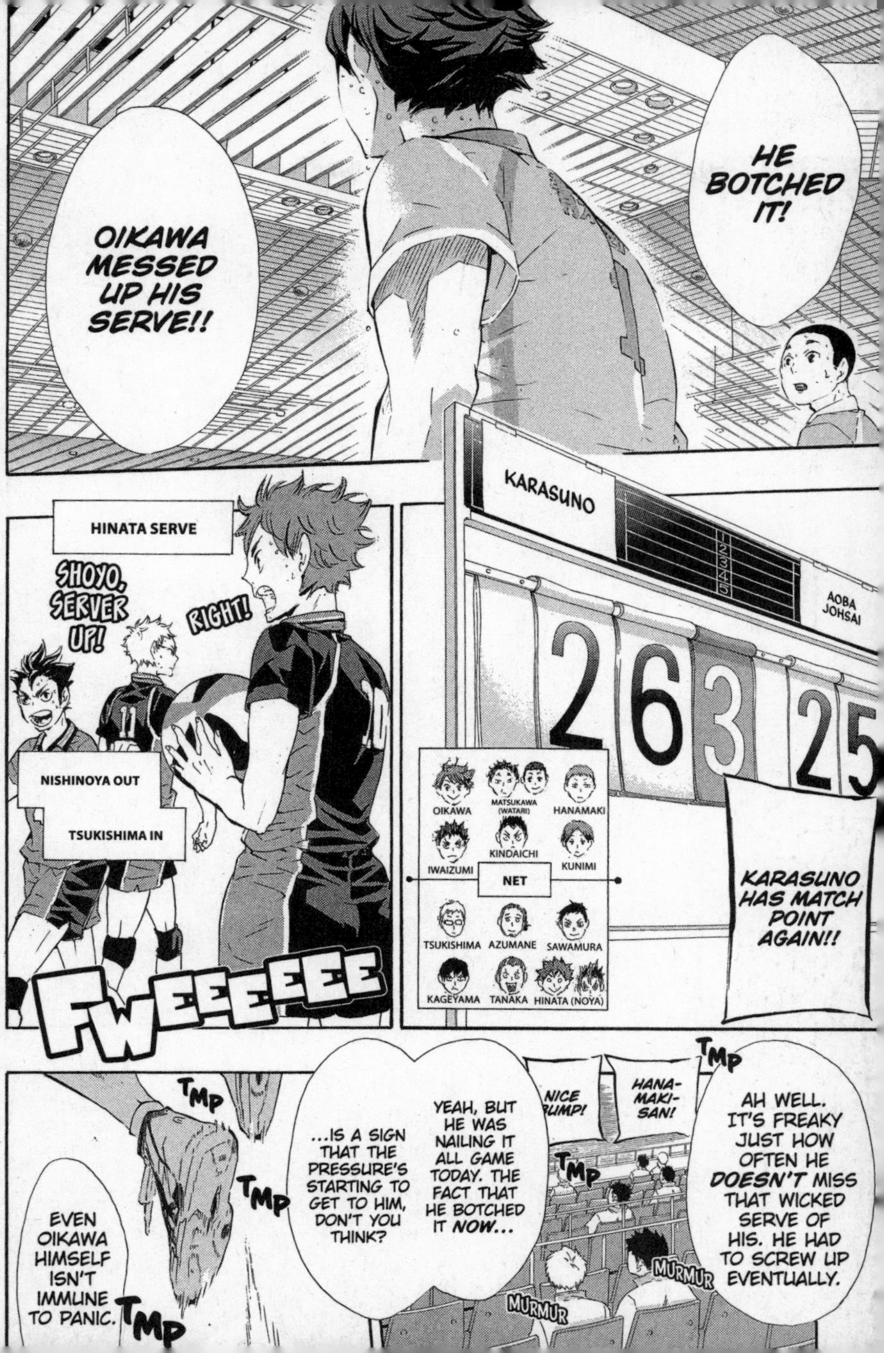
HE BOTCHED IT!
OIKAWA MESSED UP HIS SERVE!!
KARASUNO
1 2 3 4 5
AOBA JOHSAI
26
3
25
KARASUNO HAS MATCH POINT AGAIN!!
OIKAWA
MATSUKAWA (WATARI)
HANAMAKI
IWAIZUMI
KINDAICHI
KUNIMI
NET
TSUKISHIMA
AZUMANE
SAWAMURA
KAGEYAMA
TANAKA
HINATA (NOYA)
HINATA SERVE
RIGHT!
SHOYO, SERVER UP!
NISHINOYA OUT
TSUKISHIMA IN
FWEEEEEE
TMP
AH WELL. IT'S FREAKY JUST HOW OFTEN HE *DOESN'T* MISS THAT WICKED SERVE OF HIS. HE HAD TO SCREW UP EVENTUALLY.
HANA-MAKI-SAN!
NICE BUMP!
TMP
MURMUR
MURMUR
YEAH, BUT HE WAS NAILING IT ALL GAME TODAY. THE FACT THAT HE BOTCHED IT *NOW*...
...IS A SIGN THAT THE PRESSURE'S STARTING TO GET TO HIM, DON'T YOU THINK?
TMP
TMP
EVEN OIKAWA HIMSELF ISN'T IMMUNE TO PANIC.
TMP

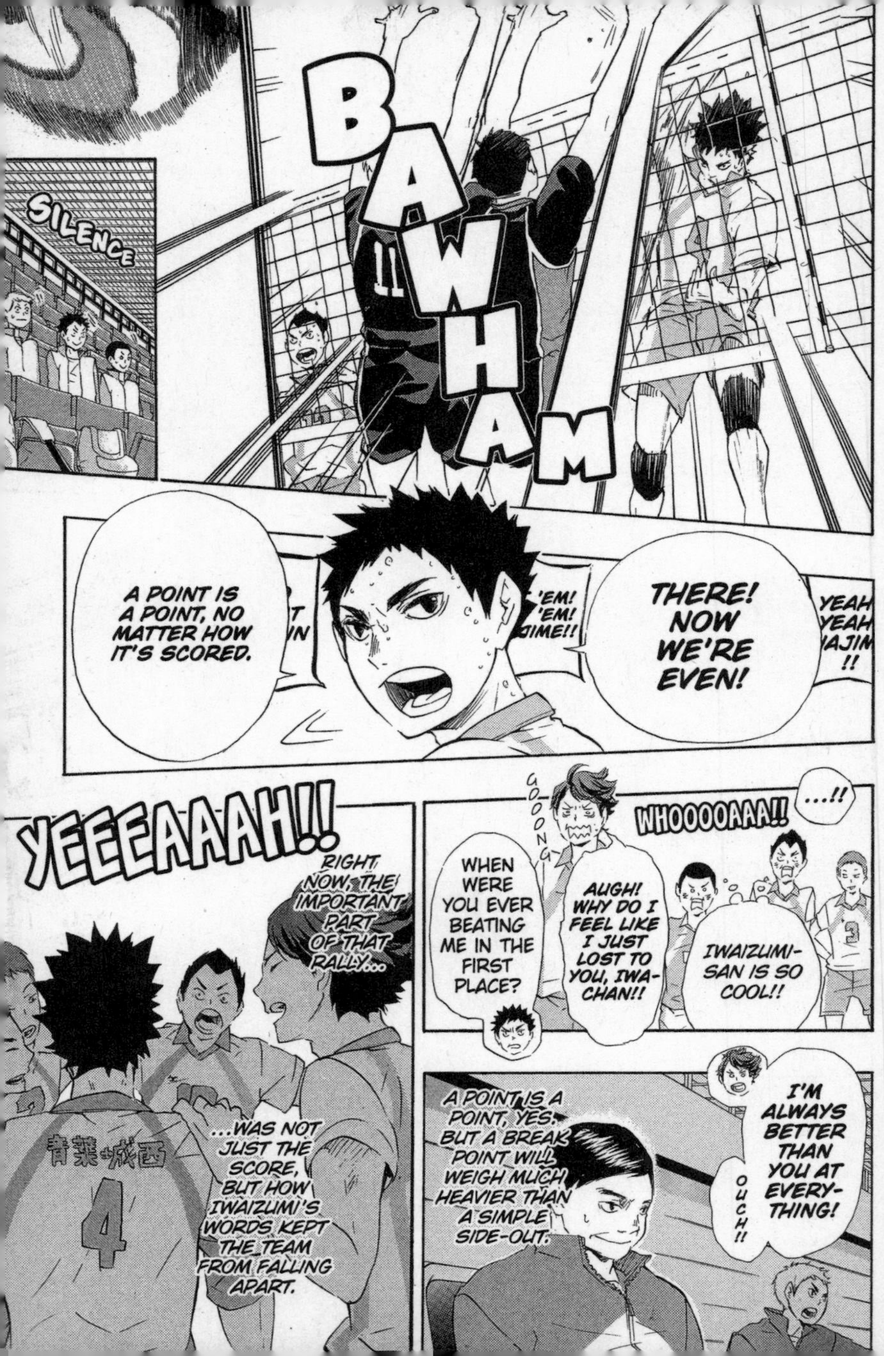
BAWHAM
SILENCE
YEAH YEAH AJIM !!
THERE! NOW WE'RE EVEN!
'EM! 'EM! JIME!!
A POINT IS A POINT, NO MATTER HOW IT'S SCORED.
WHOOOOAAA!!
...!!
GOOOONG
AUGH! WHY DO I FEEL LIKE I JUST LOST TO YOU, IWA-CHAN!!
WHEN WERE YOU EVER BEATING ME IN THE FIRST PLACE?
IWAIZUMI-SAN IS SO COOL!!
I'M ALWAYS BETTER THAN YOU AT EVERY-THING!
OUCH!!
A POINT IS A POINT, YES. BUT A BREAK POINT WILL WEIGH MUCH HEAVIER THAN A SIMPLE SIDE-OUT.
YEEEAAAH!!
RIGHT NOW, THE IMPORTANT PART OF THAT RALLY...
...WAS NOT JUST THE SCORE, BUT HOW IWAIZUMI'S WORDS KEPT THE TEAM FROM FALLING APART.

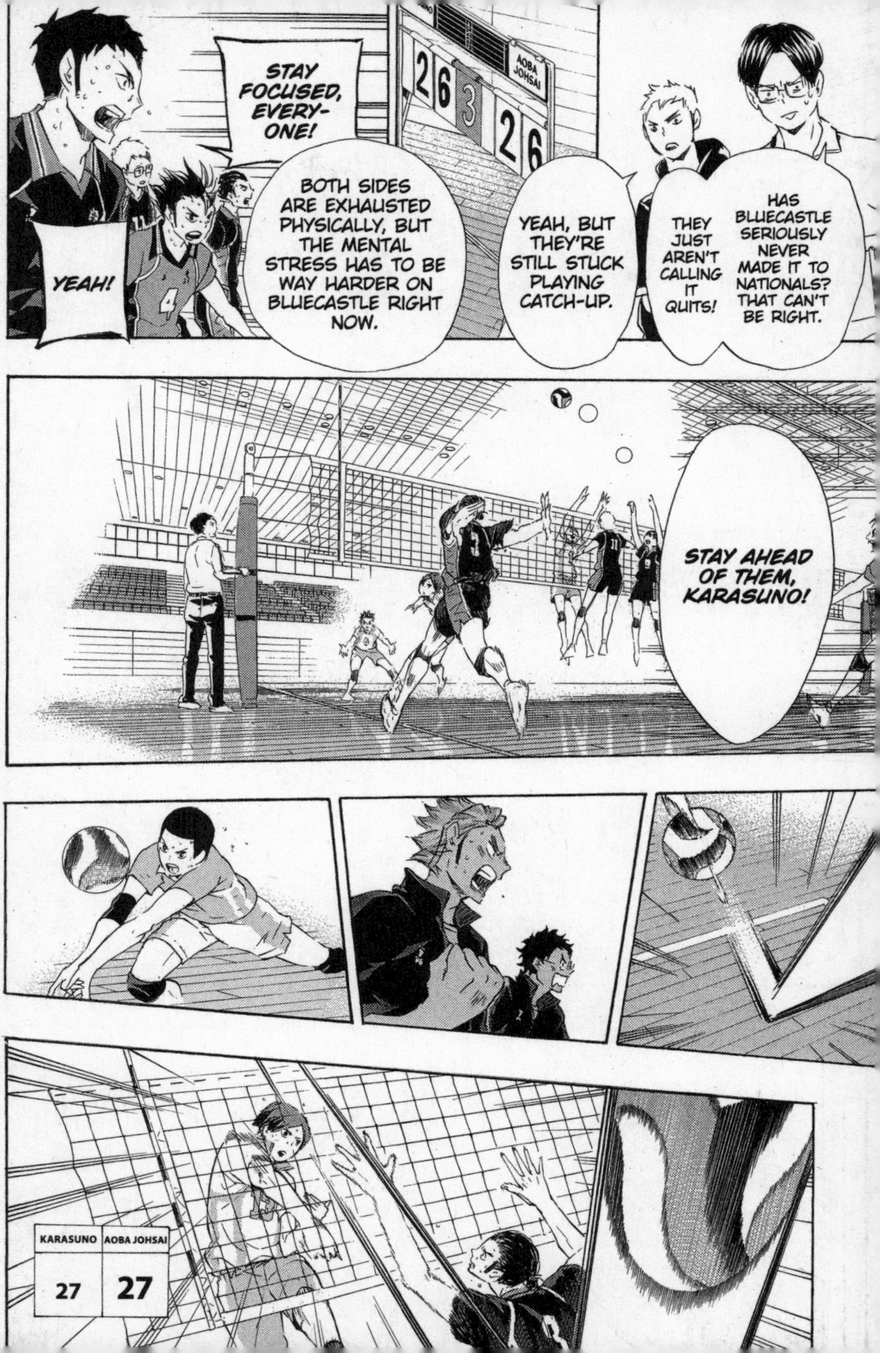
HAS BLUECASTLE SERIOUSLY NEVER MADE IT TO NATIONALS? THAT CAN'T BE RIGHT.
THEY JUST AREN'T CALLING IT QUITS!
YEAH, BUT THEY'RE STILL STUCK PLAYING CATCH-UP.
AOBA JOHSAI
BOTH SIDES ARE EXHAUSTED PHYSICALLY, BUT THE MENTAL STRESS HAS TO BE WAY HARDER ON BLUECASTLE RIGHT NOW.
STAY FOCUSED, EVERY-ONE!
YEAH!
STAY AHEAD OF THEM, KARASUNO!
KARASUNO
AOBA JOHSAI
27
27

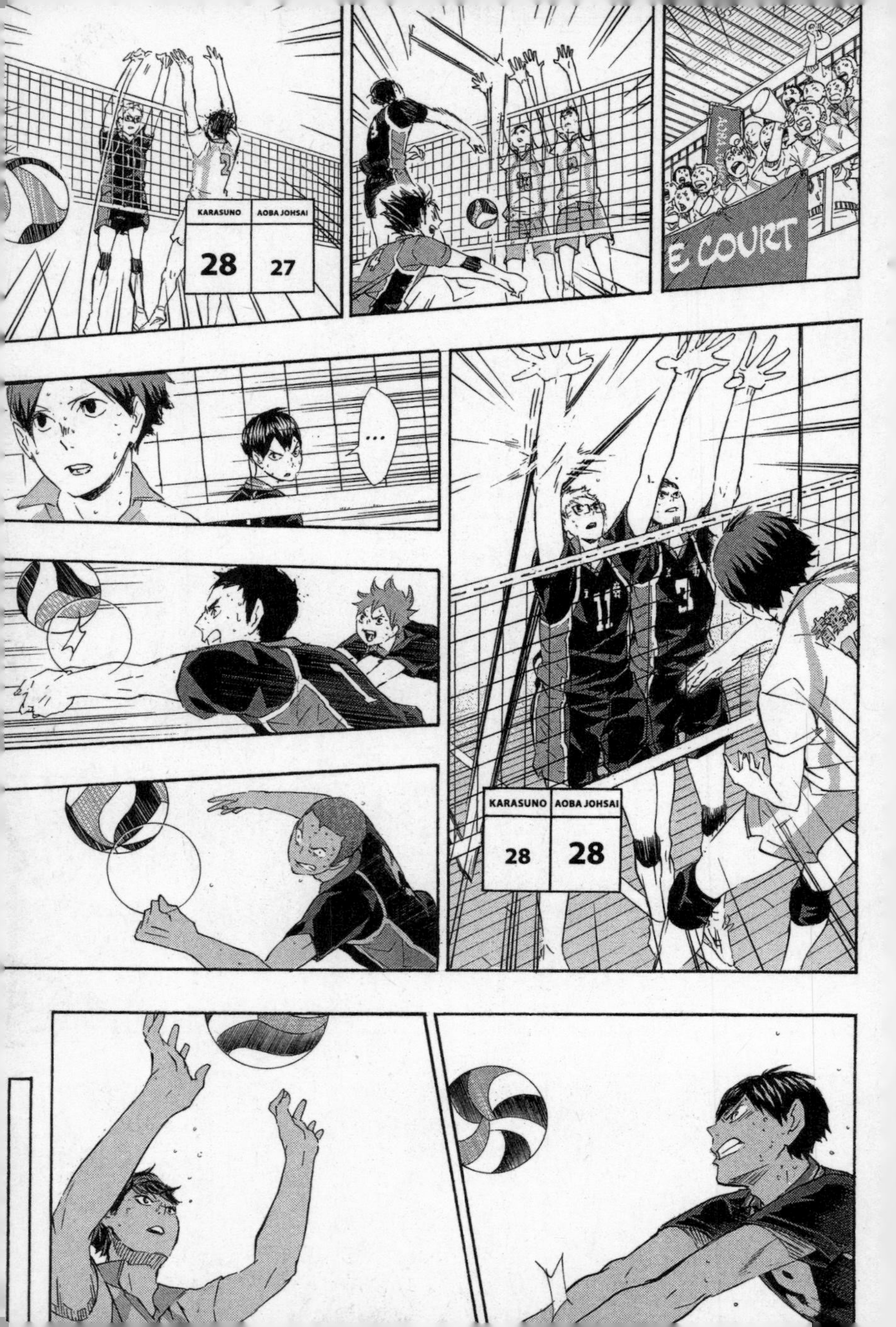
E COURT
KARASUNO
AOBA JOHSAI
28
27
...
KARASUNO
AOBA JOHSAI
28
28

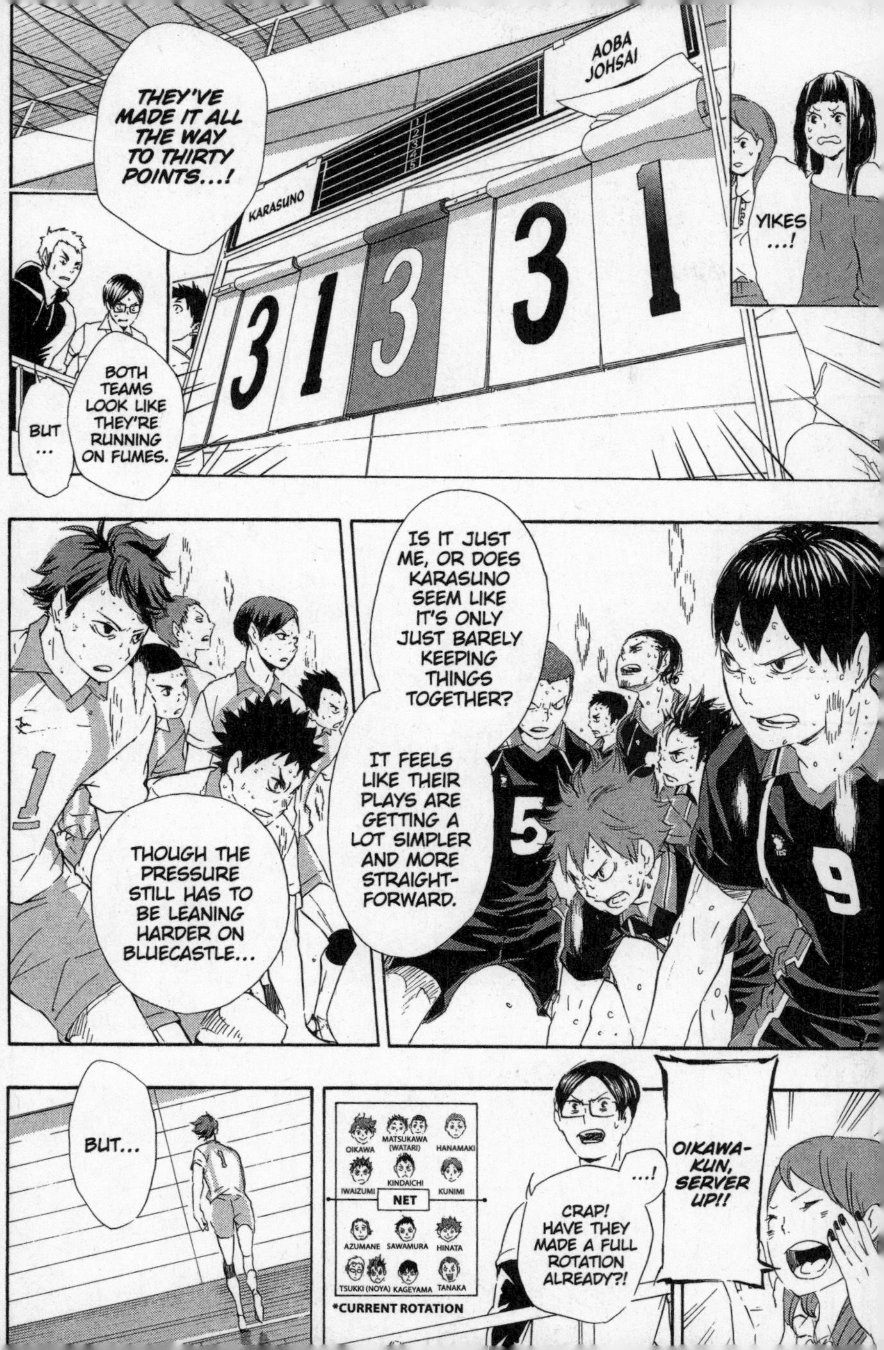
YIKES ...!
THEY'VE MADE IT ALL THE WAY TO THIRTY POINTS...!
AOBA JOHSAI
KARASUNO
1 2 3 4 5
31 31
BOTH TEAMS LOOK LIKE THEY'RE RUNNING ON FUMES.
BUT ...
IS IT JUST ME, OR DOES KARASUNO SEEM LIKE IT'S ONLY JUST BARELY KEEPING THINGS TOGETHER?
IT FEELS LIKE THEIR PLAYS ARE GETTING A LOT SIMPLER AND MORE STRAIGHT-FORWARD.
THOUGH THE PRESSURE STILL HAS TO BE LEANING HARDER ON BLUECASTLE...
OIKAWA-KUN, SERVER UP!!
...!
CRAP! HAVE THEY MADE A FULL ROTATION ALREADY?!
OIKAWA
MATSUKAWA (WATARI)
HANAMAKI
IWAIZUMI
KINDAICHI
KUNIMI
NET
AZUMANE
SAWAMURA
HINATA
TSUKKI (NOYA)
KAGEYAMA
TANAKA
*CURRENT ROTATION
BUT...

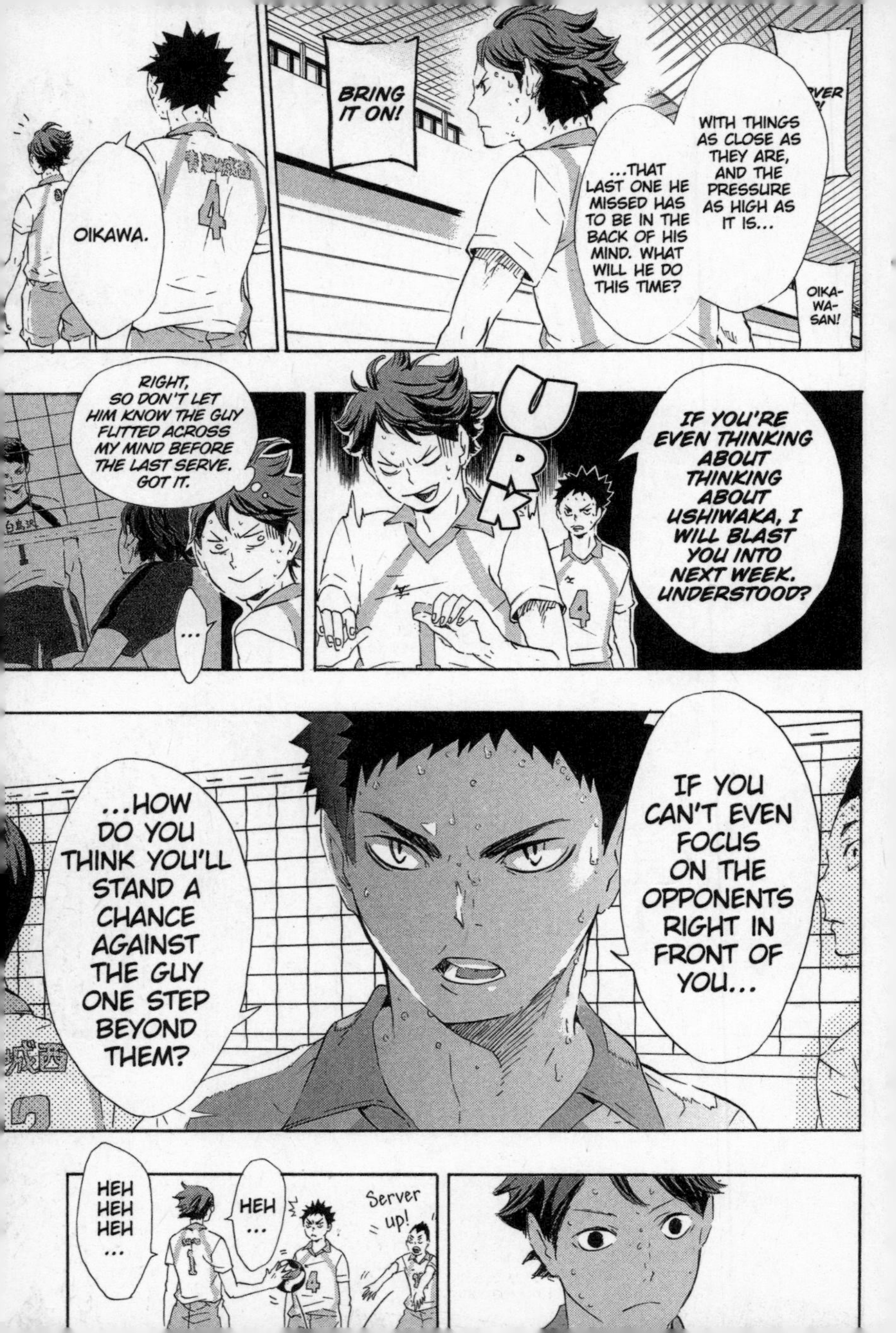
OIKA-WA-SAN!
WITH THINGS AS CLOSE AS THEY ARE, AND THE PRESSURE AS HIGH AS IT IS...
...THAT LAST ONE HE MISSED HAS TO BE IN THE BACK OF HIS MIND. WHAT WILL HE DO THIS TIME?
BRING IT ON!
OIKAWA.
IF YOU'RE EVEN THINKING ABOUT THINKING ABOUT USHIWAKA, I WILL BLAST YOU INTO NEXT WEEK. UNDERSTOOD?
URK
RIGHT, SO DON'T LET HIM KNOW THE GUY FLITTED ACROSS MY MIND BEFORE THE LAST SERVE. GOT IT.
...
IF YOU CAN'T EVEN FOCUS ON THE OPPONENTS RIGHT IN FRONT OF YOU...
...HOW DO YOU THINK YOU'LL STAND A CHANCE AGAINST THE GUY ONE STEP BEYOND THEM?
Server up!
HEH ...
HEH HEH HEH ...

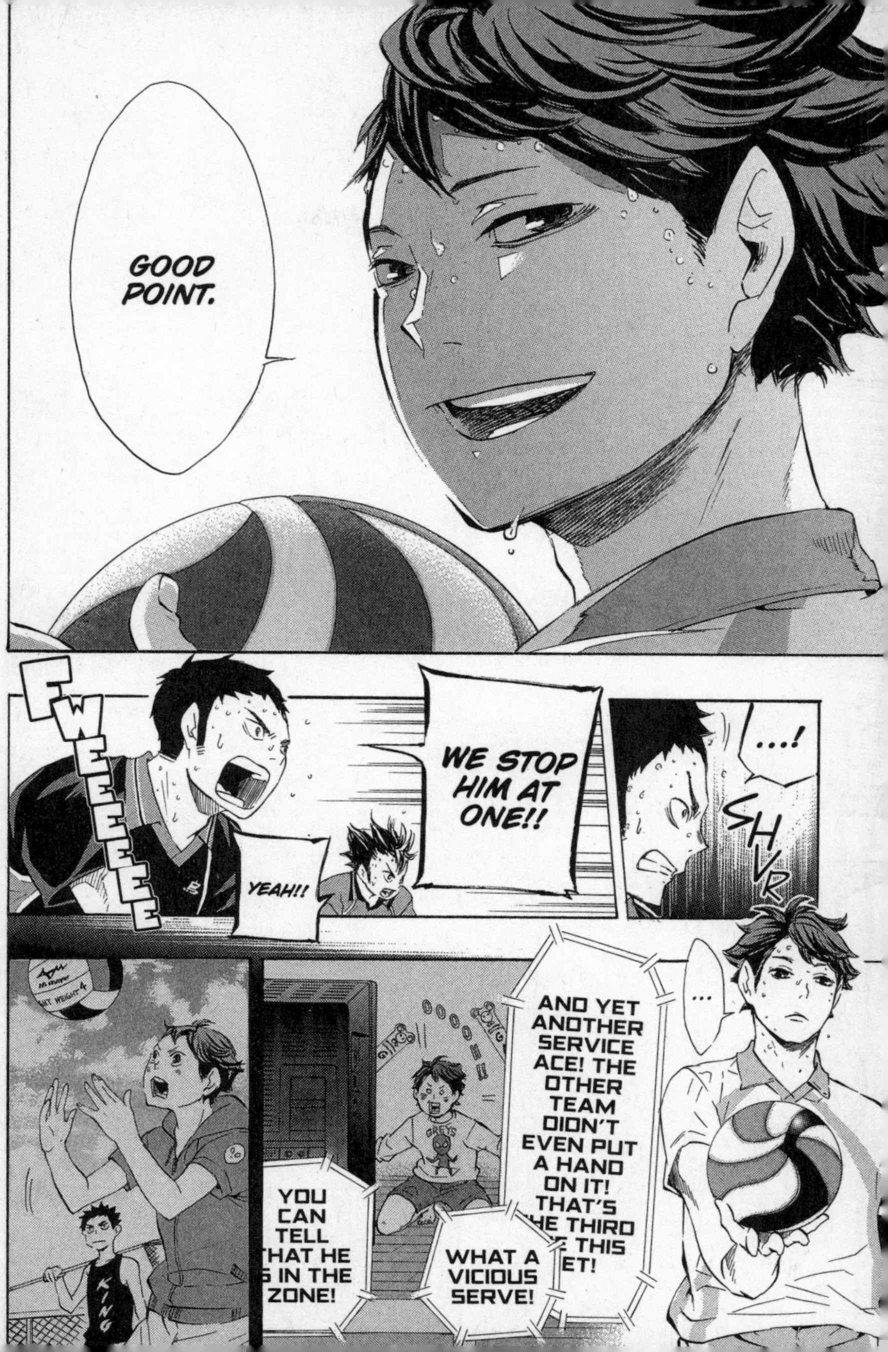
GOOD POINT.
...!
SHVR
WE STOP HIM AT ONE!!
YEAH!!
FWEEEEEE
...
AND YET ANOTHER SERVICE ACE! THE OTHER TEAM DIDN'T EVEN PUT A HAND ON IT! THAT'S HE THIRD E THIS ET!
WHAT A VICIOUS SERVE!
YOU CAN TELL THAT HE S IN THE ZONE!
GREYS
KING

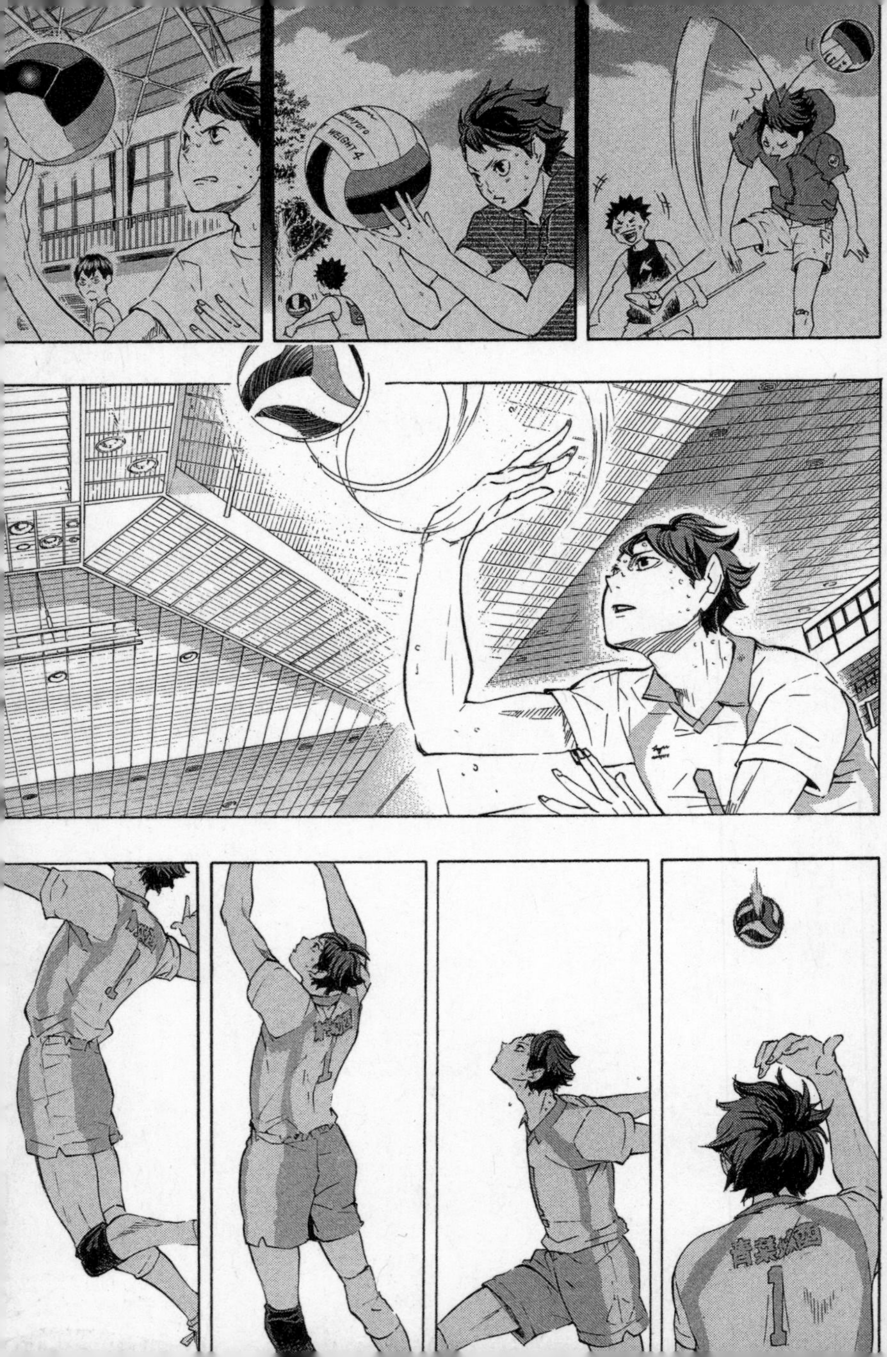
WEIGHT 4
青葉城西
1

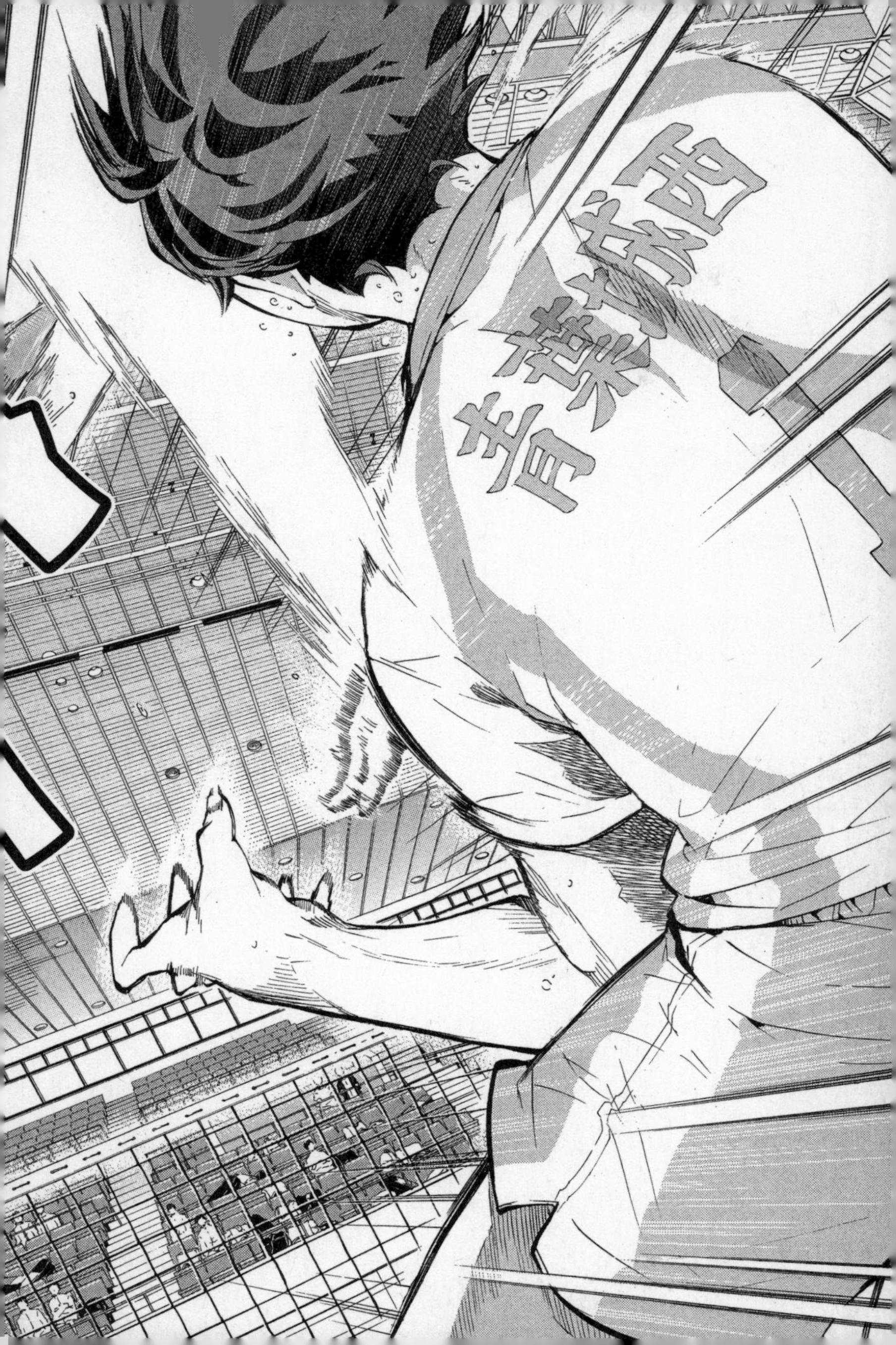
青葉城西

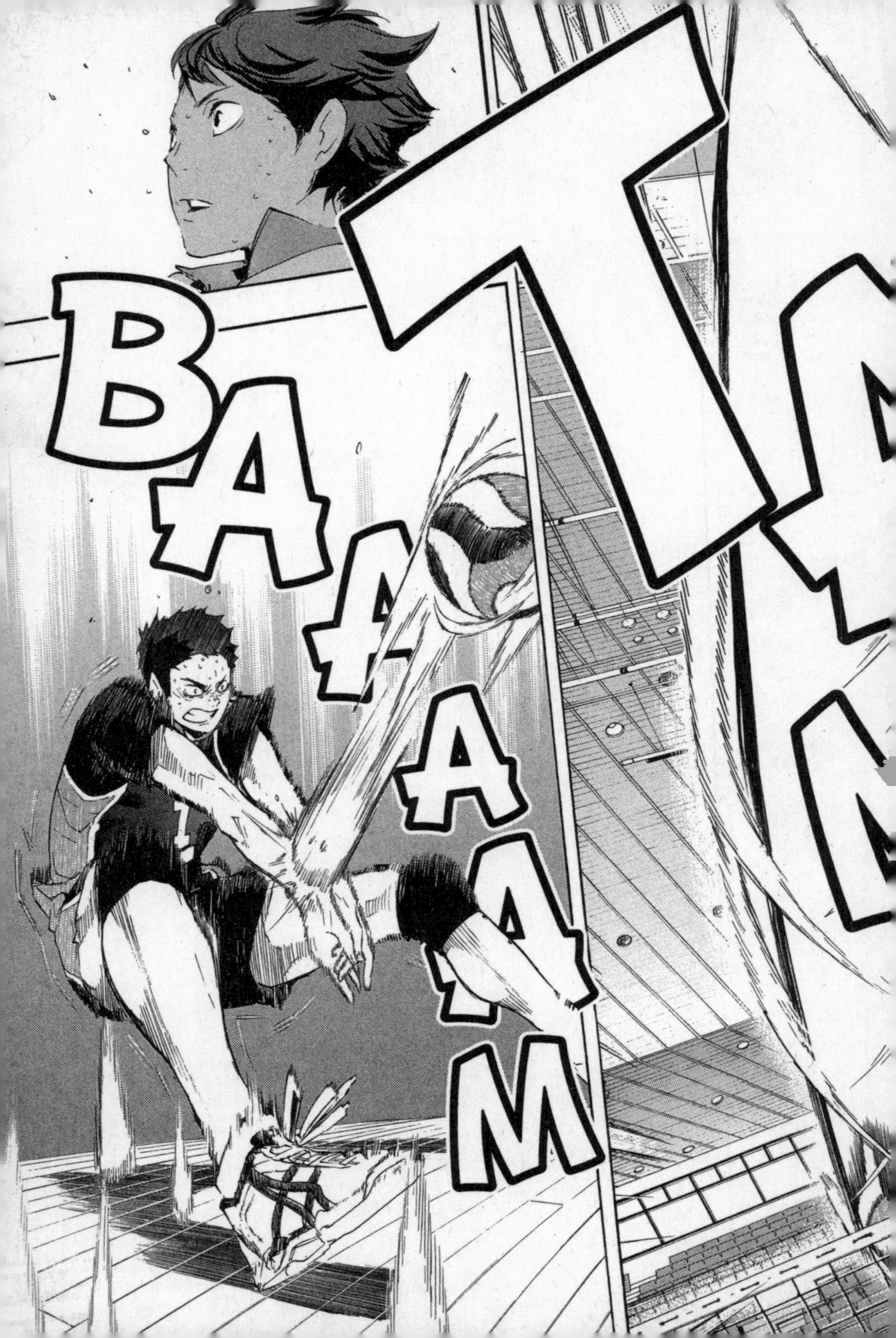
BAAAAM

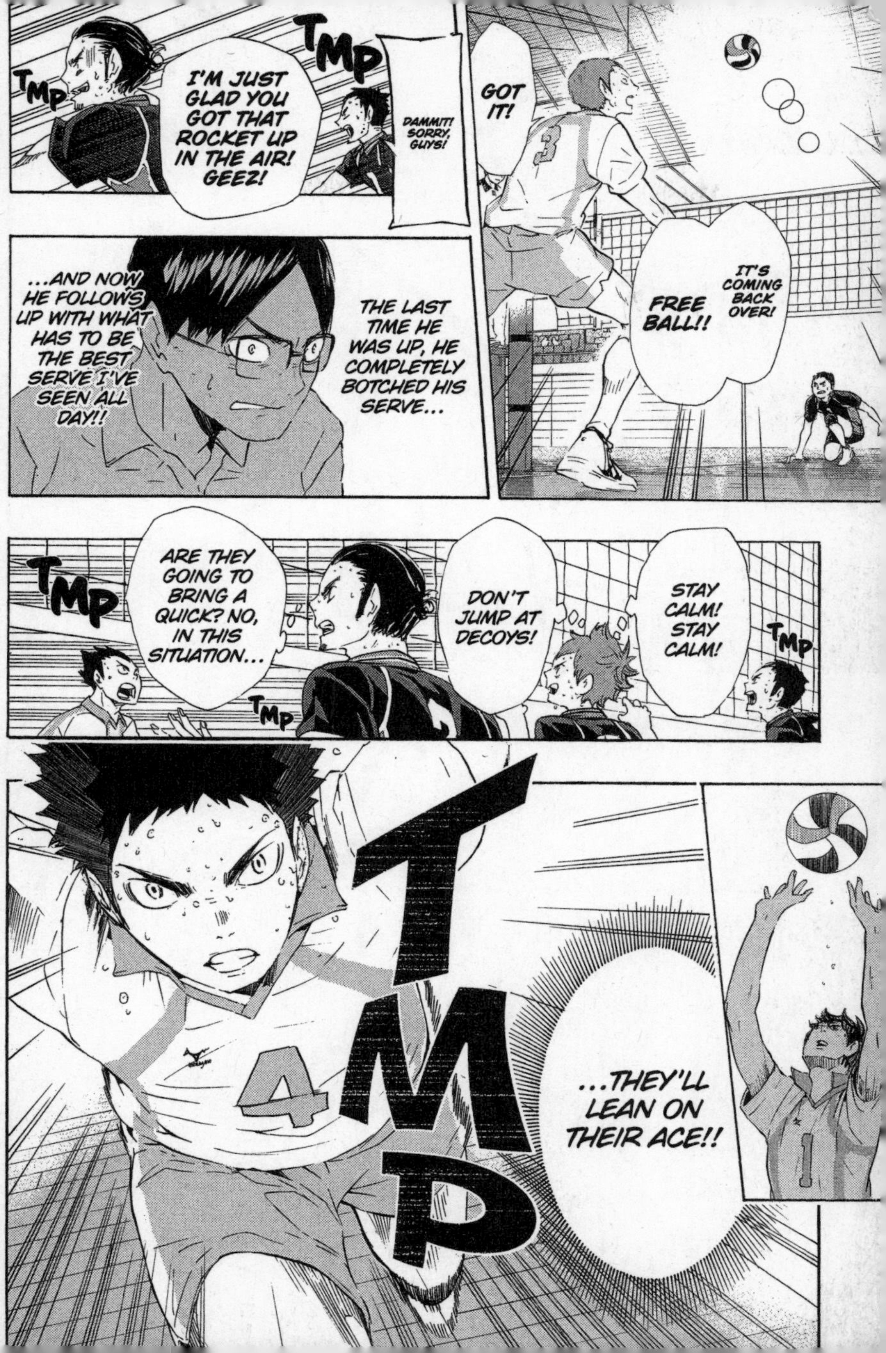
GOT IT!
IT'S COMING BACK OVER!
FREE BALL!!
DAMMIT! SORRY, GUYS!
TMP
I'M JUST GLAD YOU GOT THAT ROCKET UP IN THE AIR! GEEZ!
TMP
THE LAST TIME HE WAS UP, HE COMPLETELY BOTCHED HIS SERVE...
...AND NOW HE FOLLOWS UP WITH WHAT HAS TO BE THE BEST SERVE I'VE SEEN ALL DAY!!
TMP
STAY CALM! STAY CALM!
DON'T JUMP AT DECOYS!
ARE THEY GOING TO BRING A QUICK? NO, IN THIS SITUATION...
TMP
TMP
...THEY'LL LEAN ON THEIR ACE!!
TMP

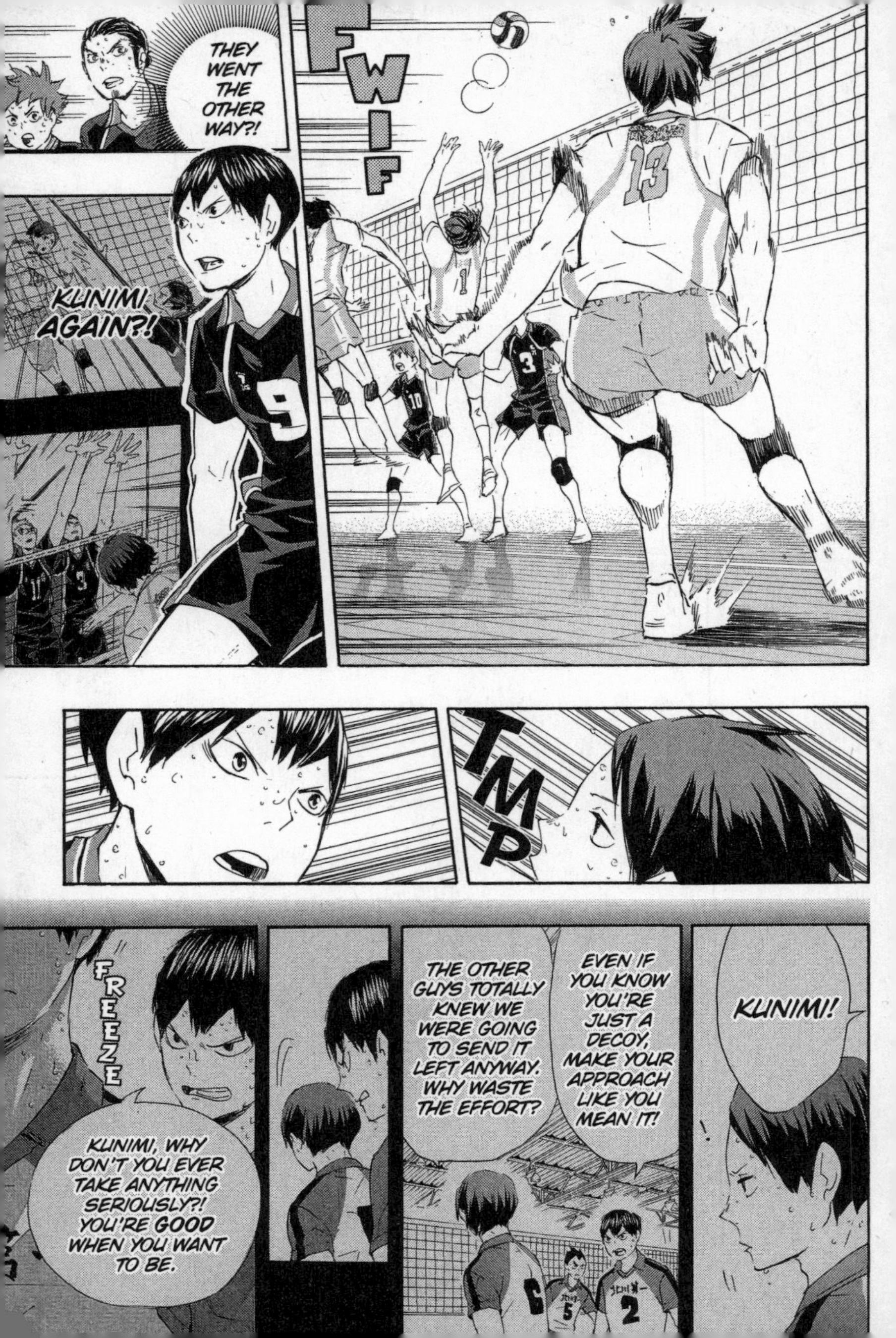
FWIF
THEY WENT THE OTHER WAY?!
KUNIMI AGAIN?!
TMP
KUNIMI!
EVEN IF YOU KNOW YOU'RE JUST A DECOY, MAKE YOUR APPROACH LIKE YOU MEAN IT!
THE OTHER GUYS TOTALLY KNEW WE WERE GOING TO SEND IT LEFT ANYWAY. WHY WASTE THE EFFORT?
FREEZE
KUNIMI, WHY DON'T YOU EVER TAKE ANYTHING SERIOUSLY?! YOU'RE GOOD WHEN YOU WANT TO BE.

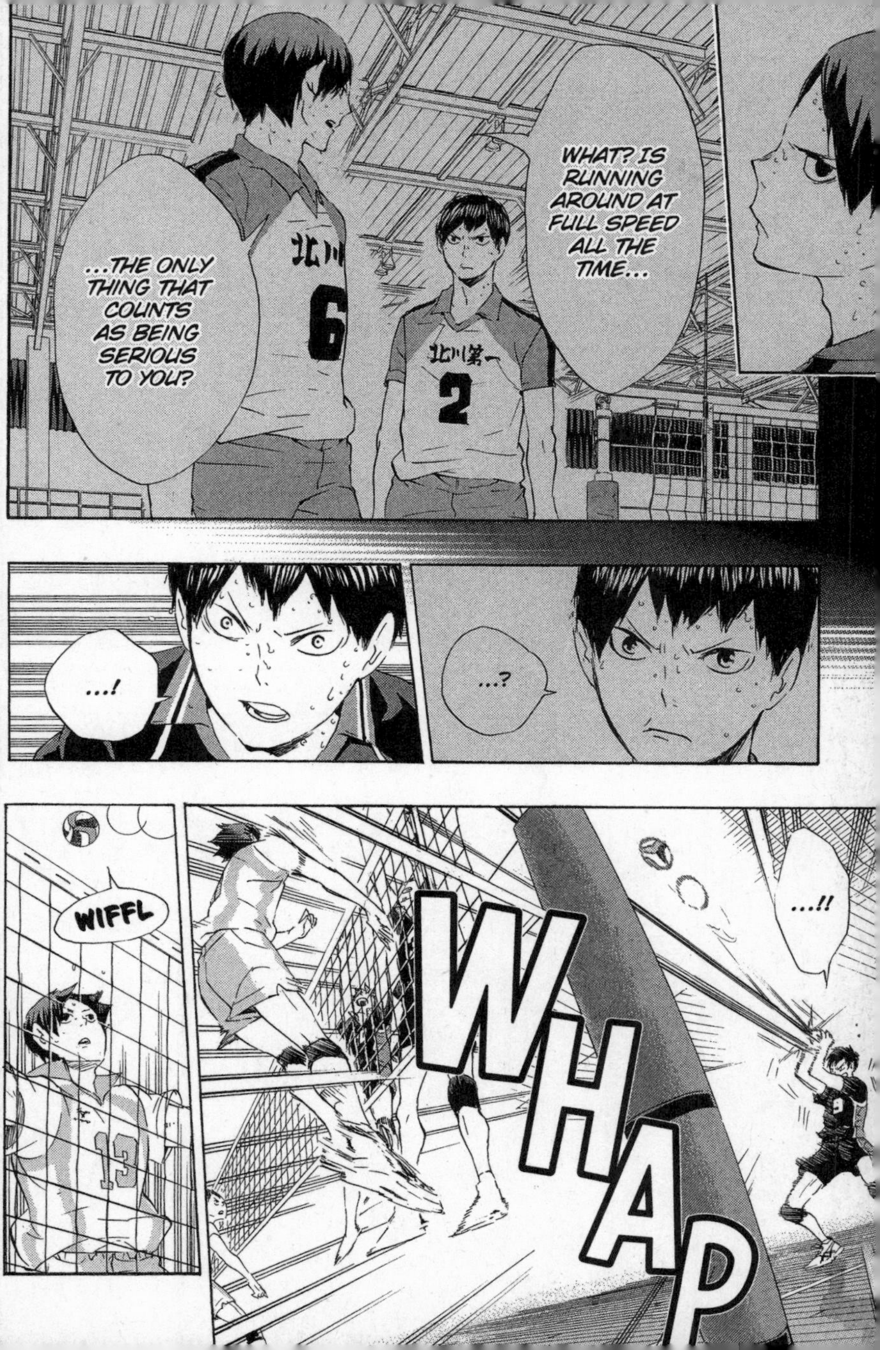
WHAT? IS RUNNING AROUND AT FULL SPEED ALL THE TIME...
...THE ONLY THING THAT COUNTS AS BEING SERIOUS TO YOU?
...?
...!
...!!
WHAP
WIFFL

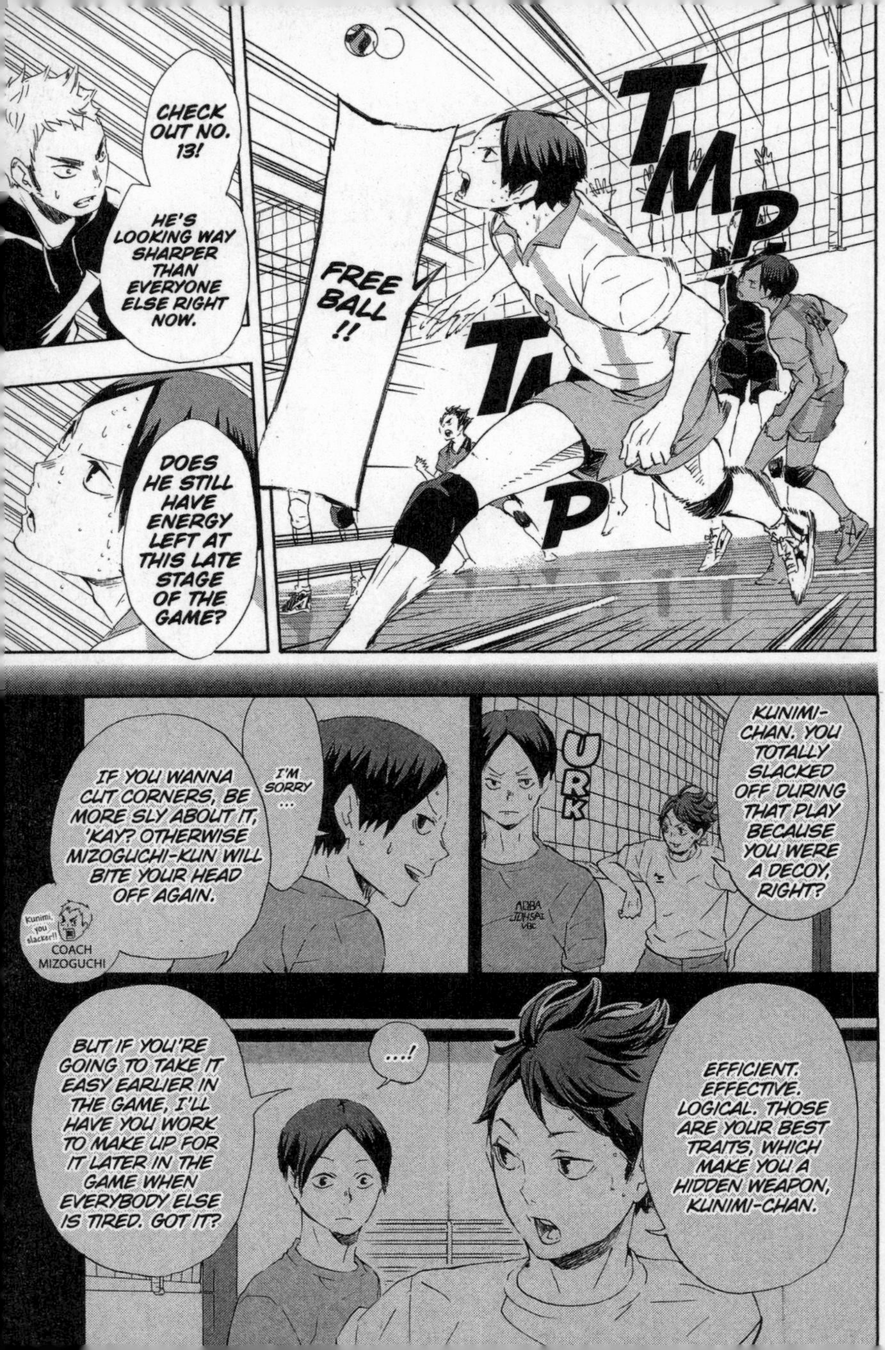
TMP
TAP
FREE BALL!!
CHECK OUT NO. 13!
HE'S LOOKING WAY SHARPER THAN EVERYONE ELSE RIGHT NOW.
DOES HE STILL HAVE ENERGY LEFT AT THIS LATE STAGE OF THE GAME?
KUNIMI-CHAN. YOU TOTALLY SLACKED OFF DURING THAT PLAY BECAUSE YOU WERE A DECOY, RIGHT?
URK
I'M SORRY...
IF YOU WANNA CUT CORNERS, BE MORE SLY ABOUT IT, 'KAY? OTHERWISE MIZOGUCHI-KUN WILL BITE YOUR HEAD OFF AGAIN.
Kunimi, you slacker!!
COACH MIZOGUCHI
EFFICIENT. EFFECTIVE. LOGICAL. THOSE ARE YOUR BEST TRAITS, WHICH MAKE YOU A HIDDEN WEAPON, KUNIMI-CHAN.
...!
BUT IF YOU'RE GOING TO TAKE IT EASY EARLIER IN THE GAME, I'LL HAVE YOU WORK TO MAKE UP FOR IT LATER IN THE GAME WHEN EVERYBODY ELSE IS TIRED. GOT IT?

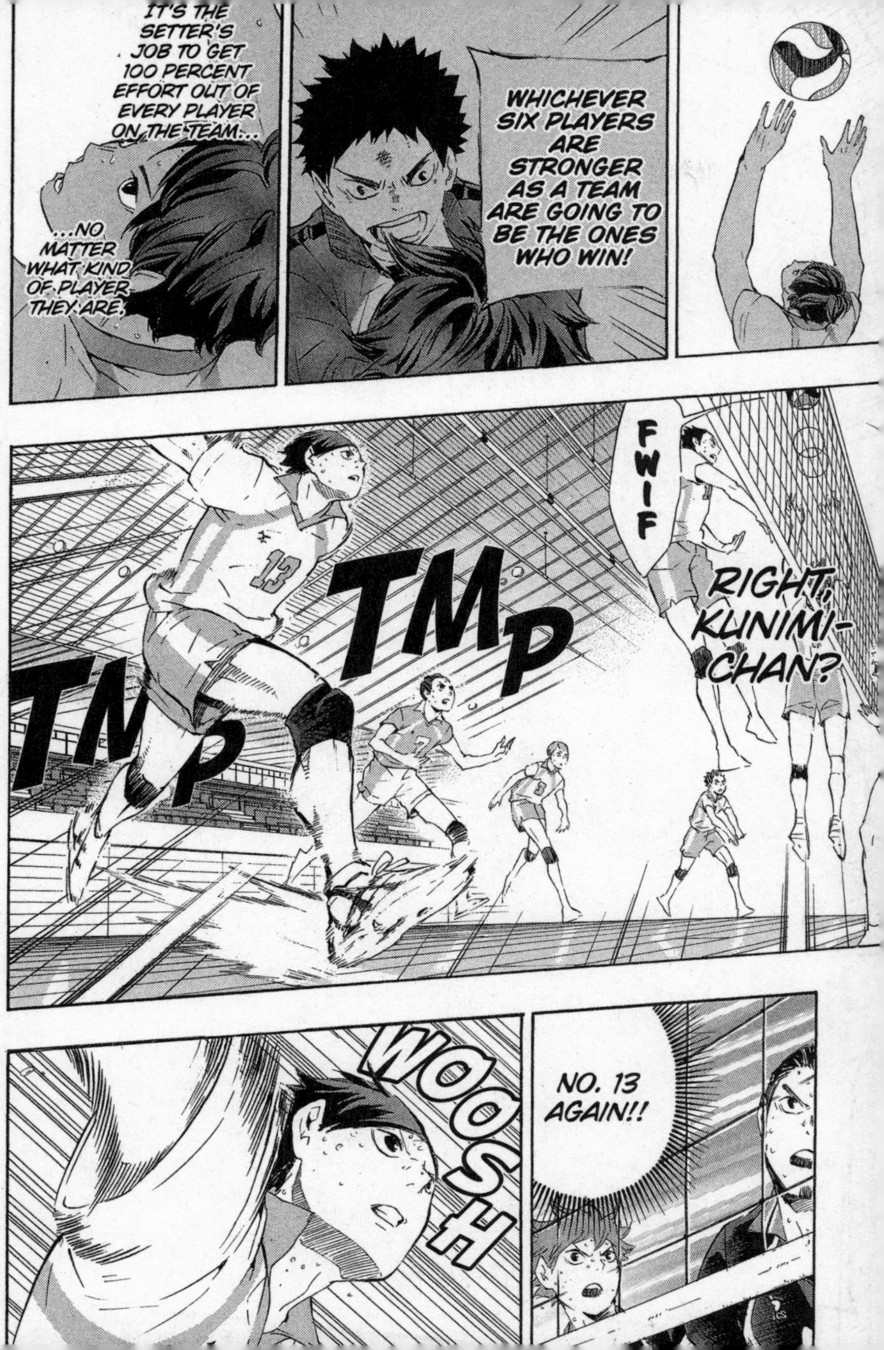
WHICHEVER SIX PLAYERS ARE STRONGER AS A TEAM ARE GOING TO BE THE ONES WHO WIN!
IT'S THE SETTER'S JOB TO GET 100 PERCENT EFFORT OUT OF EVERY PLAYER ON THE TEAM...
...NO MATTER WHAT KIND OF PLAYER THEY ARE.
FWIF
RIGHT, KUNIMI-CHAN?
TMP
TMP
NO. 13 AGAIN!!
WOOSH

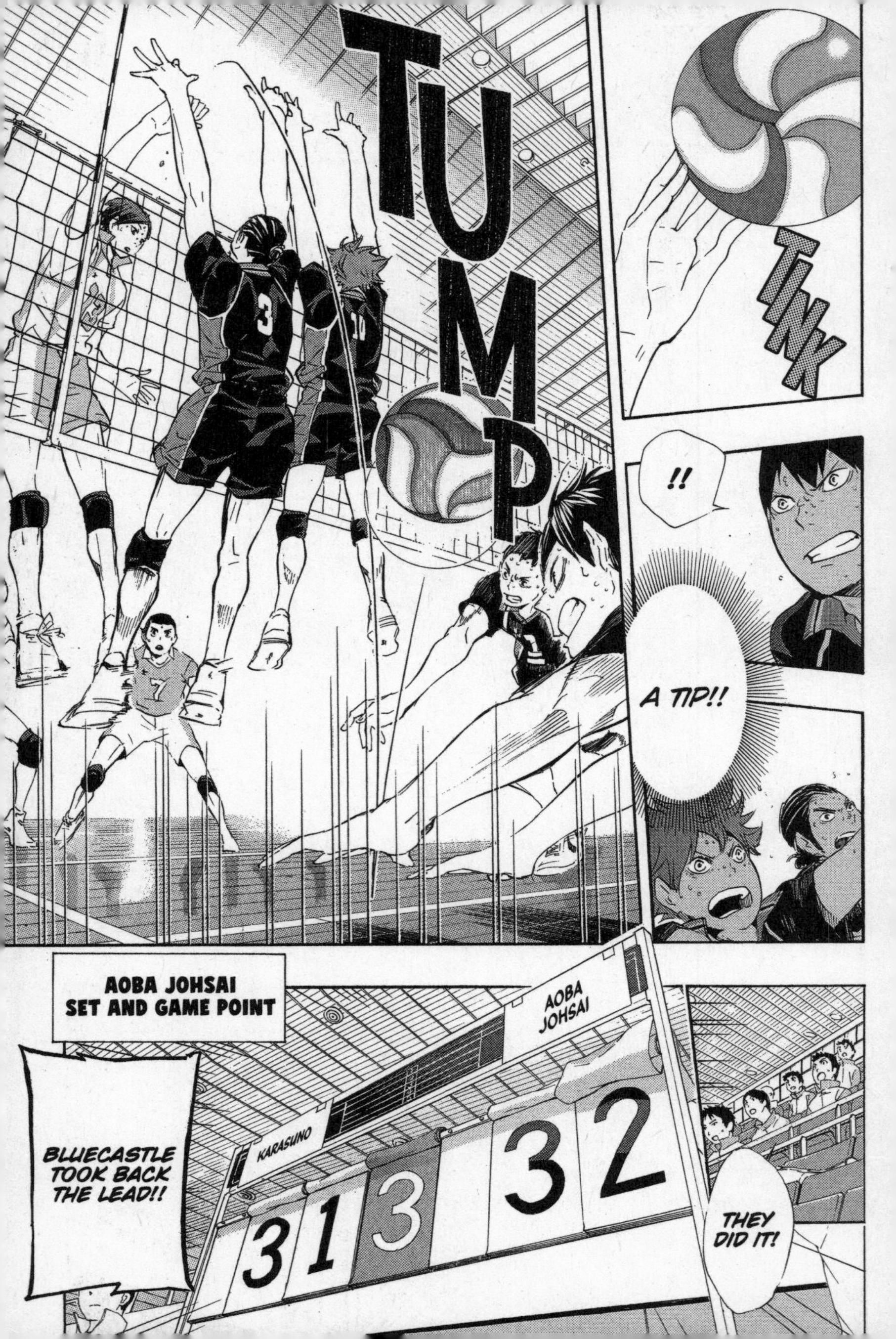
TINK
!!
A TIP!!
TUMP
THEY DID IT!
AOBA JOHSAI SET AND GAME POINT
AOBA JOHSAI
BLUECASTLE TOOK BACK THE LEAD!!
KARASUNO
31
32

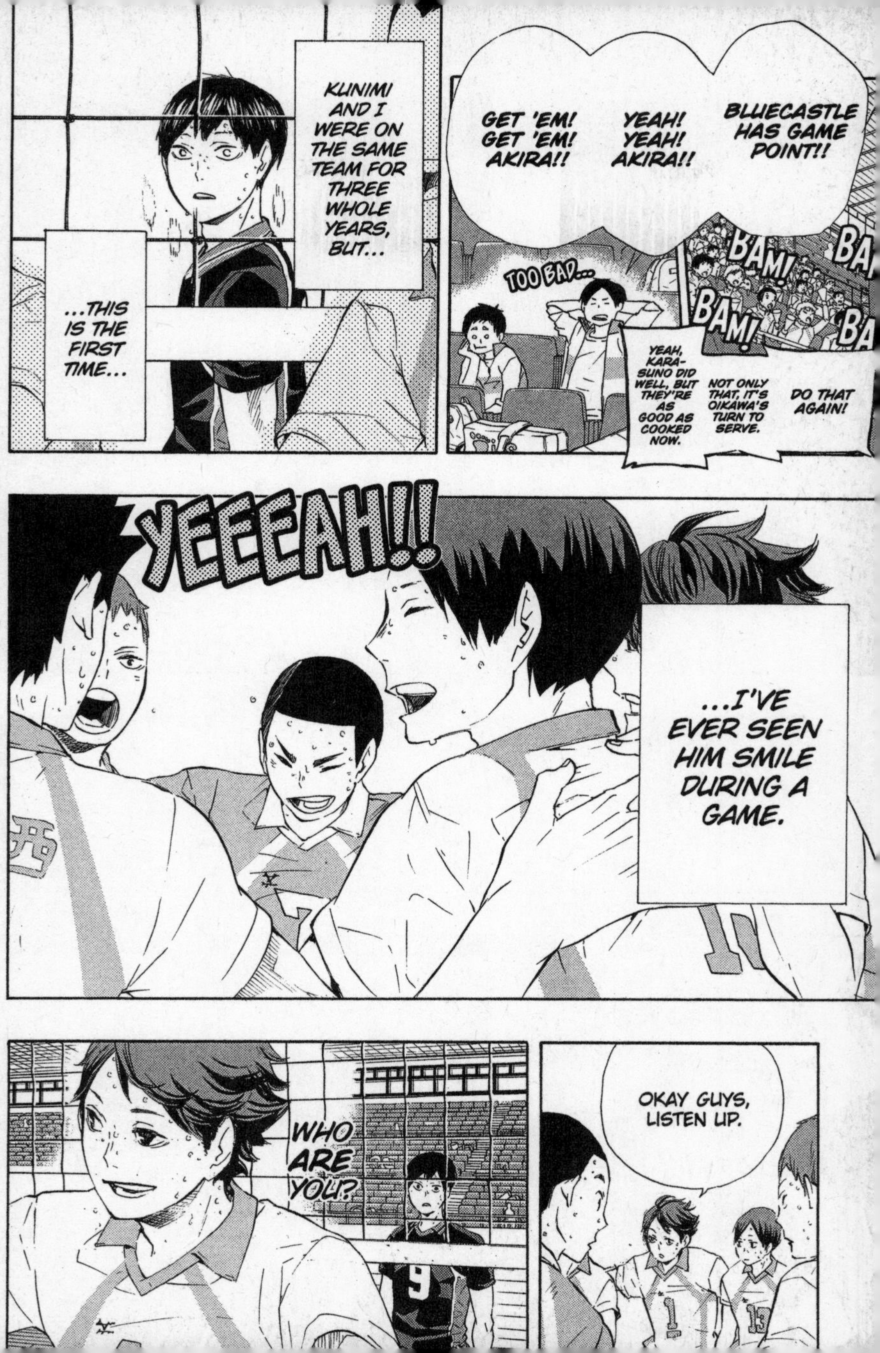
BLUECASTLE HAS GAME POINT!!
YEAH! YEAH! AKIRA!!
GET 'EM! GET 'EM! AKIRA!!
BAM!
BAM!
BA
BA
TOO BAD...
DO THAT AGAIN!
NOT ONLY THAT, IT'S OIKAWA'S TURN TO SERVE.
YEAH, KARA-SUNO DID WELL, BUT THEY'RE AS GOOD AS COOKED NOW.
KUNIMI AND I WERE ON THE SAME TEAM FOR THREE WHOLE YEARS, BUT...
...THIS IS THE FIRST TIME...
...I'VE EVER SEEN HIM SMILE DURING A GAME.
YEEEAH!!
OKAY GUYS, LISTEN UP.
WHO ARE YOU?

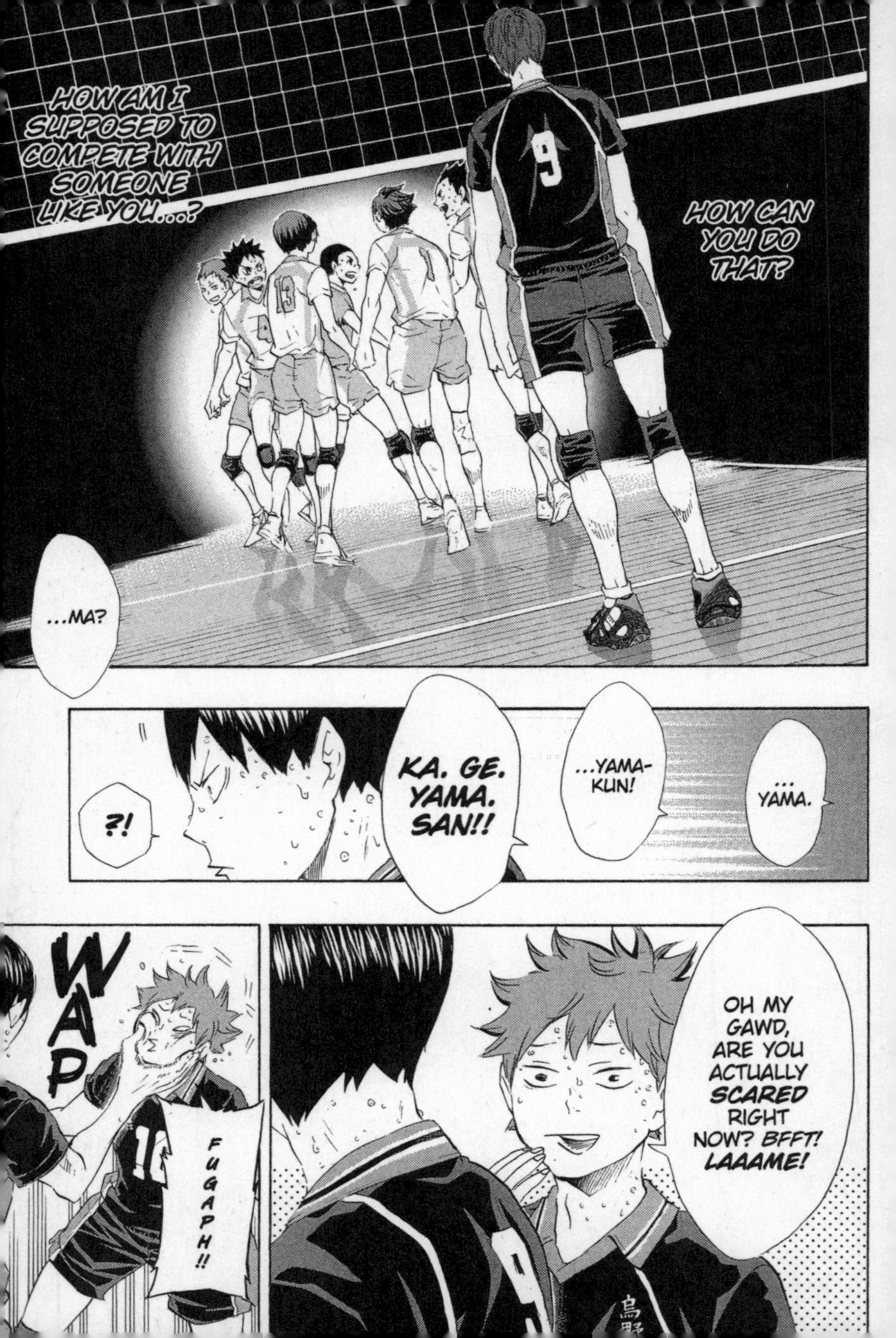
HOW CAN YOU DO THAT?
HOW AM I SUPPOSED TO COMPETE WITH SOMEONE LIKE YOU...?
...MA?
... YAMA.
...YAMA-KUN!
KA. GE. YAMA. SAN!!
?!
OH MY GAWD, ARE YOU ACTUALLY SCARED RIGHT NOW? BFFT! LAAAME!
WAP
FUGAPH!!

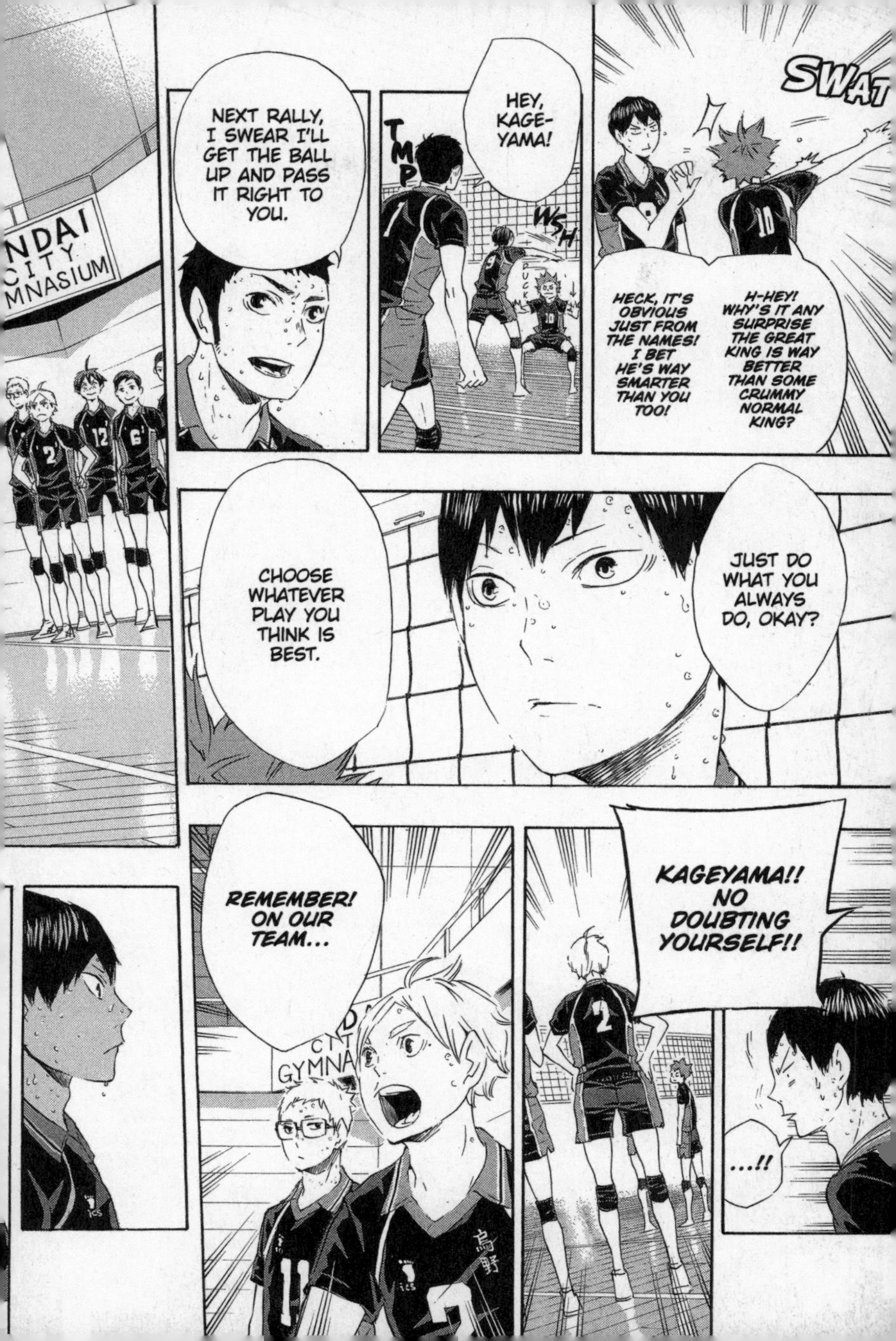
SWAT
!
H-HEY! WHY'S IT ANY SURPRISE THE GREAT KING IS WAY BETTER THAN SOME CRUMMY NORMAL KING?
HECK, IT'S OBVIOUS JUST FROM THE NAMES! I BET HE'S WAY SMARTER THAN YOU TOO!
TMP
HEY, KAGE-YAMA!
WSH
DUCK
NEXT RALLY, I SWEAR I'LL GET THE BALL UP AND PASS IT RIGHT TO YOU.
JUST DO WHAT YOU ALWAYS DO, OKAY?
CHOOSE WHATEVER PLAY YOU THINK IS BEST.
NDAI CITY MNASIUM
...!!
KAGEYAMA!! NO DOUBTING YOURSELF!!
REMEMBER! ON OUR TEAM...
CITY GYMNA

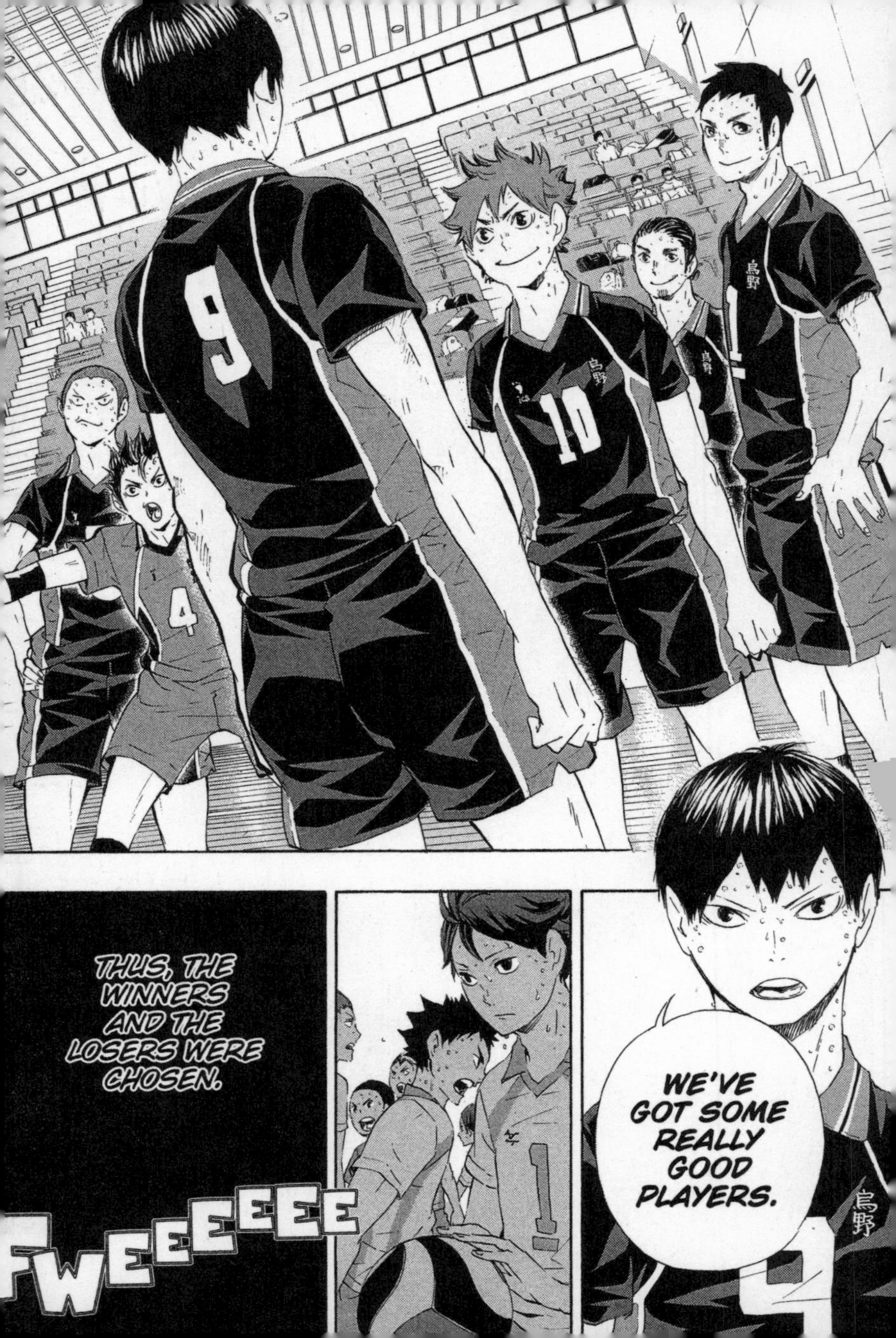
WE'VE GOT SOME REALLY GOOD PLAYERS.
THUS, THE WINNERS AND THE LOSERS WERE CHOSEN.
FWEEEEEEE

Fugashi candy

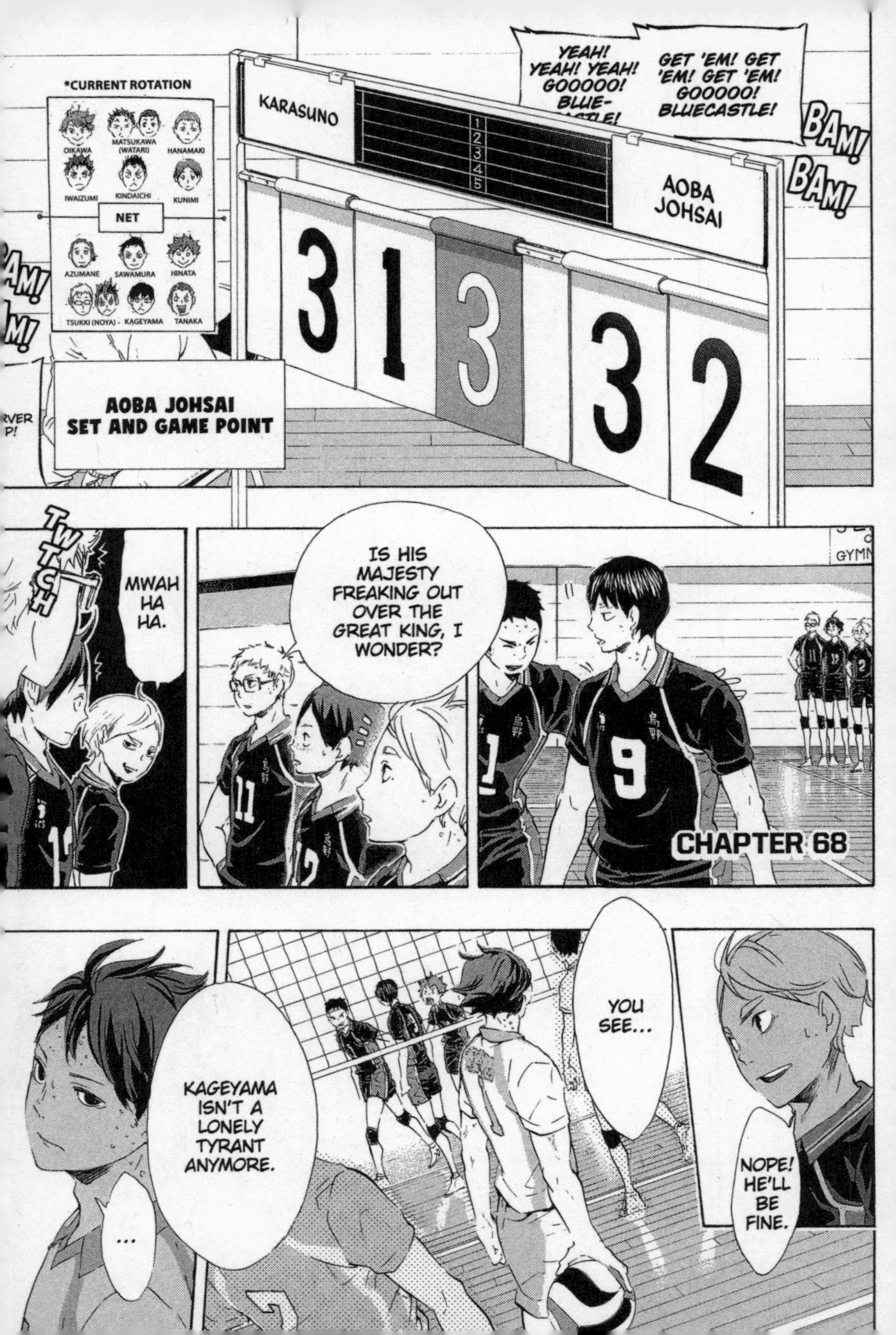
BAM! BAM!
GET 'EM! GET 'EM! GET 'EM! GOOOOO! BLUECASTLE!
YEAH! YEAH! YEAH! GOOOOO! BLUE-CASTLE!
AOBA JOHSAI
KARASUNO
3 1 3 3 2
*CURRENT ROTATION
OIKAWA
MATSUKAWA (WATARI)
HANAMAKI
IWAIZUMI
KINDAICHI
KUNIMI
NET
AZUMANE
SAWAMURA
HINATA
TSUKKI (NOYA)
KAGEYAMA
TANAKA
AOBA JOHSAI SET AND GAME POINT
CHAPTER 68
IS HIS MAJESTY FREAKING OUT OVER THE GREAT KING, I WONDER?
TWITCH
MWAH HA HA.
NOPE! HE'LL BE FINE.
YOU SEE...
KAGEYAMA ISN'T A LONELY TYRANT ANYMORE.
...

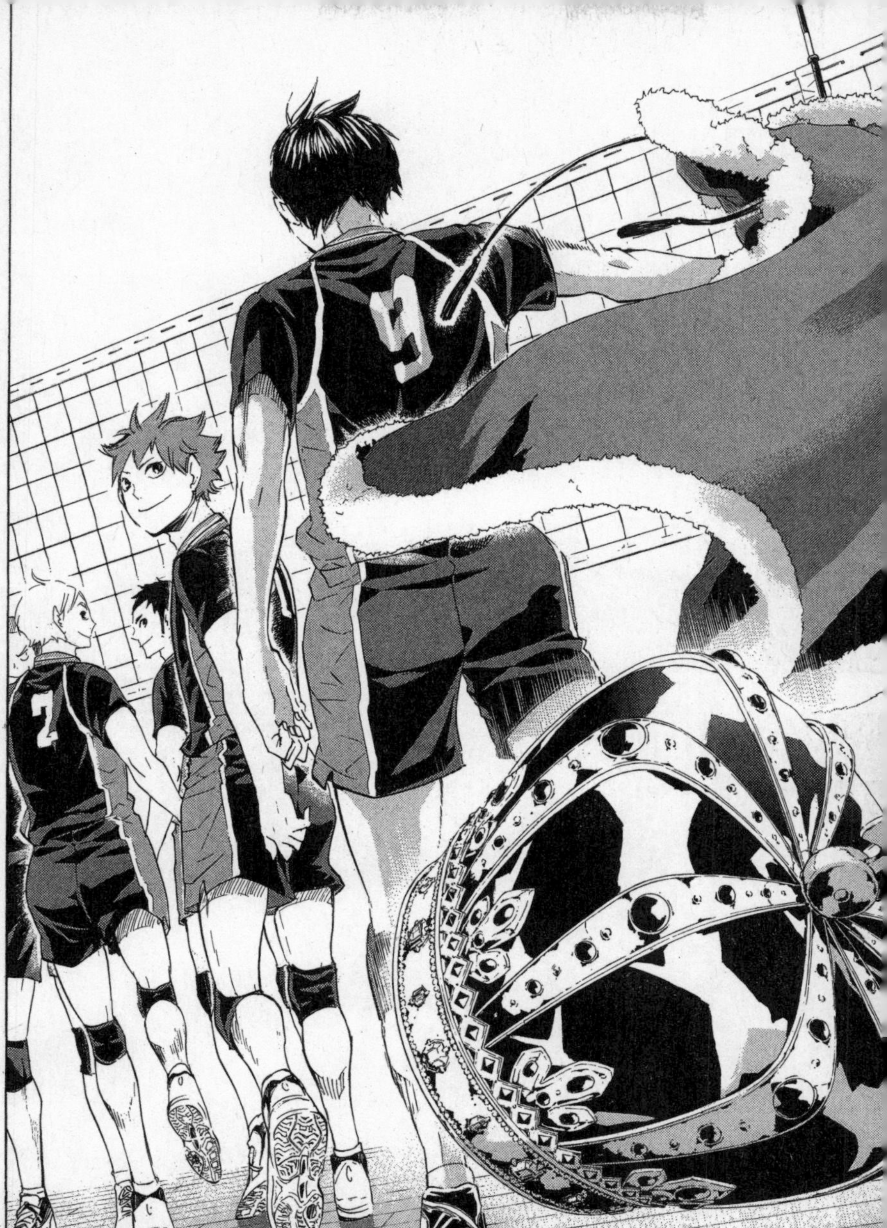

CHAPTER 68: Former Lonely Tyrant

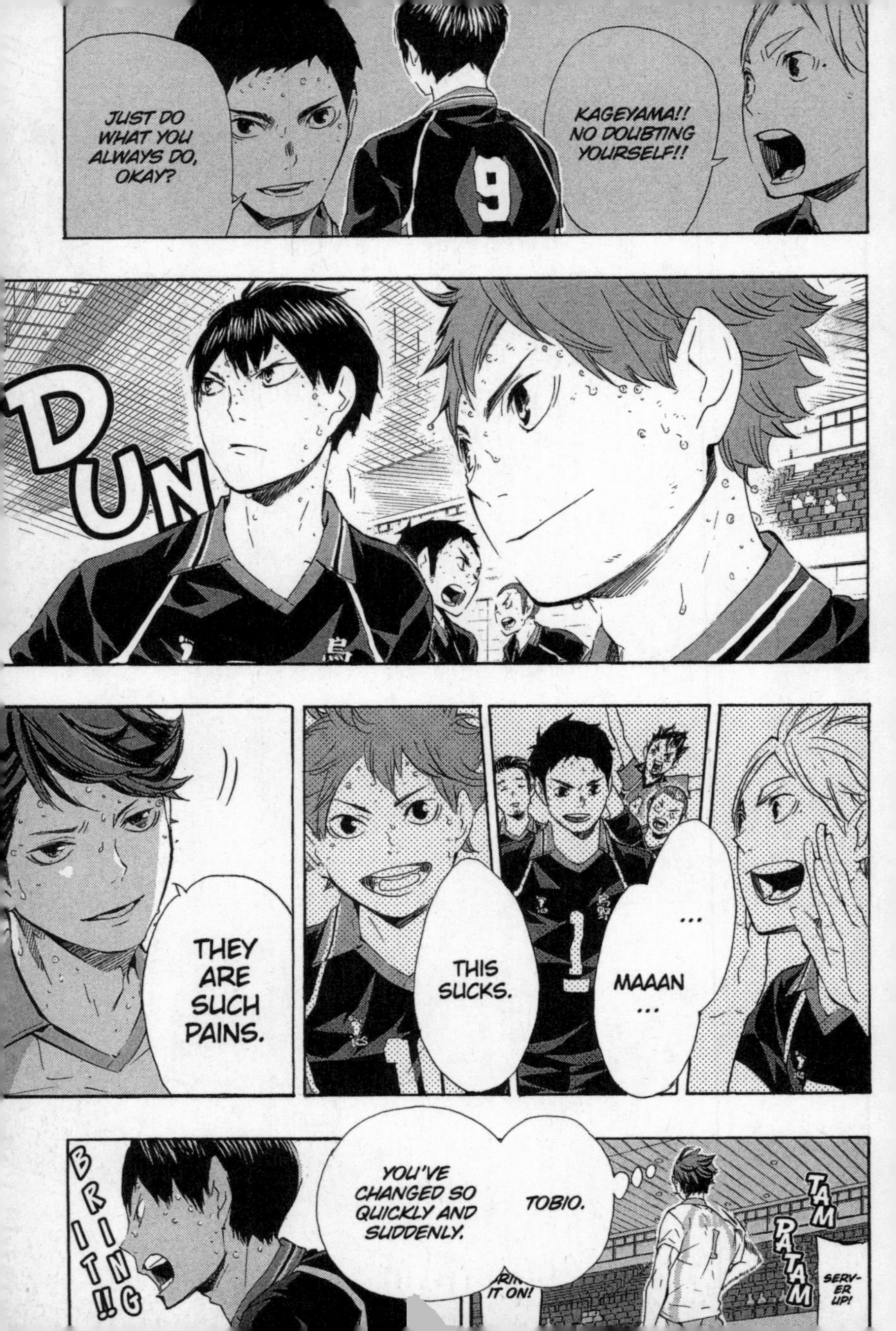

KAGEYAMA!! NO DOUBTING YOURSELF!!
JUST DO WHAT YOU ALWAYS DO, OKAY?
DUN
... MAAAN ...
THIS SUCKS.
THEY ARE SUCH PAINS.
TAM PATAM
SERV-ER UP!
TOBIO.
YOU'VE CHANGED SO QUICKLY AND SUDDENLY.
IT ON!
BRING IT!!

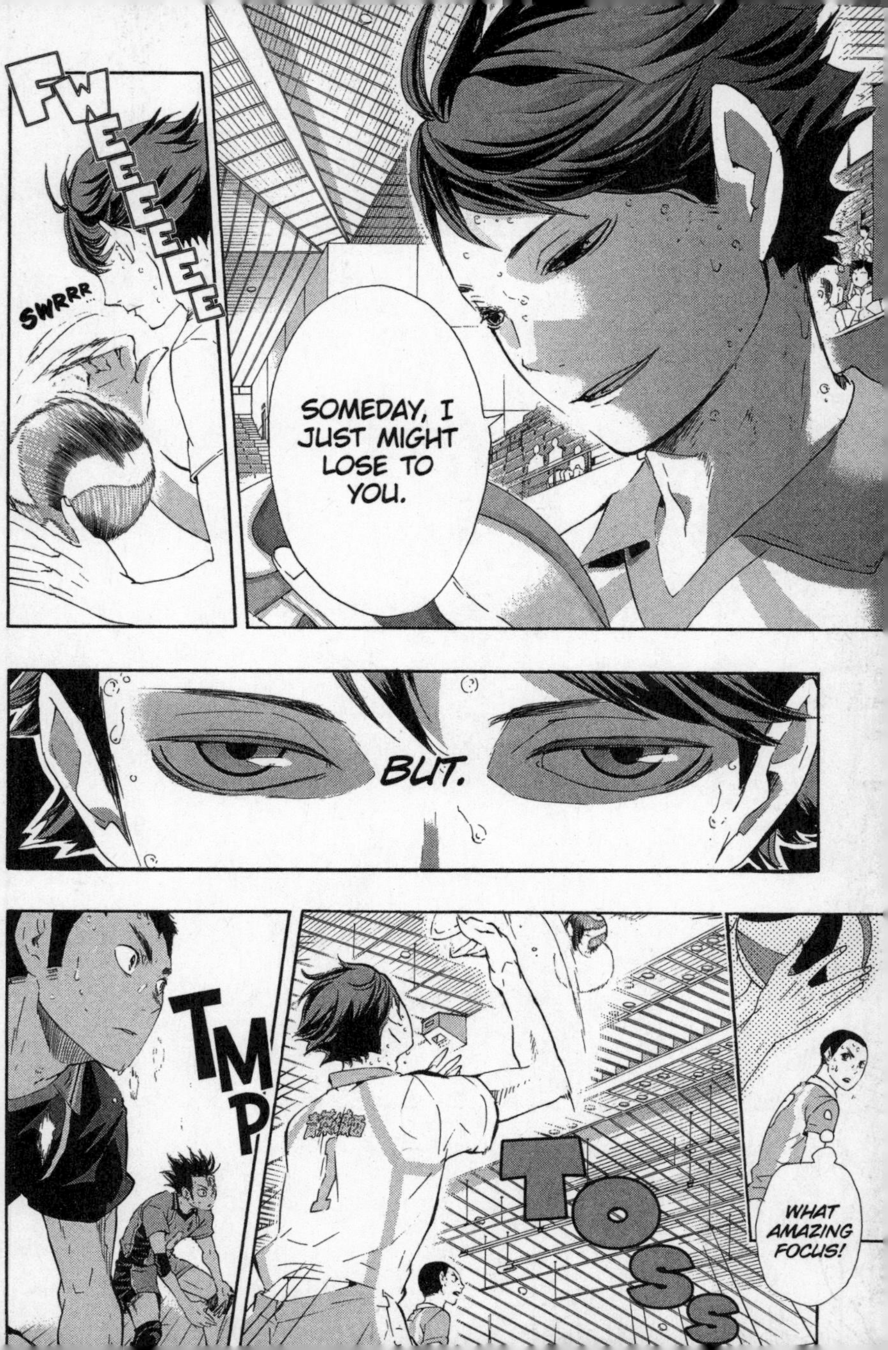
SOMEDAY, I JUST MIGHT LOSE TO YOU.
FWEEEEEEE
SWRRR
BUT.
WHAT AMAZING FOCUS!
TOSS
TMP

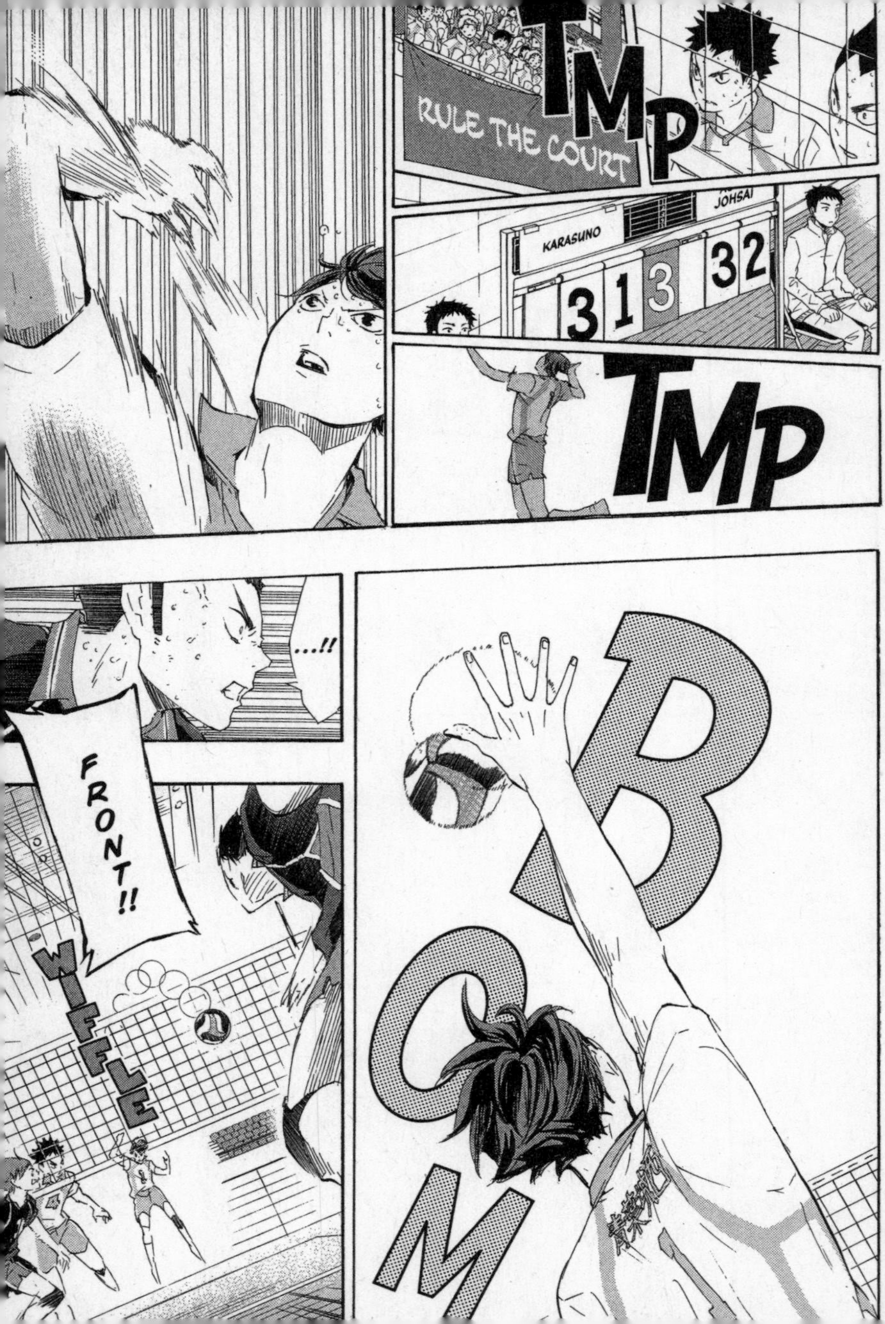

TMP
RULE THE COURT
JOHSAI
KARASUNO
31
3
32
TMP
BOOM
...!!
FRONT!!
WIFFLE

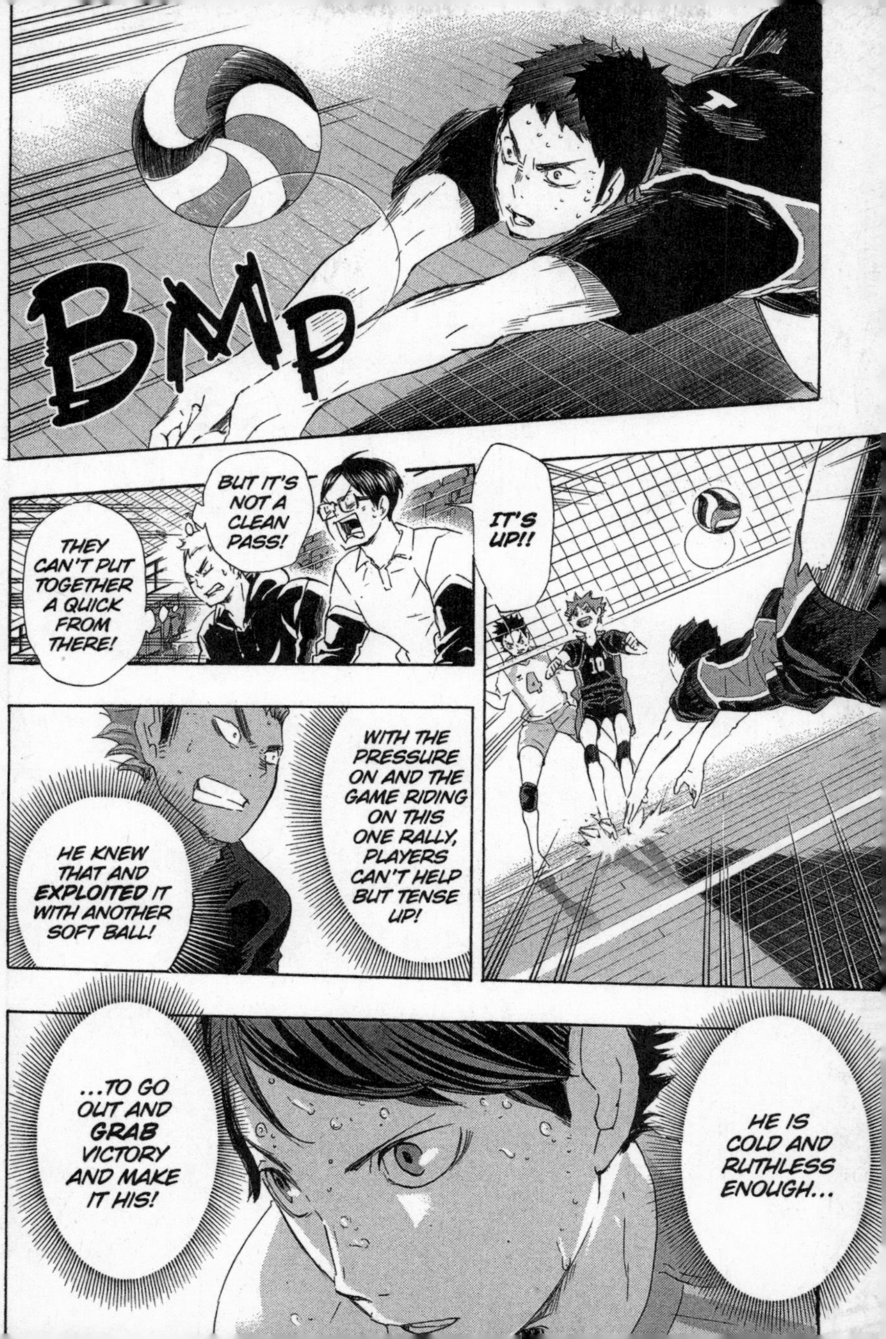
BMP
IT'S UP!!
BUT IT'S NOT A CLEAN PASS!
THEY CAN'T PUT TOGETHER A QUICK FROM THERE!
WITH THE PRESSURE ON AND THE GAME RIDING ON THIS ONE RALLY, PLAYERS CAN'T HELP BUT TENSE UP!
HE KNEW THAT AND EXPLOITED IT WITH ANOTHER SOFT BALL!
HE IS COLD AND RUTHLESS ENOUGH...
...TO GO OUT AND GRAB VICTORY AND MAKE IT HIS!

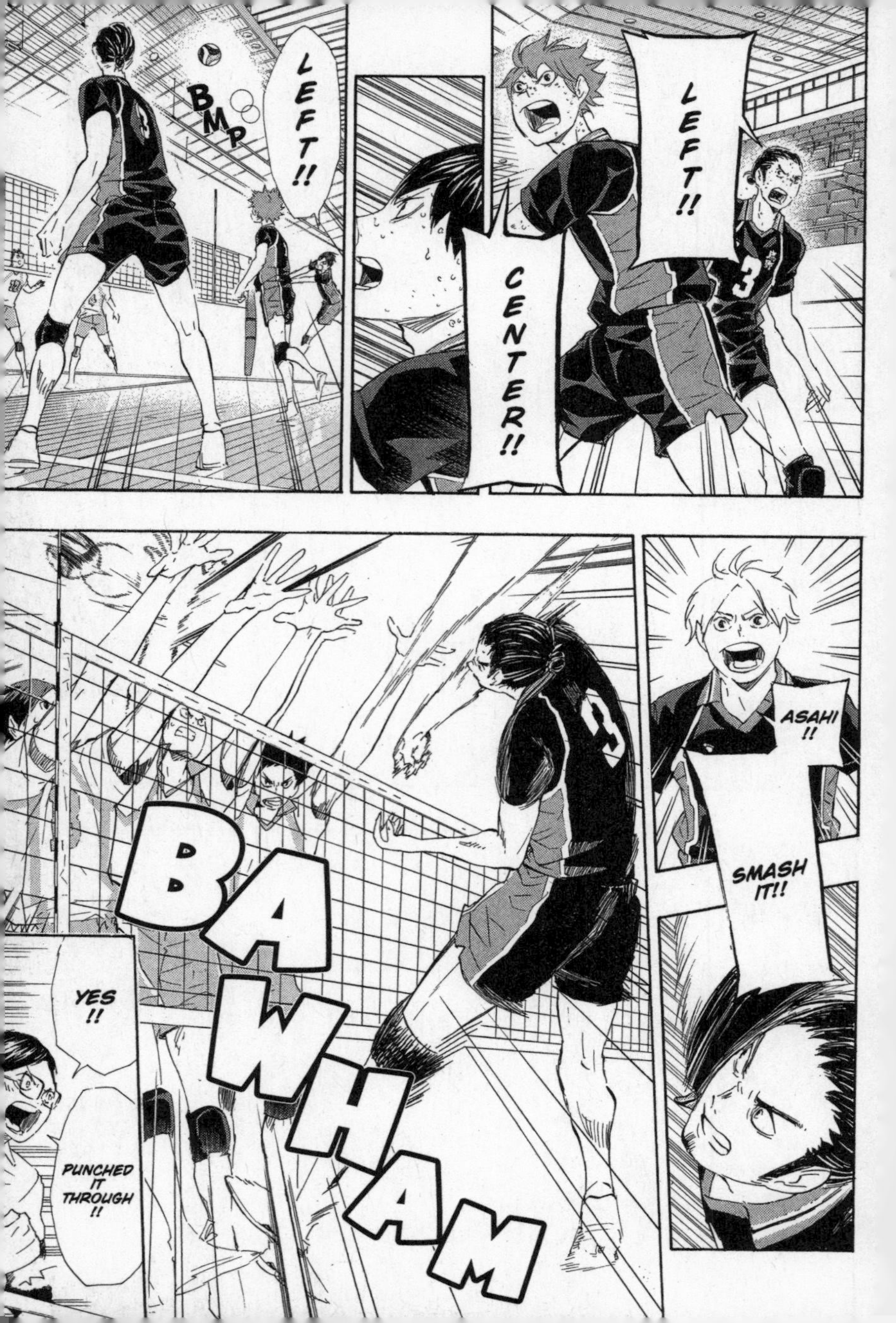
LEFT!!
CENTER!!
BMP
LEFT!!
ASAHI!!
SMASH IT!!
BAWHAM
YES!!
PUNCHED IT THROUGH!!

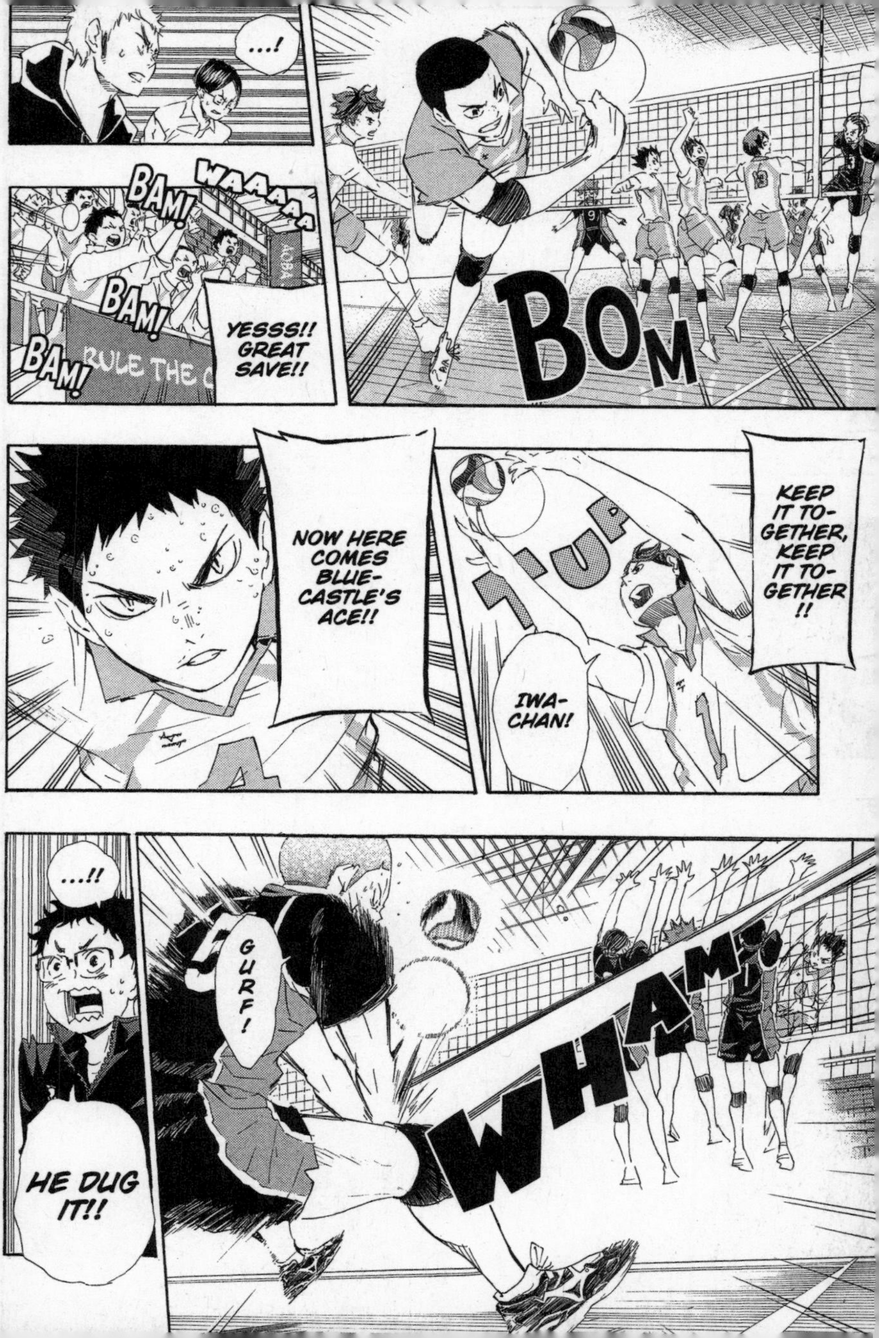
BOM
...!
WAAAAA
BAM!
YESSS!! GREAT SAVE!!
BAM!
BAM!
RULE THE C
KEEP IT TO-GETHER, KEEP IT TO-GETHER !!
T'UP
IWA-CHAN!
NOW HERE COMES BLUE-CASTLE'S ACE!!
GURF!
WHAM
...!!
HE DUG IT!!

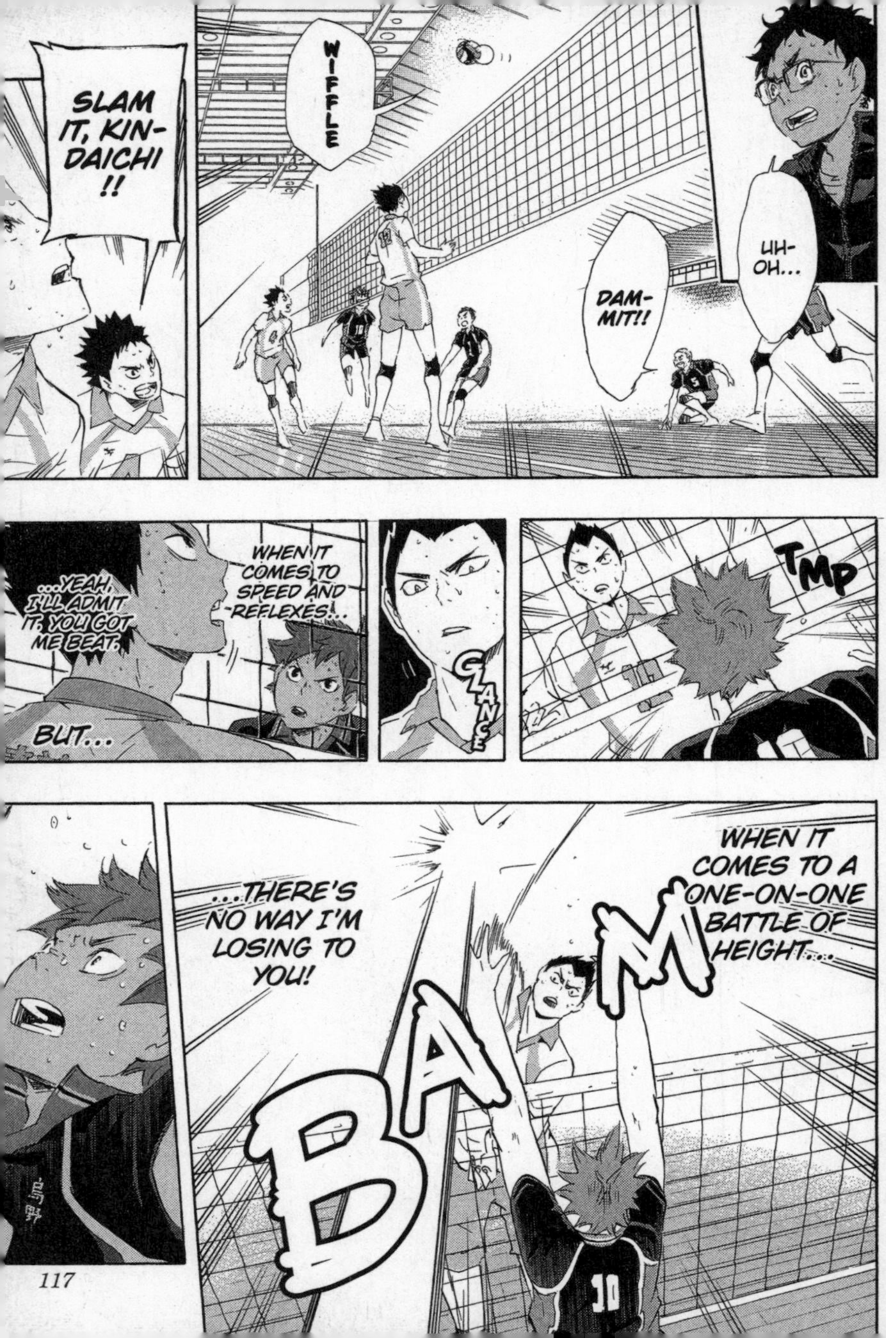
UH-OH...
WIFFLE
DAM-MIT!!
SLAM IT, KIN-DAICHI!!
TMP
GLANCE
WHEN IT COMES TO SPEED AND REFLEXES...
...YEAH, I'LL ADMIT IT. YOU GOT ME BEAT.
BUT...
WHEN IT COMES TO A ONE-ON-ONE BATTLE OF HEIGHT...
BAM
...THERE'S NO WAY I'M LOSING TO YOU!

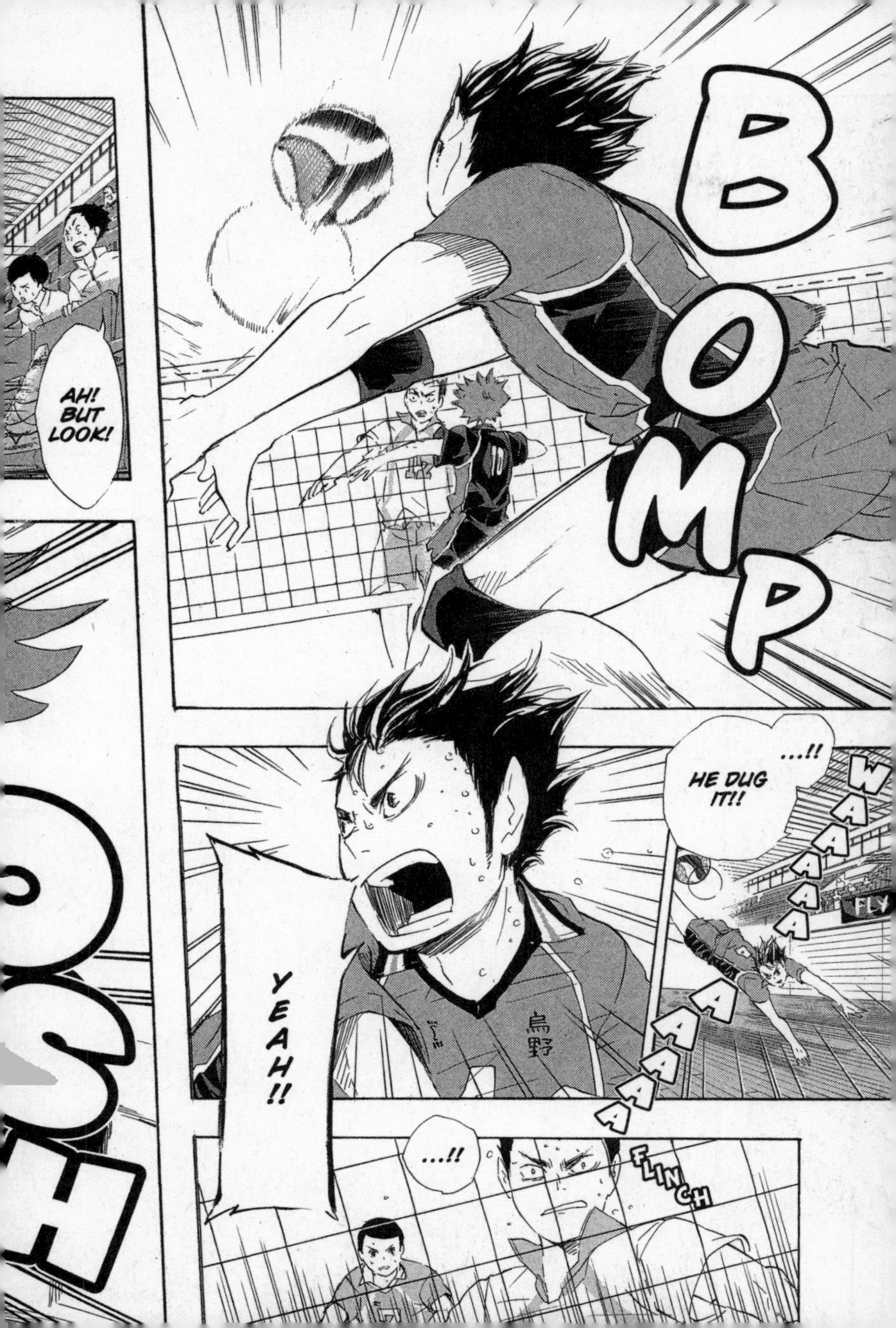
BOMP
AH! BUT LOOK!
...!! HE DUG IT!!
WAAAAAAAAAA
YEAH!!
...!!
FLINCH

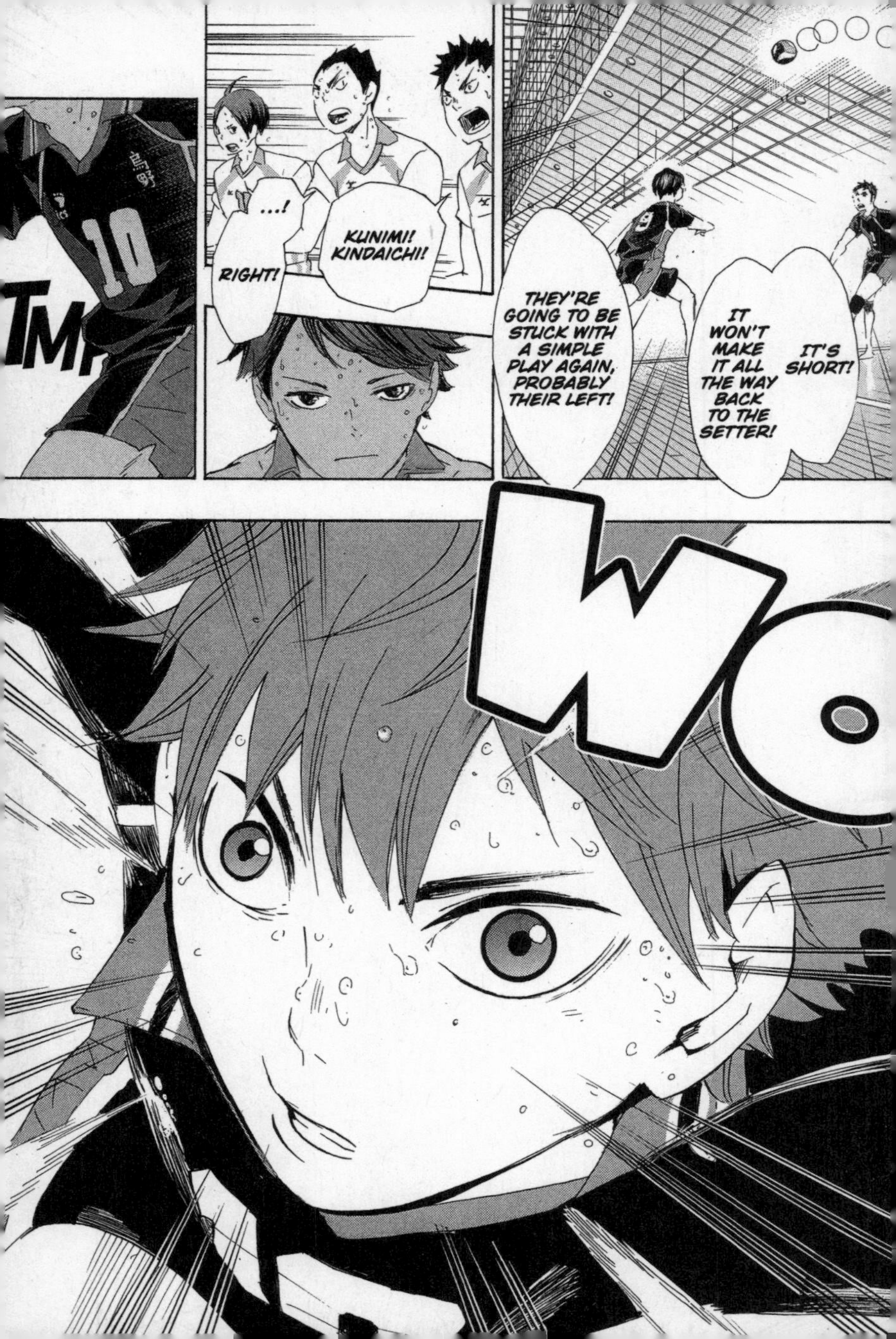
IT'S SHORT!
IT WON'T MAKE IT ALL THE WAY BACK TO THE SETTER!
THEY'RE GOING TO BE STUCK WITH A SIMPLE PLAY AGAIN, PROBABLY THEIR LEFT!
KUNIMI! KINDAICHI!
...!
RIGHT!
TMP
WO

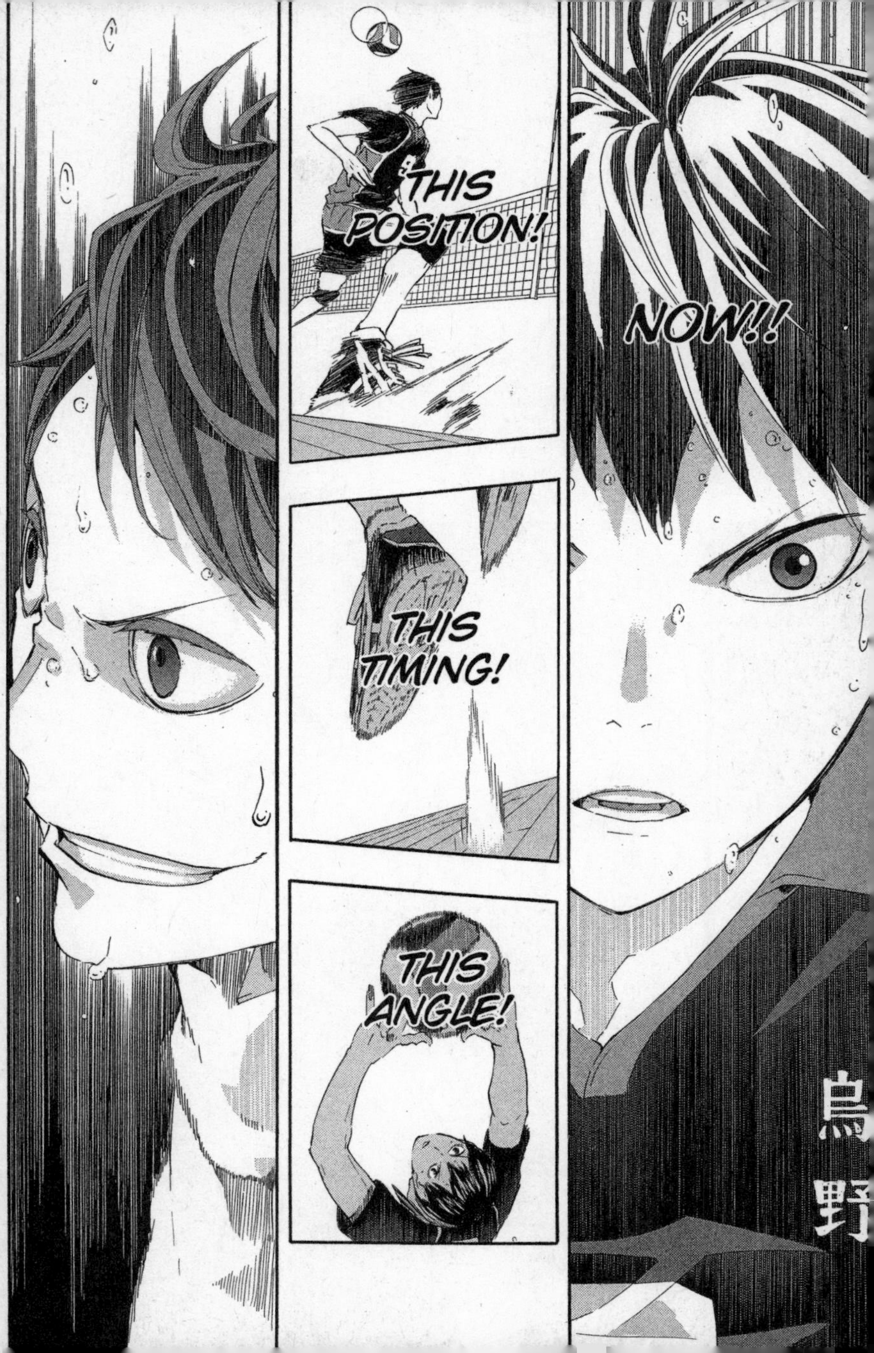
NOW!!
烏野
THIS POSITION!
THIS TIMING!
THIS ANGLE!

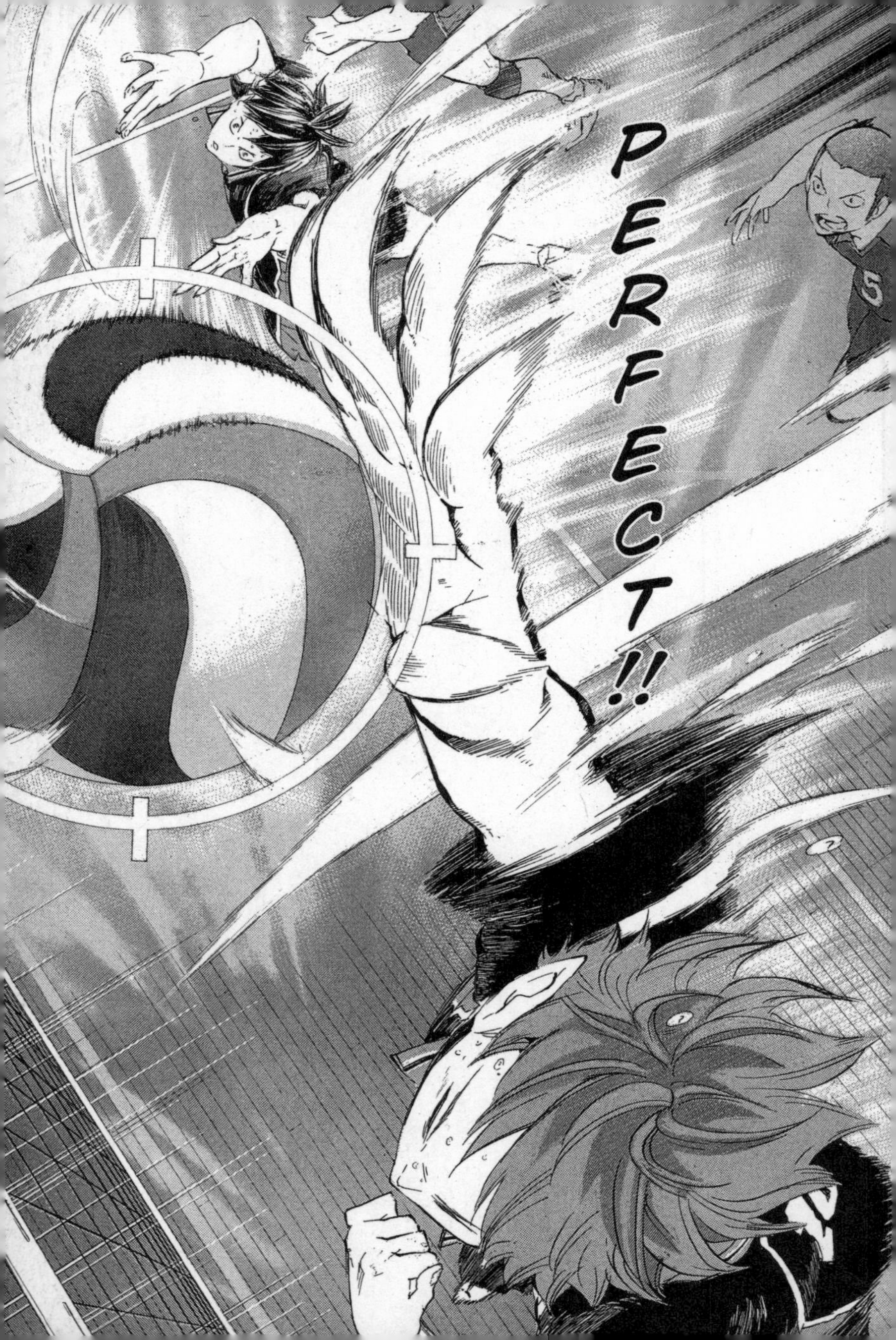
PERFECT!!

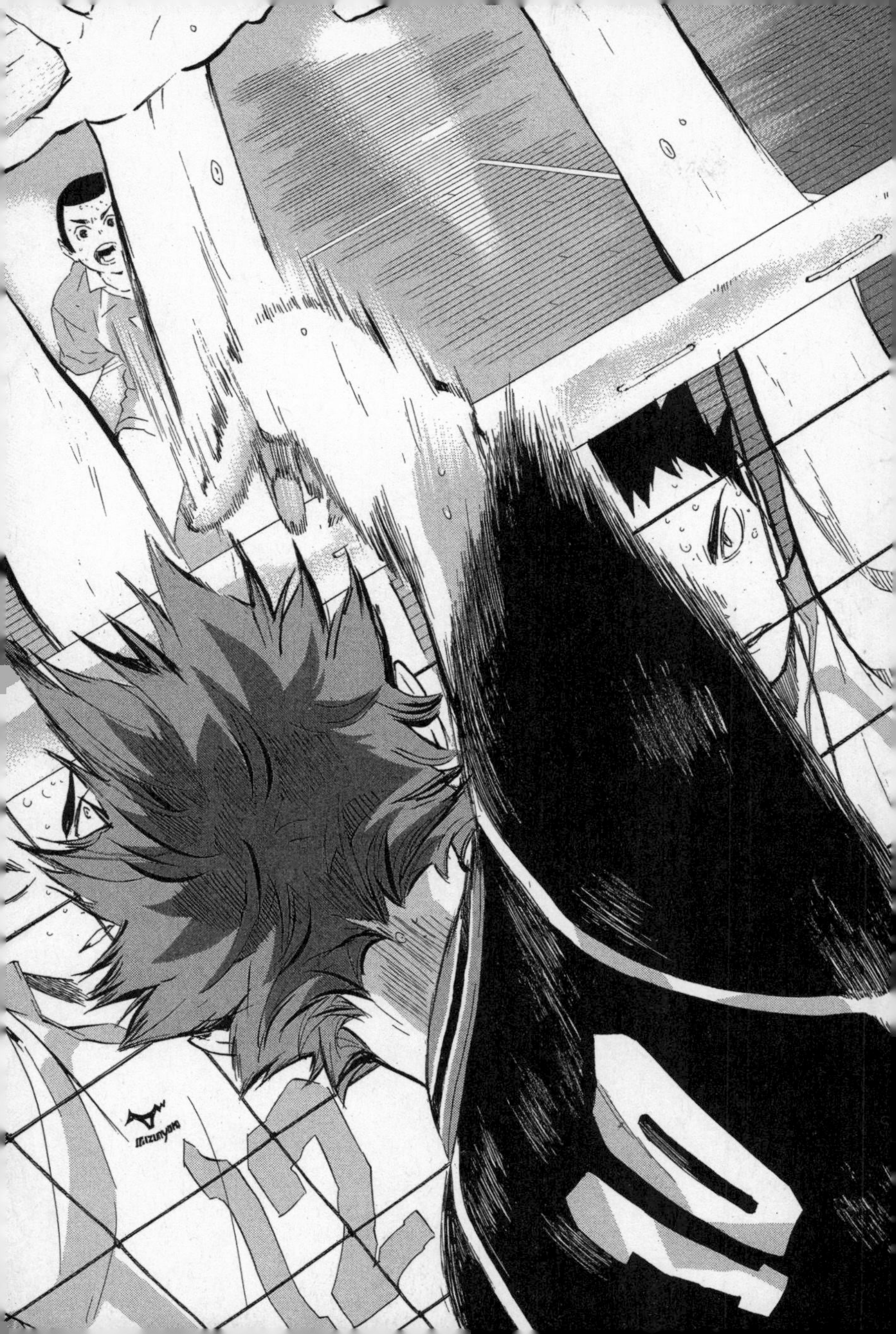

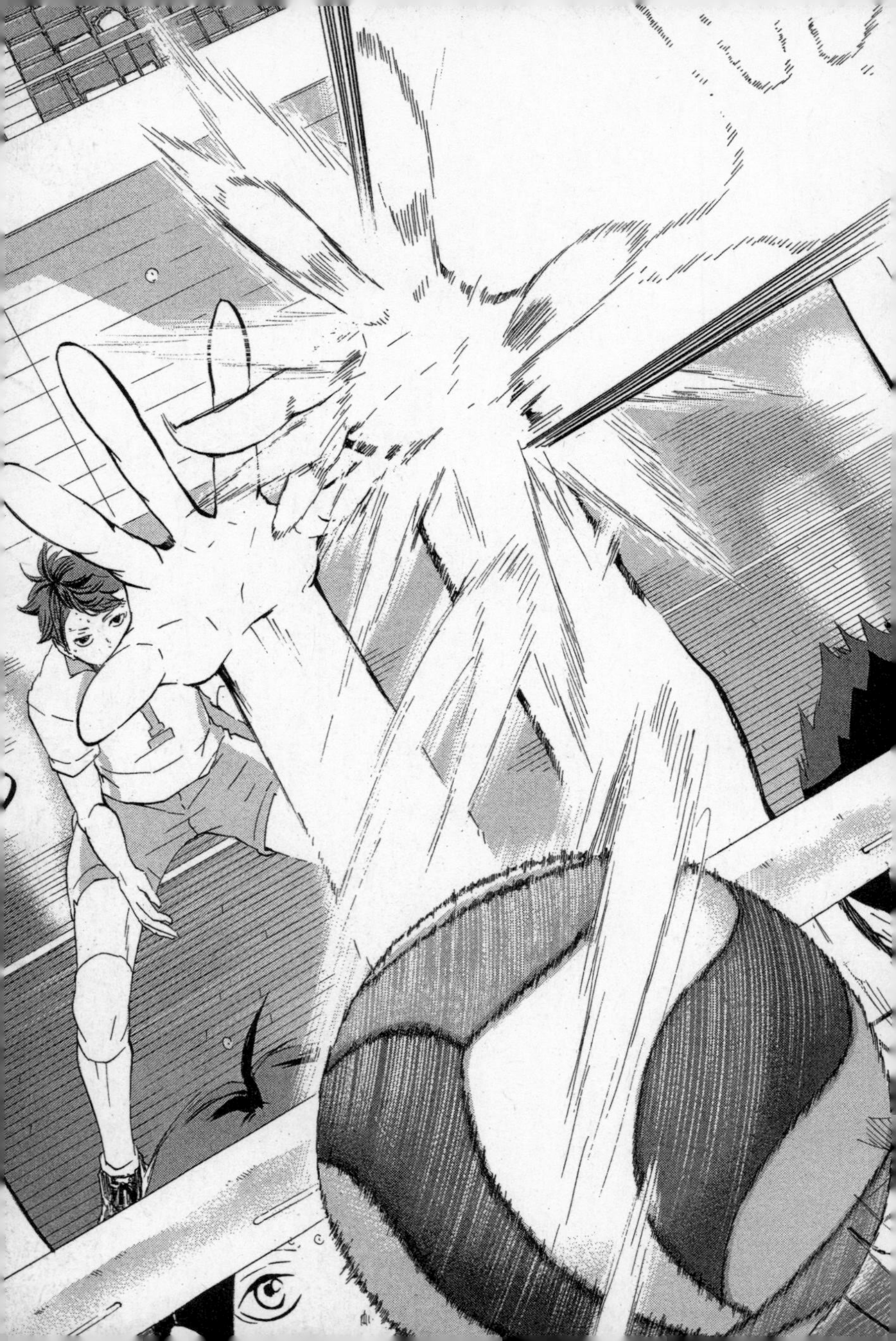

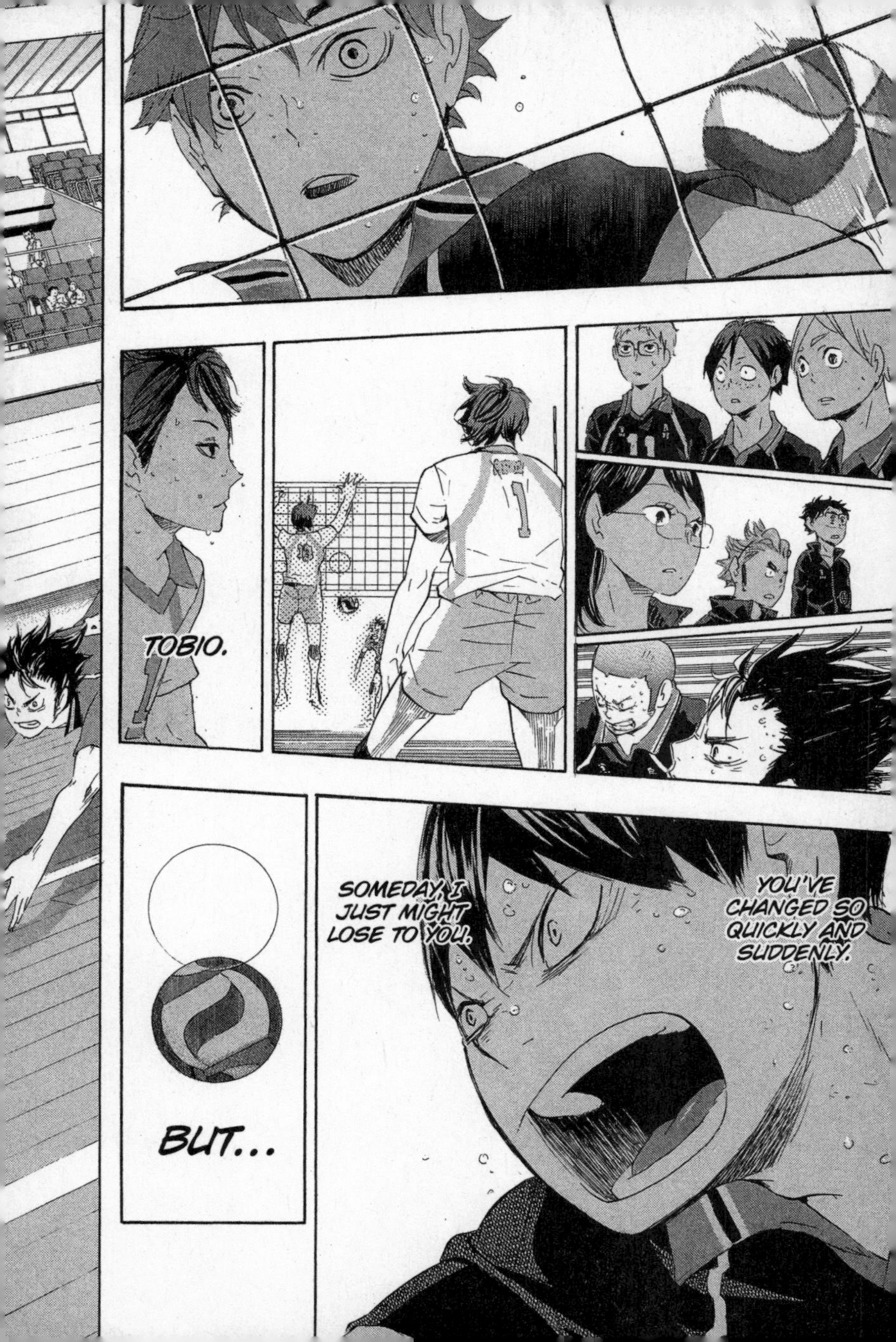
TOBIO.
YOU'VE CHANGED SO QUICKLY AND SUDDENLY.
SOMEDAY, I JUST MIGHT LOSE TO YOU.
BUT...

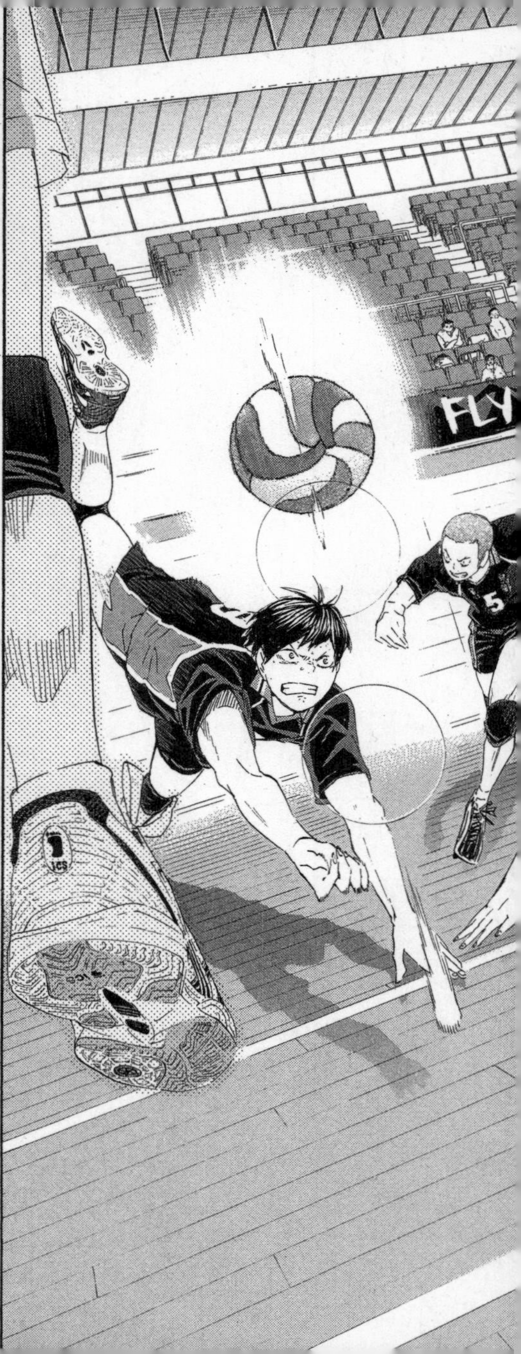
FLY

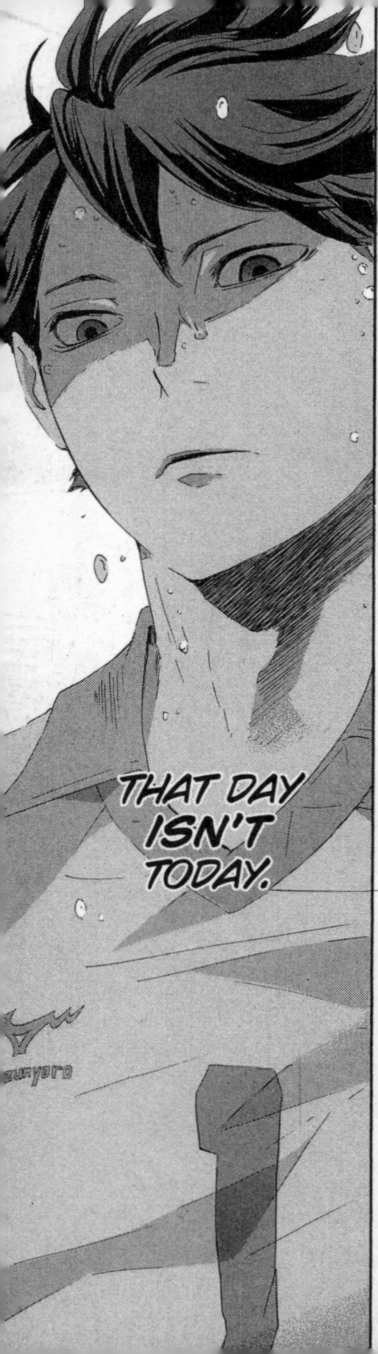
THAT DAY ISN'T TODAY.

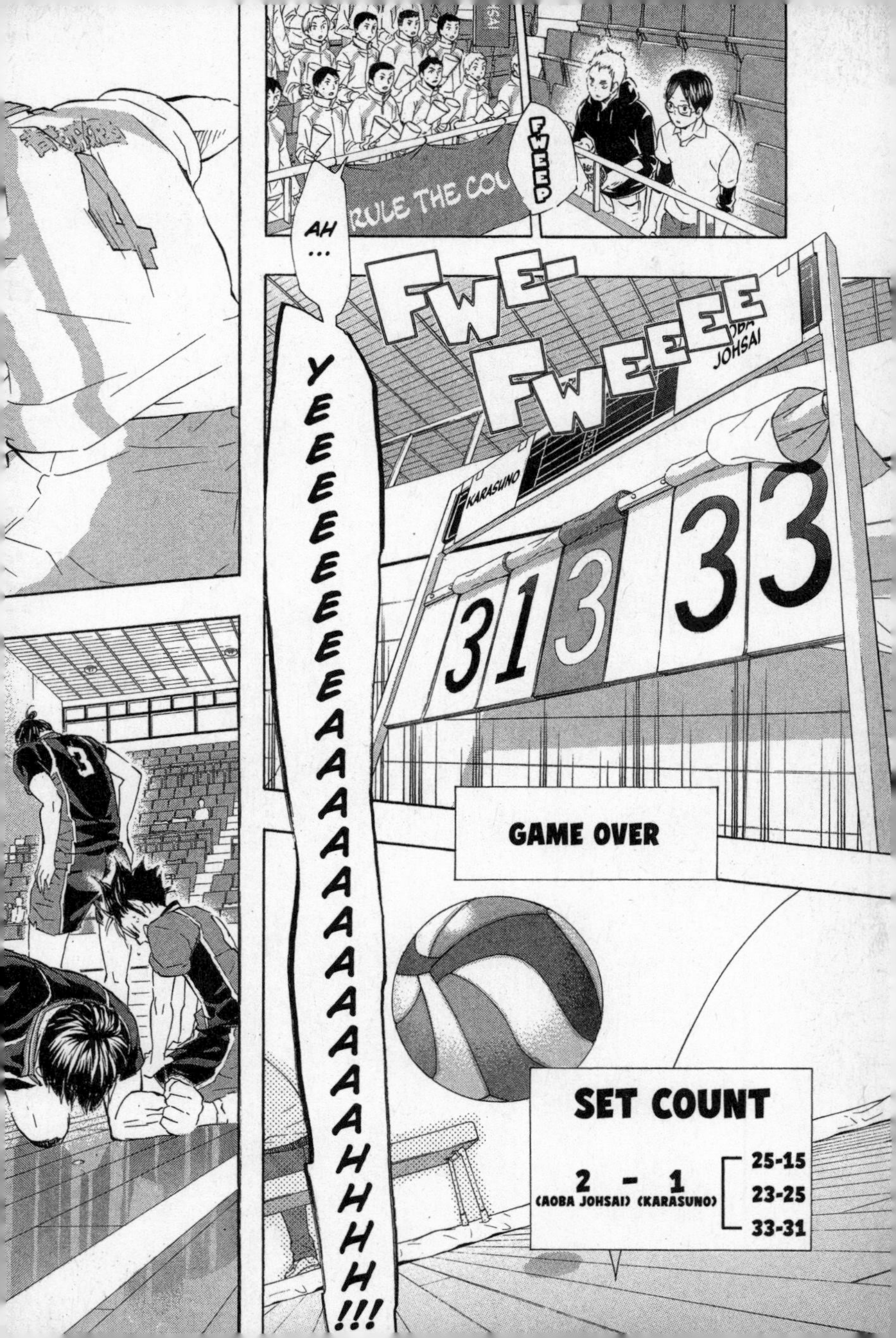
FWEEP
RULE THE COU
AH ...
FWE-FWEEEE
AOBA JOHSAI
KARASUNO
31
33
GAME OVER
YEEEEEEEEAAAAAAAAAAHHHH!!!
SET COUNT
2 - 1
(AOBA JOHSAI) (KARASUNO)
25-15
23-25
33-31

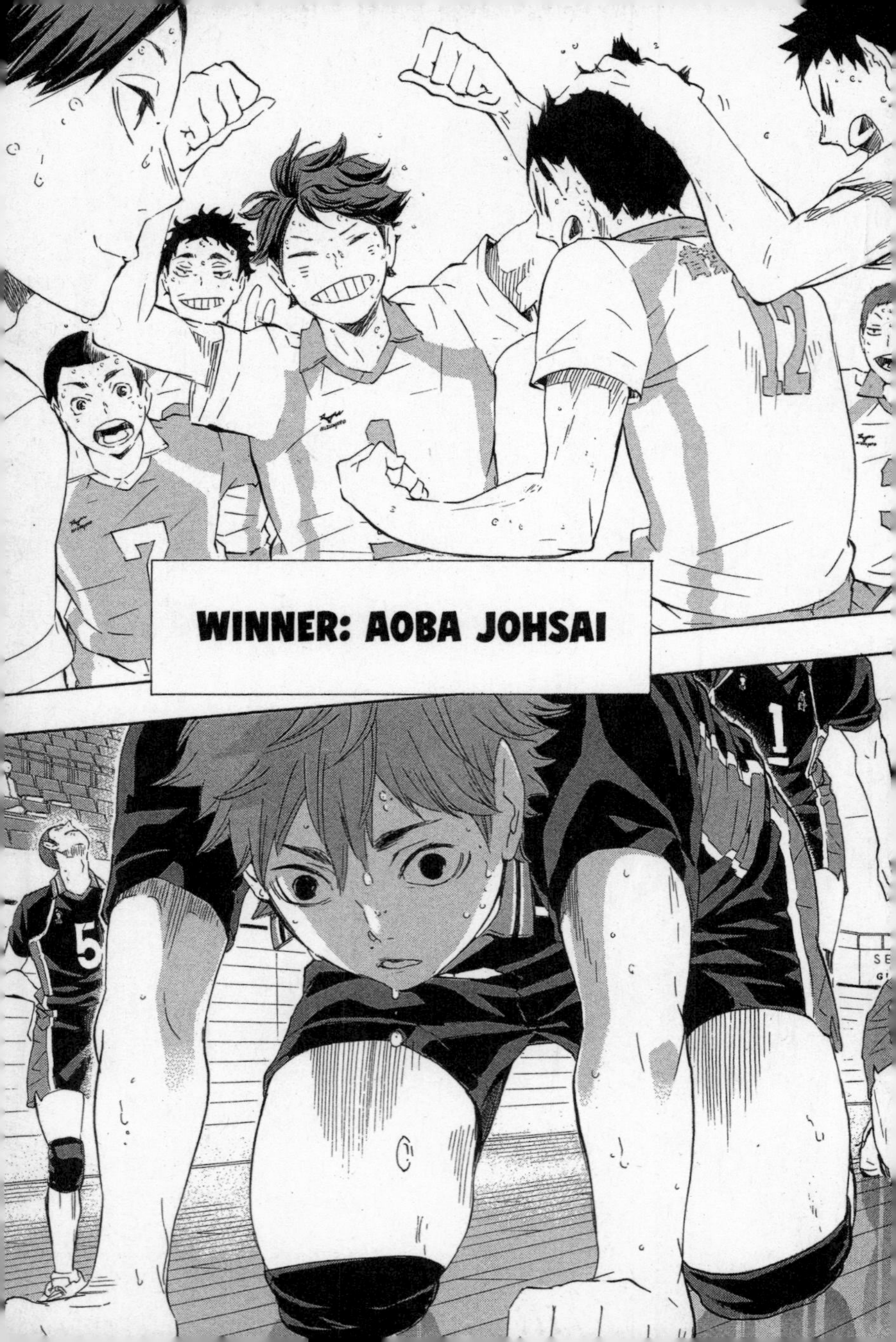
WINNER: AOBA JOHSAI

CHAPTER 69: The Losers

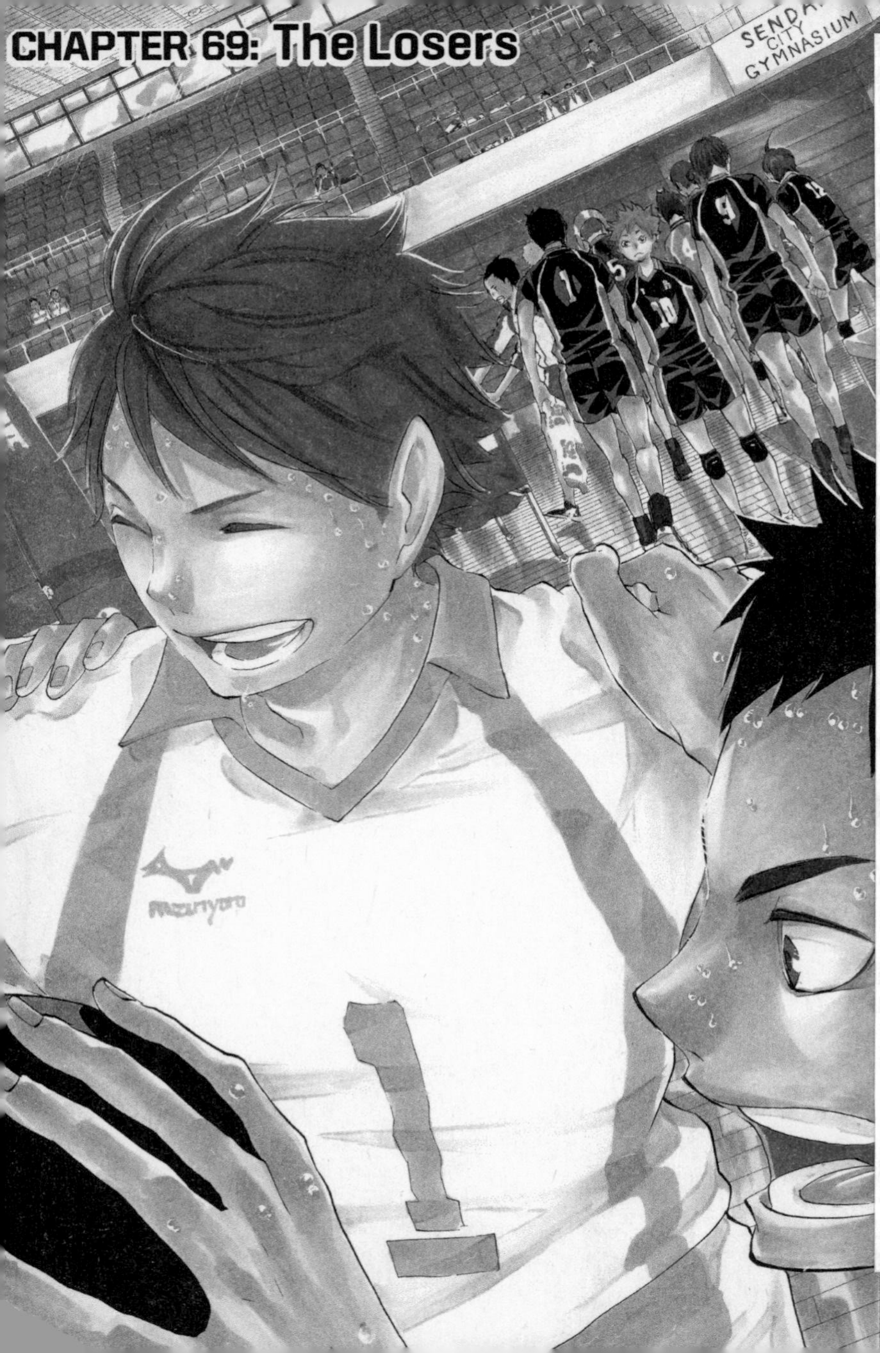
SENDA
CITY
GYMNASIUM

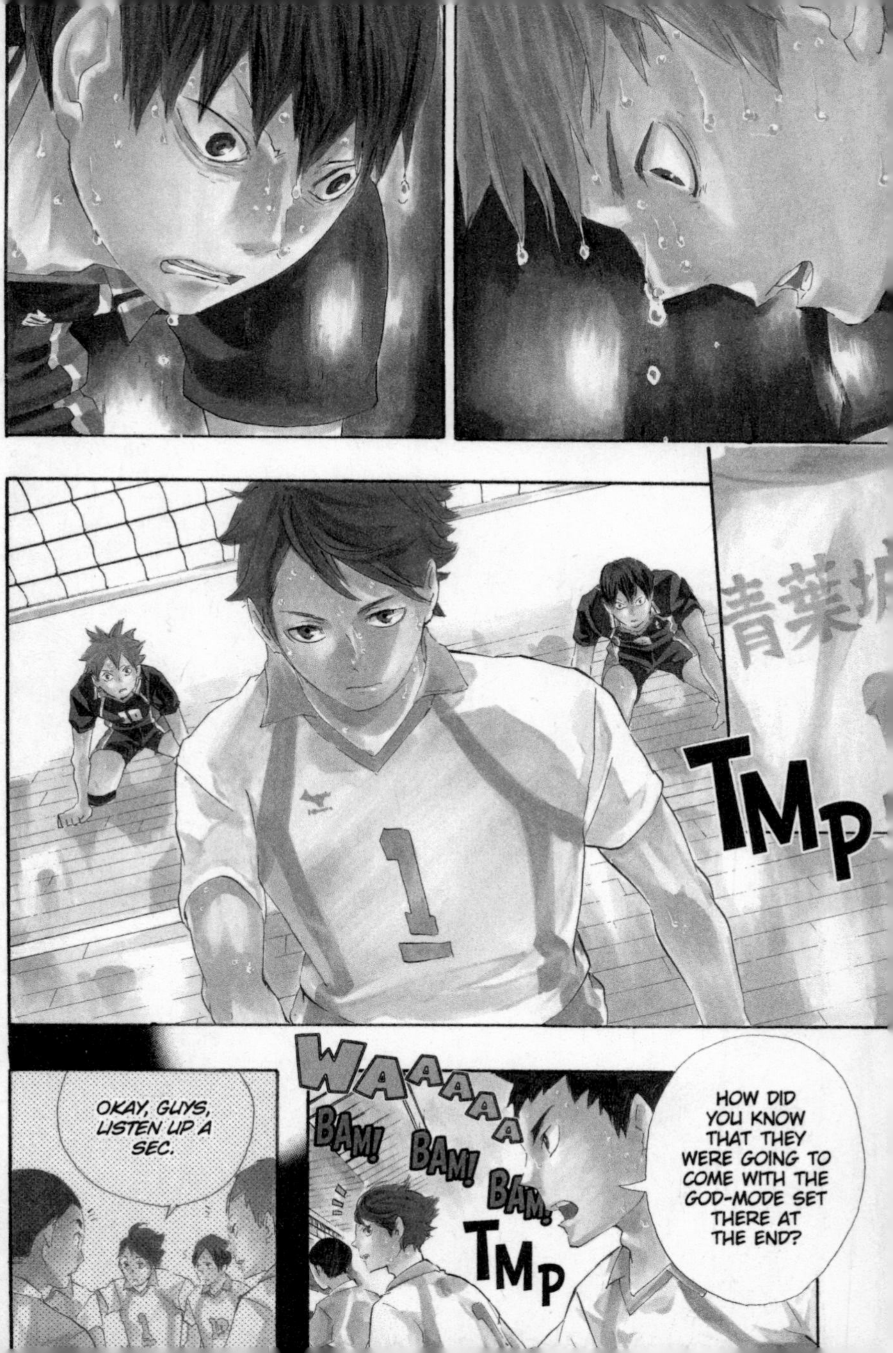
青葉
TMP
HOW DID YOU KNOW THAT THEY WERE GOING TO COME WITH THE GOD-MODE SET THERE AT THE END?
WAAAAAA
BAM! BAM! BAM!
TMP
OKAY, GUYS, LISTEN UP A SEC.

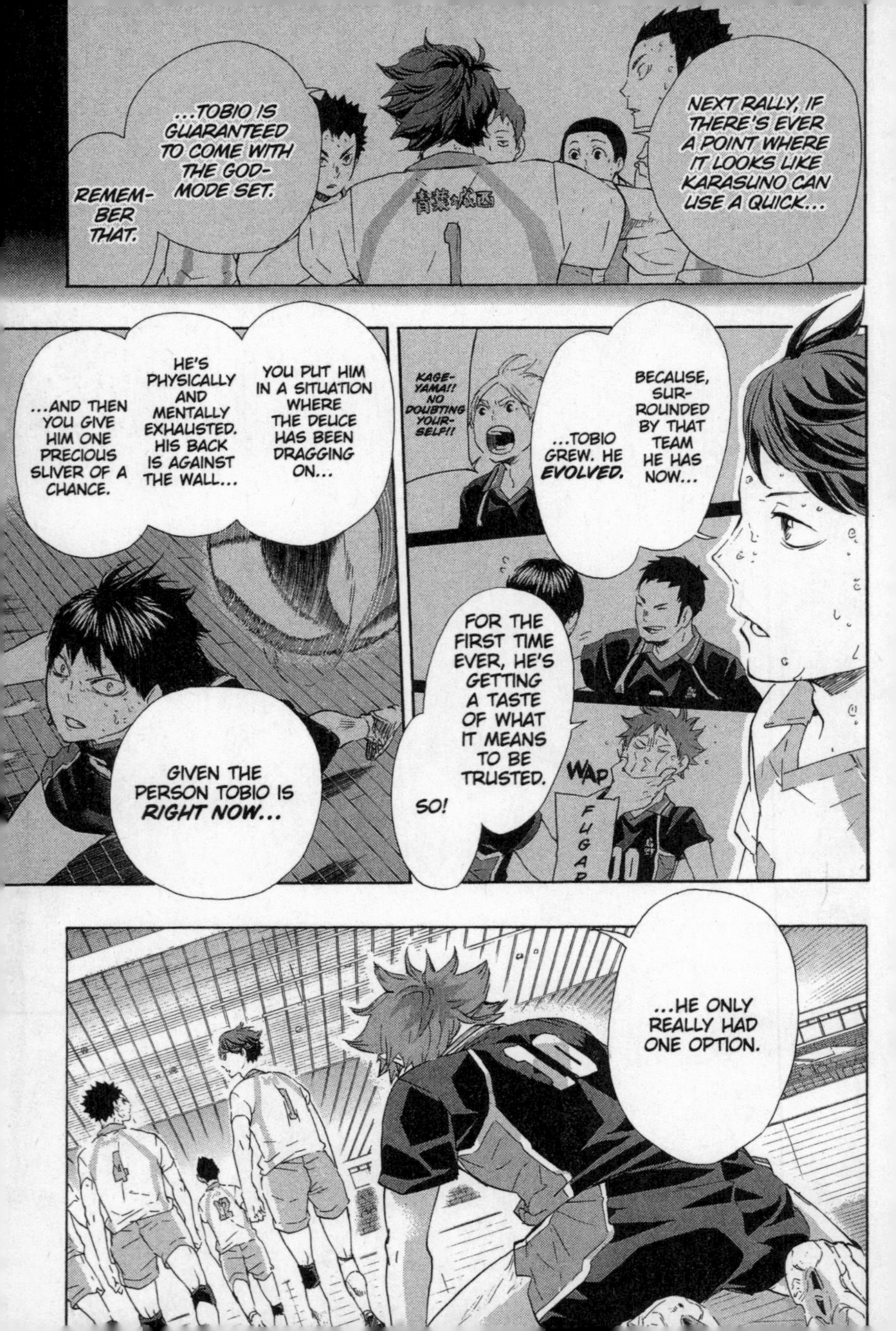
NEXT RALLY, IF THERE'S EVER A POINT WHERE IT LOOKS LIKE KARASUNO CAN USE A QUICK...
...TOBIO IS GUARANTEED TO COME WITH THE GOD-MODE SET.
REMEMBER THAT.
BECAUSE, SURROUNDED BY THAT TEAM HE HAS NOW...
...TOBIO GREW. HE *EVOLVED.*
KAGEYAMA!! NO DOUBTING YOURSELF!!
FOR THE FIRST TIME EVER, HE'S GETTING A TASTE OF WHAT IT MEANS TO BE TRUSTED.
SO!
WAP
FUGA
YOU PUT HIM IN A SITUATION WHERE THE DEUCE HAS BEEN DRAGGING ON...
HE'S PHYSICALLY AND MENTALLY EXHAUSTED. HIS BACK IS AGAINST THE WALL...
...AND THEN YOU GIVE HIM ONE PRECIOUS SLIVER OF A CHANCE.
GIVEN THE PERSON TOBIO IS *RIGHT NOW...*
...HE ONLY REALLY HAD ONE OPTION.

C'MON, YOU TWO. WE HAVE TO LINE UP.

THAT HAD TO HURT. SHORT STUFF HAS TO BE FEELING MISERABLE RIGHT NOW.

LAST RALLY OF THE GAME AND HE GETS STUFFED BY A TRIPLE BLOCK.

NONE OF US MADE A MISTAKE.

CAPTAIN ...!

...

"ALL RIGHT. WE WILL."

"WIN...!! AND KEEP WINNING, FOR US TOO!!"

I'M SORRY --

SO NO APOLOGIZING.

YOU DIDN'T MAKE A MISTAKE.

FWEEEEEE

DUN

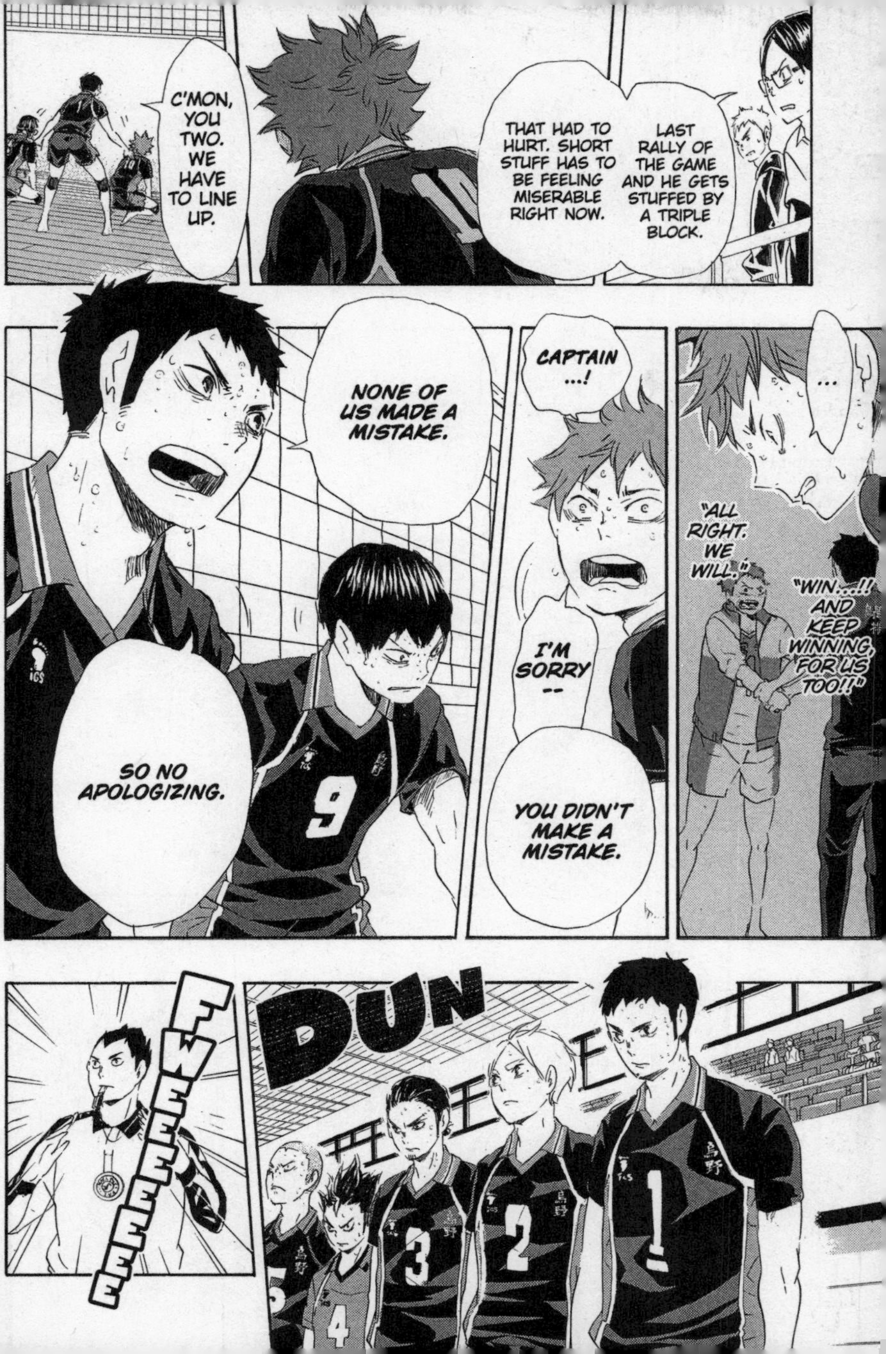
LAST RALLY OF THE GAME AND HE GETS STUFFED BY A TRIPLE BLOCK.
THAT HAD TO HURT. SHORT STUFF HAS TO BE FEELING MISERABLE RIGHT NOW.
C'MON, YOU TWO. WE HAVE TO LINE UP.
...
"WIN...!! AND KEEP WINNING, FOR US TOO!!"
"ALL RIGHT. WE WILL."
CAPTAIN ...!
I'M SORRY --
YOU DIDN'T MAKE A MISTAKE.
NONE OF US MADE A MISTAKE.
SO NO APOLOGIZING.
DUN
FWEEEEEEEE

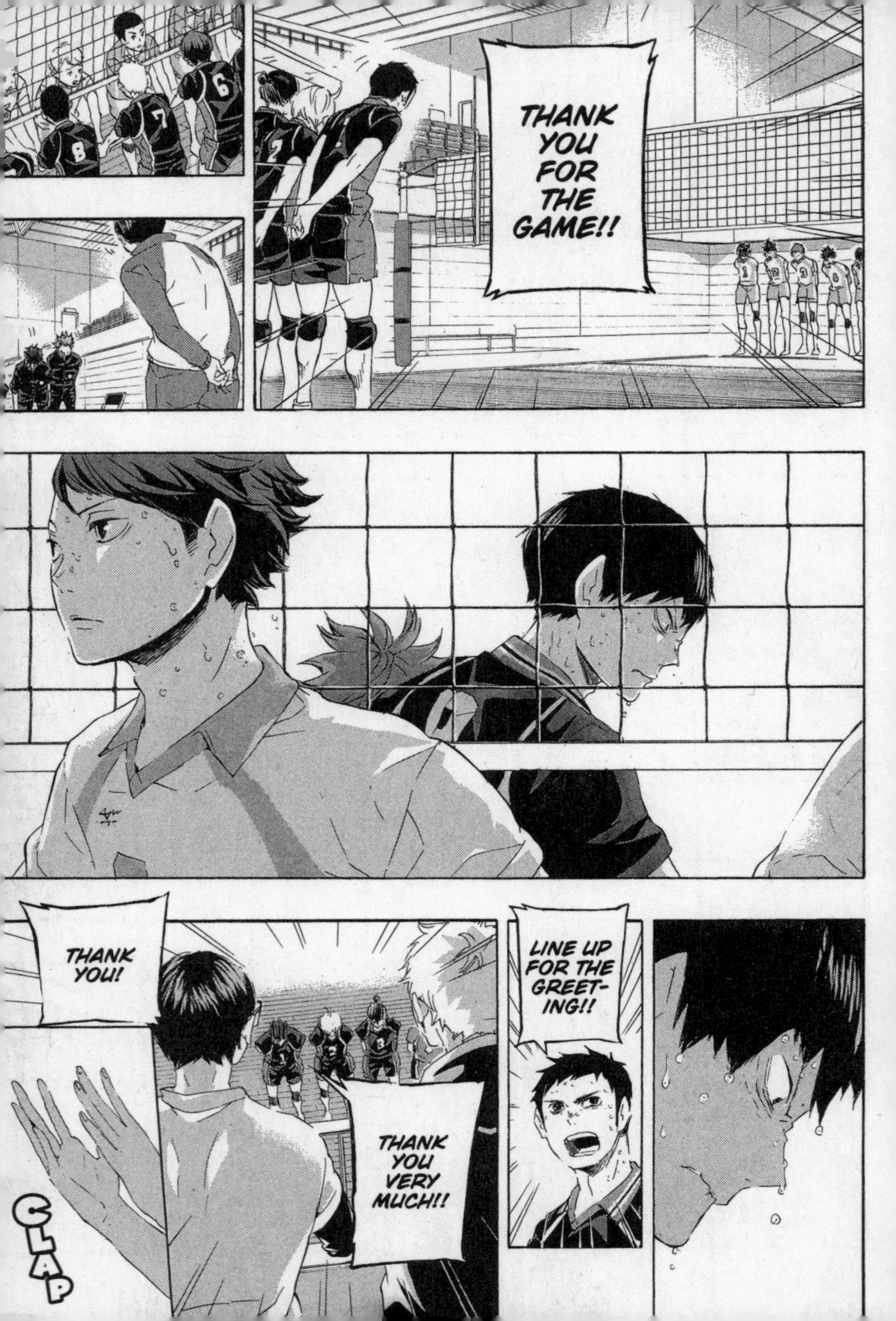
THANK YOU FOR THE GAME!!
LINE UP FOR THE GREET-ING!!
THANK YOU!
THANK YOU VERY MUCH!!
CLAP

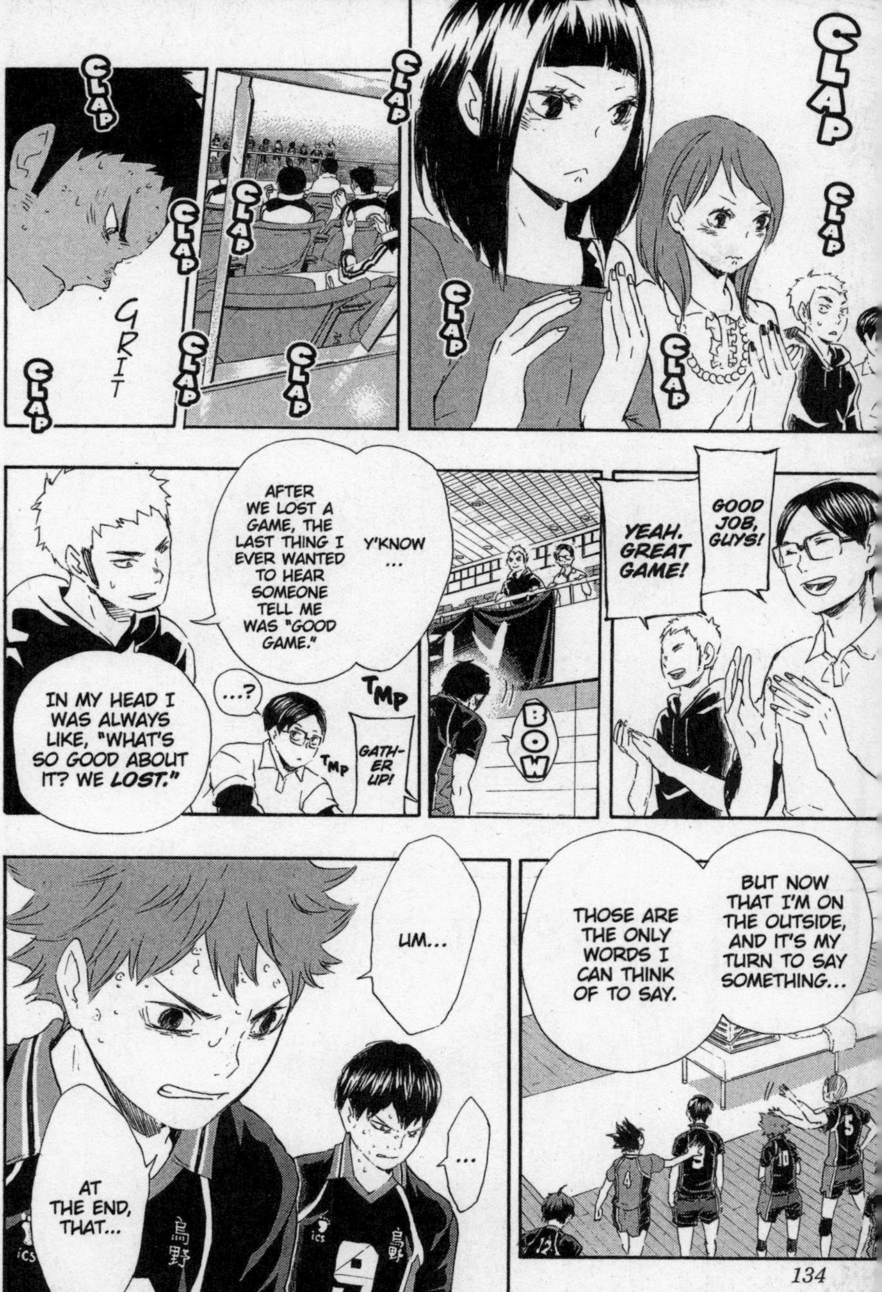
CLAP
CLAP
CLAP
CLAP
CLAP
CLAP
CLAP
CLAP
CLAP
CLAP
GRIT
CLAP
GOOD JOB, GUYS!
YEAH. GREAT GAME!
BOW
Y'KNOW...
AFTER WE LOST A GAME, THE LAST THING I EVER WANTED TO HEAR SOMEONE TELL ME WAS "GOOD GAME."
...?
TMP
TMP
GATHER UP!
IN MY HEAD I WAS ALWAYS LIKE, "WHAT'S SO GOOD ABOUT IT? WE LOST."
BUT NOW THAT I'M ON THE OUTSIDE, AND IT'S MY TURN TO SAY SOMETHING...
THOSE ARE THE ONLY WORDS I CAN THINK OF TO SAY.
UM...
...
AT THE END, THAT...

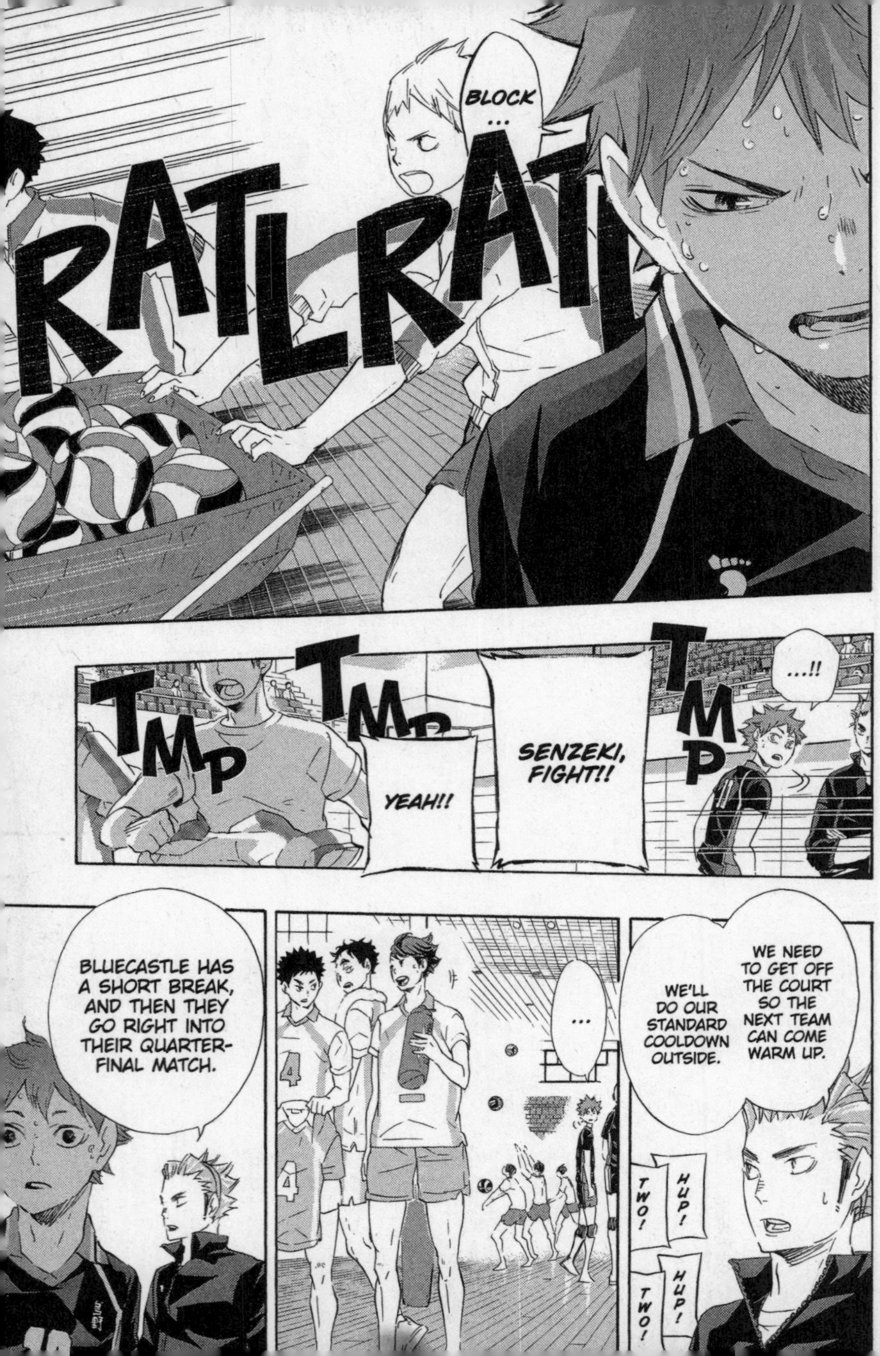

BLOCK ...
RATL RATL
...!!
TMP
SENZEKI, FIGHT!!
YEAH!!
TMP
TMP
WE NEED TO GET OFF THE COURT SO THE NEXT TEAM CAN COME WARM UP.
WE'LL DO OUR STANDARD COOLDOWN OUTSIDE.
HUP!
TWO!
HUP!
TWO!
...
BLUECASTLE HAS A SHORT BREAK, AND THEN THEY GO RIGHT INTO THEIR QUARTER-FINAL MATCH.

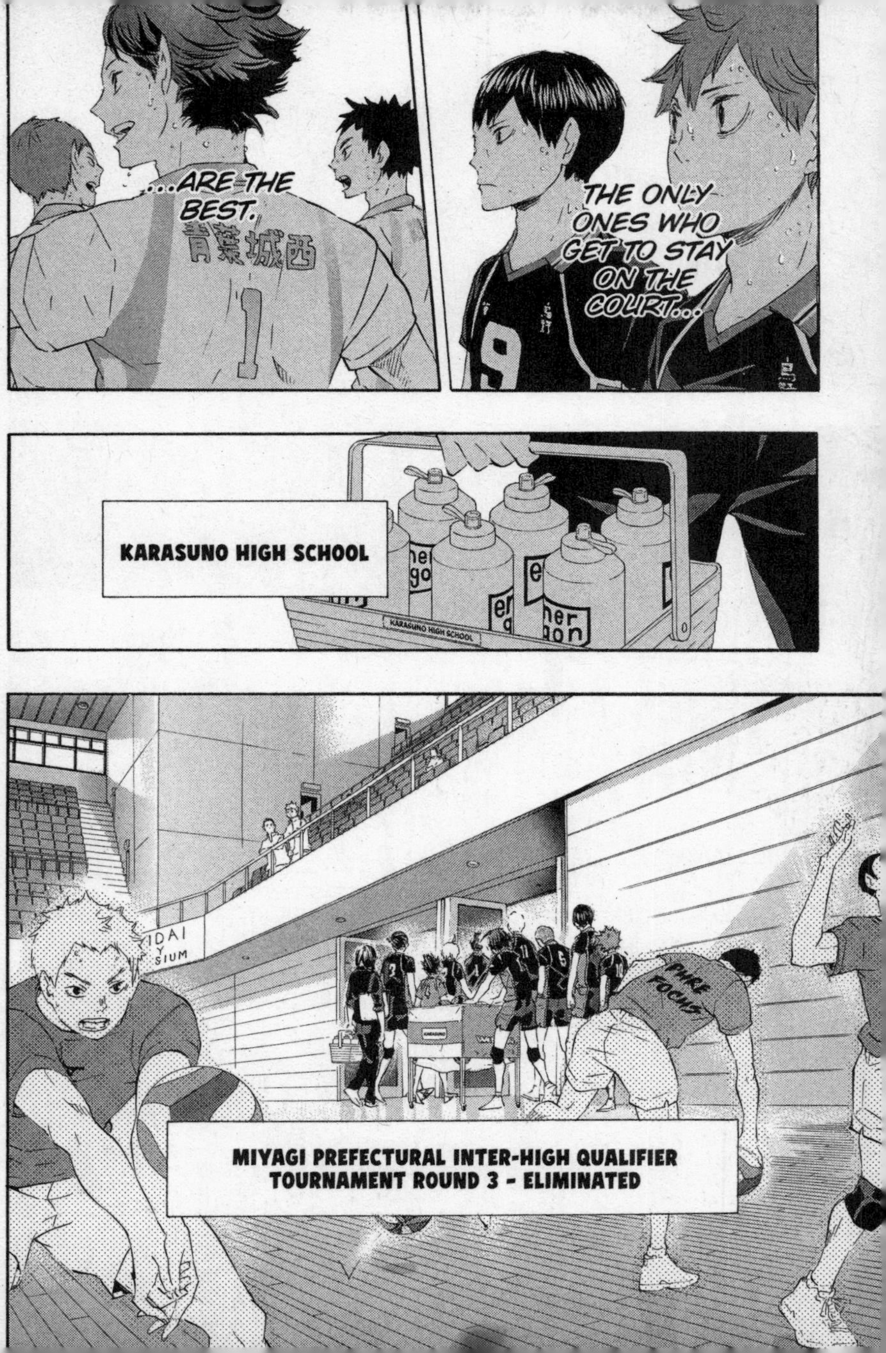
THE ONLY ONES WHO GET TO STAY ON THE COURT...
...ARE THE BEST.
KARASUNO HIGH SCHOOL
KARASUNO HIGH SCHOOL
MIYAGI PREFECTURAL INTER-HIGH QUALIFIER TOURNAMENT ROUND 3 - ELIMINATED

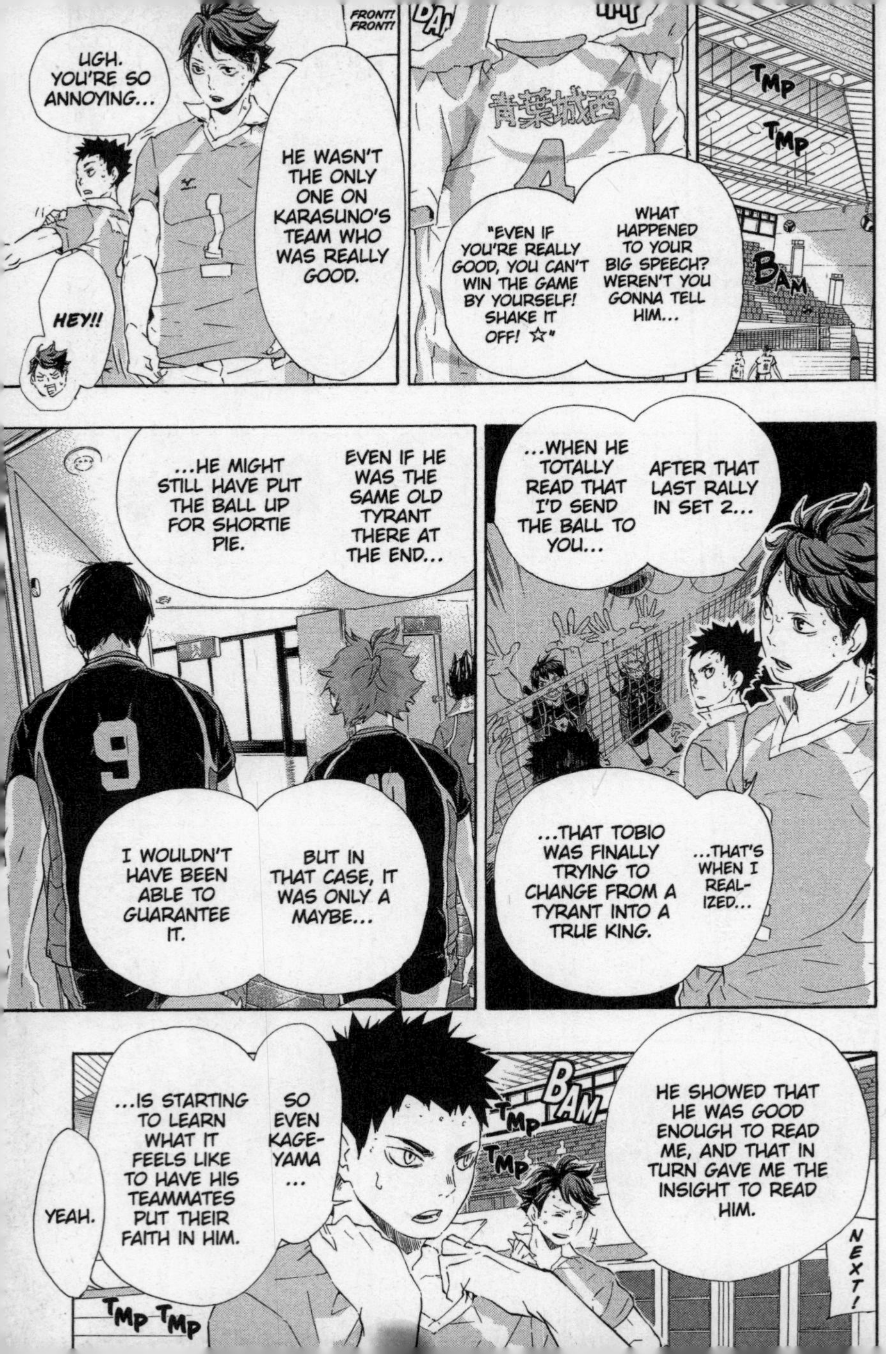
TMP
TMP
BAM
FRONT! FRONT!
BAM
WHAT HAPPENED TO YOUR BIG SPEECH? WEREN'T YOU GONNA TELL HIM...
"EVEN IF YOU'RE REALLY GOOD, YOU CAN'T WIN THE GAME BY YOURSELF! SHAKE IT OFF! ☆"
HE WASN'T THE ONLY ONE ON KARASUNO'S TEAM WHO WAS REALLY GOOD.
UGH. YOU'RE SO ANNOYING...
HEY!!
AFTER THAT LAST RALLY IN SET 2...
...WHEN HE TOTALLY READ THAT I'D SEND THE BALL TO YOU...
...THAT'S WHEN I REALIZED...
...THAT TOBIO WAS FINALLY TRYING TO CHANGE FROM A TYRANT INTO A TRUE KING.
EVEN IF HE WAS THE SAME OLD TYRANT THERE AT THE END...
...HE MIGHT STILL HAVE PUT THE BALL UP FOR SHORTIE PIE.
BUT IN THAT CASE, IT WAS ONLY A MAYBE...
I WOULDN'T HAVE BEEN ABLE TO GUARANTEE IT.
NEXT!
HE SHOWED THAT HE WAS GOOD ENOUGH TO READ ME, AND THAT IN TURN GAVE ME THE INSIGHT TO READ HIM.
BAM
TMP
TMP
SO EVEN KAGEYAMA...
...IS STARTING TO LEARN WHAT IT FEELS LIKE TO HAVE HIS TEAMMATES PUT THEIR FAITH IN HIM.
YEAH.
TMP TMP

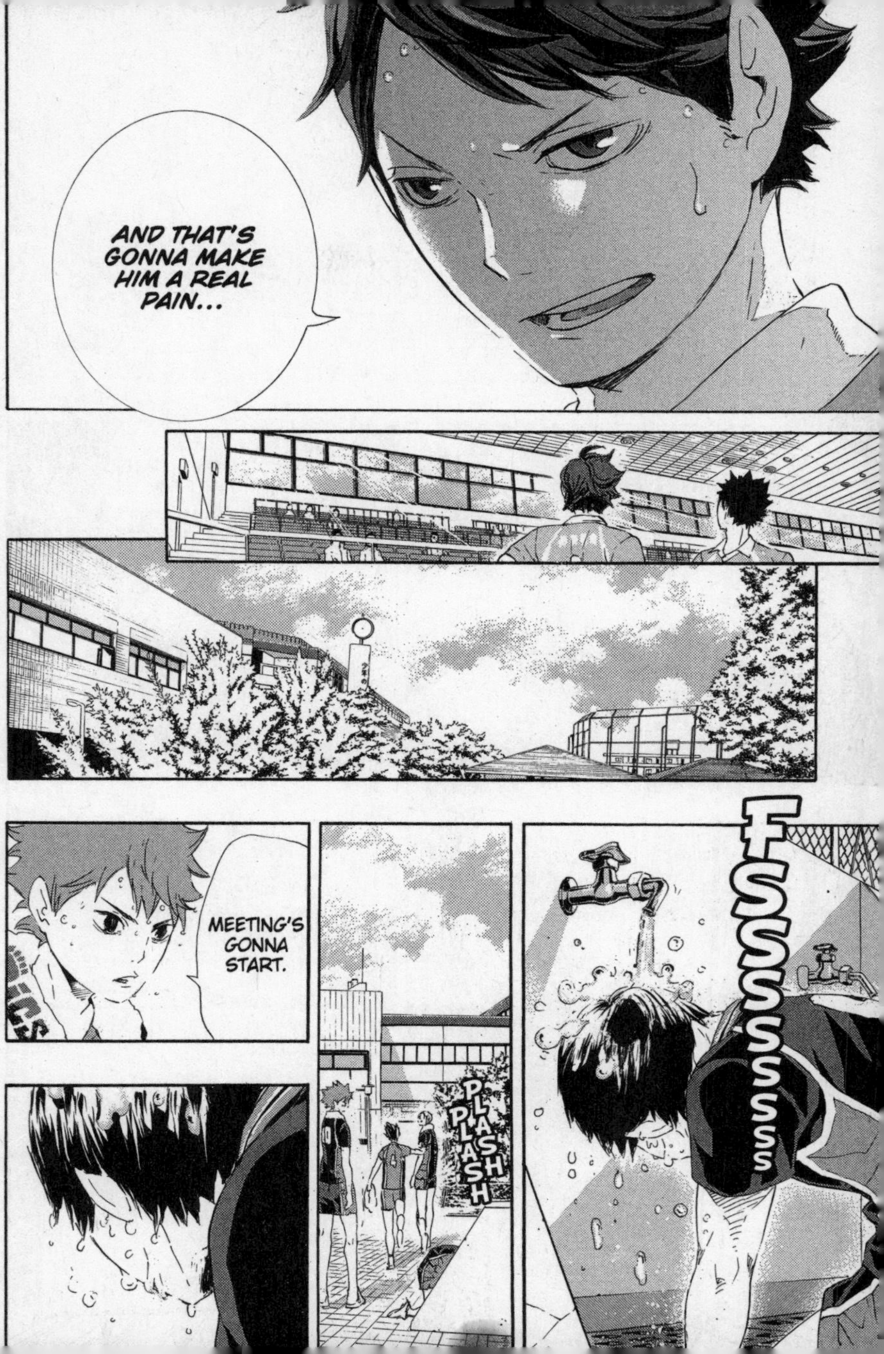
AND THAT'S GONNA MAKE HIM A REAL PAIN...
FSSSSSS
PLASH PLASH
MEETING'S GONNA START.

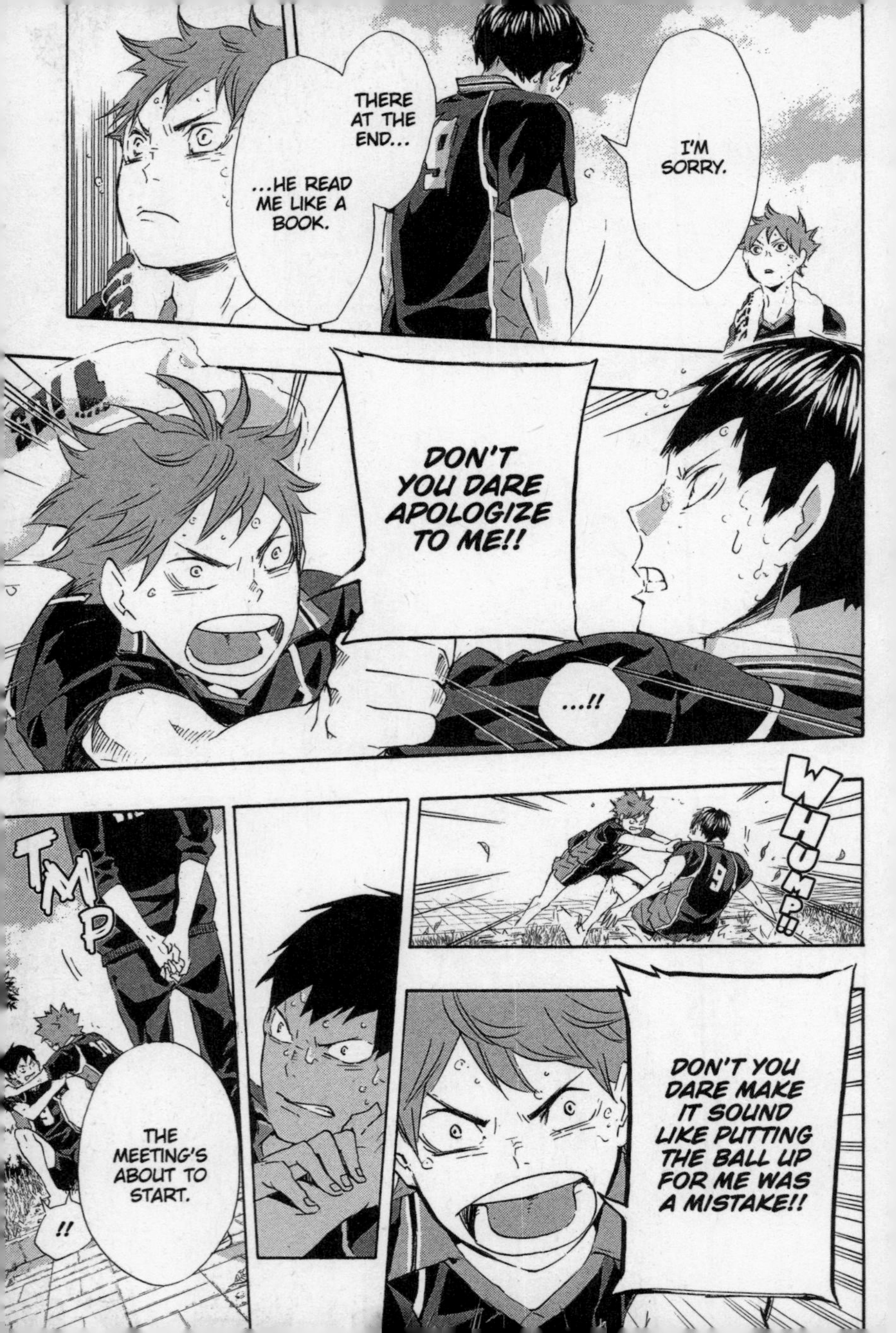
I'M SORRY.
THERE AT THE END...
...HE READ ME LIKE A BOOK.
DON'T YOU DARE APOLOGIZE TO ME!!
...!!
WHUMP!!
DON'T YOU DARE MAKE IT SOUND LIKE PUTTING THE BALL UP FOR ME WAS A MISTAKE!!
TMP
THE MEETING'S ABOUT TO START.
!!

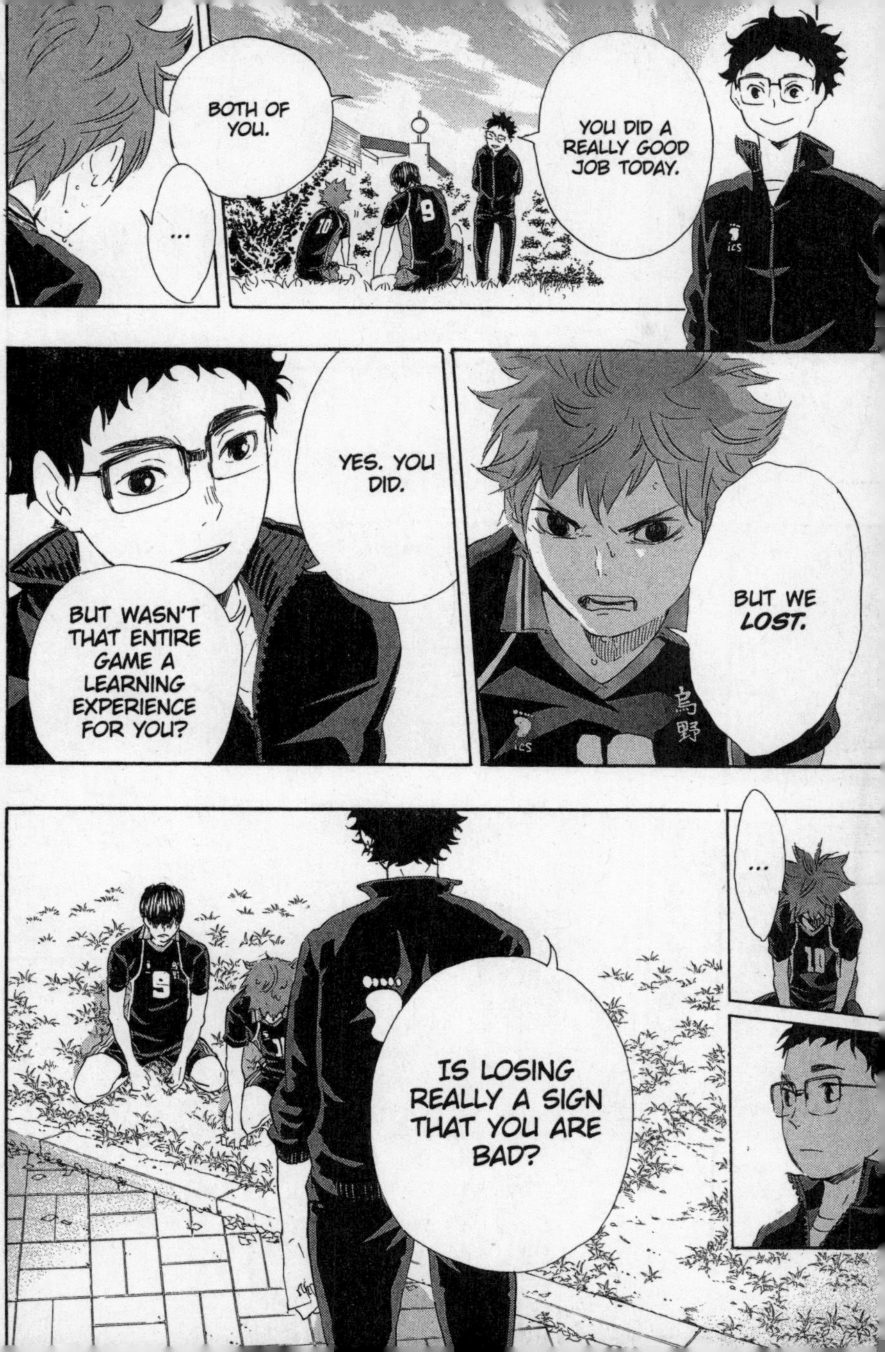
YOU DID A REALLY GOOD JOB TODAY.
BOTH OF YOU.
...
BUT WE LOST.
YES. YOU DID.
BUT WASN'T THAT ENTIRE GAME A LEARNING EXPERIENCE FOR YOU?
...
IS LOSING REALLY A SIGN THAT YOU ARE BAD?

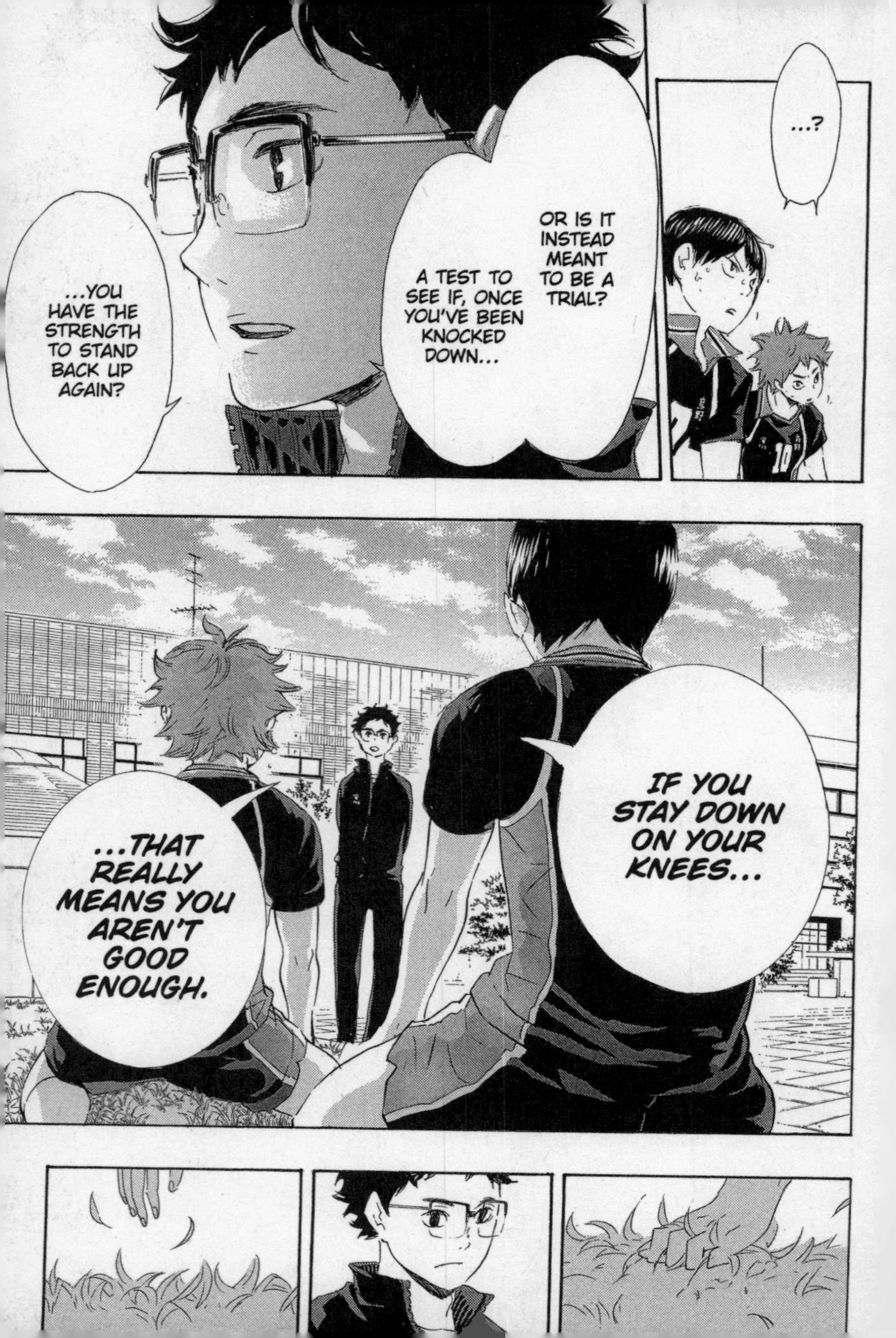
...?
OR IS IT INSTEAD MEANT TO BE A TRIAL?
A TEST TO SEE IF, ONCE YOU'VE BEEN KNOCKED DOWN...
...YOU HAVE THE STRENGTH TO STAND BACK UP AGAIN?
IF YOU STAY DOWN ON YOUR KNEES...
...THAT REALLY MEANS YOU AREN'T GOOD ENOUGH.

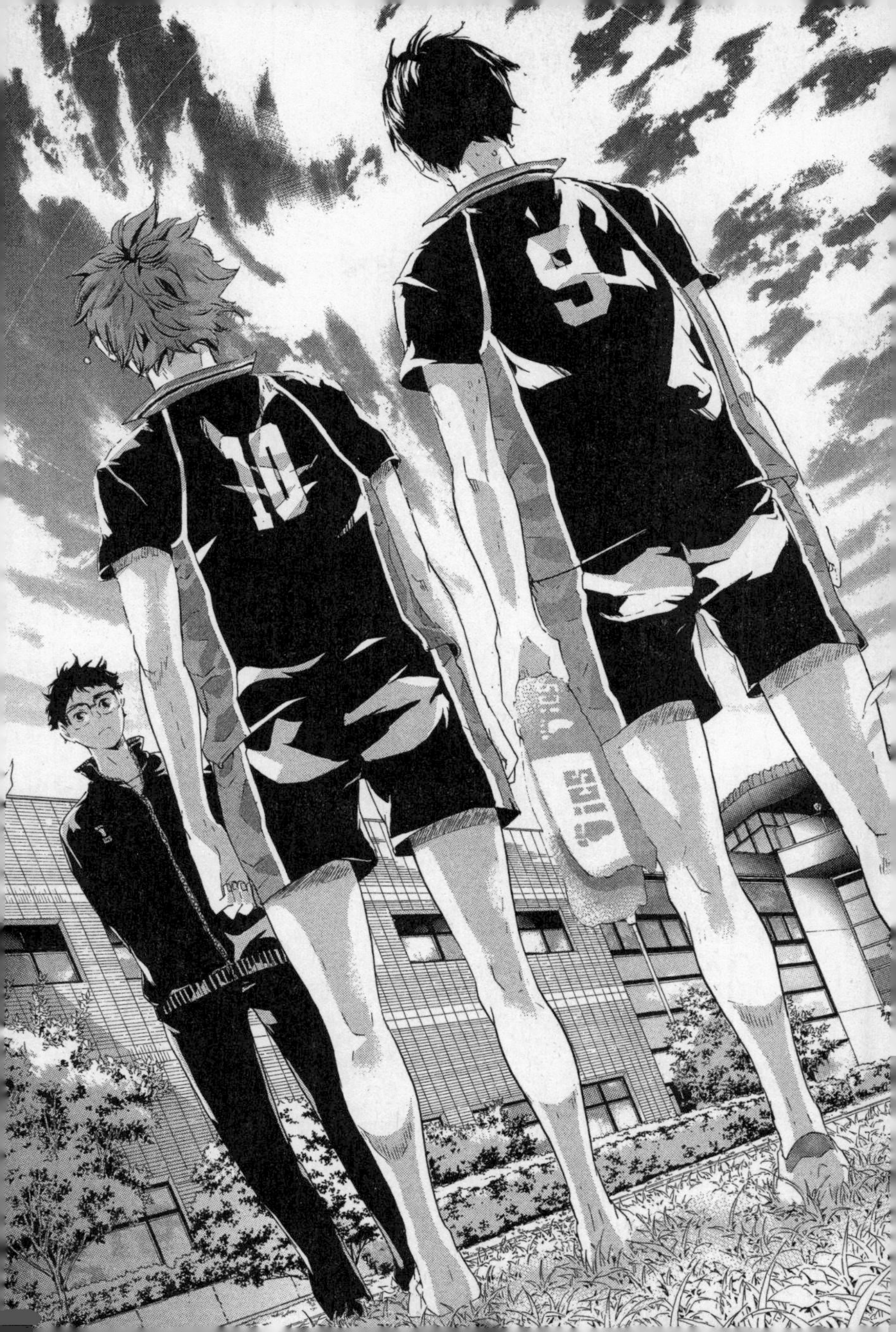

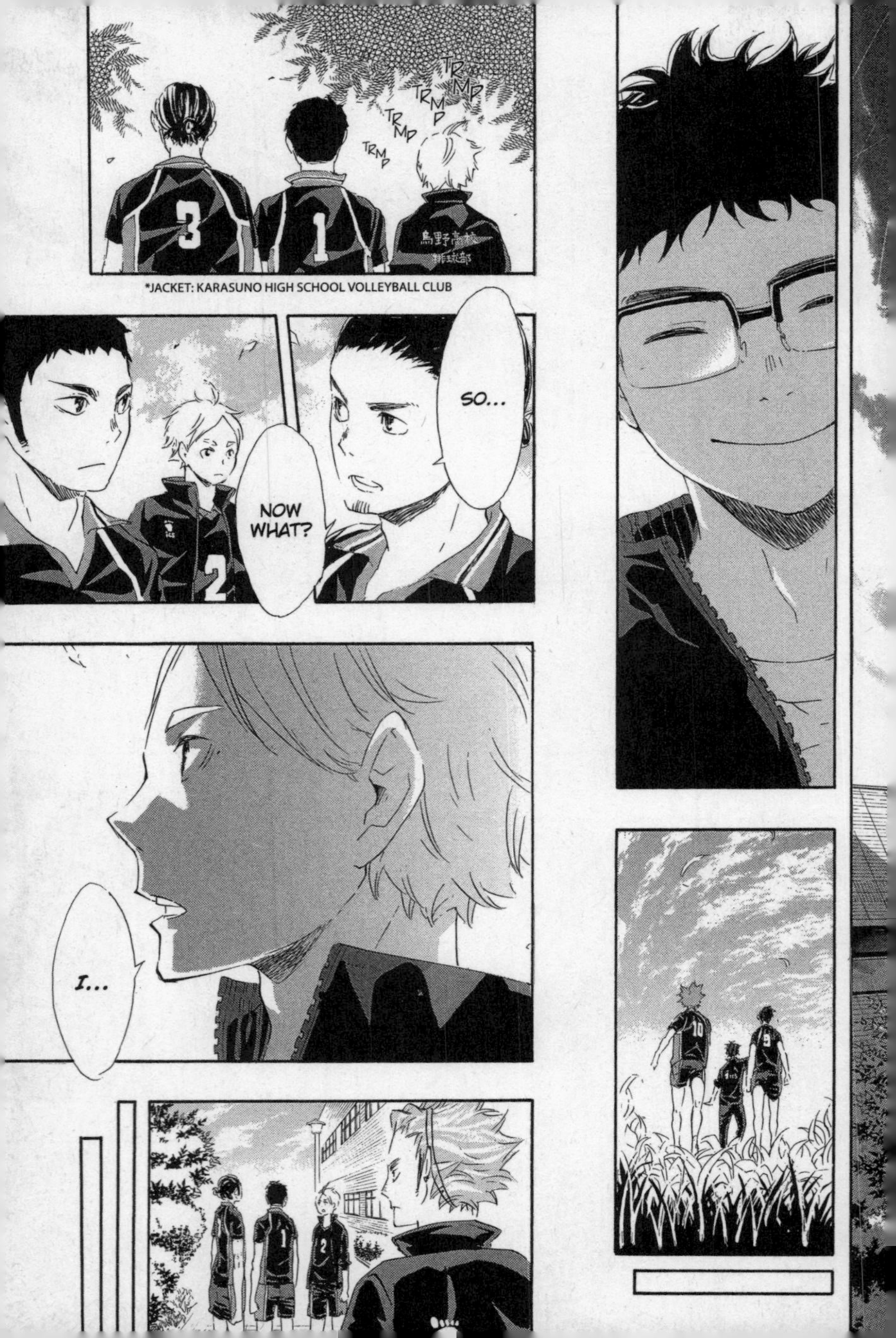
TRMP
TRMP
TRMP
TRMP
鳥野高校
排球部
*JACKET: KARASUNO HIGH SCHOOL VOLLEYBALL CLUB
SO...
NOW WHAT?
I...

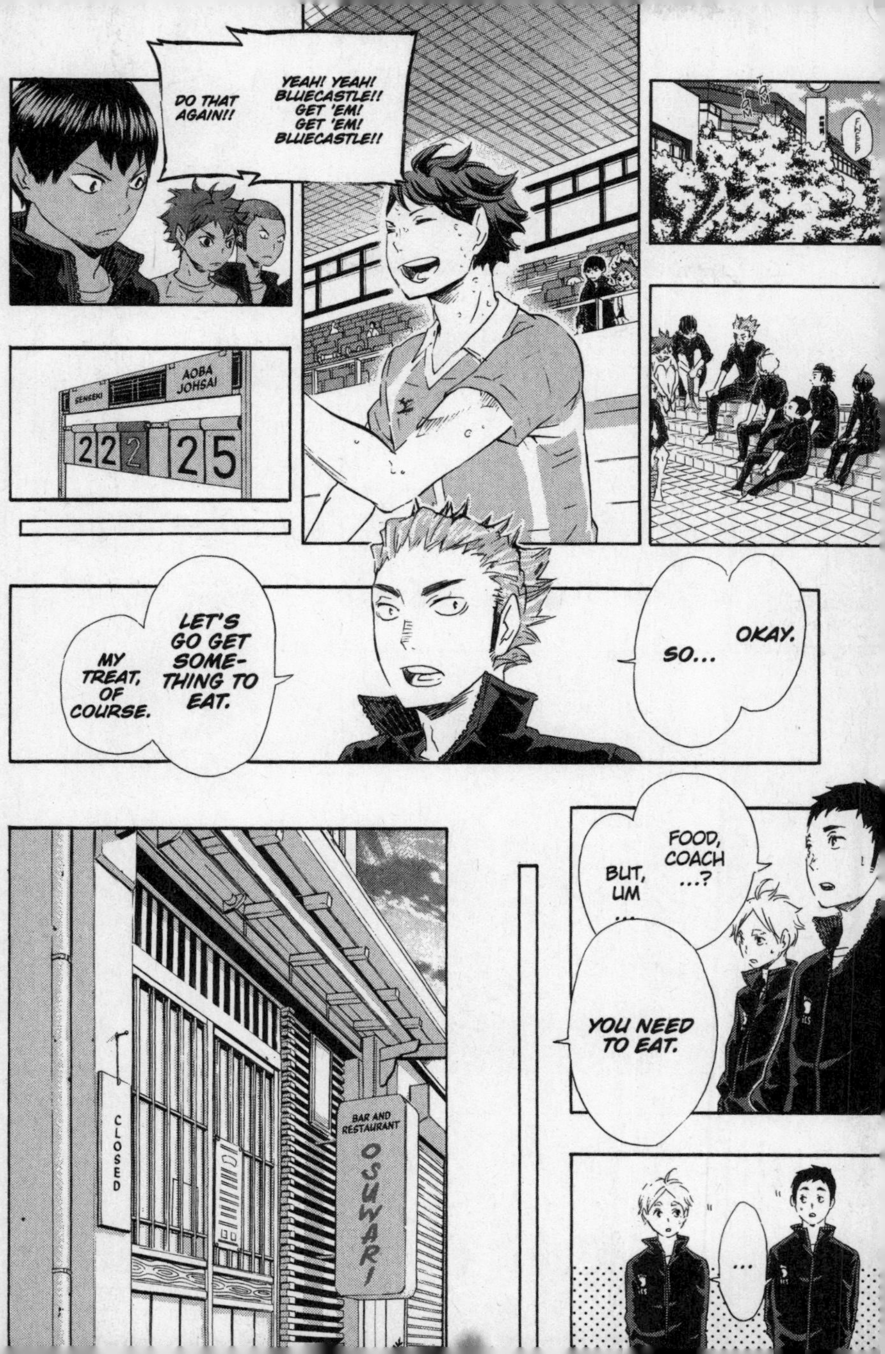
TAM TAM
FINISHED
YEAH! YEAH! BLUECASTLE!! GET 'EM! GET 'EM! BLUECASTLE!!
DO THAT AGAIN!!
SENSEKI
AOBA JOHSAI
22 25
OKAY.
SO...
LET'S GO GET SOME-THING TO EAT.
MY TREAT, OF COURSE.
FOOD, COACH ...?
BUT, UM ...
YOU NEED TO EAT.
...
CLOSED
BAR AND RESTAURANT
OSUWARI

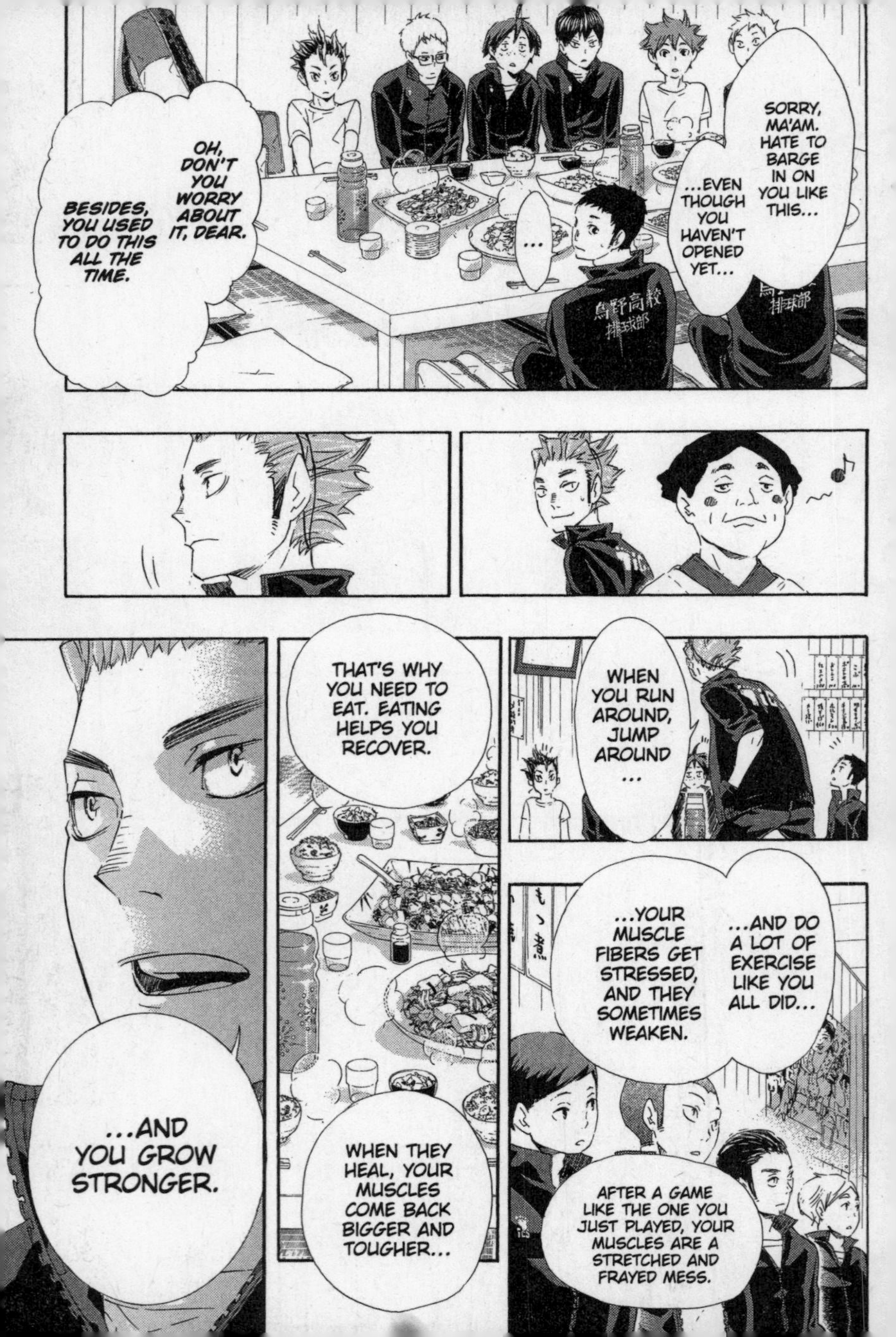
SORRY, MA'AM. HATE TO BARGE IN ON YOU LIKE THIS...
...EVEN THOUGH YOU HAVEN'T OPENED YET...
...
OH, DON'T YOU WORRY ABOUT IT, DEAR.
BESIDES, YOU USED TO DO THIS ALL THE TIME.
WHEN YOU RUN AROUND, JUMP AROUND ...
...AND DO A LOT OF EXERCISE LIKE YOU ALL DID...
...YOUR MUSCLE FIBERS GET STRESSED, AND THEY SOMETIMES WEAKEN.
AFTER A GAME LIKE THE ONE YOU JUST PLAYED, YOUR MUSCLES ARE A STRETCHED AND FRAYED MESS.
THAT'S WHY YOU NEED TO EAT. EATING HELPS YOU RECOVER.
WHEN THEY HEAL, YOUR MUSCLES COME BACK BIGGER AND TOUGHER...
...AND YOU GROW STRONGER.

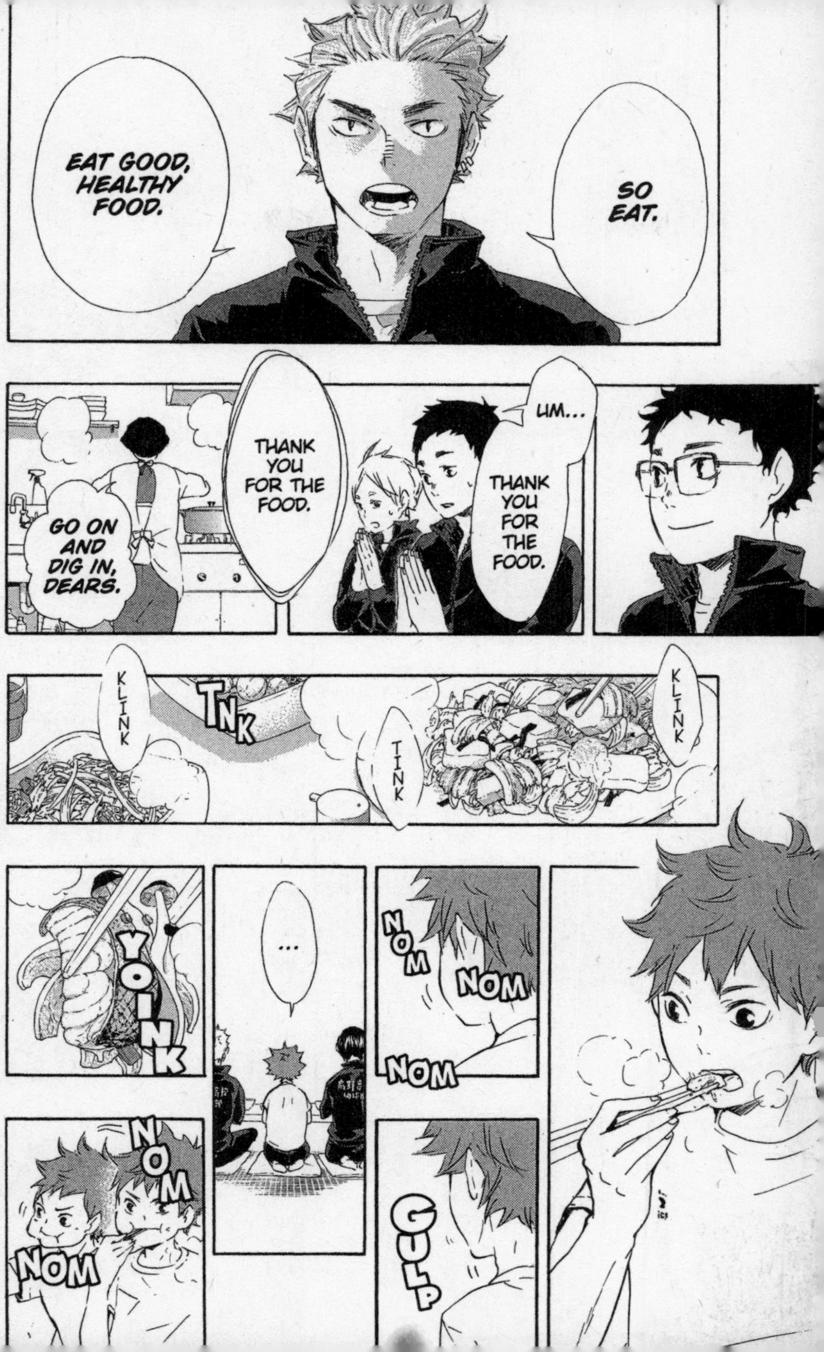
SO EAT.
EAT GOOD, HEALTHY FOOD.
UM...
THANK YOU FOR THE FOOD.
THANK YOU FOR THE FOOD.
GO ON AND DIG IN, DEARS.
KLINK
TINK
TNK
KLINK
NOM NOM
NOM
GULP
...
YOINK
NOM
NOM

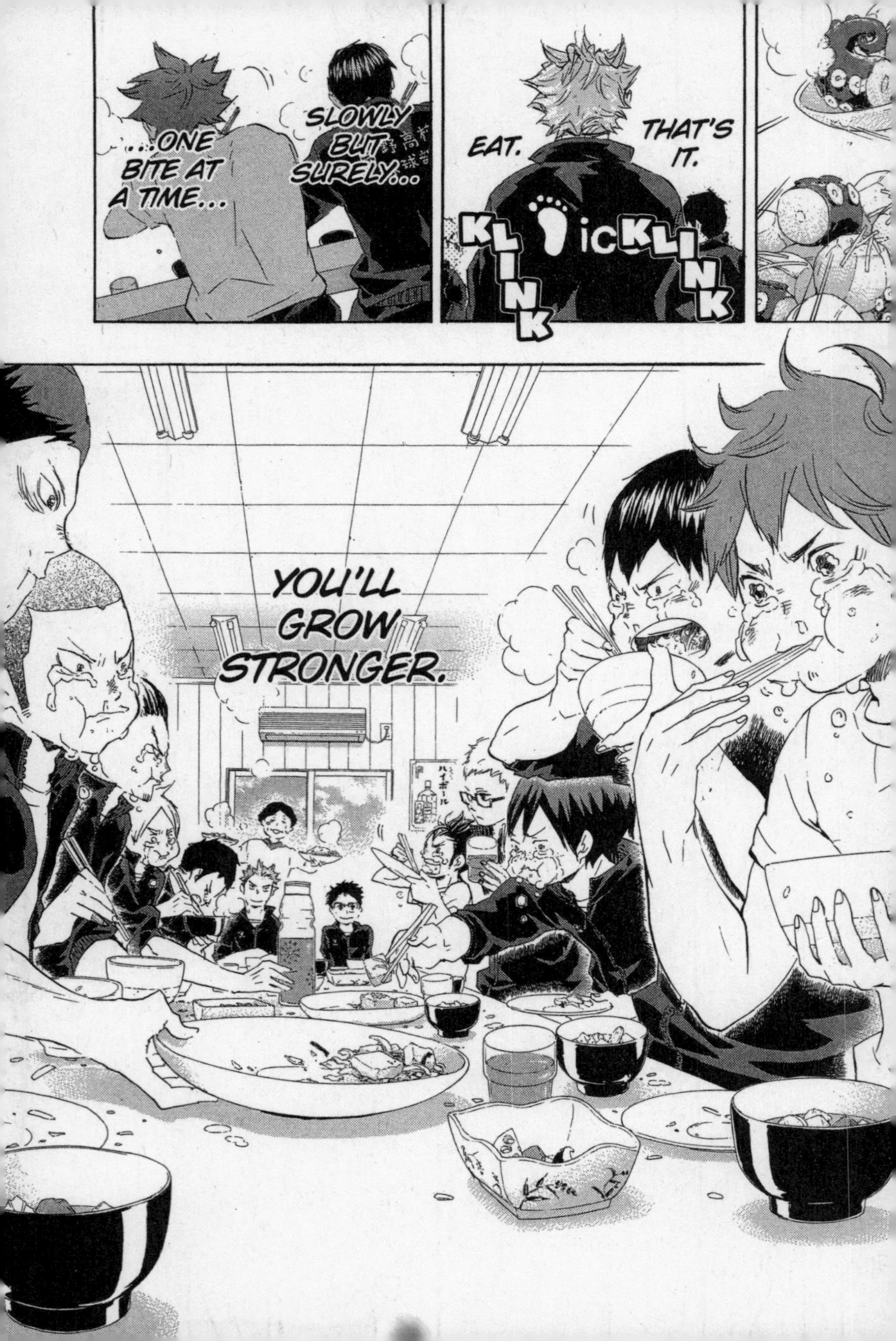
THAT'S IT.
EAT.
KLINK
iC
KLINK
SLOWLY BUT SURELY...
...ONE BITE AT A TIME...
YOU'LL GROW STRONGER.

I'm
gonna
fly now...

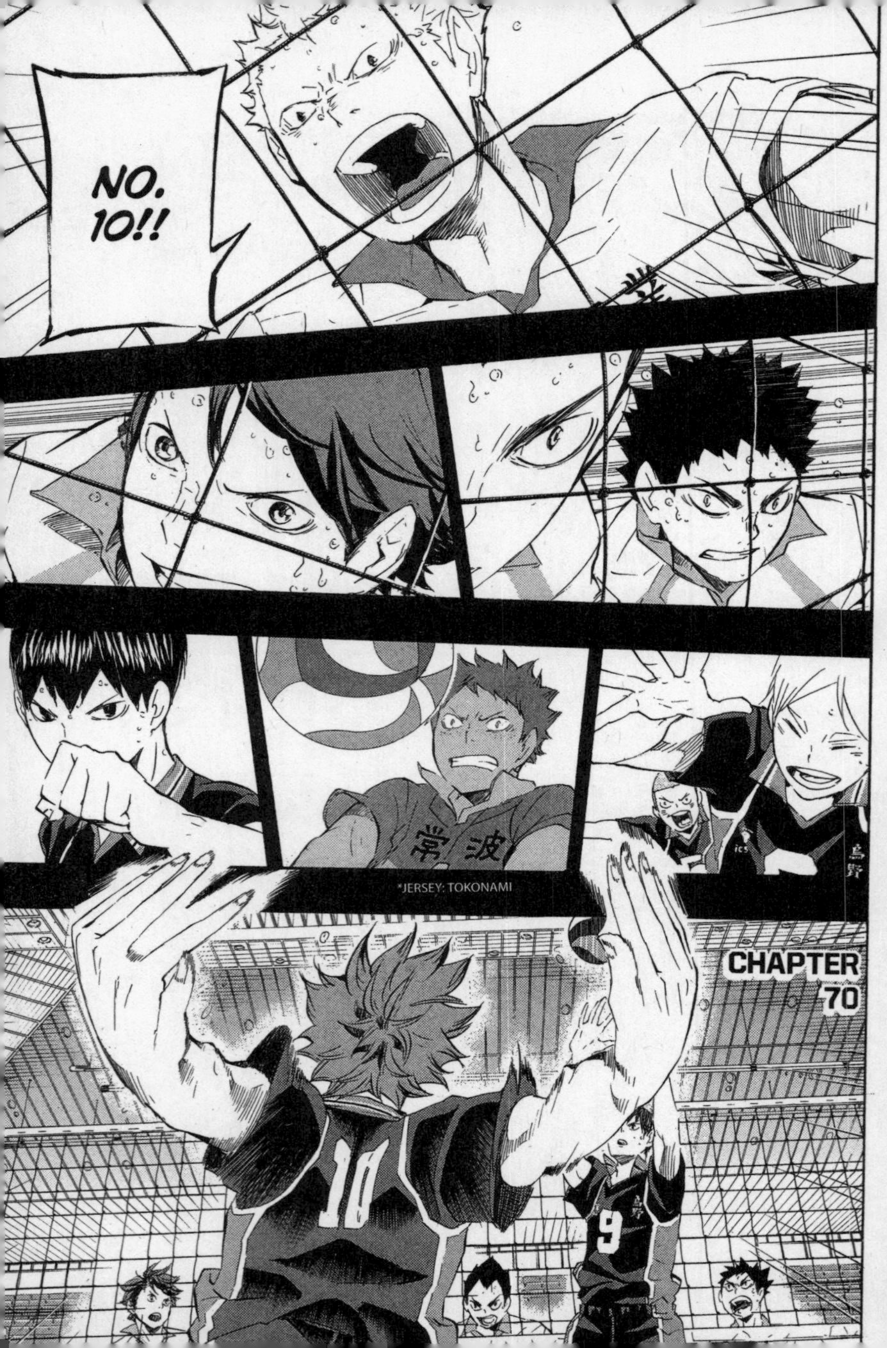
NO. 10!!
常波
*JERSEY: TOKONAMI
CHAPTER 70

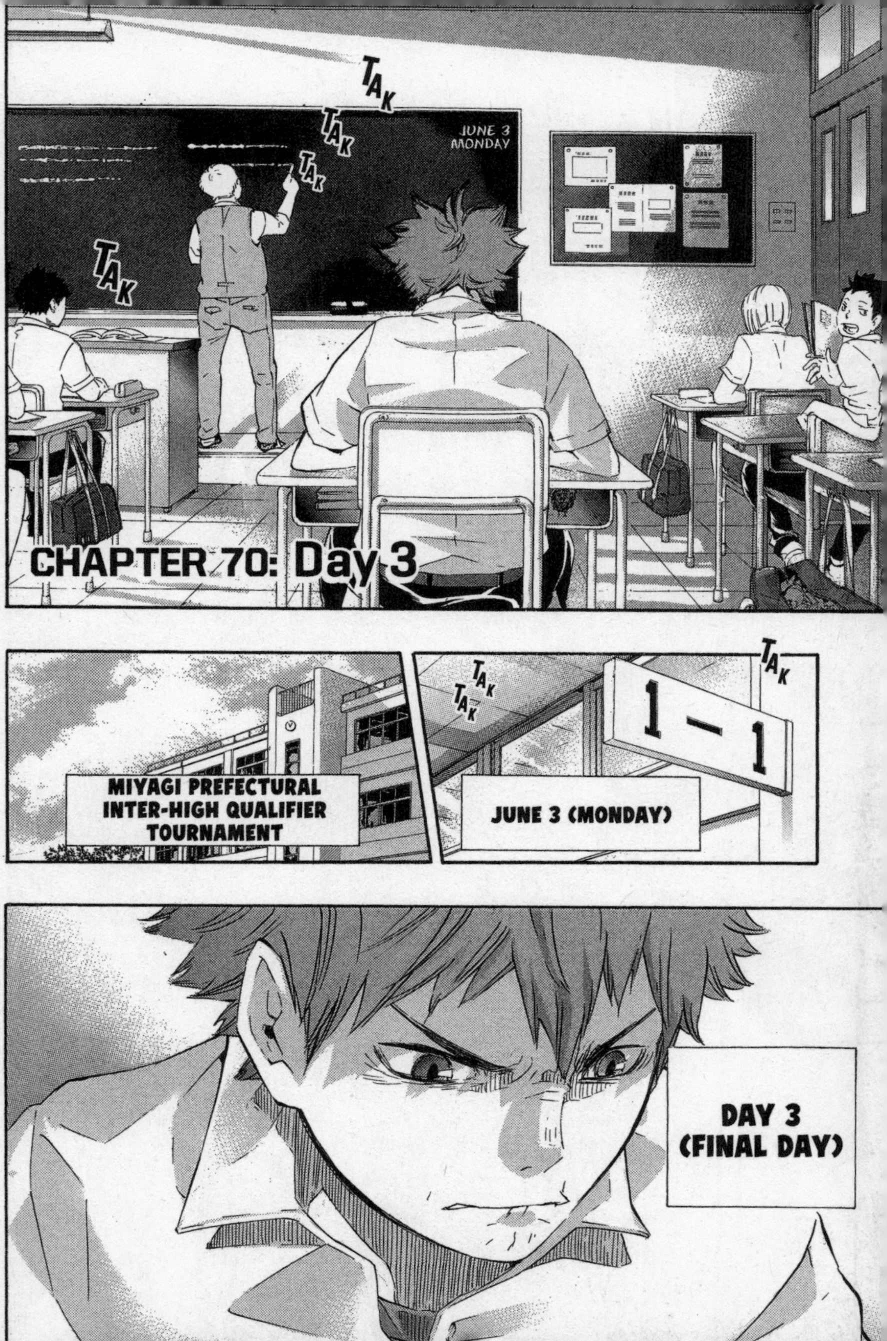
TAK
TAK
JUNE 3
MONDAY
TAK
TAK
CHAPTER 70: Day 3
TAK
1-1
TAK
TAK
JUNE 3 (MONDAY)
MIYAGI PREFECTURAL
INTER-HIGH QUALIFIER
TOURNAMENT
DAY 3
(FINAL DAY)

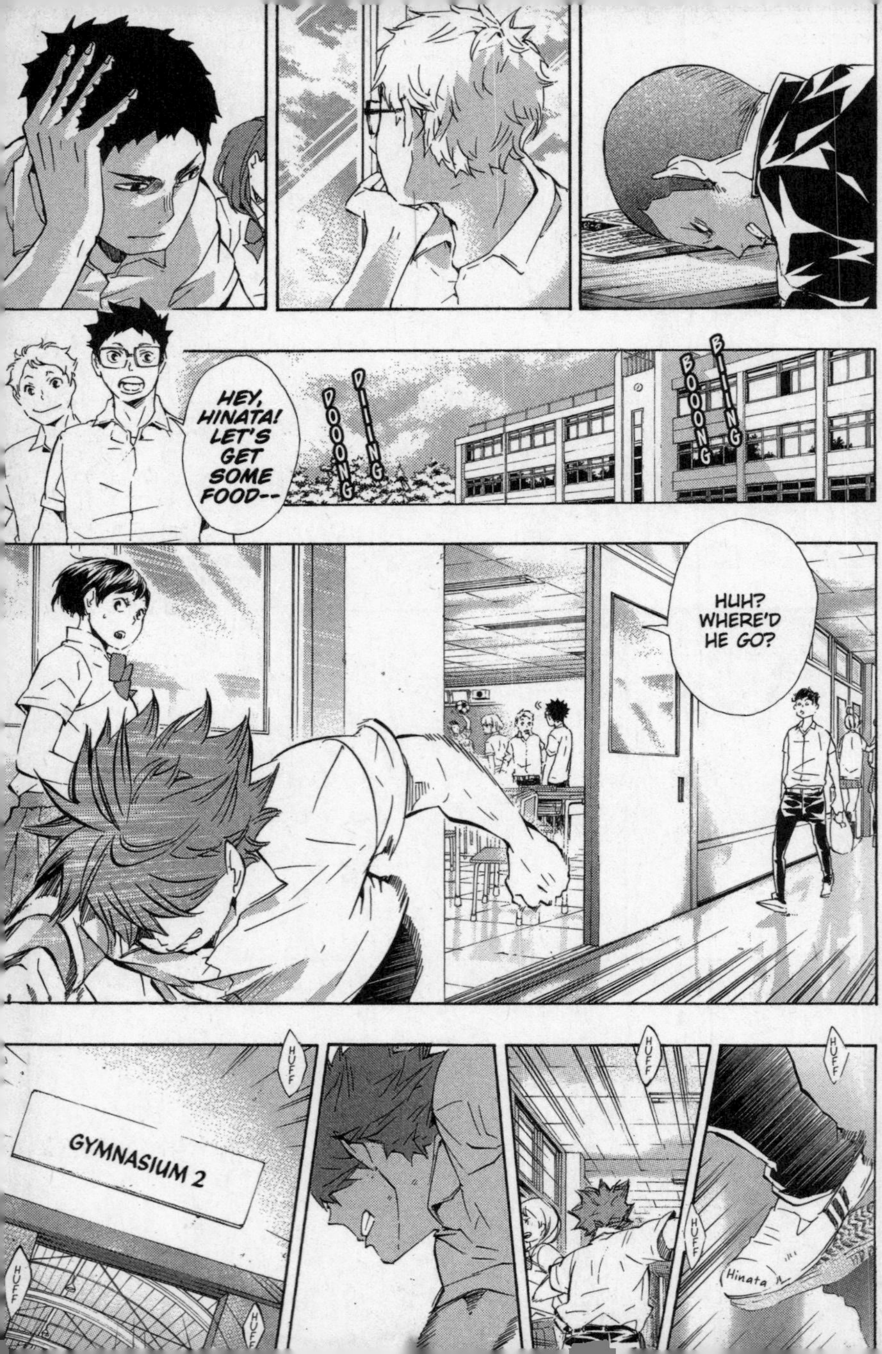
BIIING
BOOONG
DIIING
DOOONG
HEY, HINATA! LET'S GET SOME FOOD--
HUH? WHERE'D HE GO?
HUFF
Hinata
HUFF
HUFF
HUFF
GYMNASIUM 2
HUFF
HUFF

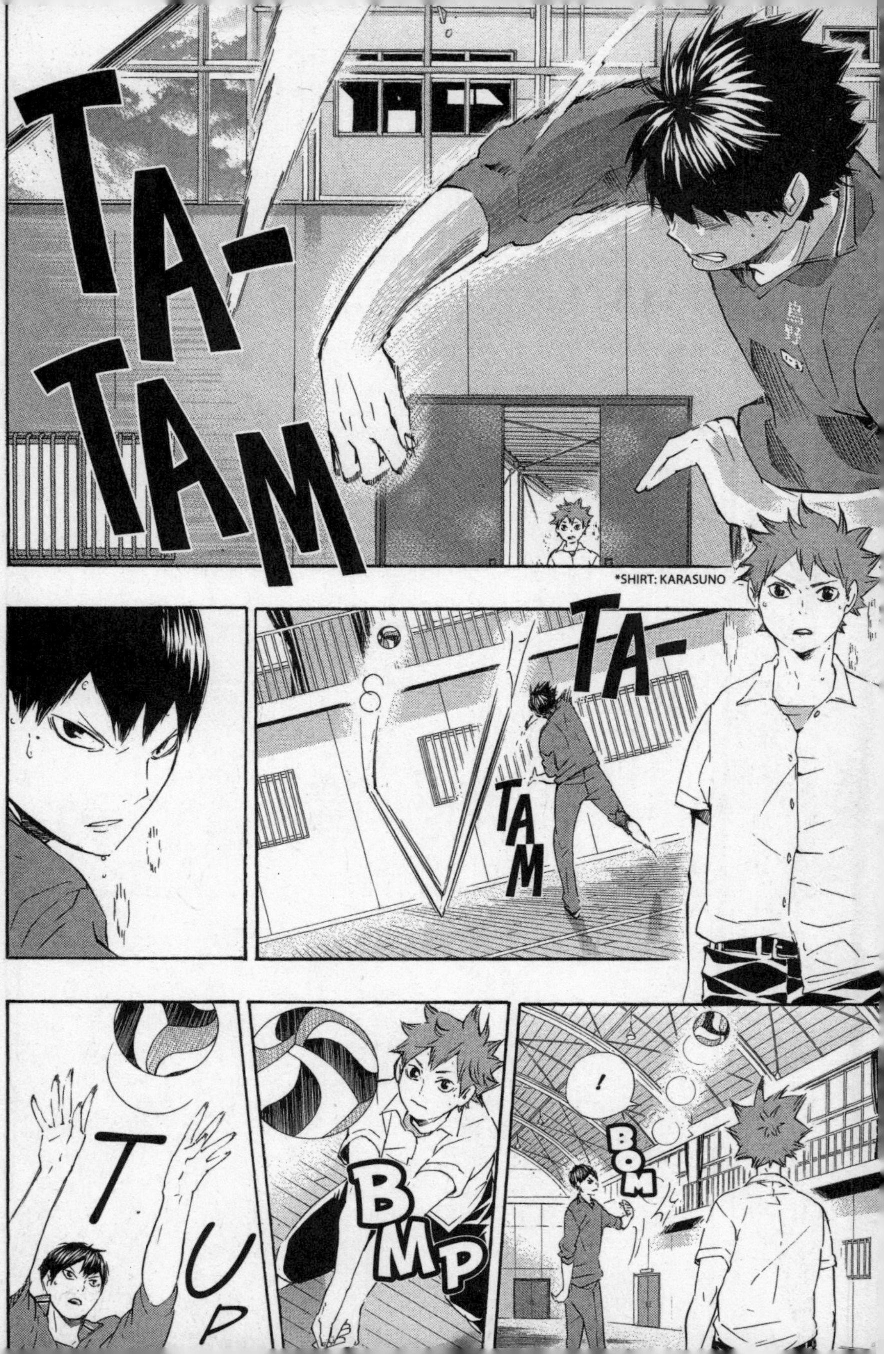
TA-TA-TAM
*SHIRT: KARASUNO
TA-
TAM
!
BOM
BMP
TUP

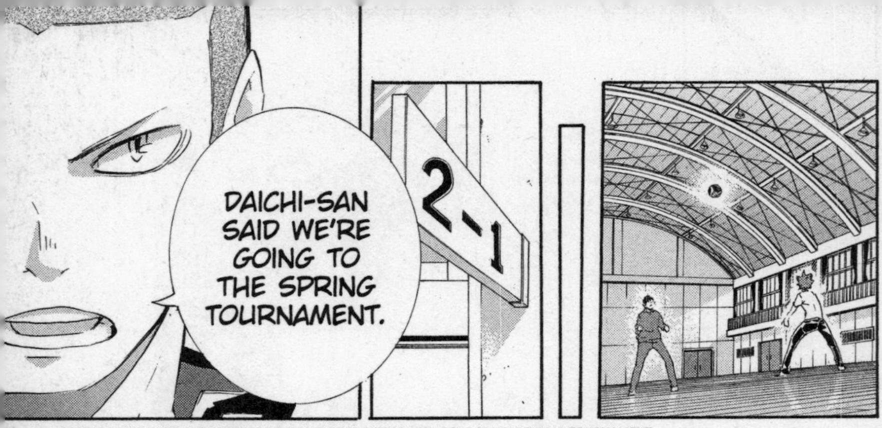
2-1
DAICHI-SAN SAID WE'RE GOING TO THE SPRING TOURNAMENT.

*SPRING TOURNAMENT IS SHORT FOR THE NATIONAL SPRING HIGH SCHOOL VOLLEYBALL TOURNAMENT.

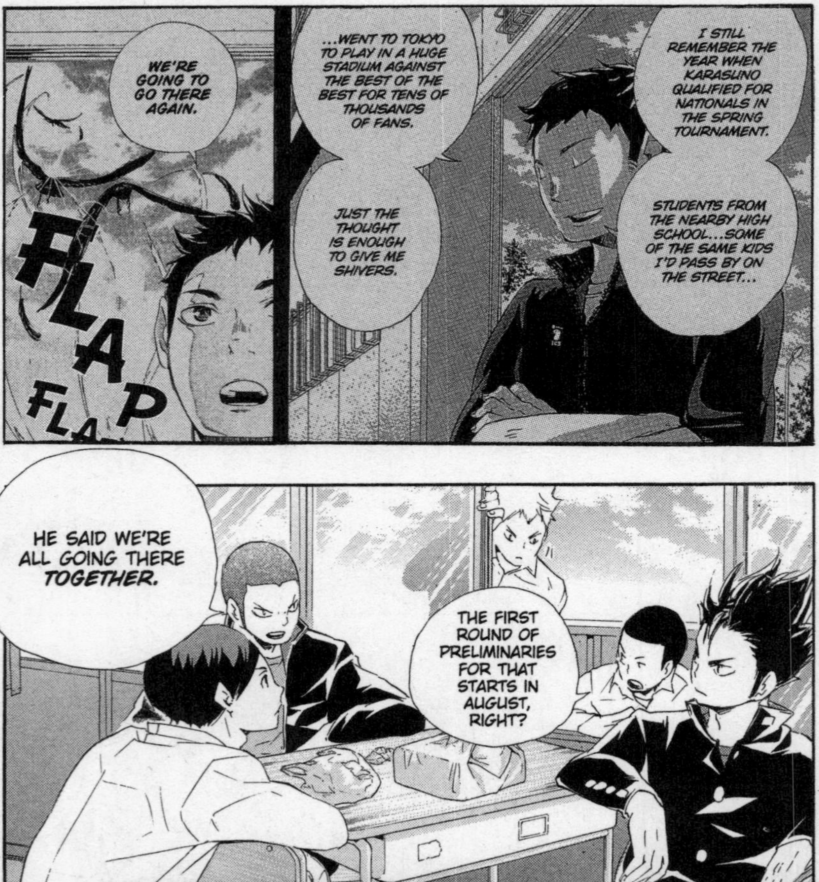
I STILL REMEMBER THE YEAR WHEN KARASUNO QUALIFIED FOR NATIONALS IN THE SPRING TOURNAMENT.
STUDENTS FROM THE NEARBY HIGH SCHOOL...SOME OF THE SAME KIDS I'D PASS BY ON THE STREET...
...WENT TO TOKYO TO PLAY IN A HUGE STADIUM AGAINST THE BEST OF THE BEST FOR TENS OF THOUSANDS OF FANS.
JUST THE THOUGHT IS ENOUGH TO GIVE ME SHIVERS.
WE'RE GOING TO GO THERE AGAIN.
FLAP
FLA
HE SAID WE'RE ALL GOING THERE *TOGETHER.*
THE FIRST ROUND OF PRELIMINARIES FOR THAT STARTS IN AUGUST, RIGHT?

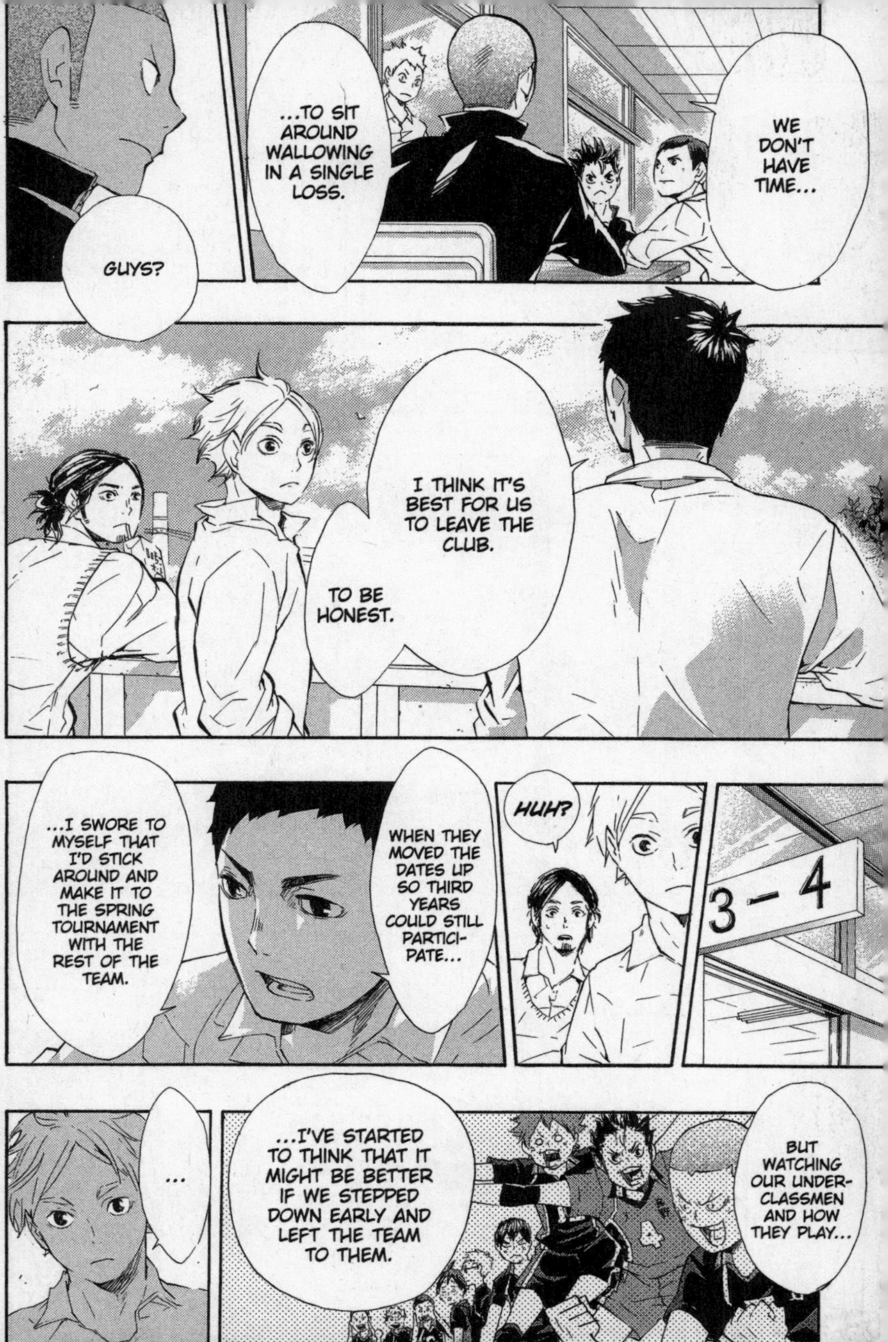
WE DON'T HAVE TIME...
...TO SIT AROUND WALLOWING IN A SINGLE LOSS.
GUYS?
I THINK IT'S BEST FOR US TO LEAVE THE CLUB.
TO BE HONEST.
3 – 4
HUH?
WHEN THEY MOVED THE DATES UP SO THIRD YEARS COULD STILL PARTICI-PATE...
...I SWORE TO MYSELF THAT I'D STICK AROUND AND MAKE IT TO THE SPRING TOURNAMENT WITH THE REST OF THE TEAM.
BUT WATCHING OUR UNDER-CLASSMEN AND HOW THEY PLAY...
...I'VE STARTED TO THINK THAT IT MIGHT BE BETTER IF WE STEPPED DOWN EARLY AND LEFT THE TEAM TO THEM.
...

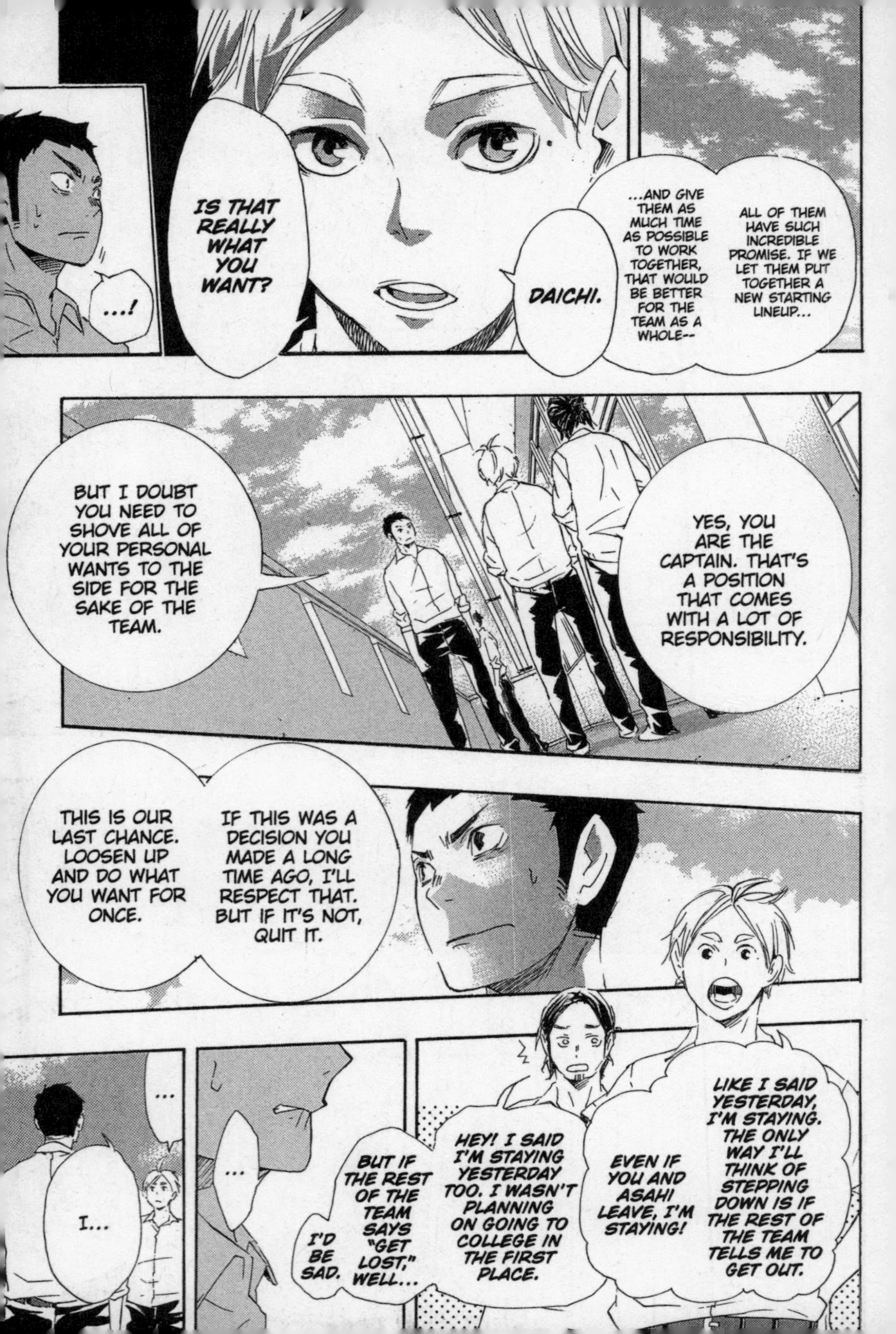
ALL OF THEM HAVE SUCH INCREDIBLE PROMISE. IF WE LET THEM PUT TOGETHER A NEW STARTING LINEUP...
...AND GIVE THEM AS MUCH TIME AS POSSIBLE TO WORK TOGETHER, THAT WOULD BE BETTER FOR THE TEAM AS A WHOLE--
DAICHI.
IS THAT REALLY WHAT YOU WANT?
...!
YES, YOU ARE THE CAPTAIN. THAT'S A POSITION THAT COMES WITH A LOT OF RESPONSIBILITY.
BUT I DOUBT YOU NEED TO SHOVE ALL OF YOUR PERSONAL WANTS TO THE SIDE FOR THE SAKE OF THE TEAM.
IF THIS WAS A DECISION YOU MADE A LONG TIME AGO, I'LL RESPECT THAT. BUT IF IT'S NOT, QUIT IT.
THIS IS OUR LAST CHANCE. LOOSEN UP AND DO WHAT YOU WANT FOR ONCE.
LIKE I SAID YESTERDAY, I'M STAYING. THE ONLY WAY I'LL THINK OF STEPPING DOWN IS IF THE REST OF THE TEAM TELLS ME TO GET OUT.
EVEN IF YOU AND ASAHI LEAVE, I'M STAYING!
HEY! I SAID I'M STAYING YESTERDAY TOO. I WASN'T PLANNING ON GOING TO COLLEGE IN THE FIRST PLACE.
BUT IF THE REST OF THE TEAM SAYS "GET LOST," WELL...
I'D BE SAD.
...
...
I...

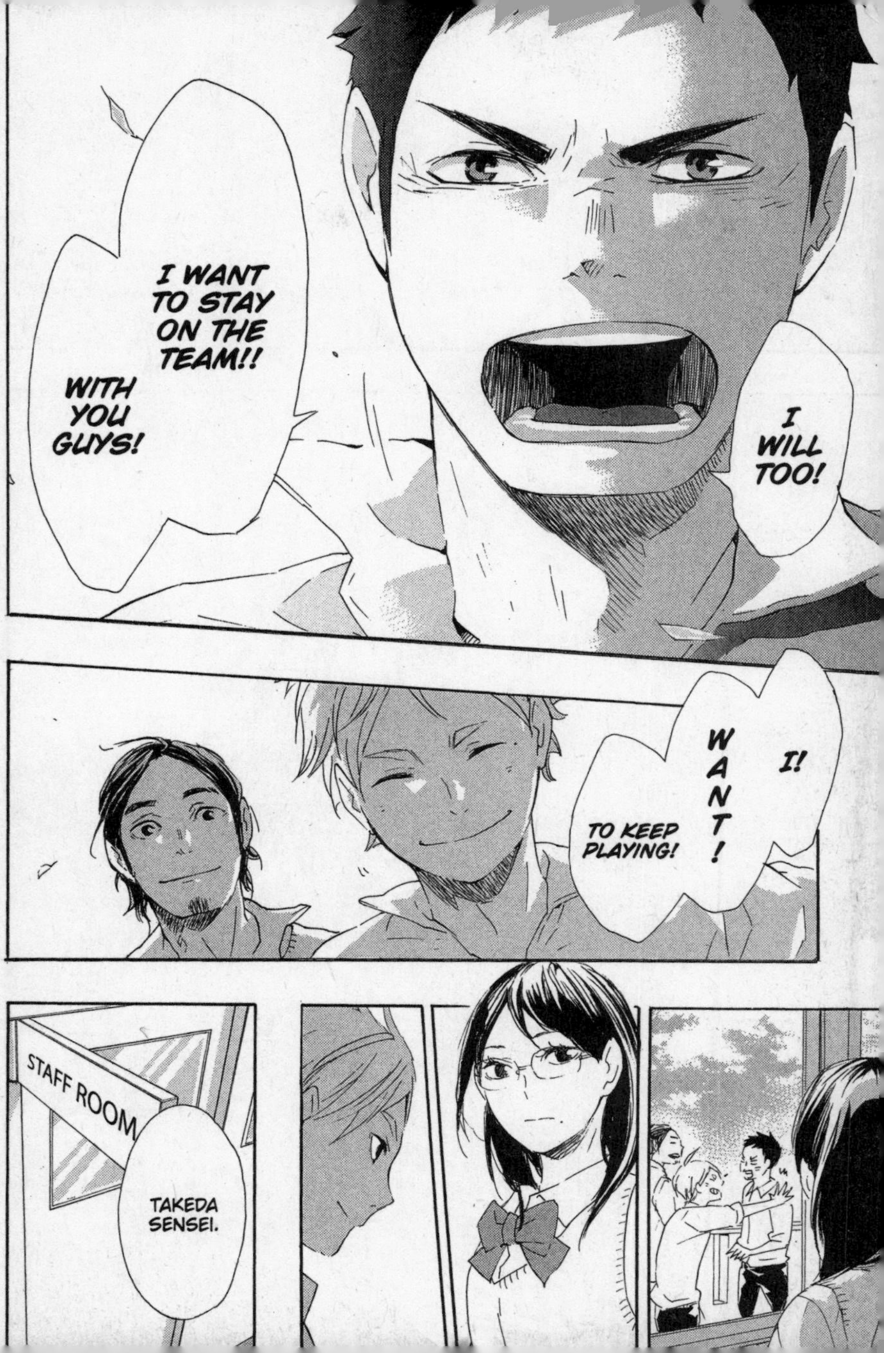
I WILL TOO!
I WANT TO STAY ON THE TEAM!!
WITH YOU GUYS!
I!
WANT!
TO KEEP PLAYING!
STAFF ROOM
TAKEDA SENSEI.

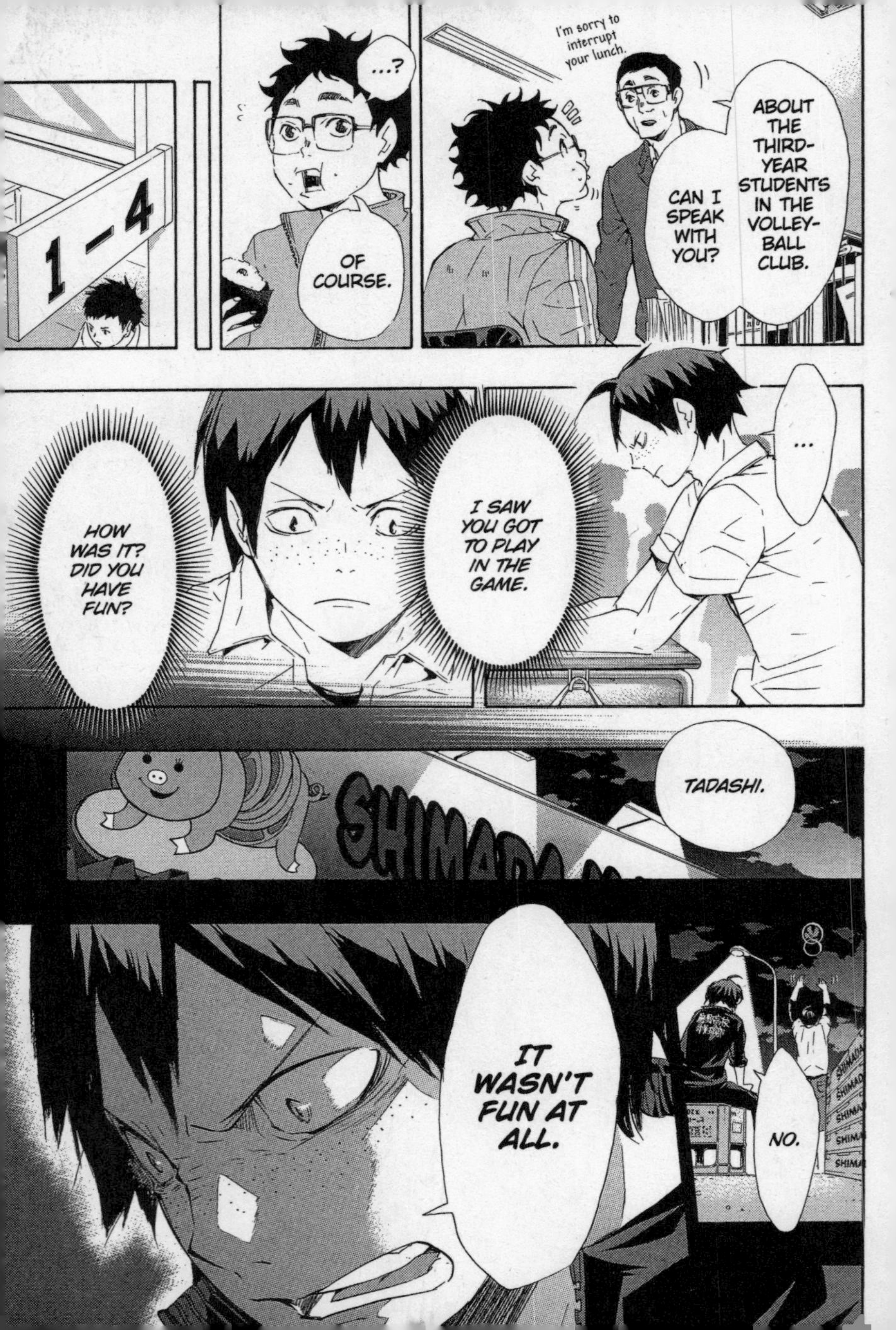
I'm sorry to interrupt your lunch.
ABOUT THE THIRD-YEAR STUDENTS IN THE VOLLEY-BALL CLUB.
CAN I SPEAK WITH YOU?
...?
OF COURSE.
...
I SAW YOU GOT TO PLAY IN THE GAME.
HOW WAS IT? DID YOU HAVE FUN?
TADASHI.
NO.
IT WASN'T FUN AT ALL.

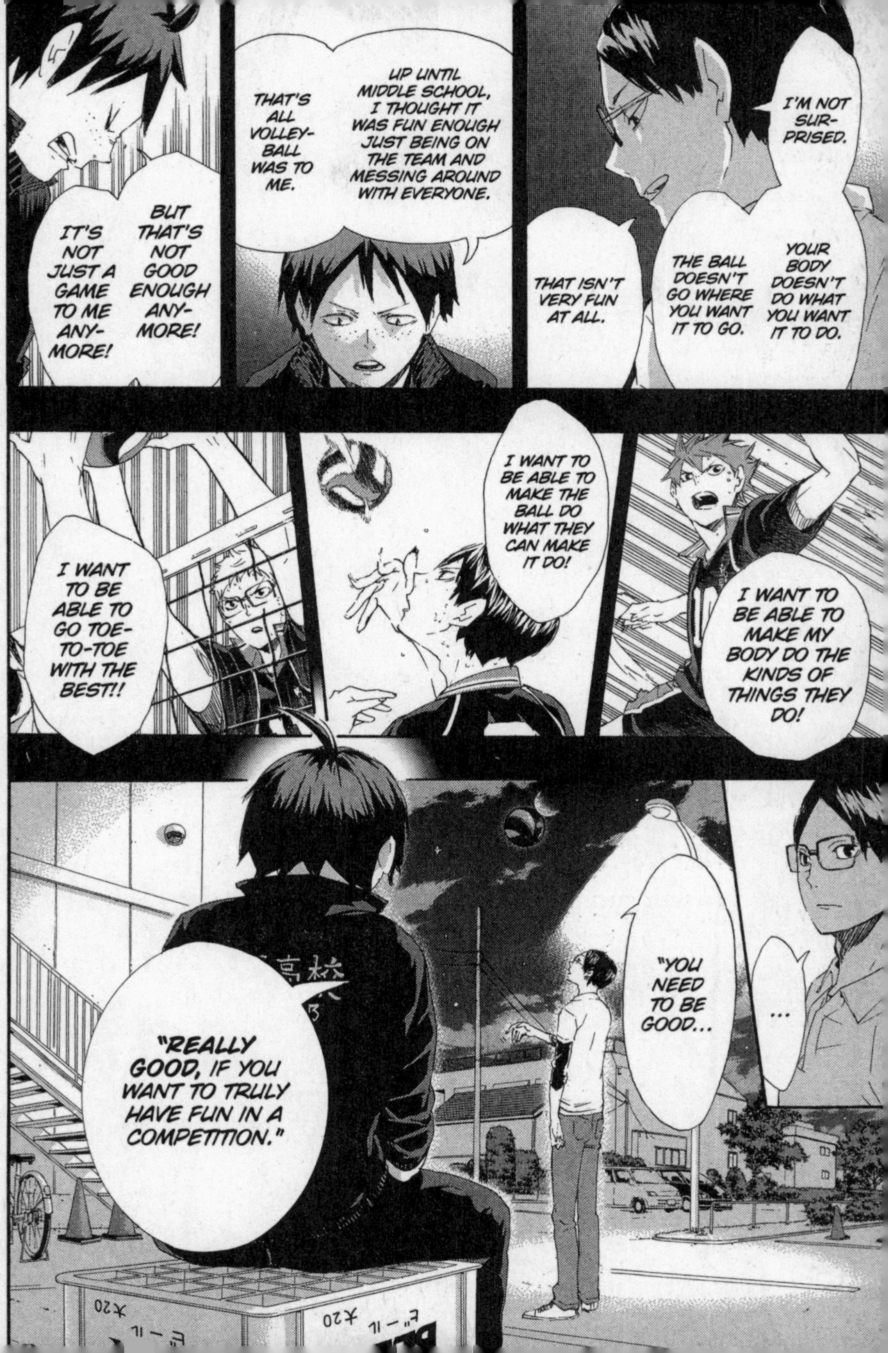
I'M NOT SURPRISED.
YOUR BODY DOESN'T DO WHAT YOU WANT IT TO DO.
THE BALL DOESN'T GO WHERE YOU WANT IT TO GO.
THAT ISN'T VERY FUN AT ALL.
UP UNTIL MIDDLE SCHOOL, I THOUGHT IT WAS FUN ENOUGH JUST BEING ON THE TEAM AND MESSING AROUND WITH EVERYONE.
THAT'S ALL VOLLEYBALL WAS TO ME.
BUT THAT'S NOT GOOD ENOUGH ANYMORE!
IT'S NOT JUST A GAME TO ME ANYMORE!
I WANT TO BE ABLE TO MAKE MY BODY DO THE KINDS OF THINGS THEY DO!
I WANT TO BE ABLE TO MAKE THE BALL DO WHAT THEY CAN MAKE IT DO!
I WANT TO BE ABLE TO GO TOE-TO-TOE WITH THE BEST!!
...
"YOU NEED TO BE GOOD...
"REALLY GOOD, IF YOU WANT TO TRULY HAVE FUN IN A COMPETITION."

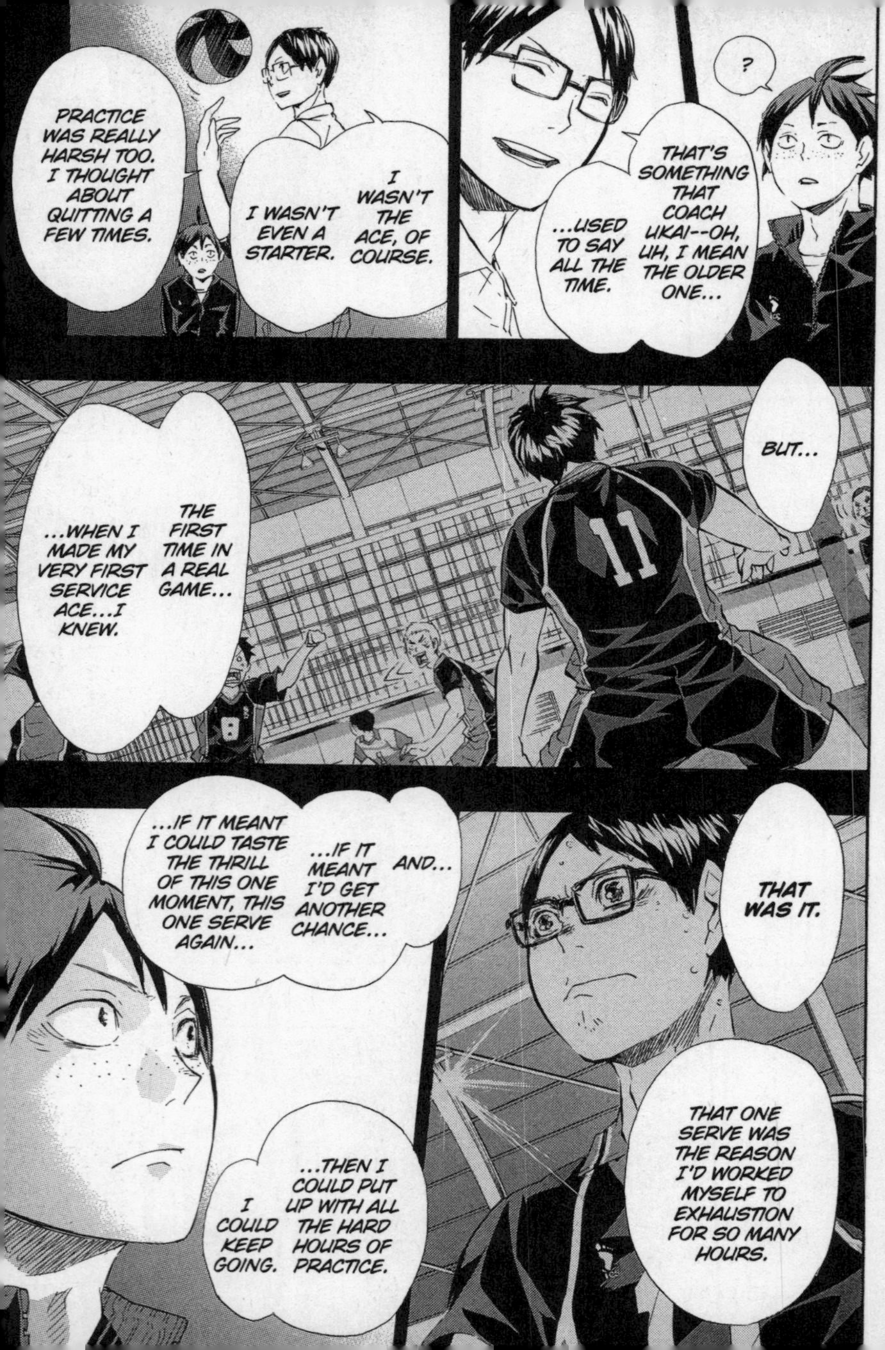
?
THAT'S SOMETHING THAT COACH UKAI--OH, UH, I MEAN THE OLDER ONE...
...USED TO SAY ALL THE TIME.
I WASN'T THE ACE, OF COURSE.
I WASN'T EVEN A STARTER.
PRACTICE WAS REALLY HARSH TOO. I THOUGHT ABOUT QUITTING A FEW TIMES.
BUT...
THE FIRST TIME IN A REAL GAME...
...WHEN I MADE MY VERY FIRST SERVICE ACE...I KNEW.
THAT WAS IT.
THAT ONE SERVE WAS THE REASON I'D WORKED MYSELF TO EXHAUSTION FOR SO MANY HOURS.
AND...
...IF IT MEANT I'D GET ANOTHER CHANCE...
...IF IT MEANT I COULD TASTE THE THRILL OF THIS ONE MOMENT, THIS ONE SERVE AGAIN...
...THEN I COULD PUT UP WITH ALL THE HARD HOURS OF PRACTICE.
I COULD KEEP GOING.

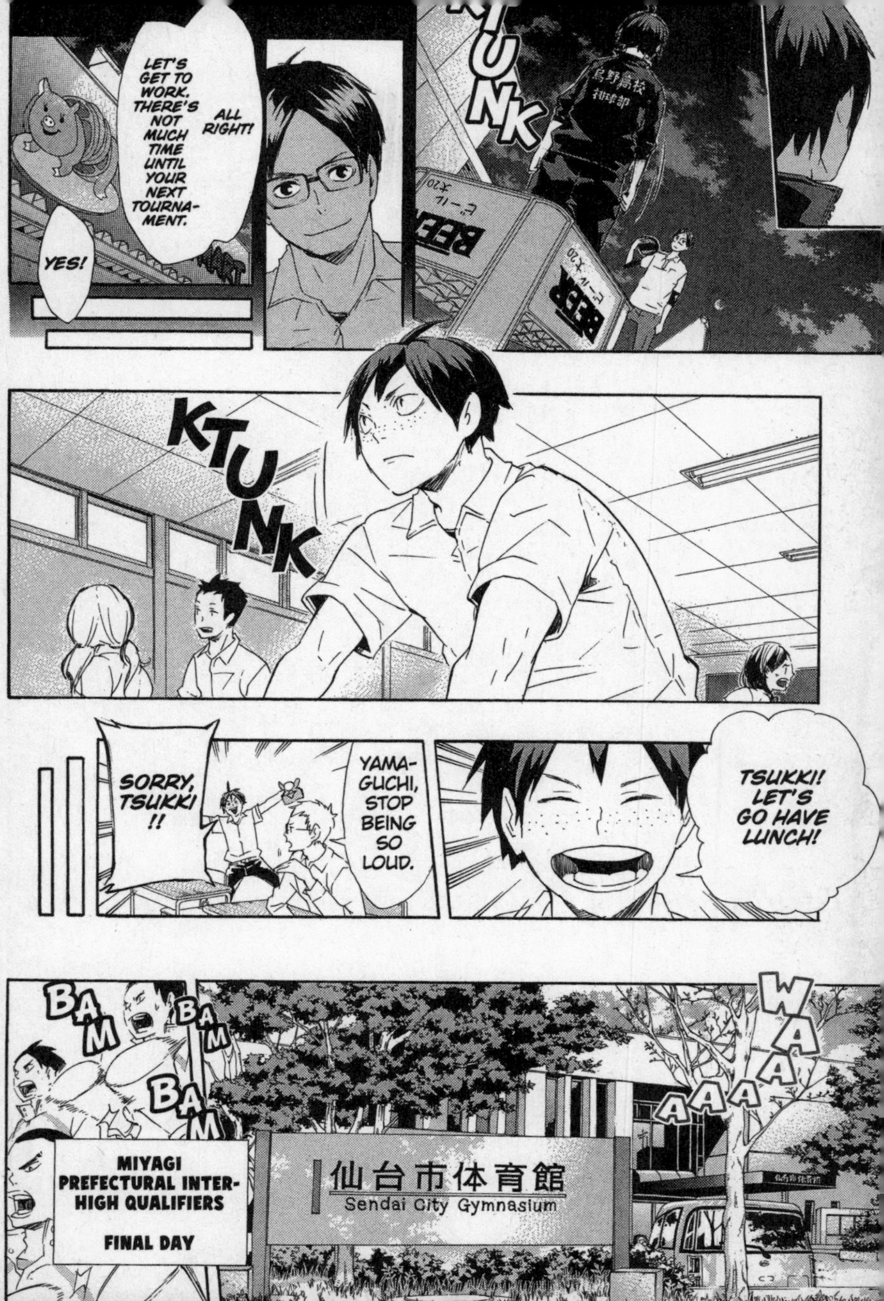
KTUNK
LET'S GET TO WORK. THERE'S NOT MUCH TIME UNTIL YOUR NEXT TOURNAMENT.
ALL RIGHT!
YES!
KTUNK
TSUKKI! LET'S GO HAVE LUNCH!
YAMAGUCHI, STOP BEING SO LOUD.
SORRY, TSUKKI!!
WAAAAAA
仙台市体育館
Sendai City Gymnasium
BAM BAM BAM
MIYAGI PREFECTURAL INTER-HIGH QUALIFIERS
FINAL DAY

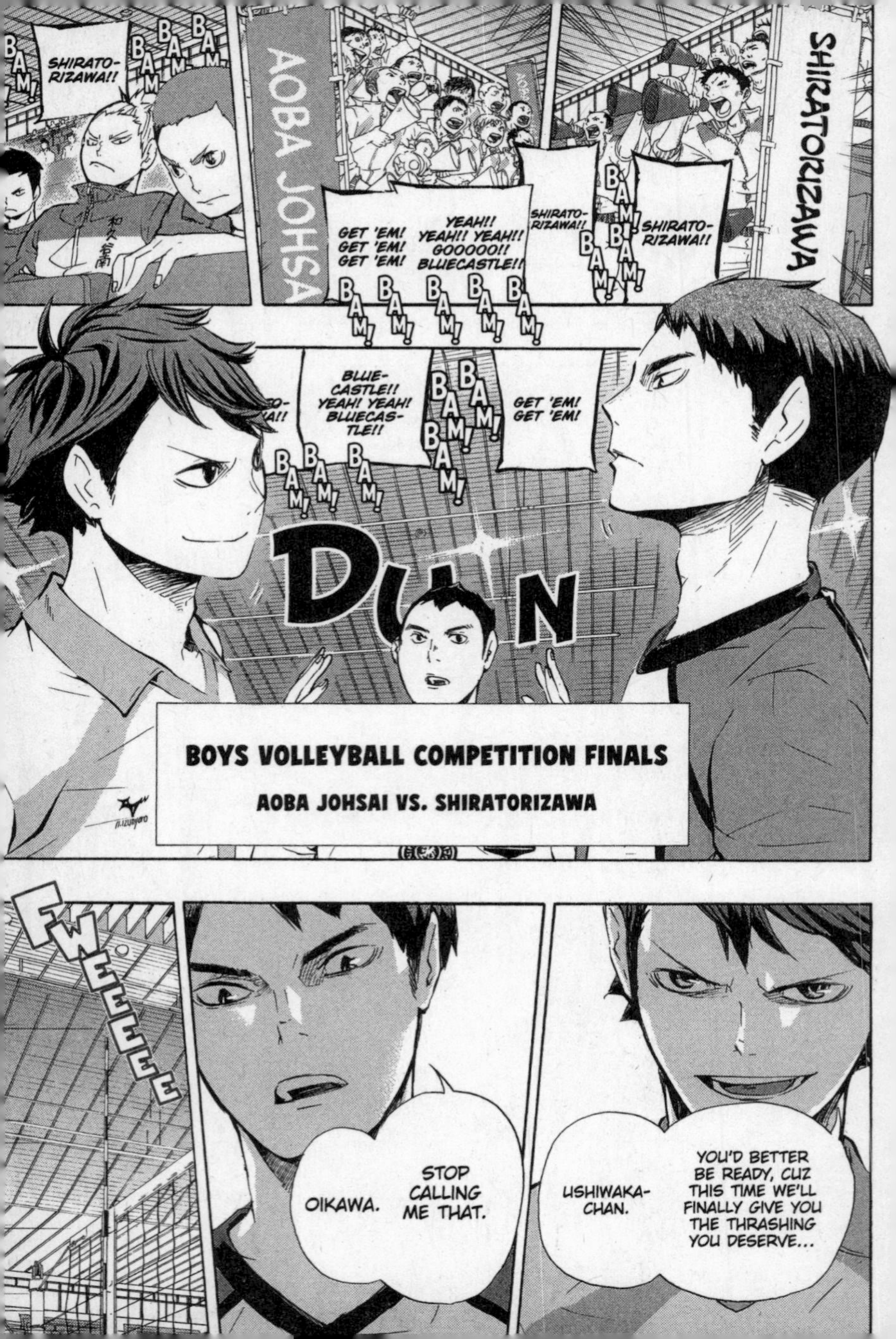
SHIRATORIZAWA
SHIRATO-RIZAWA!!
SHIRATO-RIZAWA!!
BAM! BAM! BAM!
AOBA JOHSA
YEAH!! YEAH!! YEAH!! GOOOOO!! BLUECASTLE!!
GET 'EM! GET 'EM! GET 'EM!
BAM! BAM! BAM! BAM! BAM!
SHIRATO-RIZAWA!!
BAM! BAM! BAM!
GET 'EM! GET 'EM!
BLUE-CASTLE!! YEAH! YEAH! BLUECAS-TLE!!
BAM! BAM! BAM! BAM! BAM!
DUN
BOYS VOLLEYBALL COMPETITION FINALS
AOBA JOHSAI VS. SHIRATORIZAWA
YOU'D BETTER BE READY, CUZ THIS TIME WE'LL FINALLY GIVE YOU THE THRASHING YOU DESERVE...
USHIWAKA-CHAN.
STOP CALLING ME THAT.
OIKAWA.
FWEEEEE

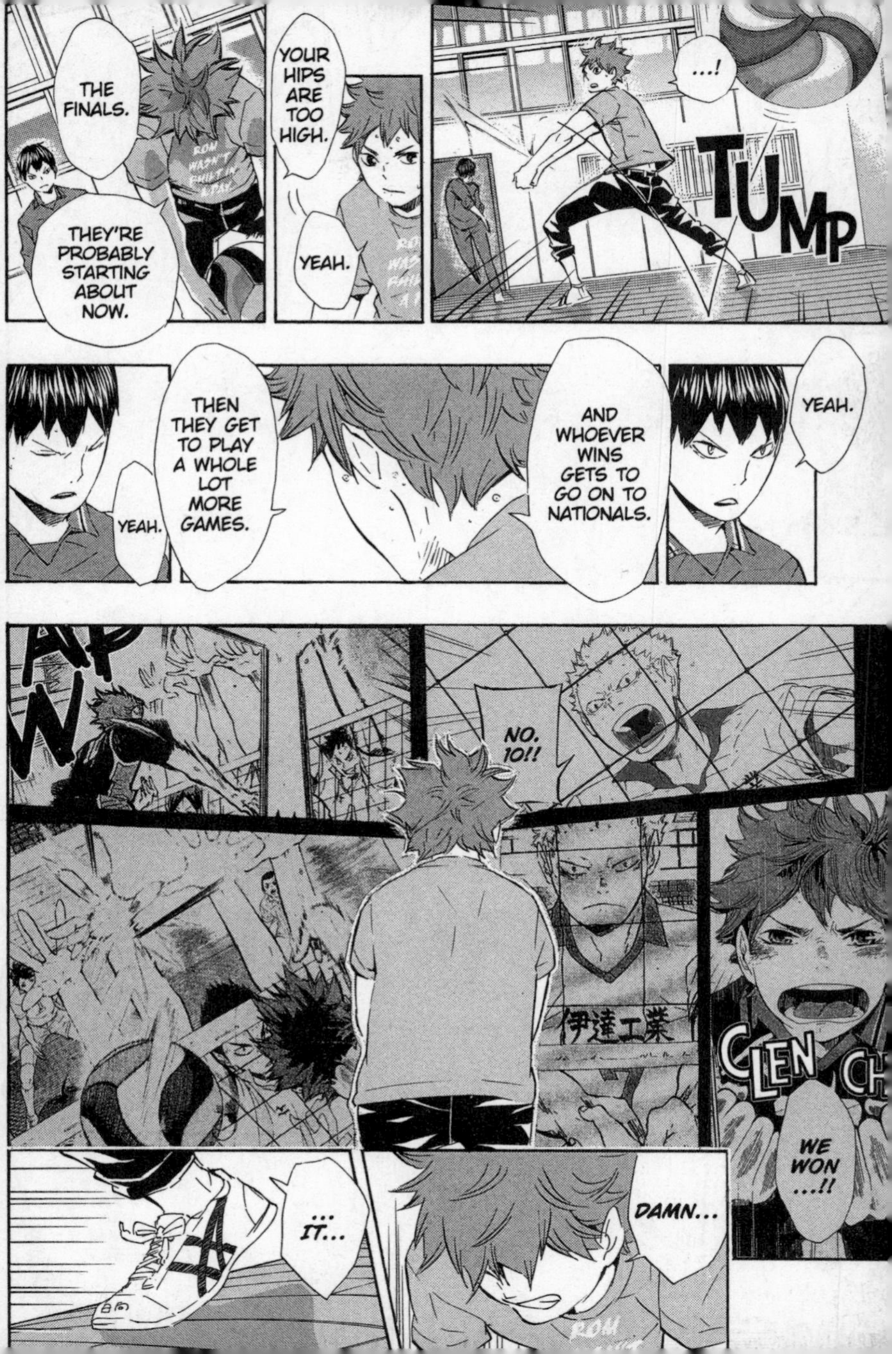

...!
TUMP
YOUR HIPS ARE TOO HIGH.
YEAH.
THE FINALS.
THEY'RE PROBABLY STARTING ABOUT NOW.
YEAH.
AND WHOEVER WINS GETS TO GO ON TO NATIONALS.
THEN THEY GET TO PLAY A WHOLE LOT MORE GAMES.
YEAH.
NO. 10!!
伊達工業
CLEN CH
WE WON ...!!
DAMN...
... IT...

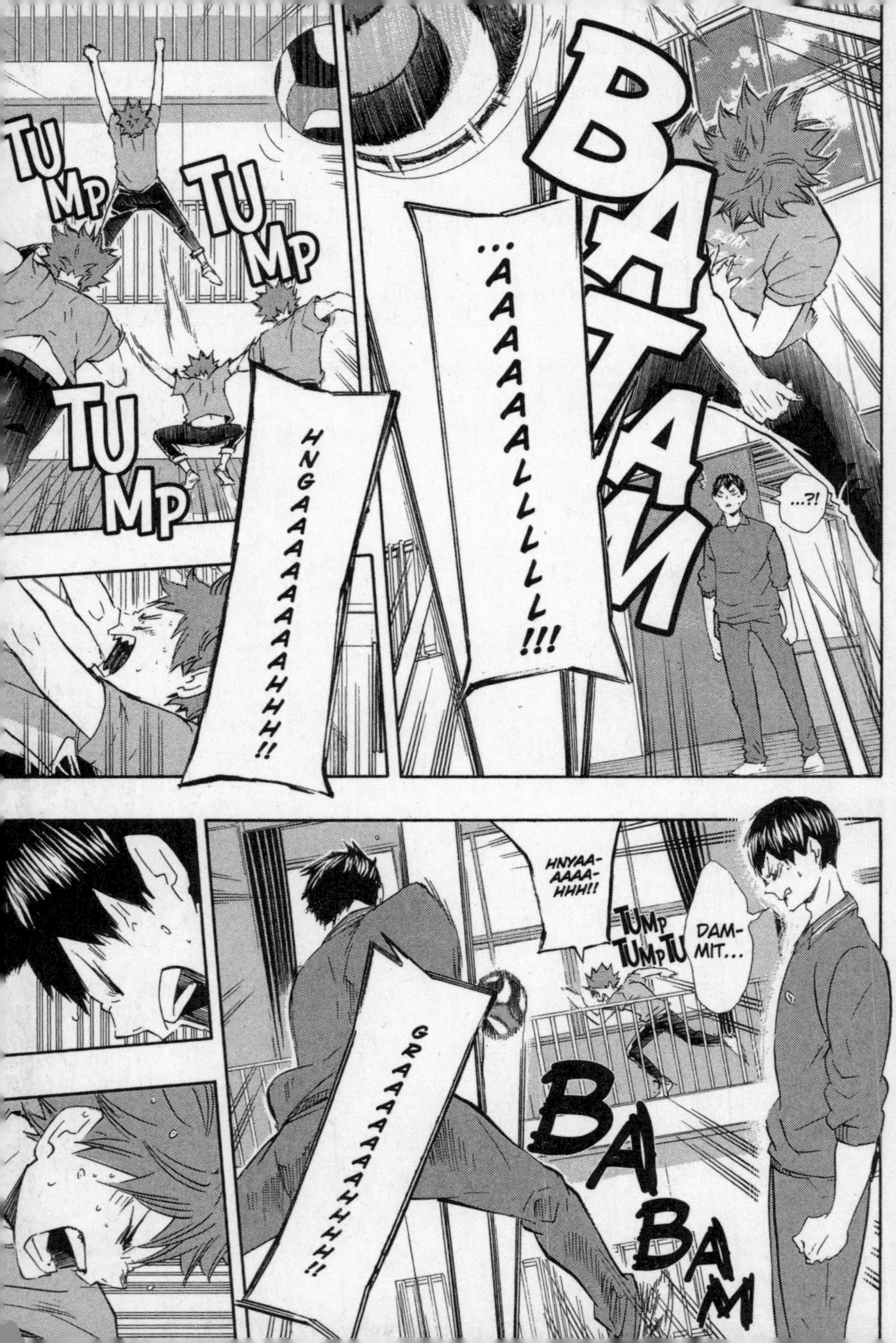
BATAM
...ÄAAAAALLLLLL!!!
...?!
TUMP
TUMP
TUMP
HNGAAAAAAAAAAHHHH!!
DAM-
MIT...
HNYAA-
AAAA-
HHH!!
TUMP
TUMP TU
BABAM
GRAAAAAAAAAAHHHHH!!

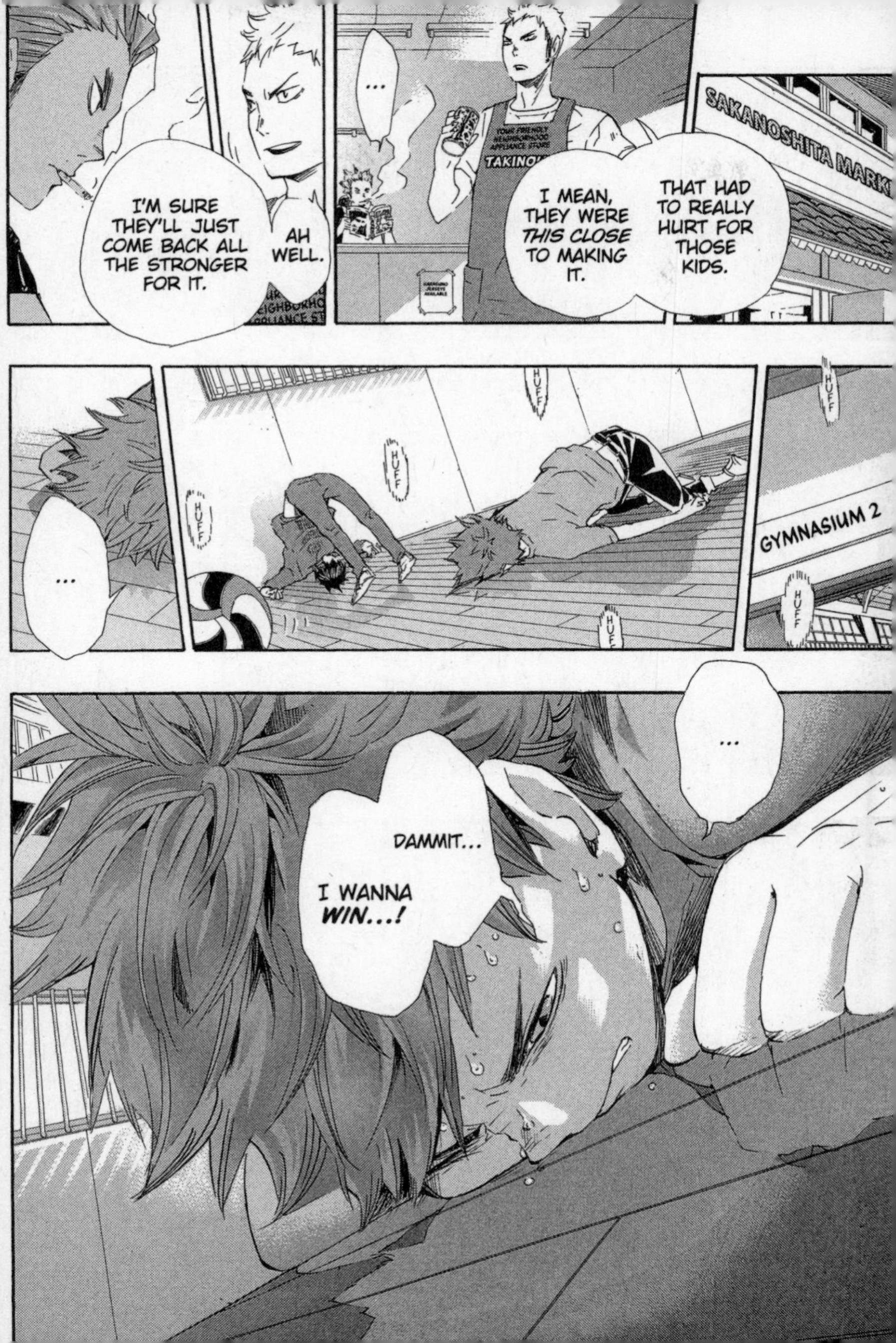
THAT HAD TO REALLY HURT FOR THOSE KIDS.
I MEAN, THEY WERE *THIS CLOSE* TO MAKING IT.
...
AH WELL.
I'M SURE THEY'LL JUST COME BACK ALL THE STRONGER FOR IT.
GYMNASIUM 2
HUFF
HUFF
HUFF
HUFF
HUFF
HUFF
...
...
DAMMIT...
I WANNA *WIN...!*

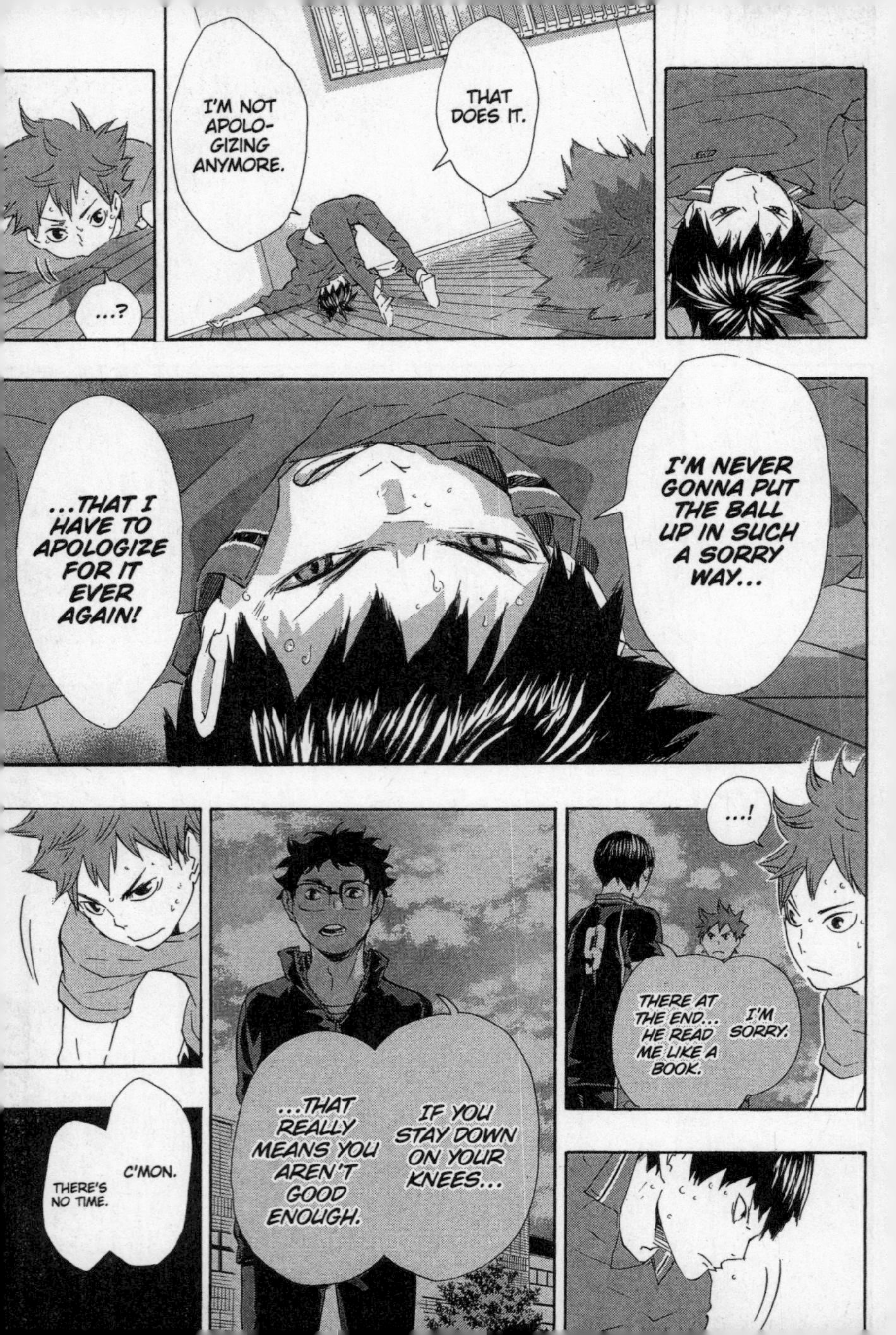
THAT DOES IT.
I'M NOT APOLO-GIZING ANYMORE.
...?
I'M NEVER GONNA PUT THE BALL UP IN SUCH A SORRY WAY...
...THAT I HAVE TO APOLOGIZE FOR IT EVER AGAIN!
...!
I'M SORRY.
THERE AT THE END... HE READ ME LIKE A BOOK.
IF YOU STAY DOWN ON YOUR KNEES...
...THAT REALLY MEANS YOU AREN'T GOOD ENOUGH.
C'MON.
THERE'S NO TIME.

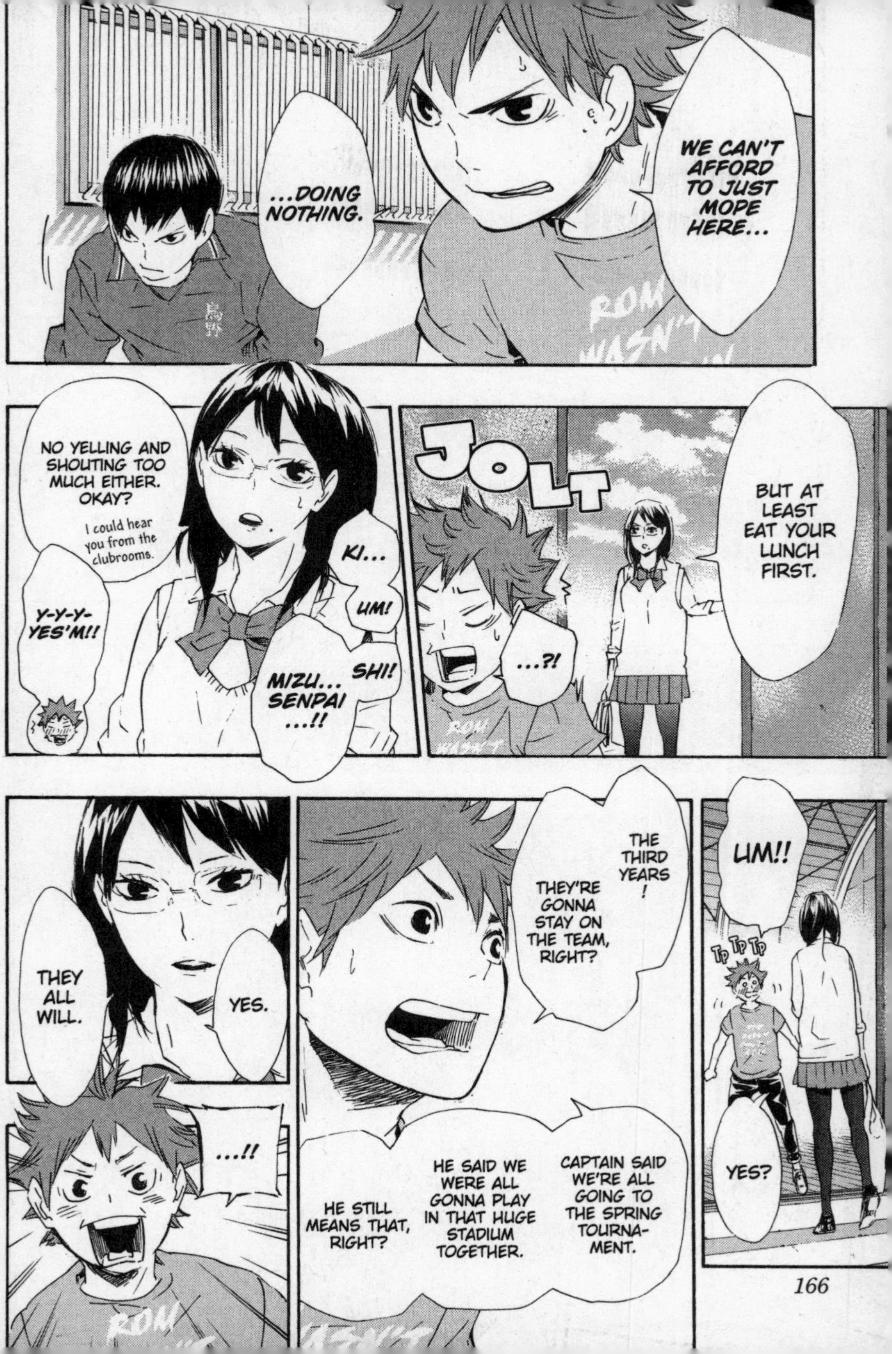
WE CAN'T AFFORD TO JUST MOPE HERE...
...DOING NOTHING.
BUT AT LEAST EAT YOUR LUNCH FIRST.
JOLT
...?!
KI...
UM!
SHI!
MIZU... SENPAI ...!!
NO YELLING AND SHOUTING TOO MUCH EITHER. OKAY?
I could hear you from the clubrooms.
Y-Y-Y-YES'M!!
UM!!
Tp Tp Tp
YES?
THE THIRD YEARS!
THEY'RE GONNA STAY ON THE TEAM, RIGHT?
CAPTAIN SAID WE'RE ALL GOING TO THE SPRING TOURNAMENT.
HE SAID WE WERE ALL GONNA PLAY IN THAT HUGE STADIUM TOGETHER.
HE STILL MEANS THAT, RIGHT?
YES.
THEY ALL WILL.
...!!

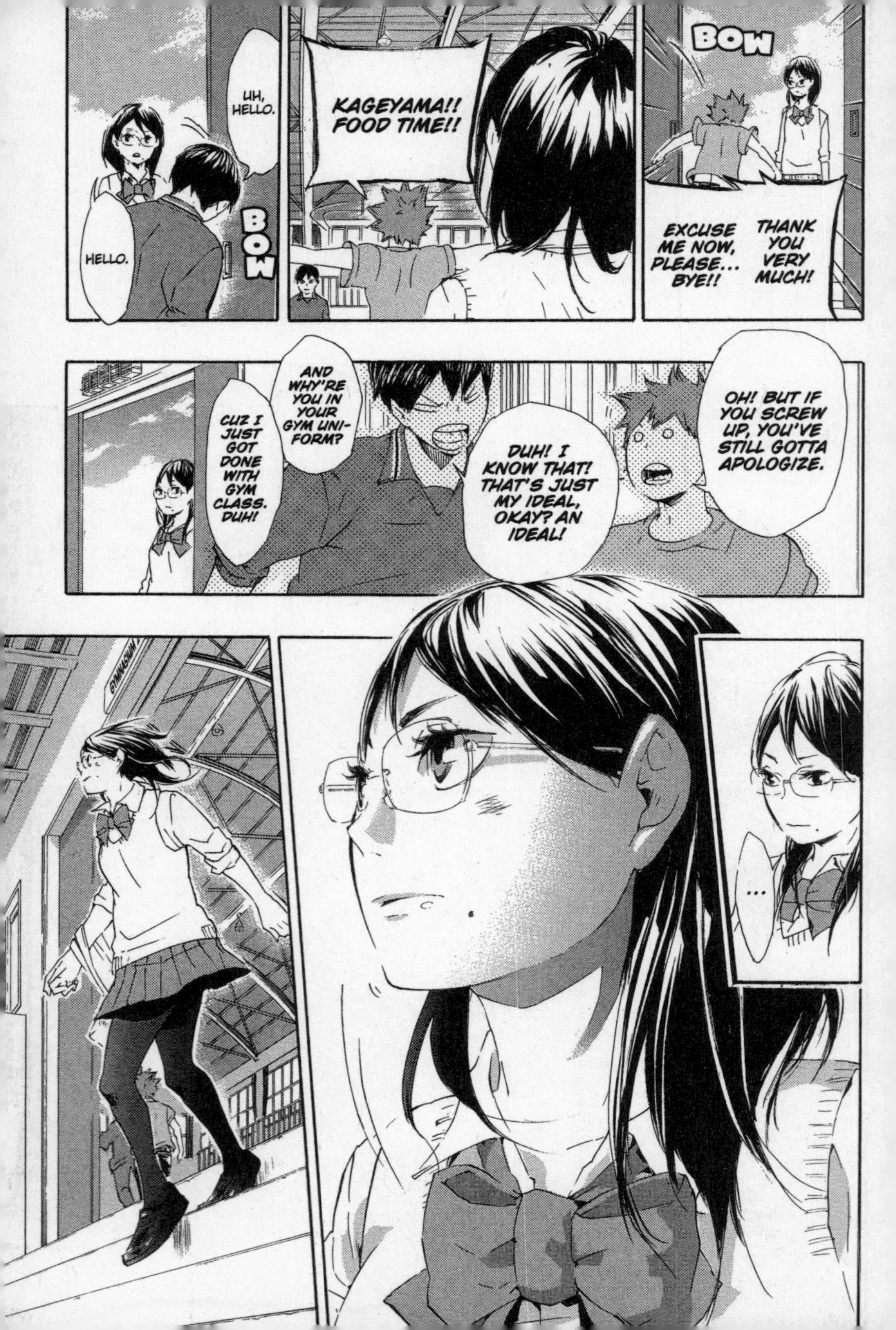
BOW
THANK YOU VERY MUCH!
EXCUSE ME NOW, PLEASE... BYE!!
KAGEYAMA!! FOOD TIME!!
UH, HELLO.
BOW
HELLO.
OH! BUT IF YOU SCREW UP, YOU'VE STILL GOTTA APOLOGIZE.
DUH! I KNOW THAT! THAT'S JUST MY IDEAL, OKAY? AN IDEAL!
AND WHY'RE YOU IN YOUR GYM UNI-FORM?
CUZ I JUST GOT DONE WITH GYM CLASS. DUH!
...

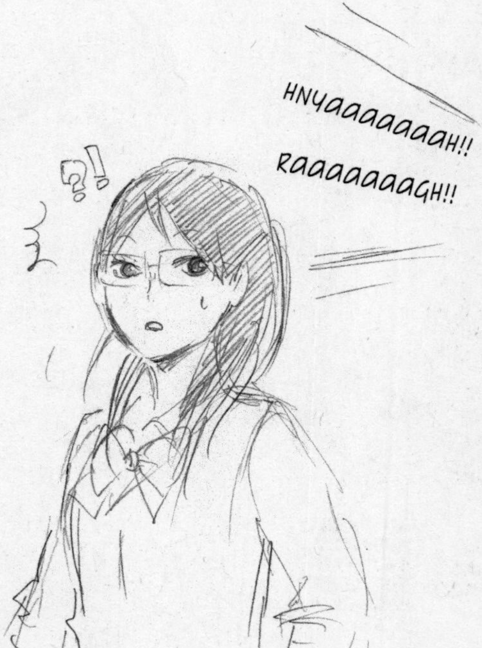

HNYAAAAAAAAH!!
RAAAAAAAAGH!!
?!

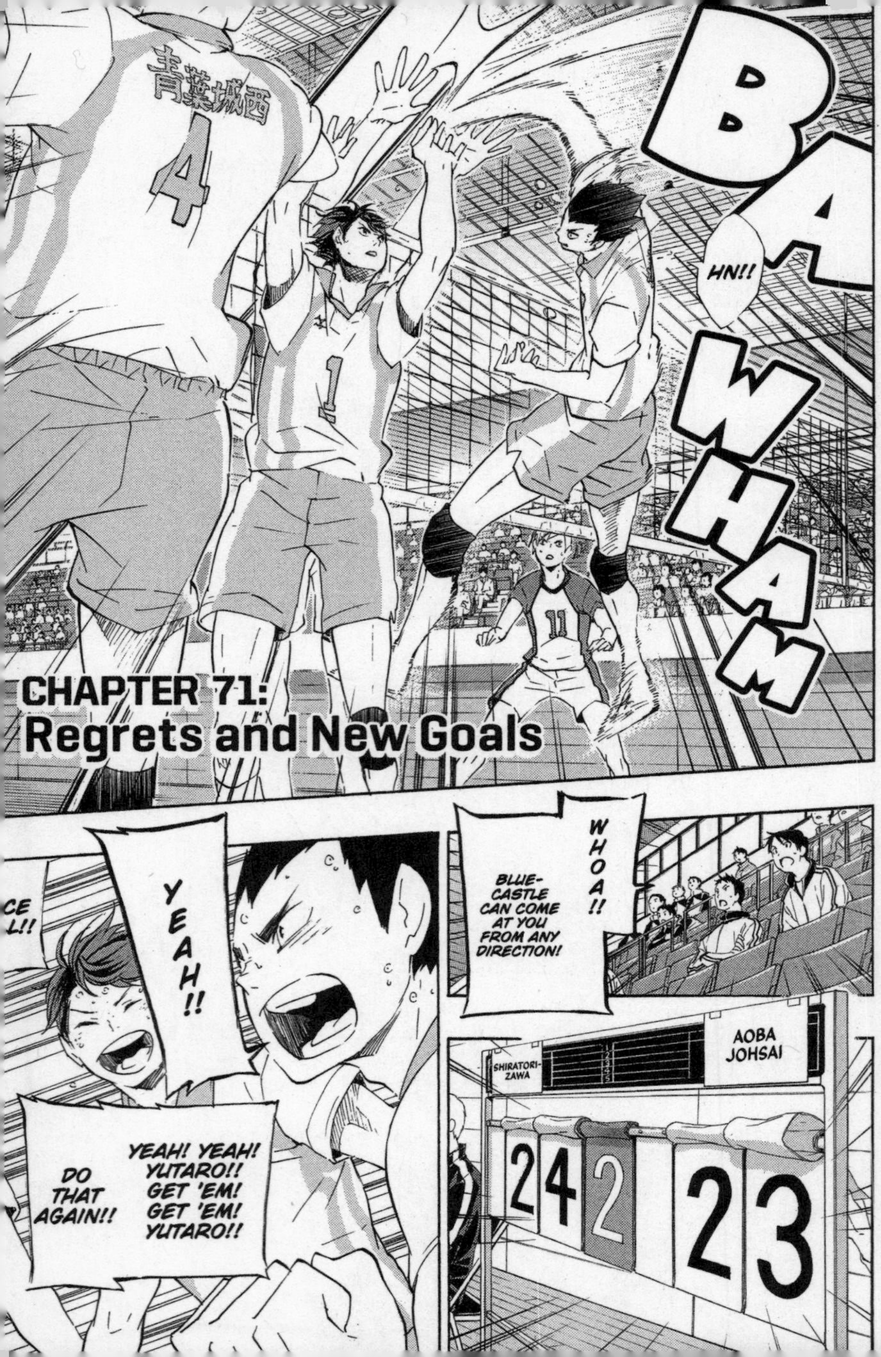

BA
WHAM
HN!!
青葉城西
CHAPTER 71:
Regrets and New Goals
WHOA!!
BLUE-CASTLE CAN COME AT YOU FROM ANY DIRECTION!
SHIRATORIZAWA
AOBA JOHSAI
24
2
23
YEAH!!
YEAH! YEAH! YUTARO!! GET 'EM! GET 'EM! YUTARO!!
DO THAT AGAIN!!

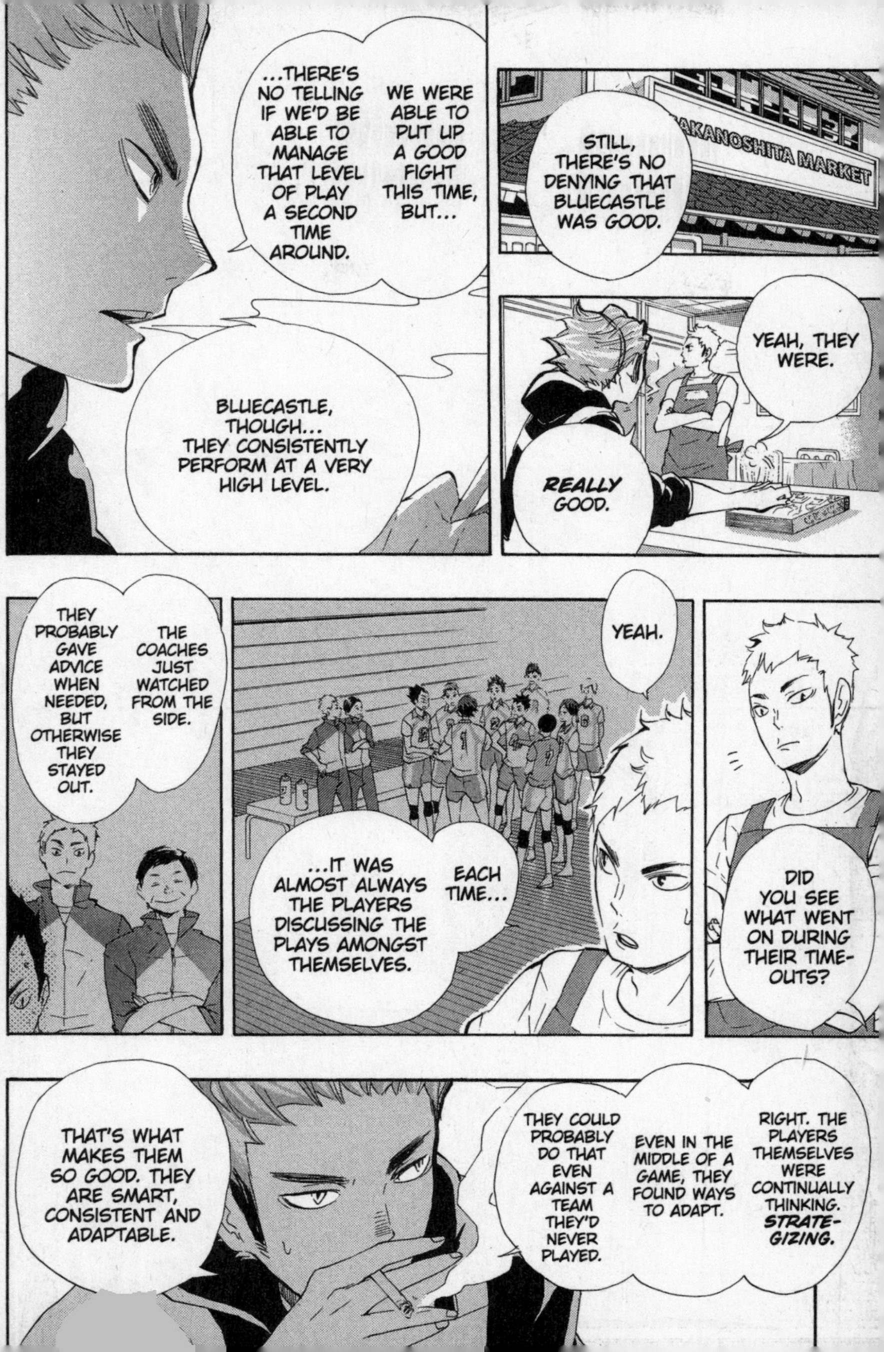
STILL, THERE'S NO DENYING THAT BLUECASTLE WAS GOOD.
AKANOSHITA MARKET
YEAH, THEY WERE.
REALLY GOOD.
WE WERE ABLE TO PUT UP A GOOD FIGHT THIS TIME, BUT...
...THERE'S NO TELLING IF WE'D BE ABLE TO MANAGE THAT LEVEL OF PLAY A SECOND TIME AROUND.
BLUECASTLE, THOUGH... THEY CONSISTENTLY PERFORM AT A VERY HIGH LEVEL.
DID YOU SEE WHAT WENT ON DURING THEIR TIME-OUTS?
YEAH.
EACH TIME...
...IT WAS ALMOST ALWAYS THE PLAYERS DISCUSSING THE PLAYS AMONGST THEMSELVES.
THE COACHES JUST WATCHED FROM THE SIDE.
THEY PROBABLY GAVE ADVICE WHEN NEEDED, BUT OTHERWISE THEY STAYED OUT.
RIGHT. THE PLAYERS THEMSELVES WERE CONTINUALLY THINKING. *STRATE-GIZING.*
EVEN IN THE MIDDLE OF A GAME, THEY FOUND WAYS TO ADAPT.
THEY COULD PROBABLY DO THAT EVEN AGAINST A TEAM THEY'D NEVER PLAYED.
THAT'S WHAT MAKES THEM SO GOOD. THEY ARE SMART, CONSISTENT AND ADAPTABLE.

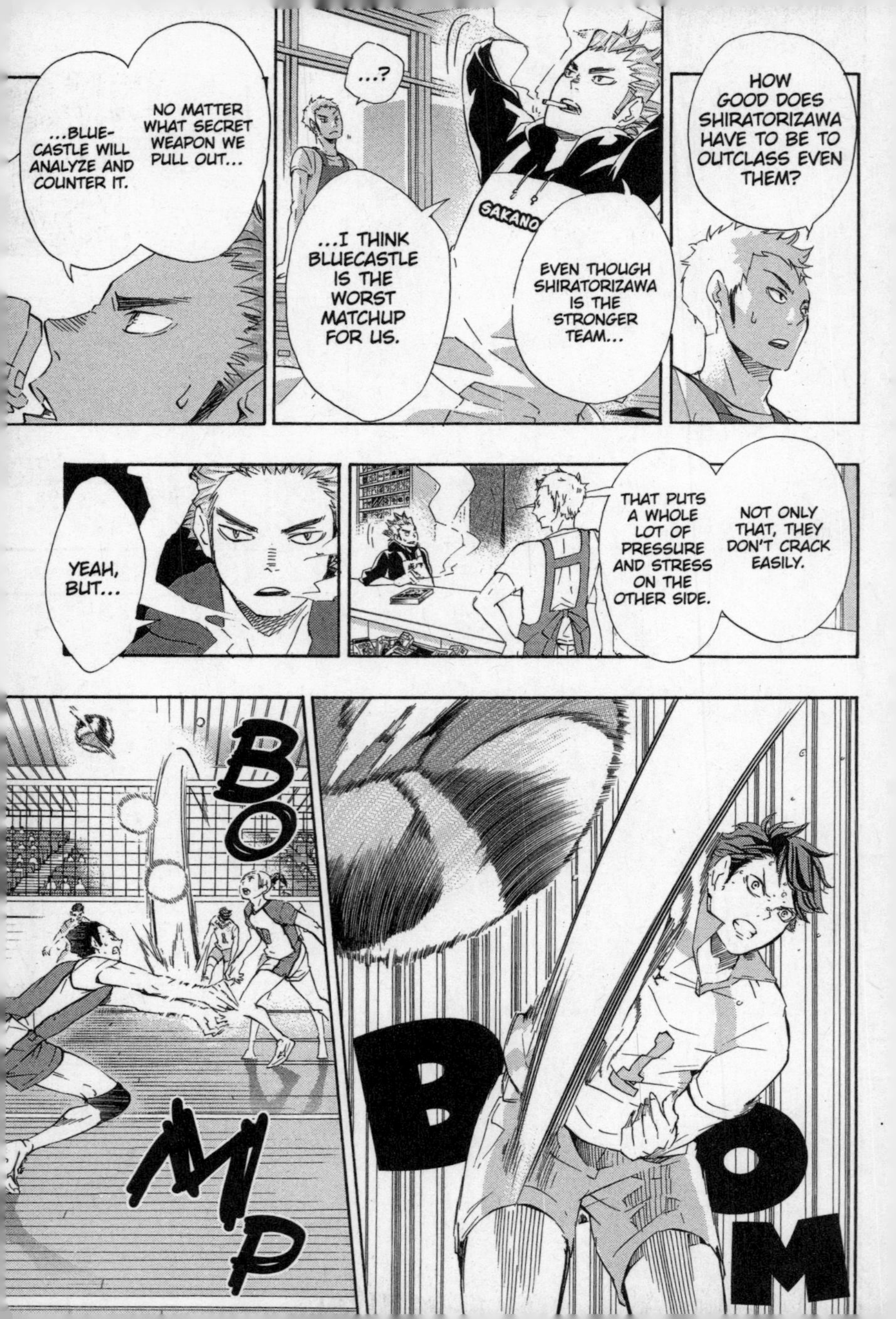
HOW GOOD DOES SHIRATORIZAWA HAVE TO BE TO OUTCLASS EVEN THEM?
...?
SAKANO
EVEN THOUGH SHIRATORIZAWA IS THE STRONGER TEAM...
...I THINK BLUECASTLE IS THE WORST MATCHUP FOR US.
NO MATTER WHAT SECRET WEAPON WE PULL OUT...
...BLUE-CASTLE WILL ANALYZE AND COUNTER IT.
NOT ONLY THAT, THEY DON'T CRACK EASILY.
THAT PUTS A WHOLE LOT OF PRESSURE AND STRESS ON THE OTHER SIDE.
YEAH, BUT...
BOM
BOMP

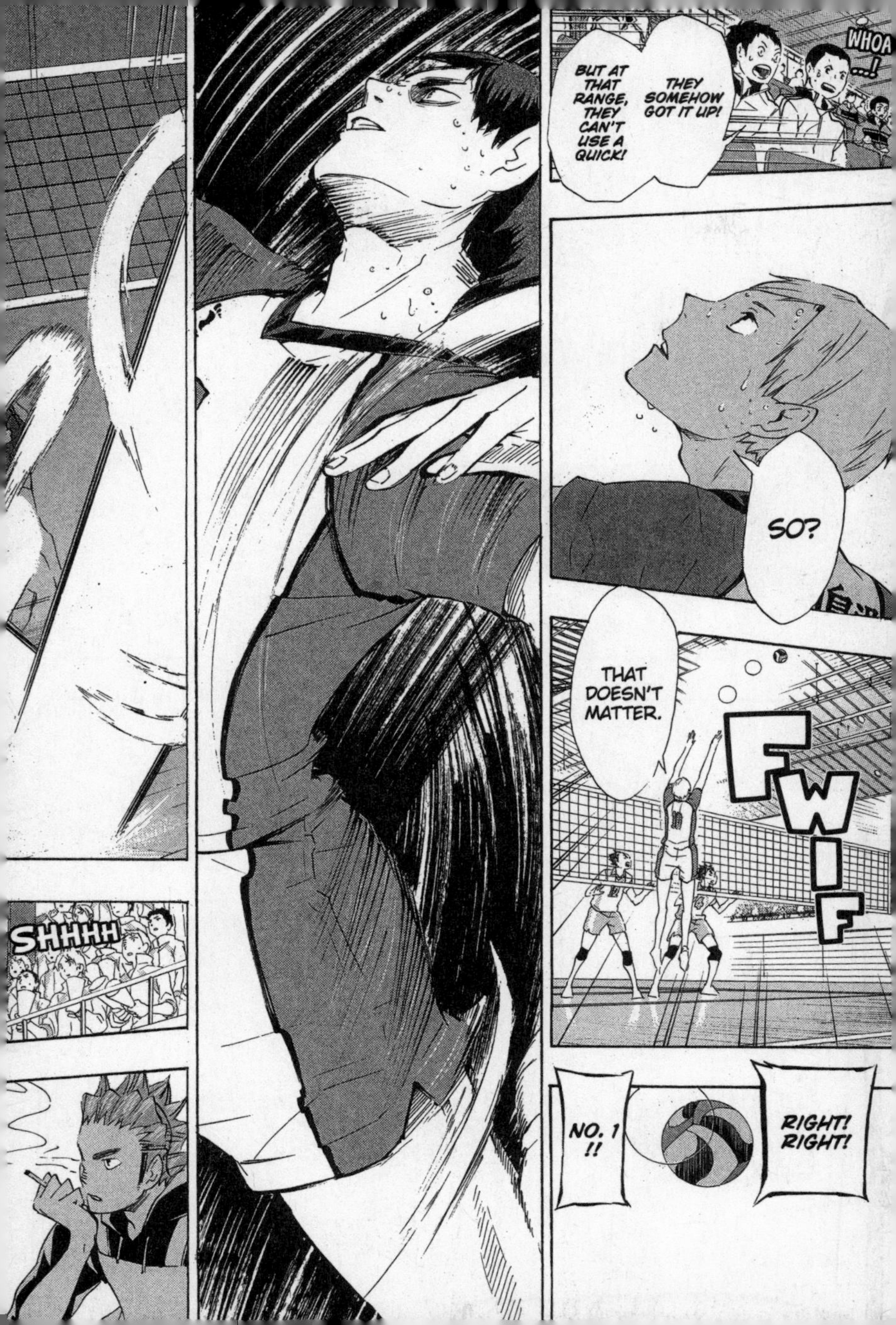
WHOA ...!
THEY SOMEHOW GOT IT UP!
BUT AT THAT RANGE, THEY CAN'T USE A QUICK!
SO?
THAT DOESN'T MATTER.
FWIF
RIGHT! RIGHT!
NO. 1 !!
SHHHH

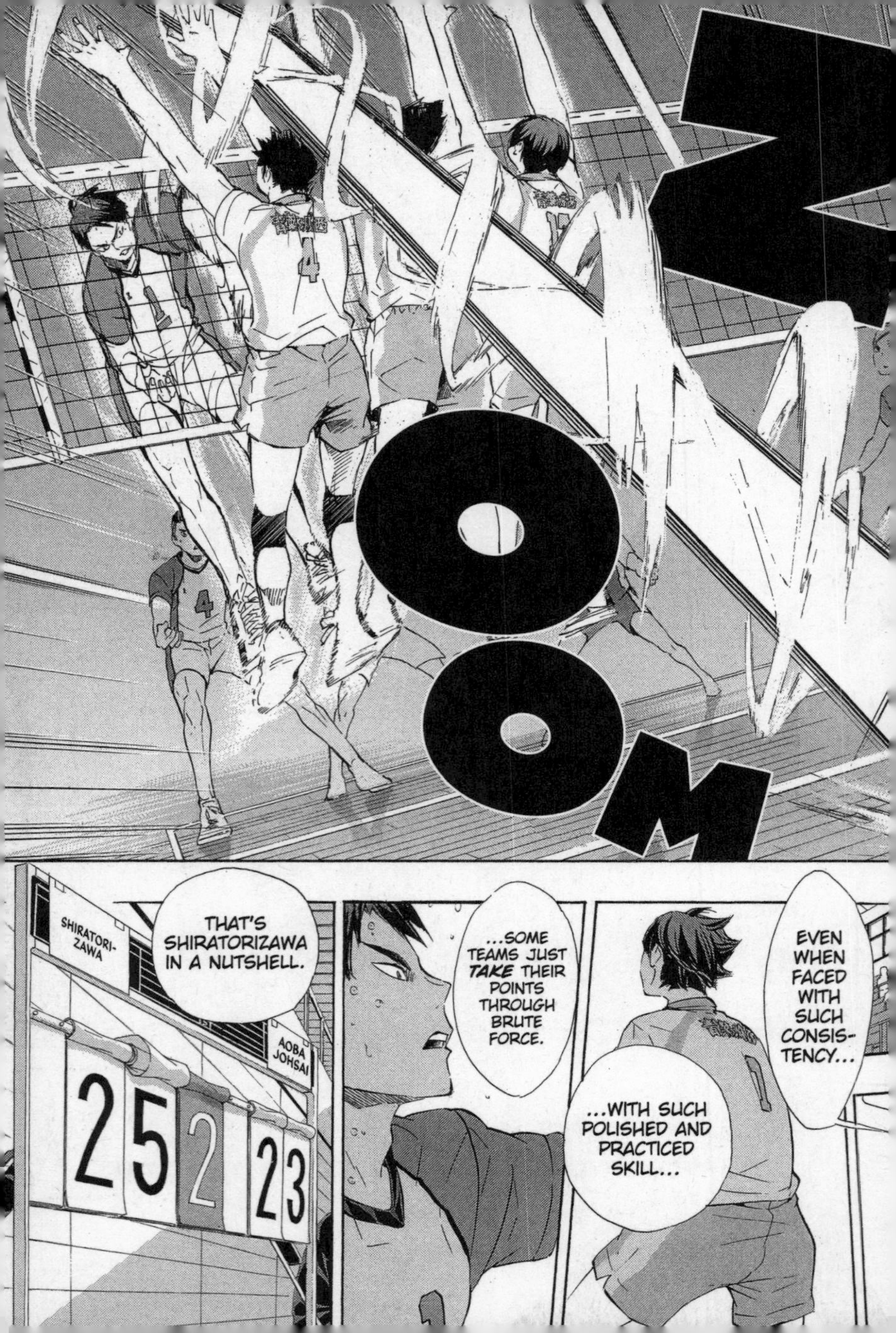
ZOOM
EVEN WHEN FACED WITH SUCH CONSISTENCY...
...WITH SUCH POLISHED AND PRACTICED SKILL...
...SOME TEAMS JUST ***TAKE*** THEIR POINTS THROUGH BRUTE FORCE.
THAT'S SHIRATORIZAWA IN A NUTSHELL.
SHIRATORIZAWA
AOBA JOHSAI
25
2
23

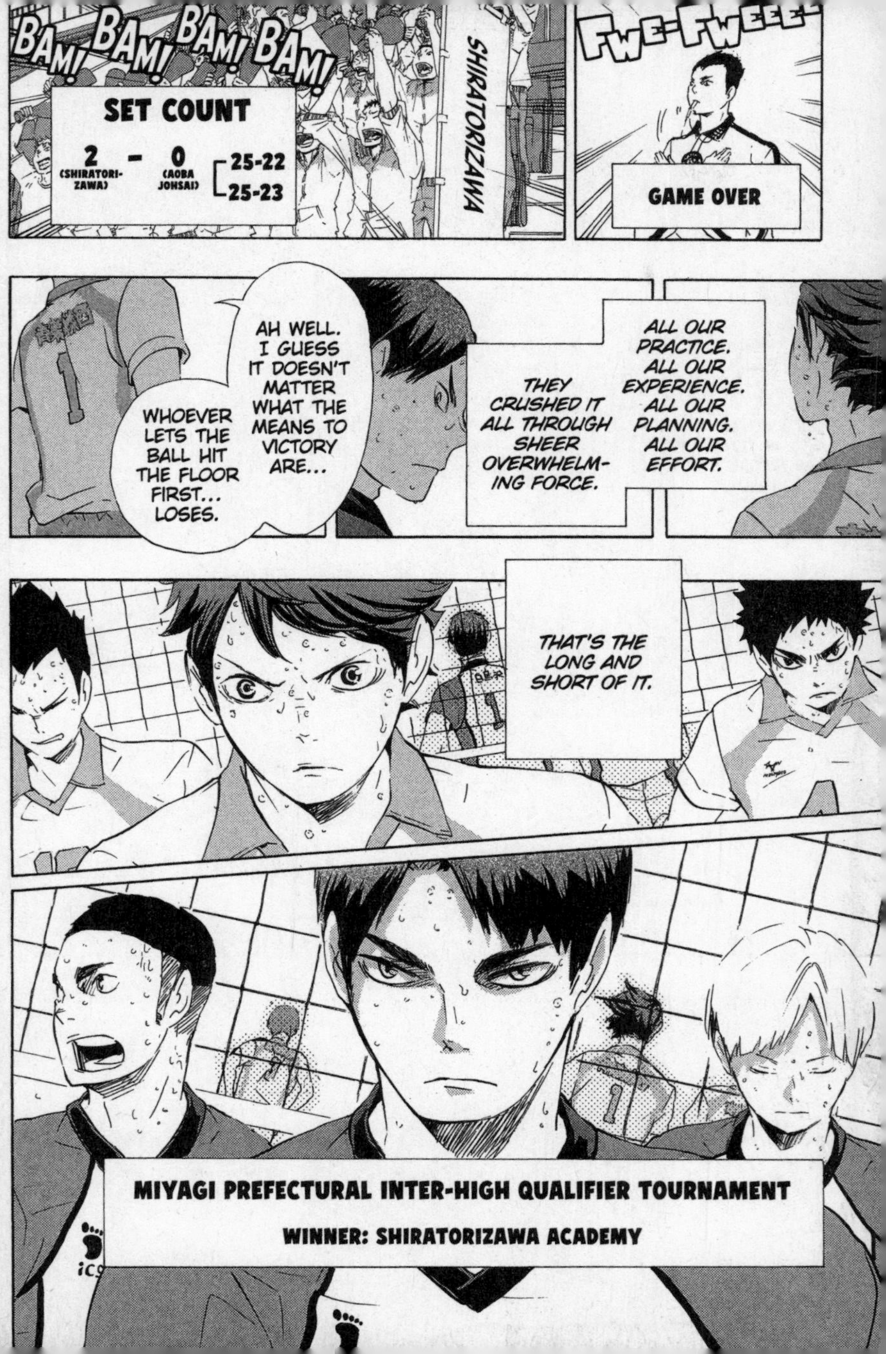
FWE-FWEEE-
GAME OVER
SHIRATORIZAWA
BAM! BAM! BAM! BAM!
SET COUNT
2 (SHIRATORI-ZAWA) - 0 (AOBA JOHSAI) 25-22 25-23
ALL OUR PRACTICE. ALL OUR EXPERIENCE. ALL OUR PLANNING. ALL OUR EFFORT.
THEY CRUSHED IT ALL THROUGH SHEER OVERWHELMING FORCE.
AH WELL. I GUESS IT DOESN'T MATTER WHAT THE MEANS TO VICTORY ARE...
WHOEVER LETS THE BALL HIT THE FLOOR FIRST... LOSES.
THAT'S THE LONG AND SHORT OF IT.
MIYAGI PREFECTURAL INTER-HIGH QUALIFIER TOURNAMENT
WINNER: SHIRATORIZAWA ACADEMY

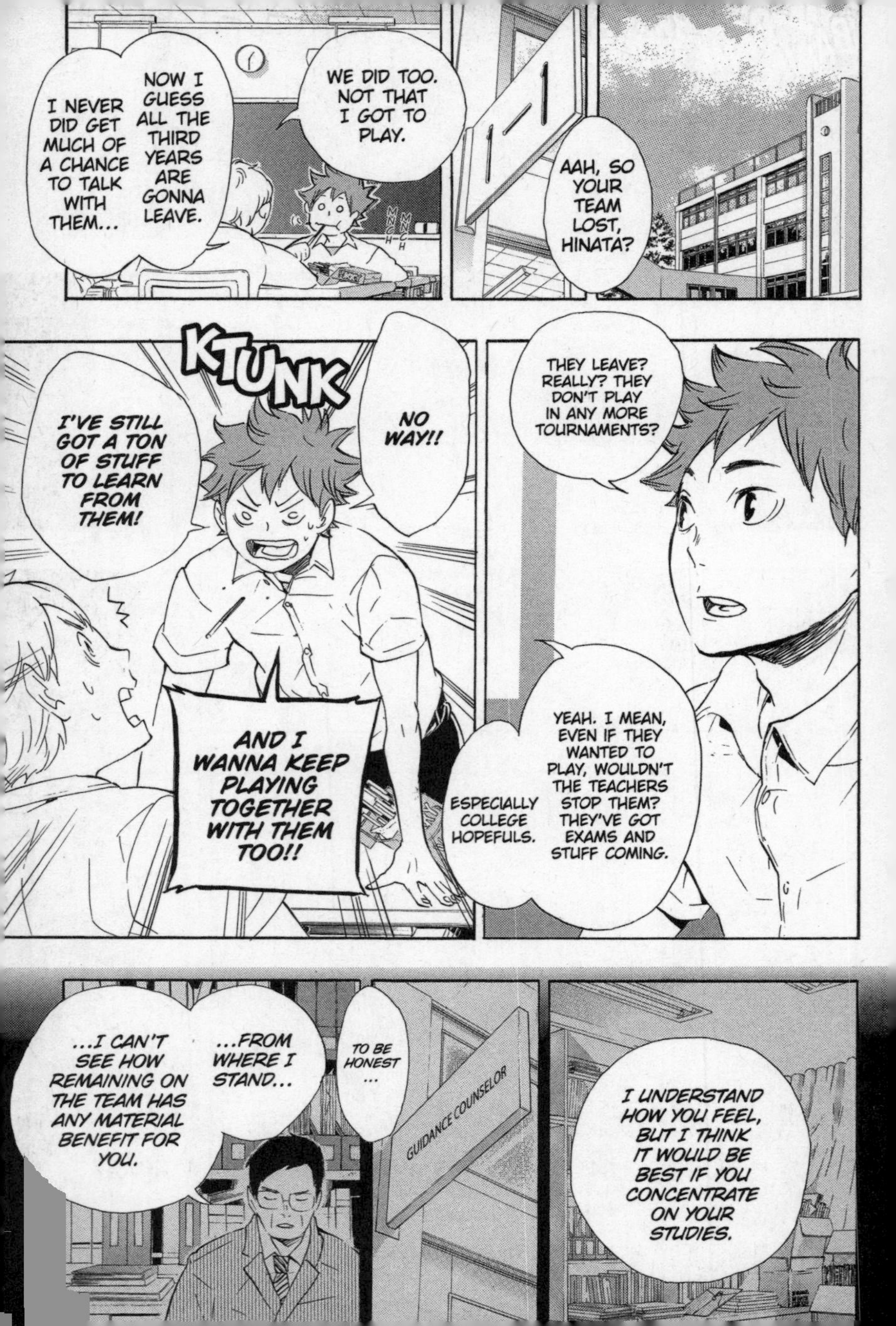
AAH, SO YOUR TEAM LOST, HINATA?
WE DID TOO. NOT THAT I GOT TO PLAY.
MNCH MNCH
NOW I GUESS ALL THE THIRD YEARS ARE GONNA LEAVE.
I NEVER DID GET MUCH OF A CHANCE TO TALK WITH THEM...
THEY LEAVE? REALLY? THEY DON'T PLAY IN ANY MORE TOURNAMENTS?
YEAH. I MEAN, EVEN IF THEY WANTED TO PLAY, WOULDN'T THE TEACHERS STOP THEM? THEY'VE GOT EXAMS AND STUFF COMING.
ESPECIALLY COLLEGE HOPEFULS.
KTUNK
NO WAY!!
I'VE STILL GOT A TON OF STUFF TO LEARN FROM THEM!
AND I WANNA KEEP PLAYING TOGETHER WITH THEM TOO!!
I UNDERSTAND HOW YOU FEEL, BUT I THINK IT WOULD BE BEST IF YOU CONCENTRATE ON YOUR STUDIES.
GUIDANCE COUNSELOR
TO BE HONEST...
...FROM WHERE I STAND...
...I CAN'T SEE HOW REMAINING ON THE TEAM HAS ANY MATERIAL BENEFIT FOR YOU.

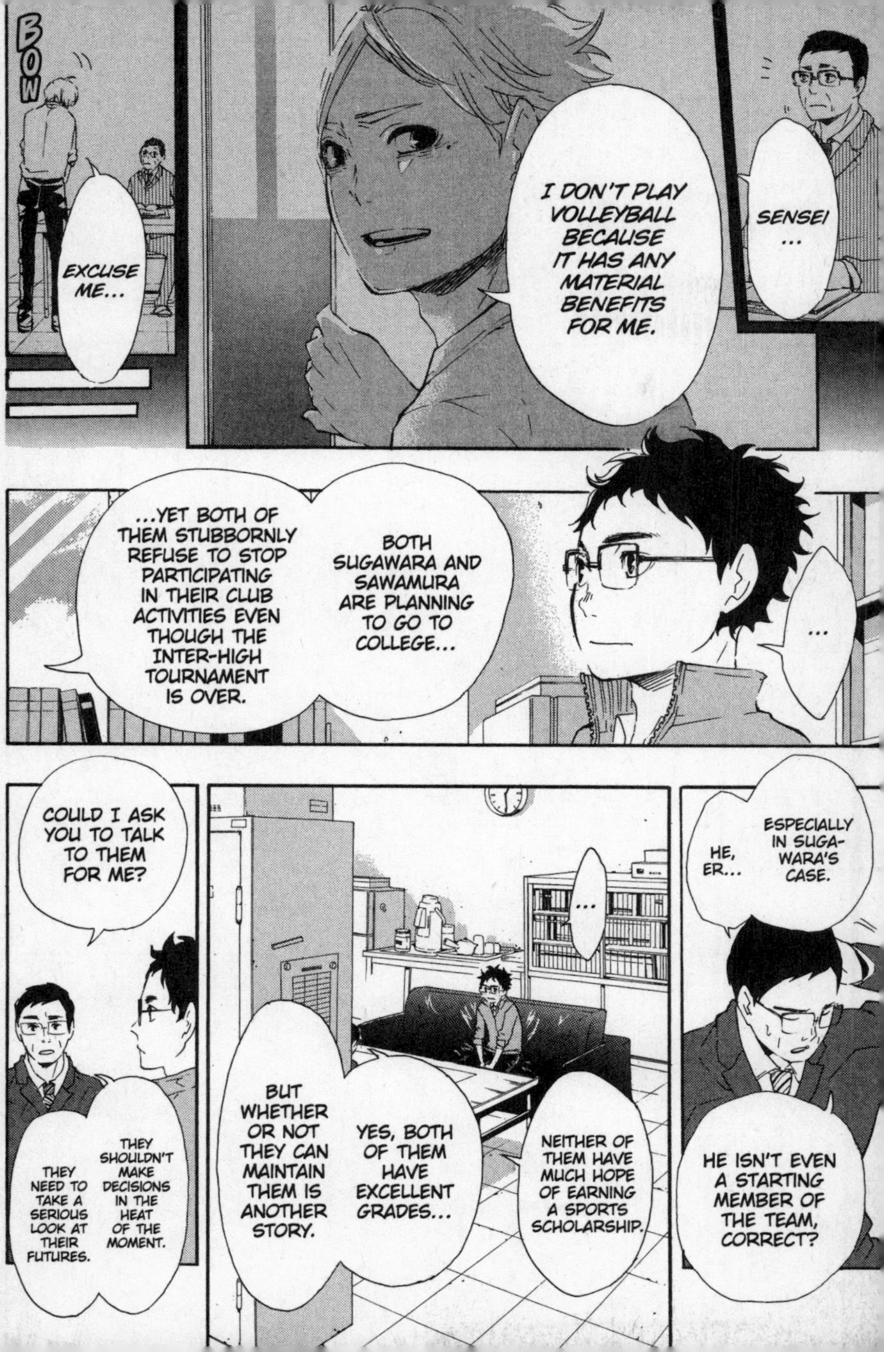
SENSEI ...
I DON'T PLAY VOLLEYBALL BECAUSE IT HAS ANY MATERIAL BENEFITS FOR ME.
BOW
EXCUSE ME...
...
BOTH SUGAWARA AND SAWAMURA ARE PLANNING TO GO TO COLLEGE...
...YET BOTH OF THEM STUBBORNLY REFUSE TO STOP PARTICIPATING IN THEIR CLUB ACTIVITIES EVEN THOUGH THE INTER-HIGH TOURNAMENT IS OVER.
ESPECIALLY IN SUGA-WARA'S CASE.
HE, ER...
HE ISN'T EVEN A STARTING MEMBER OF THE TEAM, CORRECT?
...
NEITHER OF THEM HAVE MUCH HOPE OF EARNING A SPORTS SCHOLARSHIP.
YES, BOTH OF THEM HAVE EXCELLENT GRADES...
BUT WHETHER OR NOT THEY CAN MAINTAIN THEM IS ANOTHER STORY.
COULD I ASK YOU TO TALK TO THEM FOR ME?
THEY SHOULDN'T MAKE DECISIONS IN THE HEAT OF THE MOMENT.
THEY NEED TO TAKE A SERIOUS LOOK AT THEIR FUTURES.

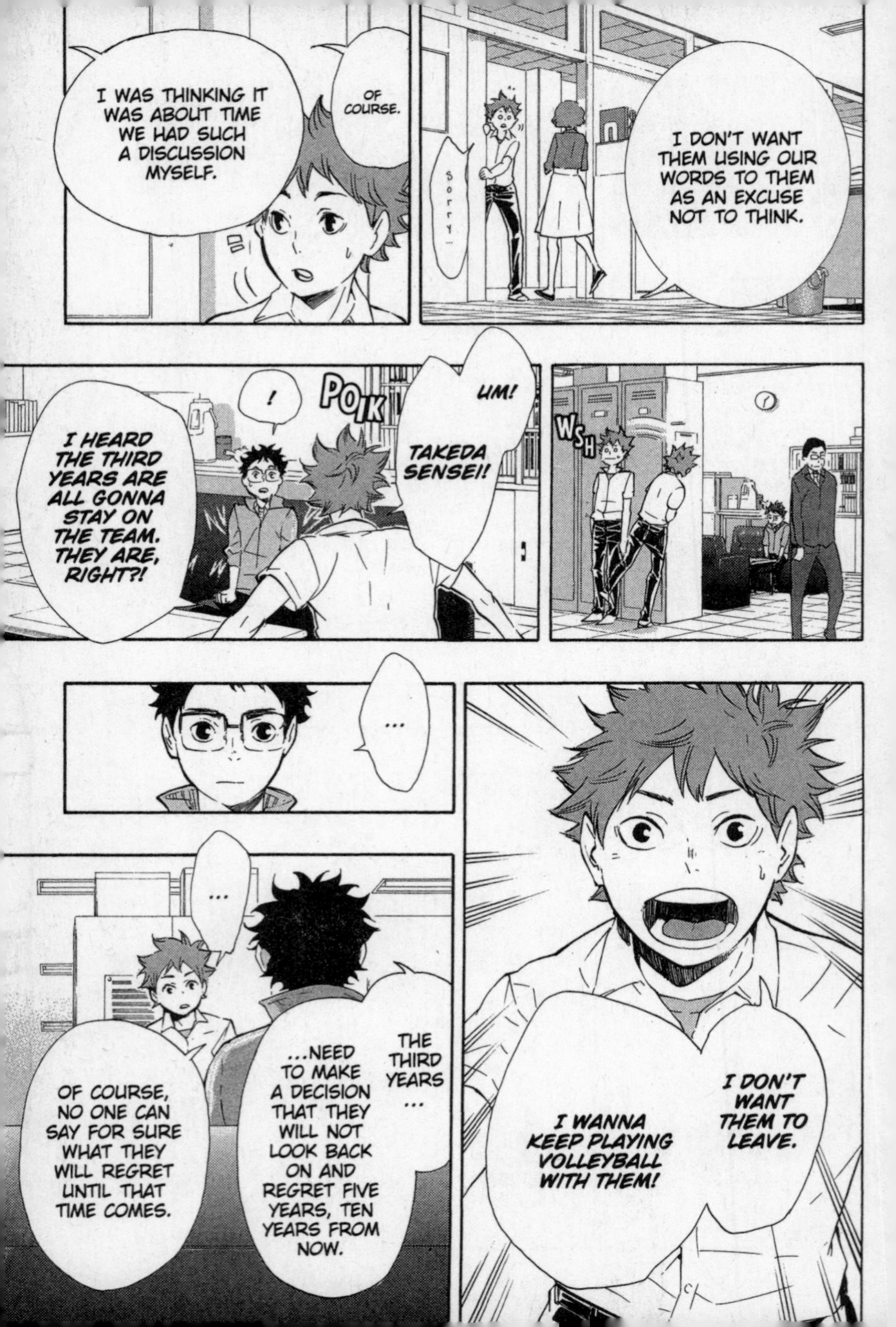
I DON'T WANT THEM USING OUR WORDS TO THEM AS AN EXCUSE NOT TO THINK.
Sorry...
OF COURSE.
I WAS THINKING IT WAS ABOUT TIME WE HAD SUCH A DISCUSSION MYSELF.
WSH
UM! TAKEDA SENSEI!
POIK
!
I HEARD THE THIRD YEARS ARE ALL GONNA STAY ON THE TEAM. THEY ARE, RIGHT?!
I DON'T WANT THEM TO LEAVE.
I WANNA KEEP PLAYING VOLLEYBALL WITH THEM!
...
...
THE THIRD YEARS...
...NEED TO MAKE A DECISION THAT THEY WILL NOT LOOK BACK ON AND REGRET FIVE YEARS, TEN YEARS FROM NOW.
OF COURSE, NO ONE CAN SAY FOR SURE WHAT THEY WILL REGRET UNTIL THAT TIME COMES.

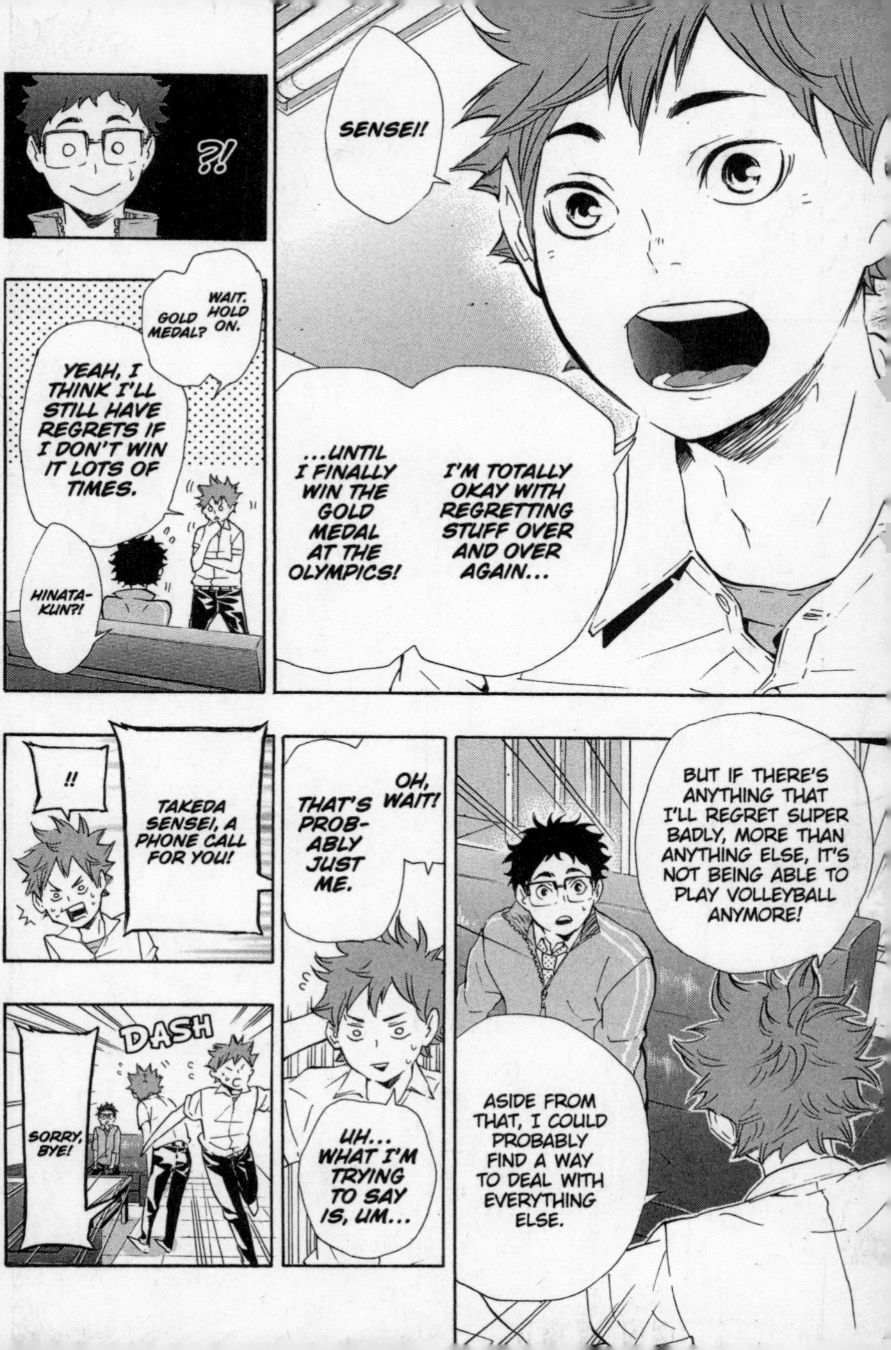
SENSEI!
I'M TOTALLY OKAY WITH REGRETTING STUFF OVER AND OVER AGAIN...
...UNTIL I FINALLY WIN THE GOLD MEDAL AT THE OLYMPICS!
?!
WAIT. HOLD ON.
GOLD MEDAL?
YEAH, I THINK I'LL STILL HAVE REGRETS IF I DON'T WIN IT LOTS OF TIMES.
HINATA-KUN?!
BUT IF THERE'S ANYTHING THAT I'LL REGRET SUPER BADLY, MORE THAN ANYTHING ELSE, IT'S NOT BEING ABLE TO PLAY VOLLEYBALL ANYMORE!
ASIDE FROM THAT, I COULD PROBABLY FIND A WAY TO DEAL WITH EVERYTHING ELSE.
OH, WAIT!
THAT'S PROB-ABLY JUST ME.
UH... WHAT I'M TRYING TO SAY IS, UM...
TAKEDA SENSEI, A PHONE CALL FOR YOU!
!!
DASH
SORRY, BYE!

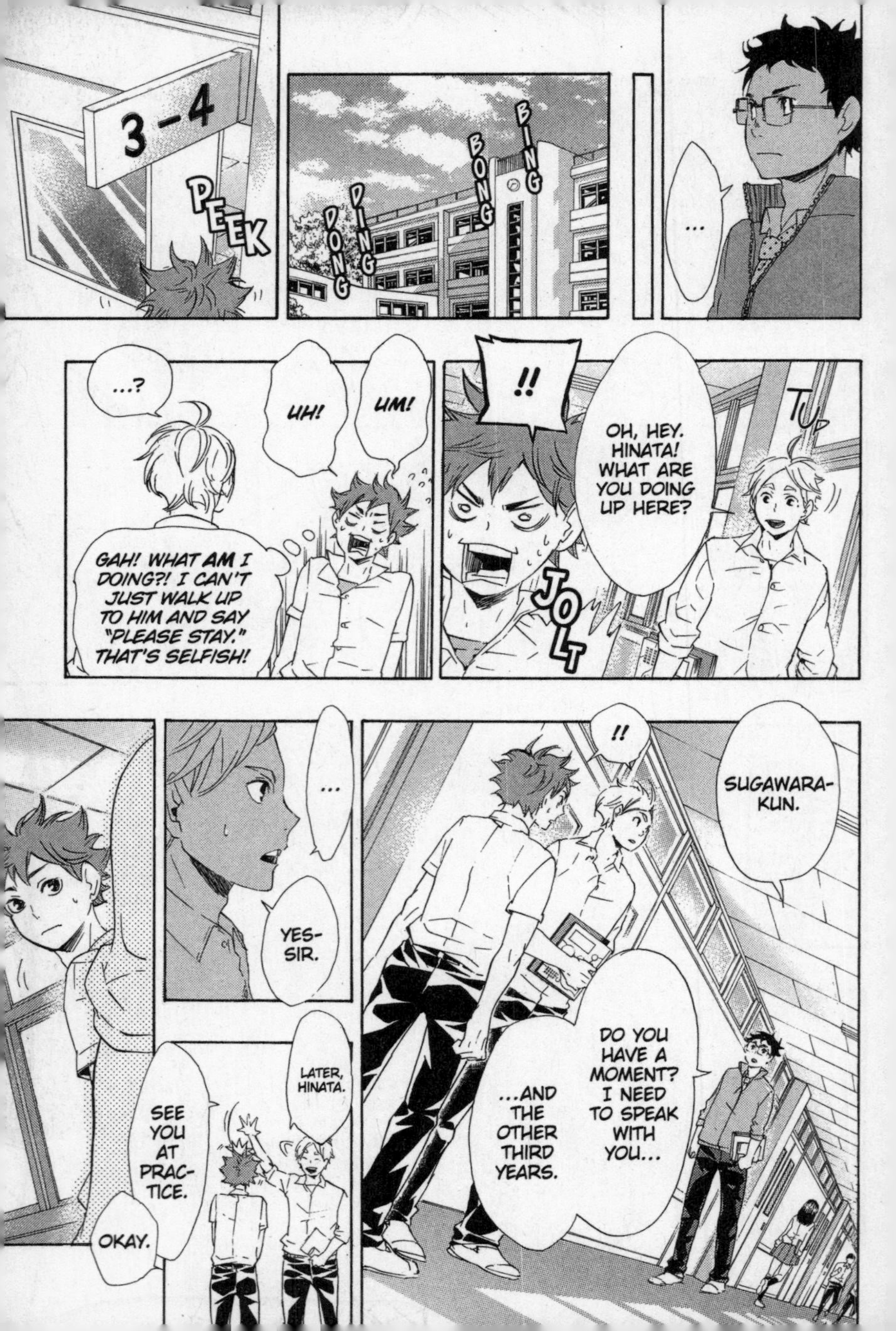
...
BING
BONG
DING
DONG
3-4
PEEEK
TUP
OH, HEY. HINATA! WHAT ARE YOU DOING UP HERE?
!!
JOLT
UM!
UH!
...?
GAH! WHAT AM I DOING?! I CAN'T JUST WALK UP TO HIM AND SAY "PLEASE STAY." THAT'S SELFISH!
SUGAWARA-KUN.
!!
DO YOU HAVE A MOMENT? I NEED TO SPEAK WITH YOU...
...AND THE OTHER THIRD YEARS.
...
YES-SIR.
LATER, HINATA.
SEE YOU AT PRAC-TICE.
OKAY.

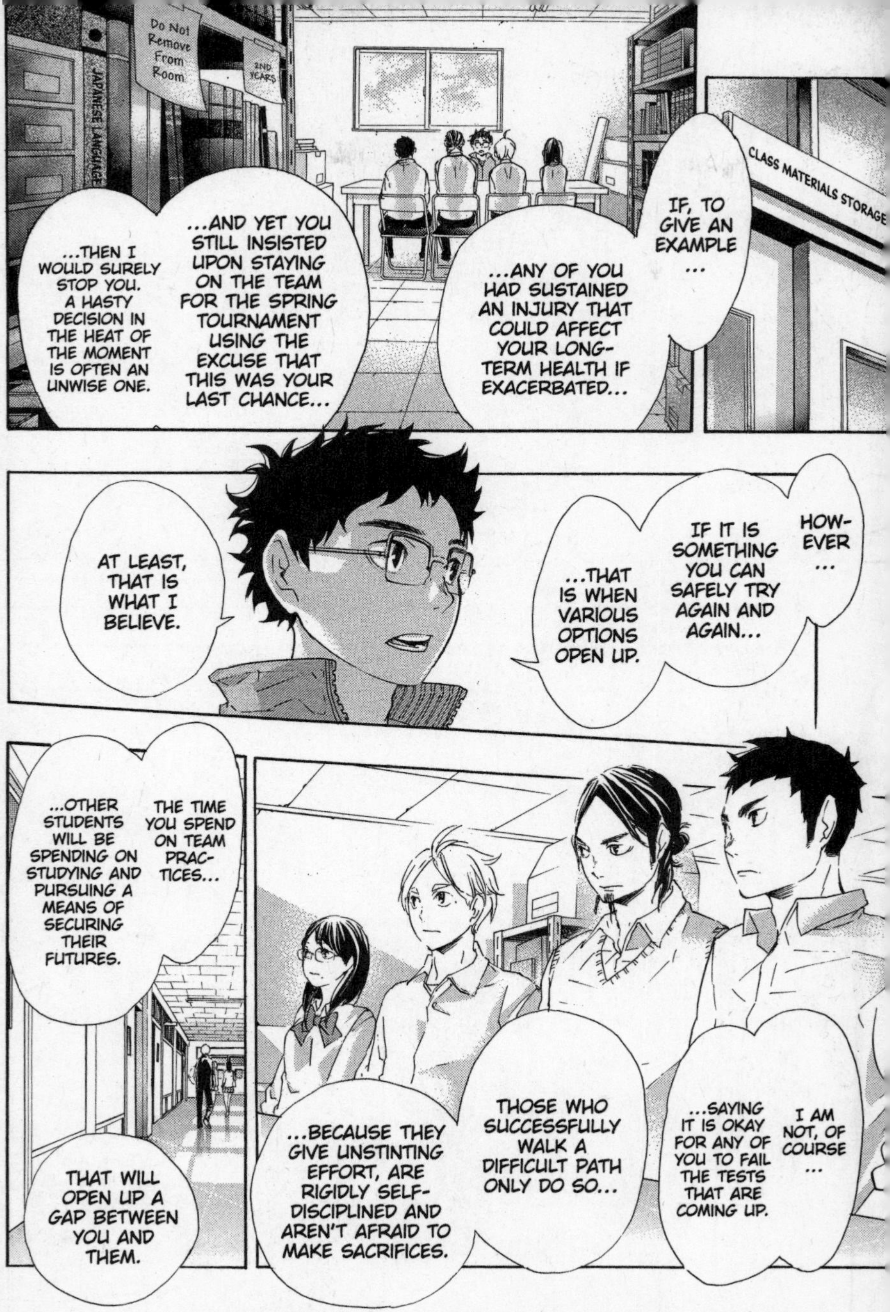

CLASS MATERIALS STORAGE
2ND YEARS
Do Not Remove From Room
JAPANESE LANGUAGE
IF, TO GIVE AN EXAMPLE ...
...ANY OF YOU HAD SUSTAINED AN INJURY THAT COULD AFFECT YOUR LONG-TERM HEALTH IF EXACERBATED...
...AND YET YOU STILL INSISTED UPON STAYING ON THE TEAM FOR THE SPRING TOURNAMENT USING THE EXCUSE THAT THIS WAS YOUR LAST CHANCE...
...THEN I WOULD SURELY STOP YOU. A HASTY DECISION IN THE HEAT OF THE MOMENT IS OFTEN AN UNWISE ONE.
HOW-EVER ...
IF IT IS SOMETHING YOU CAN SAFELY TRY AGAIN AND AGAIN...
...THAT IS WHEN VARIOUS OPTIONS OPEN UP.
AT LEAST, THAT IS WHAT I BELIEVE.
I AM NOT, OF COURSE ...
...SAYING IT IS OKAY FOR ANY OF YOU TO FAIL THE TESTS THAT ARE COMING UP.
THOSE WHO SUCCESSFULLY WALK A DIFFICULT PATH ONLY DO SO...
...BECAUSE THEY GIVE UNSTINTING EFFORT, ARE RIGIDLY SELF-DISCIPLINED AND AREN'T AFRAID TO MAKE SACRIFICES.
THE TIME YOU SPEND ON TEAM PRAC-TICES...
...OTHER STUDENTS WILL BE SPENDING ON STUDYING AND PURSUING A MEANS OF SECURING THEIR FUTURES.
THAT WILL OPEN UP A GAP BETWEEN YOU AND THEM.

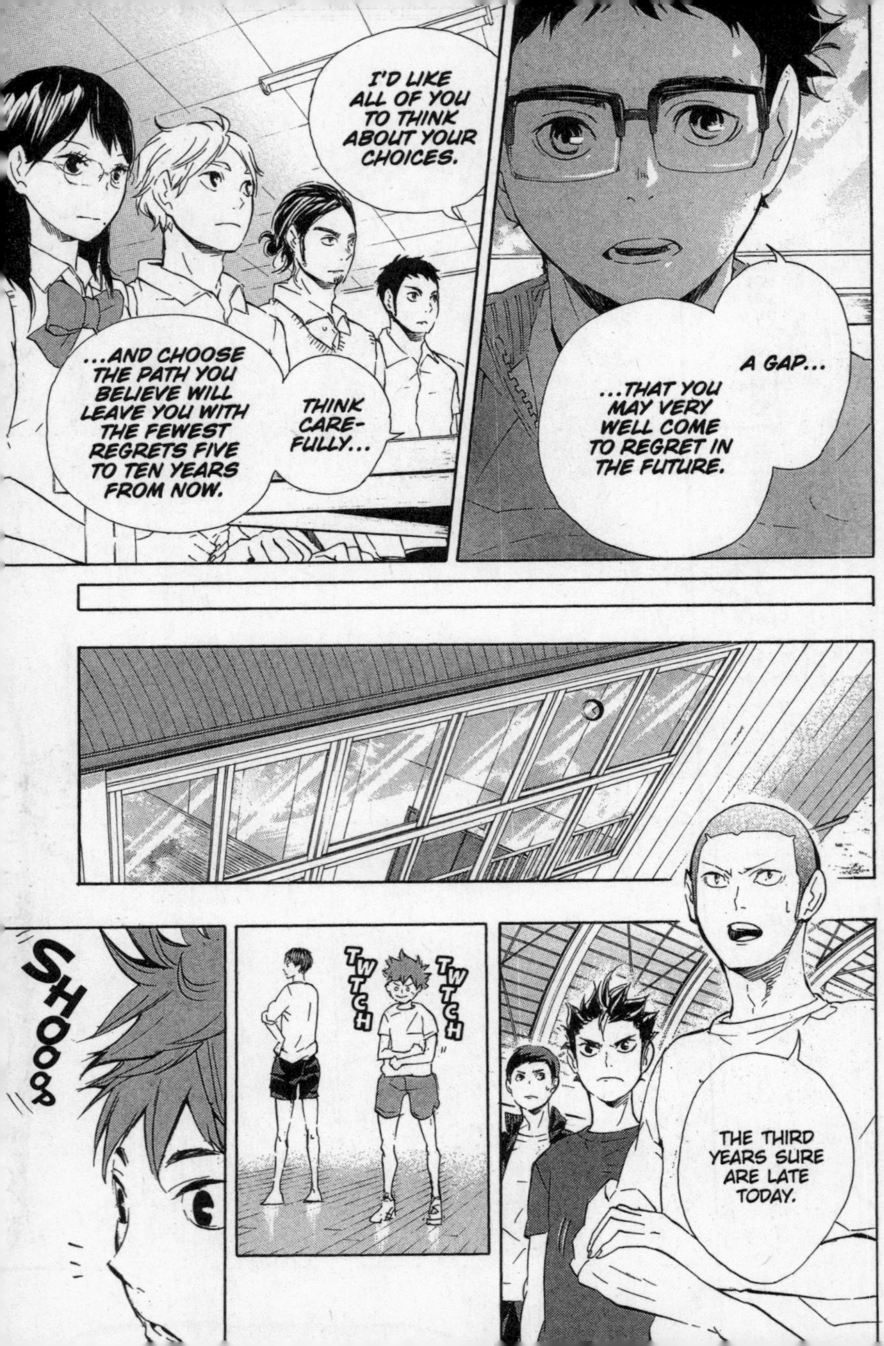
A GAP...
...THAT YOU MAY VERY WELL COME TO REGRET IN THE FUTURE.
I'D LIKE ALL OF YOU TO THINK ABOUT YOUR CHOICES.
THINK CARE-FULLY...
...AND CHOOSE THE PATH YOU BELIEVE WILL LEAVE YOU WITH THE FEWEST REGRETS FIVE TO TEN YEARS FROM NOW.
THE THIRD YEARS SURE ARE LATE TODAY.
TWTCH
TWTCH
SHOOOP

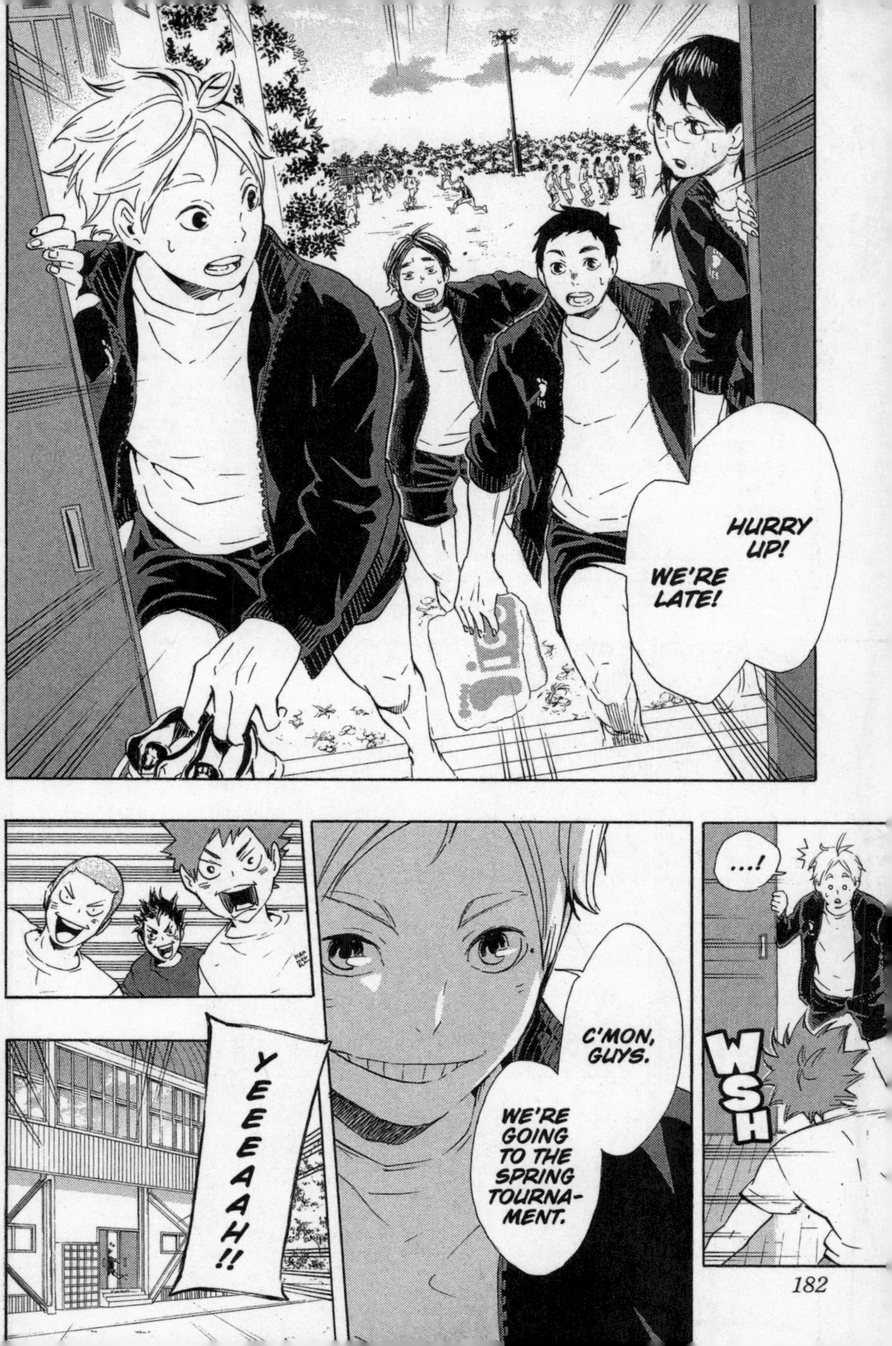
HURRY UP!
WE'RE LATE!
...!
WSH
C'MON, GUYS.
WE'RE GOING TO THE SPRING TOURNAMENT.
YEEEAAAH!!

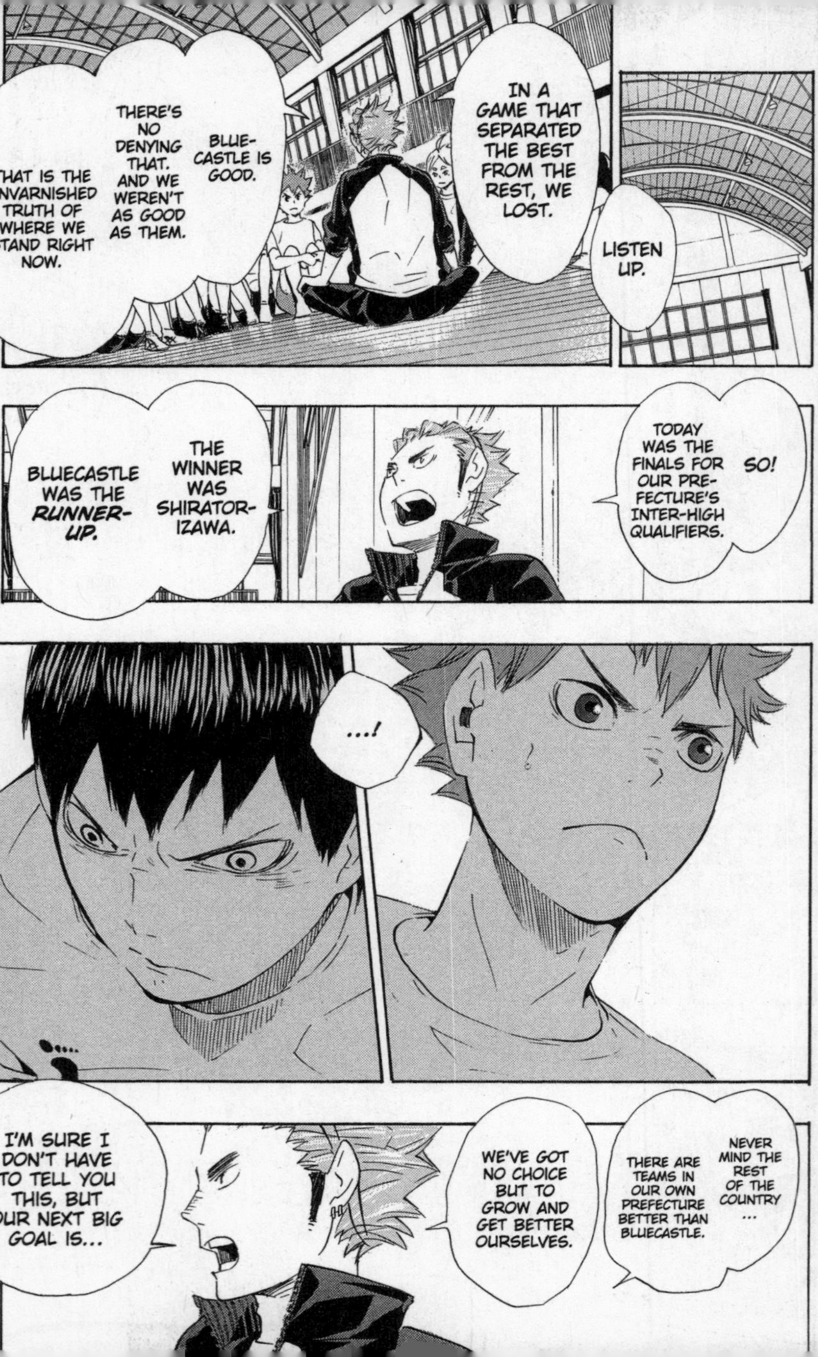
LISTEN UP.
IN A GAME THAT SEPARATED THE BEST FROM THE REST, WE LOST.
BLUE-CASTLE IS GOOD.
THERE'S NO DENYING THAT. AND WE WEREN'T AS GOOD AS THEM.
THAT IS THE UNVARNISHED TRUTH OF WHERE WE STAND RIGHT NOW.
SO!
TODAY WAS THE FINALS FOR OUR PRE-FECTURE'S INTER-HIGH QUALIFIERS.
THE WINNER WAS SHIRATOR-IZAWA.
BLUECASTLE WAS THE *RUNNER-UP.*
...!
NEVER MIND THE REST OF THE COUNTRY ...
THERE ARE TEAMS IN OUR OWN PREFECTURE BETTER THAN BLUECASTLE.
WE'VE GOT NO CHOICE BUT TO GROW AND GET BETTER OURSELVES.
I'M SURE I DON'T HAVE TO TELL YOU THIS, BUT OUR NEXT BIG GOAL IS...

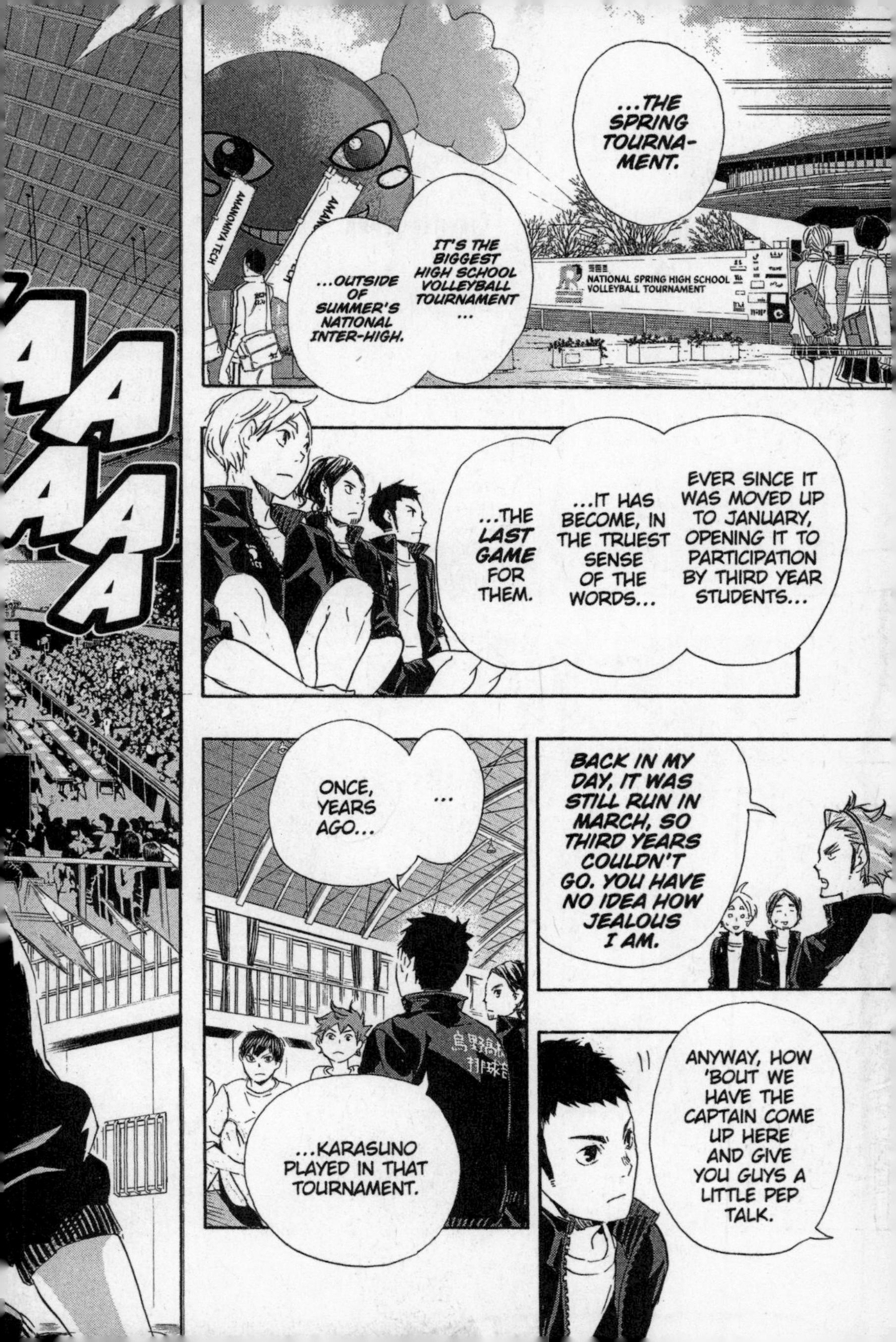
...THE SPRING TOURNAMENT.
IT'S THE BIGGEST HIGH SCHOOL VOLLEYBALL TOURNAMENT...
...OUTSIDE OF SUMMER'S NATIONAL INTER-HIGH.
NATIONAL SPRING HIGH SCHOOL VOLLEYBALL TOURNAMENT
AMANOMIYA TECH
EVER SINCE IT WAS MOVED UP TO JANUARY, OPENING IT TO PARTICIPATION BY THIRD YEAR STUDENTS...
...IT HAS BECOME, IN THE TRUEST SENSE OF THE WORDS...
...THE LAST GAME FOR THEM.
BACK IN MY DAY, IT WAS STILL RUN IN MARCH, SO THIRD YEARS COULDN'T GO. YOU HAVE NO IDEA HOW JEALOUS I AM.
ANYWAY, HOW 'BOUT WE HAVE THE CAPTAIN COME UP HERE AND GIVE YOU GUYS A LITTLE PEP TALK.
...
ONCE, YEARS AGO...
...KARASUNO PLAYED IN THAT TOURNAMENT.
AAAA

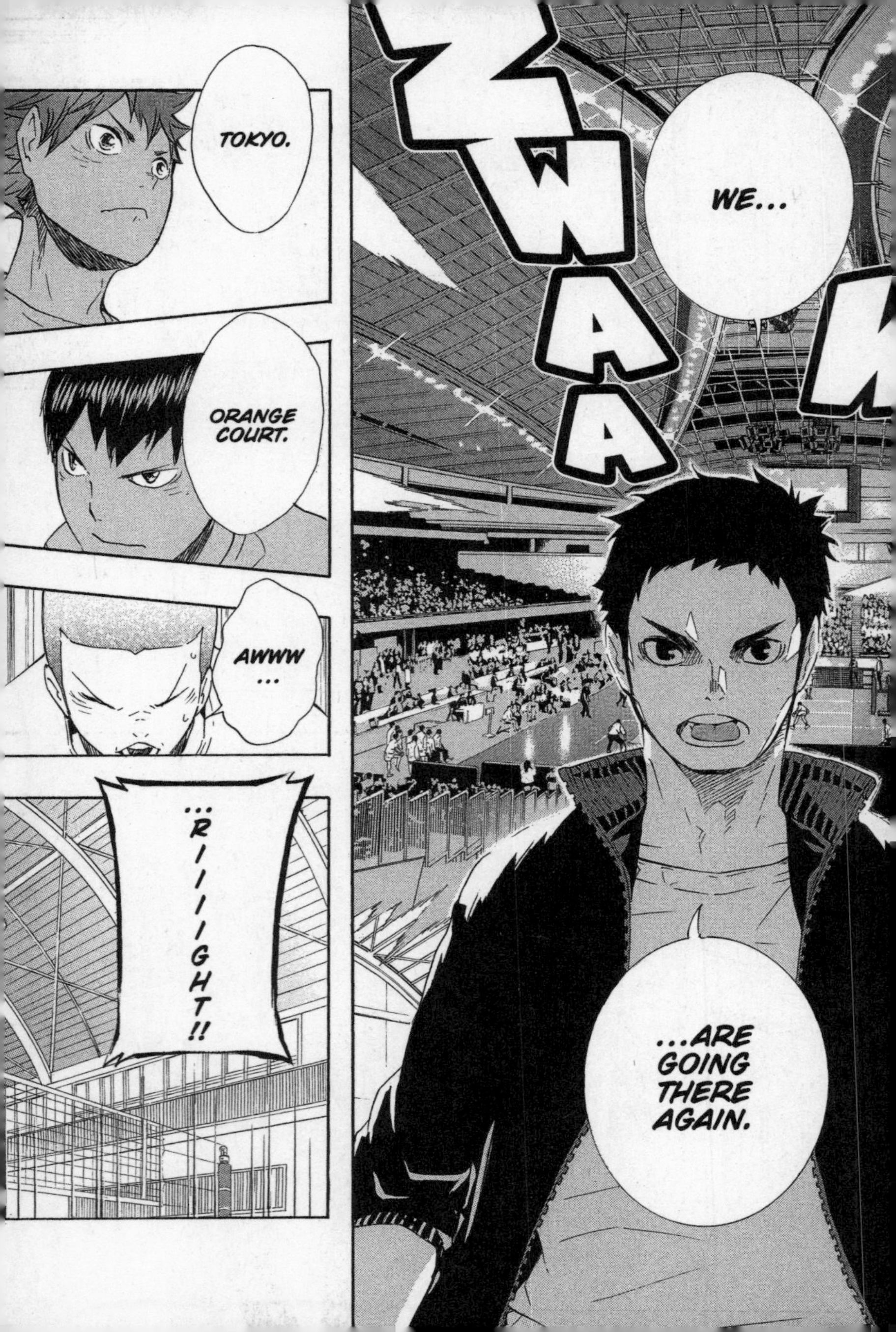
WE...
WAAK
...ARE GOING THERE AGAIN.
TOKYO.
ORANGE COURT.
AWWW ...
...R-I-I-I-I-GHT!!

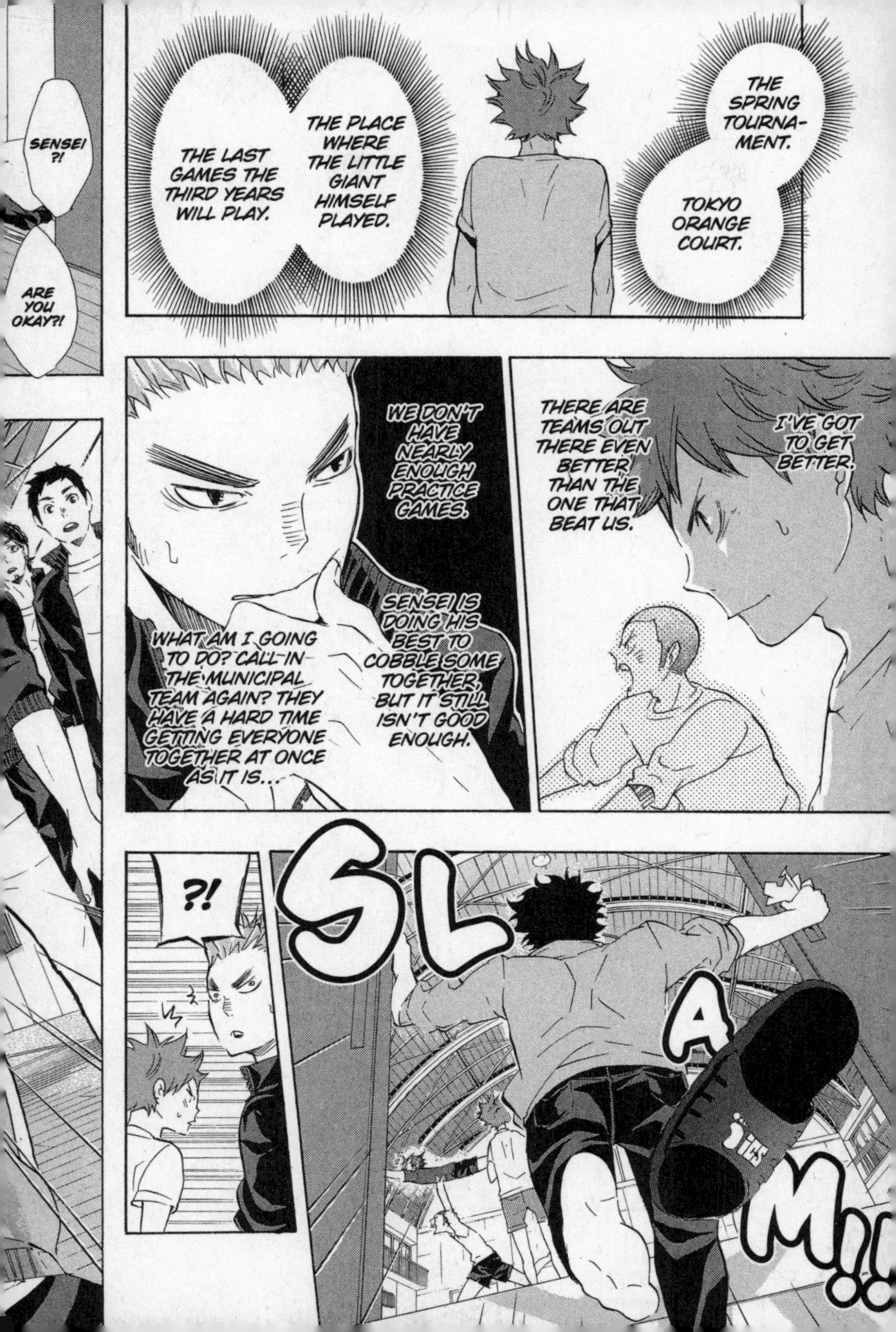
THE SPRING TOURNAMENT.
TOKYO ORANGE COURT.
THE PLACE WHERE THE LITTLE GIANT HIMSELF PLAYED.
THE LAST GAMES THE THIRD YEARS WILL PLAY.
I'VE GOT TO GET BETTER.
THERE ARE TEAMS OUT THERE EVEN BETTER THAN THE ONE THAT BEAT US.
WE DON'T HAVE NEARLY ENOUGH PRACTICE GAMES.
SENSEI IS DOING HIS BEST TO COBBLE SOME TOGETHER, BUT IT STILL ISN'T GOOD ENOUGH.
WHAT AM I GOING TO DO? CALL IN THE MUNICIPAL TEAM AGAIN? THEY HAVE A HARD TIME GETTING EVERYONE TOGETHER AT ONCE AS IT IS...
SLAM!!
?!
SENSEI ?!
ARE YOU OKAY?!

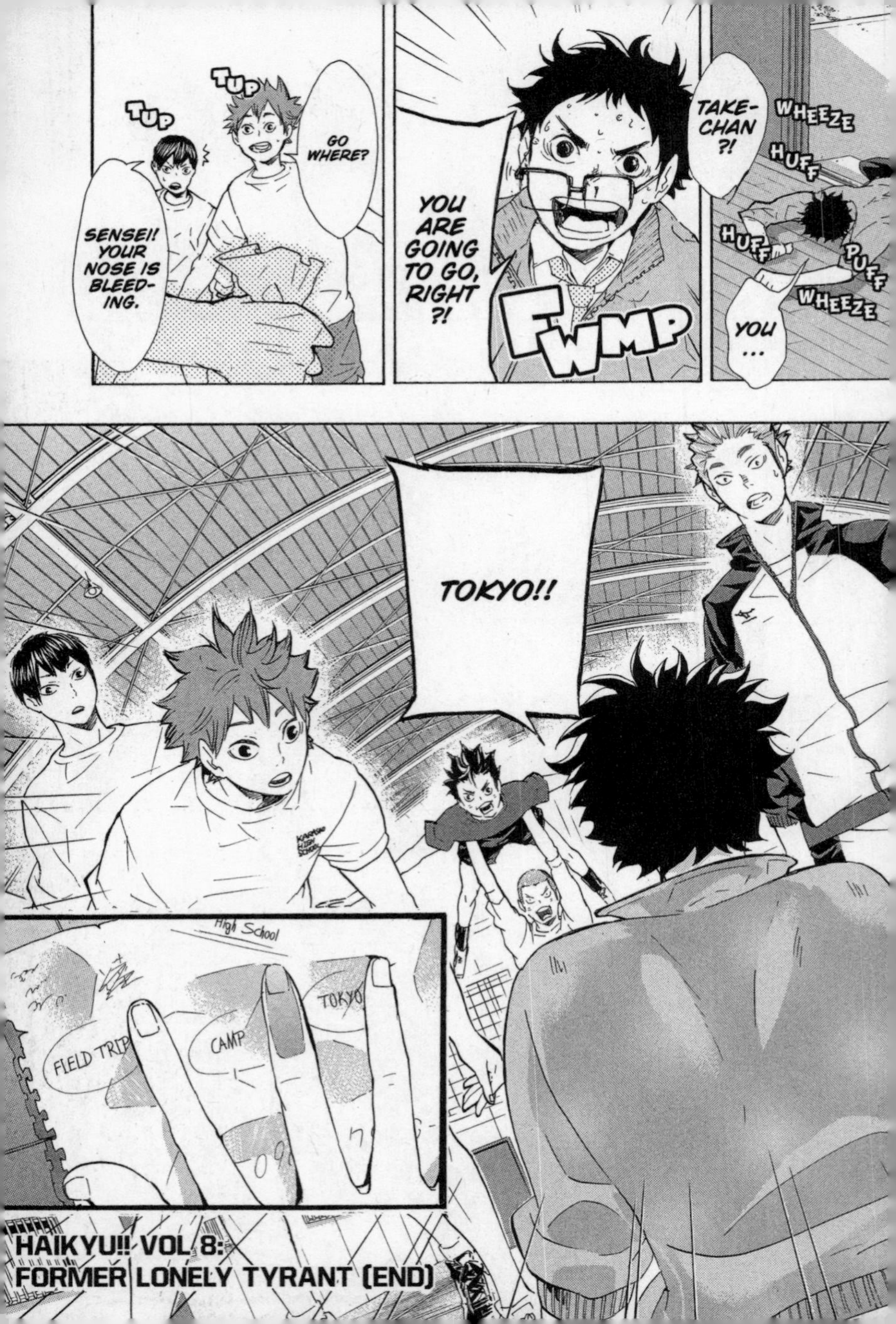
TAKE-CHAN ?!
WHEEZE
HUFF
HUFF
PUFF
WHEEZE
YOU ...
YOU ARE GOING TO GO, RIGHT ?!
FWMP
TUP
TUP
GO WHERE?
SENSEI! YOUR NOSE IS BLEED-ING.
TOKYO!!
High School
TOKYO
CAMP
FIELD TRIP
HAIKYU!! VOL 8:
FORMER LONELY TYRANT (END)

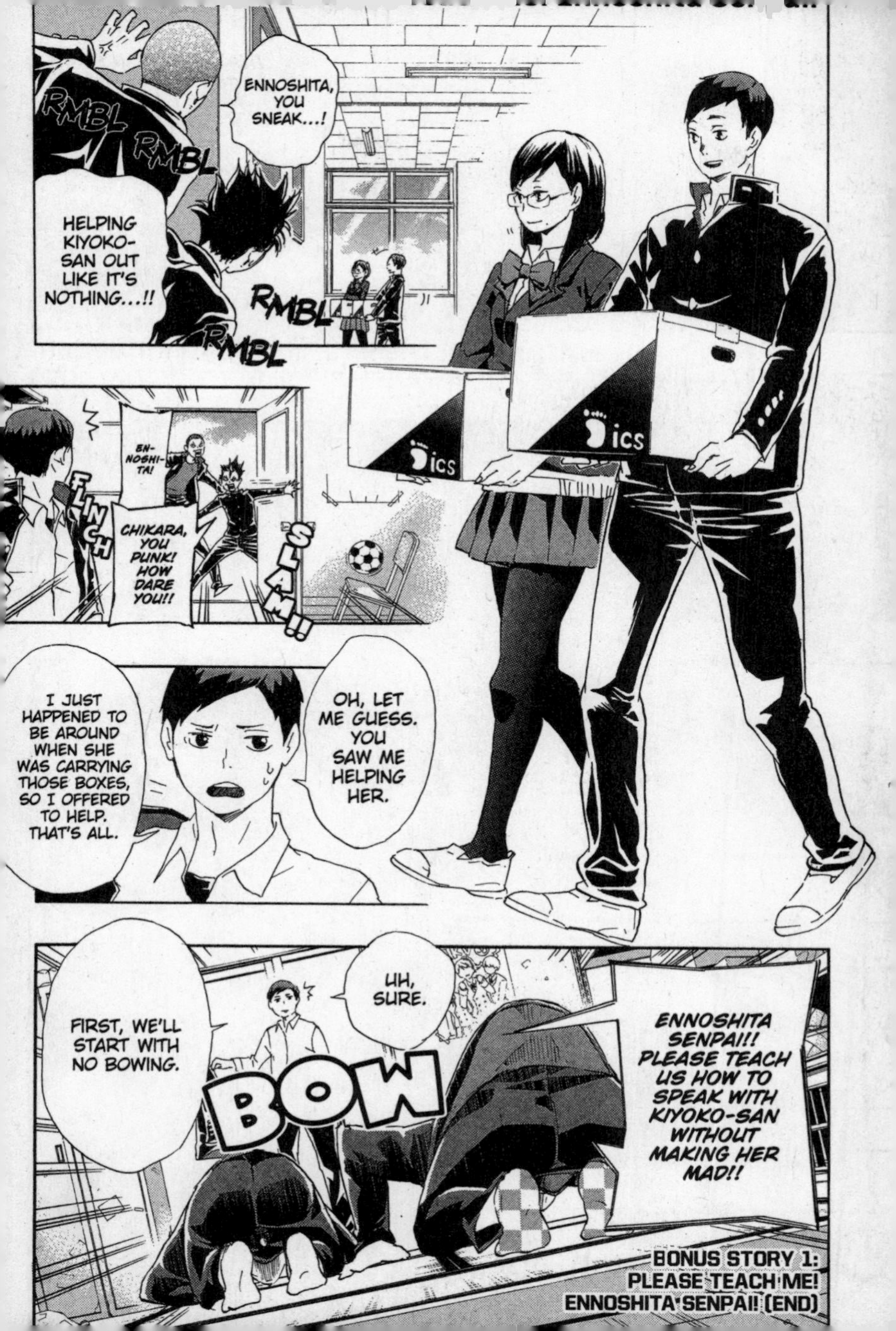
ENNOSHITA, YOU SNEAK...!
RMBL
RMBL
HELPING KIYOKO-SAN OUT LIKE IT'S NOTHING...!!
RMBL
RMBL
SLAM!!
EN-NOSHI-TA!
CHIKARA, YOU PUNK! HOW DARE YOU!!
FLINCH
OH, LET ME GUESS. YOU SAW ME HELPING HER.
I JUST HAPPENED TO BE AROUND WHEN SHE WAS CARRYING THOSE BOXES, SO I OFFERED TO HELP. THAT'S ALL.
ENNOSHITA SENPAI!! PLEASE TEACH US HOW TO SPEAK WITH KIYOKO-SAN WITHOUT MAKING HER MAD!!
BOW
UH, SURE.
FIRST, WE'LL START WITH NO BOWING.
BONUS STORY 1: PLEASE TEACH ME! ENNOSHITA SENPAI! (END)

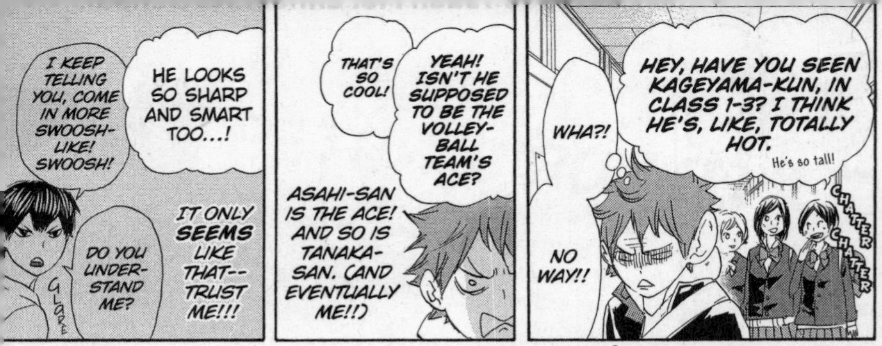
HEY, HAVE YOU SEEN KAGEYAMA-KUN, IN CLASS 1-3? I THINK HE'S, LIKE, TOTALLY HOT.
He's so tall!
CHATTER CHATTER
WHA?!
NO WAY!!
YEAH! ISN'T HE SUPPOSED TO BE THE VOLLEYBALL TEAM'S ACE?
THAT'S SO COOL!
ASAHI-SAN IS THE ACE! AND SO IS TANAKA-SAN. (AND EVENTUALLY ME!!)
HE LOOKS SO SHARP AND SMART TOO...!
I KEEP TELLING YOU, COME IN MORE SWOOSH-LIKE! SWOOSH!
IT ONLY SEEMS LIKE THAT--TRUST ME!!!
DO YOU UNDERSTAND ME?
GLARE

BONUS STORY 2: Class 1-3's Kageyama-Kun

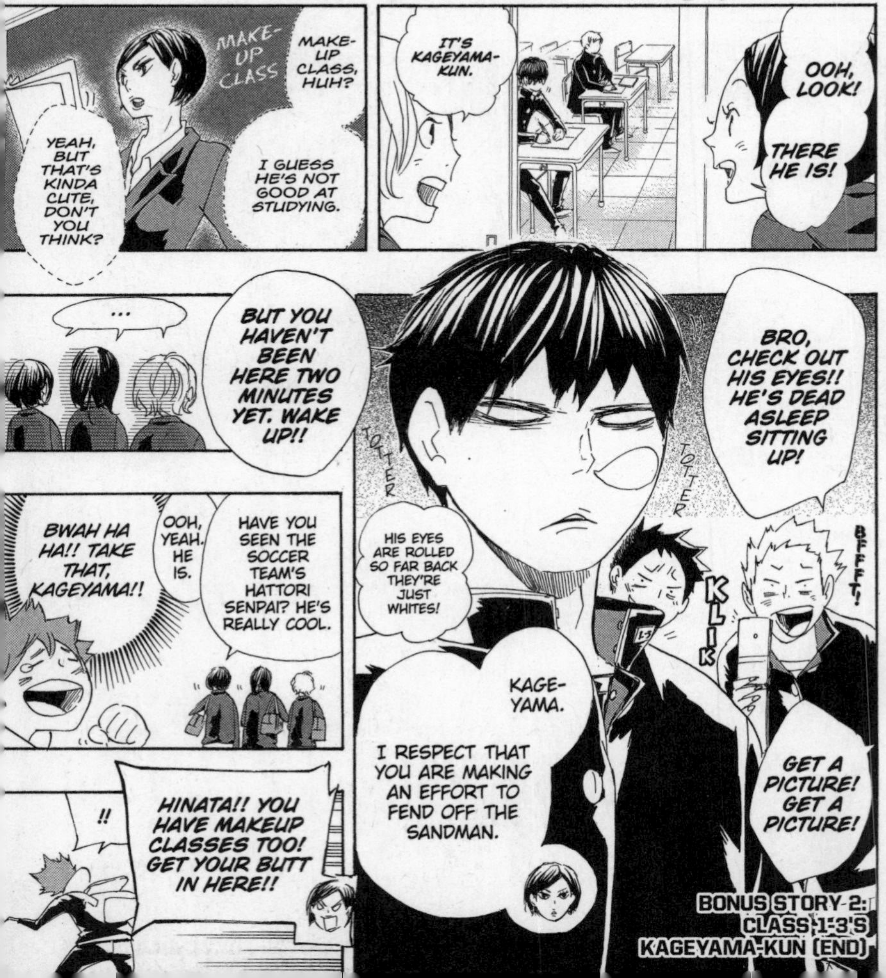
OOH, LOOK!
THERE HE IS!
IT'S KAGEYAMA-KUN.
MAKE-UP CLASS, HUH?
MAKE-UP CLASS
I GUESS HE'S NOT GOOD AT STUDYING.
YEAH, BUT THAT'S KINDA CUTE, DON'T YOU THINK?
BRO, CHECK OUT HIS EYES!! HE'S DEAD ASLEEP SITTING UP!
TOTTER
TOTTER
BFFFT!
KLIK
HIS EYES ARE ROLLED SO FAR BACK THEY'RE JUST WHITES!
GET A PICTURE! GET A PICTURE!
KAGE-YAMA.
I RESPECT THAT YOU ARE MAKING AN EFFORT TO FEND OFF THE SANDMAN.
BUT YOU HAVEN'T BEEN HERE TWO MINUTES YET. WAKE UP!!
...
HAVE YOU SEEN THE SOCCER TEAM'S HATTORI SENPAI? HE'S REALLY COOL.
OOH, YEAH. HE IS.
BWAH HA HA!! TAKE THAT, KAGEYAMA!!
HINATA!! YOU HAVE MAKEUP CLASSES TOO! GET YOUR BUTT IN HERE!!
!!
BONUS STORY 2: CLASS 1-3'S KAGEYAMA-KUN (END)

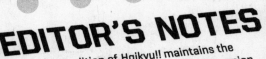

EDITOR'S NOTES

The English edition of Haikyu!! maintains the honorifics used in the original Japanese version. For those of you who are new to these terms, here's a brief explanation to help with your reading experience!

When saying someone's name in Japanese, a suffix is often attached to indicate how familiar the speaker is with the person. Some are more polite and respectful, while others are endearing.

1 *-kun* is often used for young men or boys, usually someone you are familiar with.

2 *-chan* is used for young children and can be used as a term of endearment.

3 *-san* is used for someone you respect or are not close to, or to be polite.

4 *Senpai* is used for someone who is older than you or in a higher position or grade in school.

5 *Kohai* is used for someone who is younger than you or in a lower position or grade in school.

6 *Sensei* means teacher.

7 *Bluecastle* is a nickname for Aoba Johsai. It is a combination of *Ao* (blue) and *Joh* (castle).

You're Reading the WRONG WAY!

HAIKYU!! reads from right to left, starting in the upper-right corner. Japanese is read from right to left, meaning that action, sound effects and word-balloon order are completely reversed from English order.

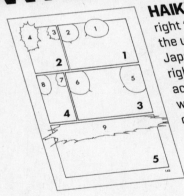